Creating Water Gardens

Meredith® Books
Des Moines, Iowa

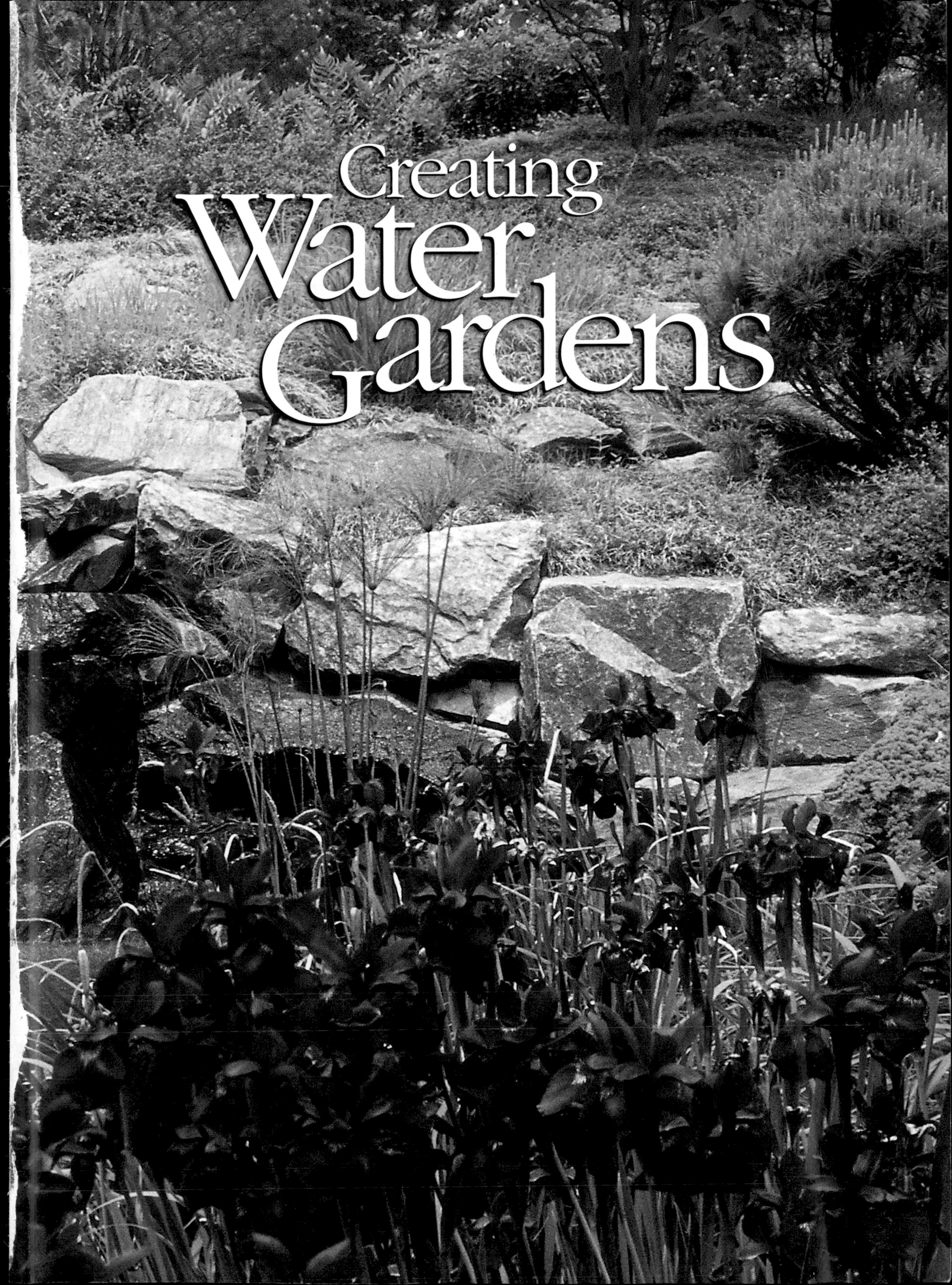
Creating
Water
Gardens

MAINTENANCE (continued)

AQUATIC LIFE 108

WATER WILDLIFE 168

PROJECTS 190

The Wonders of Water Gardening

In This Section

Water gardening is many things. It's gardening, fish-keeping, bird-watching, and nature and habitat restoration. It's part hobby, part educational, part spiritual. Although a pond may be defined by liner and stone, it is ever changing and waiting to be explored. Each day brings a new surprise or an unseen challenge.

Water gardening can be as easy or complex as you want it to be. People with busy schedules like water gardening because of the ease of care and the satisfying results they get with minimal maintenance. People new to pond-keeping have learned how easy it is to create a lush garden and wildlife habitat.

The bane of many new gardeners is figuring out when to water, how to water, and how much to water. Water gardening eliminates those dilemmas, because you can't overwater water plants!

Imagine being able to walk out into your yard, stroll over to your pond, and watch bright goldfish darting beneath the spreading leaves of jewel-toned water lilies. A water garden provides a cool oasis in a hectic world, a place to retreat to and relax.

Water cascading down a waterfall, babbling in a brook, or lying still in a reflective pool soothes the spirit and refreshes the soul. It reflects a simpler, less demanding time. It may remind you of a lakeside vacation or a pond where as a child you caught frogs and explored for underwater treasures. Water gardening is all of these pleasures and more.

Water gardening brings a world of wonder and excitement to any backyard. Whether you are a beginning or experienced gardener, you'll find that darting fish, colorful blossoms, and splashing water easily add to the beauty and enjoyment of your home.

WATER GARDENS IN HISTORY

Water gardening and water gardens have been around for a long time. This fascination with water can be traced throughout history. The Egyptians planted water lilies for their fragrance and for use in religious ceremonies. Thousands of water lilies were cultivated for the priests, who drank wine through the stems of the native varieties for a slightly narcotic experience. Papyrus, a water plant that grows at the margins of ponds or in bogs, was planted and harvested to make scrolls, the precursor to paper.

In Asia, water gardening was even more central to the culture because many of the area's staple foods are aquatic or semiaquatic. The main food, rice, has been cultivated in water-flooded fields for thousands of years. Taros (often called elephant's ears) and lotuses are just as old and still have a special place in water gardens, used to symbolize the heavens. In early Asian water gardens, goldfish and koi were objects of wealth and status, possessed mainly by the ruling classes.

Moorish and Turkish nobles used water features to cool their surroundings. Muslims shaped pools into geometric designs, and the features became stylized versions of irrigation canals and reservoirs. Later, French and German rulers used water to rival the glory days of the Roman Empire, displaying wealth and power with huge fountains as well as constructed streams, waterfalls, and lakes.

In Victorian times, rulers and the wealthy used water gardens to display the new, exotic plants and animals brought back to England from all over the world. In the United States, 19th-century landscape architects such as Jens Jensen and Frederick Law Olmsted used water in the landscape to bring nature and recreation to the inhabitants of the country's burgeoning cities.

Most homeowners of the time, however, were not able to afford such a luxury. Building a water garden took a great deal of time, effort, and money, far more than the average person was willing or able to invest. Because the pond was usually made of concrete, it was difficult to build naturally shaped ponds; and once a pond was built, little could be done to change its design or configuration. Moving the pond was out of the question.

Water features play a role in the history of many countries. With flexible liners now available, almost anyone can create a water garden almost anywhere.

WATER GARDENS AT HOME

All this changed in the 1960s with the advent of flexible liners, which have altered the very nature of water gardening. No longer just for the wealthy, a water garden can be built by anyone just about anywhere.

As a life-giving and -sustaining element, water is an essential part of any landscape. Moving or still, water in your landscape will entrance you and reward you with a variety of benefits. Water delights the beholder, whether it is peaceful and contemplative in a reflective pool or a quiet bog or exciting in a rushing waterfall or stream. A water feature that includes aquatic plants and fish captivates viewers with its fascinating rhythm of life and continual change. The magic of waterfalls captivates no matter the climate, garden design, home architecture, or lifestyle.

WATER GARDENS OFFER SOMETHING FOR EVERYONE

Create a water garden for your home and reap the many joys it can bring:

- An oasis of tranquillity to which you can retreat from the stress of everyday life.
- The refreshing sound of moving water to wash away worries and calm nerves.
- The visual excitement of spilling, cascading, rippling, and sparkling water.
- The intriguing dance of nature among plants, fish, insects, birds, and other wildlife attracted to the water through the seasons.
- The pleasure of feeding ornamental fish that come to

Landscaping with water can create a tranquil family gathering spot with opportunities for learning and relaxing. Guests, too, will be drawn outdoors to the sound of moving water.

the surface to greet you and hearing the peaceful songs of frogs.

- The magical presence of water running through the garden that draws you outside.
- A center of activity for viewing, sharing, and learning for people of all ages.

GETTING STARTED

Landscaping with water presents a wealth of design opportunities as well as a challenge to the imagination. Because water is part of the natural world, it easily harmonizes with any landscape, any regional climate, and any architectural style. In dry areas, a water feature is a welcome oasis; in cold regions, it brings year-round interest.

Despite all the compelling reasons to make a beautiful water feature, some people hesitate. Construction can be intimidating and may discourage the start of a project. That's where this book comes in, helping you to bring the many pleasures of water gardening to your home. Use this thorough guide to simplify the process and organize your plans. With instructions for design and installation, tips for stocking and maintenance, and how-to ideas for all kinds of water features, these pages provide guidance and inspiration for creating a wonderful water garden of your own.

Container gardens add movement and beauty to small decks and porches. Water and plants soften the surroundings and bring nature close—even to patios twenty stories up.

DESIGNING A WATER GARDEN

Water gardens are popular because they transform an ordinary garden into a delightful retreat. Choose from a wealth of possibilities, from a small, simple container garden or a fountain to a still pool or a cascading stream.

A CREATIVE OUTLET

Designing a water feature offers lots of appeal, whether you seek a creative outlet or a way to challenge your mechanical or building skills. Even if you don't view its design as an art form, a water feature becomes an artful addition to the landscape. Making a waterfall, a stream, a reflecting pool, or a koi pond also offers new gardening opportunities as you decide which plants to include and how to incorporate aquatic plants. Whatever your goals, completing the project—a permanent addition to your garden—will give you a sense of accomplishment.

HOME IMPROVEMENT

In addition, a well-designed landscape that includes a carefully constructed water feature could increase your property's resale value. Depending on the design, you can use a water feature to resolve a landscape problem, such as an uninteresting or sloping site, turning it into a decorative asset. Your design might help you build on top of soil that retains water or won't support much plant life other than weeds. Following a trend toward more environmentally friendly landscapes, the newest aquascape technology and concepts in constructing water features imitate nature and give you ways to transform your property into a beautiful oasis.

IN THIS SECTION

Ponds should complement and enhance the landscape, fitting into the surrounding scheme and placed where they look most natural. They should also complement your ideas for using the space.

SELECTING A SITE

Water gardens are now within the budget and skill level of most homeowners, and the tools and materials available today make water garden installation easier than ever. You can put a water garden almost anywhere: in a large, expansive landscape; in a small, urban backyard; or on a balcony or porch. However, for the water garden to be successful—and for you to get the most enjoyment from it—you must build it on the right site.

Before you decide on the final location, there are a number of things to keep in mind: your site conditions, including slope, soil, sun, shade, and wind; your intended use of the feature; climatic conditions in your region; and the location of utility lines. Finding the perfect spot requires balancing all of these elements. Here's what to look for.

An earth-bottom pond can bring depth and texture to an otherwise flat expanse of lawn if tied into the surrounding landscape with rocky edging and marginal plants that blend in naturally.

LOCATION, LOCATION, LOCATION

SLOPE: Check out your site. Consider the slope and grade of your yard and work with it. The lowest spot may look like the best place for a pond, but it's actually the worst. Rainwater flows into a low-lying pond, muddying the water, washing away your fish, and knocking over plants. Poor drainage can also cause runoff to well up underneath the pond liner, creating undesirable bubbles that rise to the surface and make your pond water look foul. Placing the pond just above the lowest spot avoids these problems.

If your site slopes, you'll have to put in some extra time preparing it for the water garden. You'll need to level it, either by grading it and building a retaining wall or by building up the downhill side of the pond by adding soil or rock. Otherwise, water will run out of the pond and down the hill.

Fortunately, a sloped site has its benefits, too. It's a perfect spot to add a waterfall, and you can lay out a slope to include a stream that runs from an upper pond to a lower one. When building on a slope, make sure you have a clear, safe, and easy path on which to carry materials to the pond site.

SOIL: Take into account the kind of soil you have. It can have a lot to do with whether your installation is easy or difficult. If the soil is especially hard and rocky, save yourself the digging and install an aboveground pond with either a flexible or preformed liner supported by a wood, stone, or masonry structure.

Sandy soil comes with problems as well. It is difficult to work with when you're trying to install an in-ground pond formed from a flexible liner, because the sand may cave in along the sides of the pond. Here, a preformed liner may be the answer. To use a flexible liner, you'll need to use cinder block under the liner to shore up the sides and hold the edging.

Clay soil, although sometimes difficult to excavate, can be ideal for in-ground installations

Taking advantage of an existing grade, this waterfall fits naturally among the rocky outcroppings. Design a waterfall in scale with the rest of the pond to keep water loss from splashing to a minimum.

(and, as you'll see later, for growing healthy water garden plants). Clay soil holds its shape, and flexible liners will conform to whatever configuration you dig.

SUN, SHADE, WIND: Take an inventory of the sun and shade patterns in your yard so you can make sure your water garden location will give your plants the sunlight (or the shade) they require. Wind can affect plant life, too. Strong winds speed evaporation from the pond and can break the stems of some tender plants and harm plants that thrive in tranquil water. If you must locate the pond in a windprone spot, erect a windscreen, or plant shrubs as a natural wall.

ACCESS: Choose a location that's far enough away from potential obstacles that you'll have easy access to all sides of the pond. Existing landscape features such as fences, utility sheds, and other structures can affect easy access to the pond when you're performing maintenance chores. If there's a fence in the vicinity, put your water garden several feet away from it (local codes often specify a distance of 5 feet from a fence).

UTILITIES: Call local utility companies before you dig and ask them to locate the buried lines that run through your property. Most utilities will mark the locations without charge. Even if a utility line is deeper than your pond will be, don't put the pond over an existing line—any future repairs on the line will tear up the pond.

FUNCTION

After site conditions, one of the most important aspects to consider when choosing a pond location is how you want to use the pond. Whatever the function and view of your garden pond, make sure it's an integral part of the design, not an add-on. Connect the pond to the perennial bed, the patio, the deck, or other existing features. Study the configuration of the land and tuck your water garden into its contours. Here are some examples of your options.

Will you look out your family room window to see the waterfall? If so, place the waterfall at the back of the pond, facing the window. Add plantings behind it to frame the view.

If your vision of the water garden includes enjoying it while sitting on a deck, you'll want the pond close by, perhaps almost under the deck so it looks like water under a dock.

If the deck is elevated, make sure that any waterfall you might have is high enough to be seen over the railing.

If your water garden will be the primary focal point of your entire landscape design, you'll want to situate it so you can take in the entire landscape in one view.

Lushly planted container water gardens bring nature into small spaces, creating new views in the enclosed balcony of an apartment or on an urban high-rise patio.

If you want a water garden to fit in with your love of bird-watching, make sure to locate the bird feeders away from and downwind of the pond to help reduce cleanup problems from hulls and spilled birdseed. A pond that's a natural wildlife setting might fit better in a less-used part of the yard, connected to the rest of the landscape with a pebble or mulch path.

A raised pool with room to sit at the edge works well in a formal patio. Add a birdbath to soften the design.

SELECTING A SITE
continued

A small pond tucked into a shady corner of the yard takes advantage of an unused area and creates a private, peaceful spot to relax. Shade- and moisture-loving marginal and companion plants add color and texture to the aquascape, while rocky outcroppings tie the cool retreat to its terrestrial surroundings.

DESIGN ELEMENTS

Water gardens affect the perspective of your landscape and add an element of surprise. Placement of the pond in relation to the rest of your landscape is crucial. If you simply plunk a water garden in the middle of the yard, it will look adrift in a sea of green lawn. Adding a neat, symmetrical row of rocks around its edge just makes matters worse, creating an unnatural perimeter that looks as though you are trying to hide something.

Think about how the location of the pond can enhance your landscape. For example, a rectangular pond set with its length parallel to the main view from the house will make a yard seem longer. An informal design with the longer sides perpendicular to your line of sight will exaggerate the perspective and make the yard seem larger. Small pools are surprises in the landscape, adding interest for visitors who happen upon them. You can achieve this sense of delight by tucking a small pond into a side yard or around the bend of a curving flower bed. Add an arbored bench to complete your garden retreat. Whatever you do, integrate the size, scale, and other elements of your water garden with all the features of your landscape.

SIZE: Backyard ponds can be installed in any size, shape, or configuration. Tuck one into a corner of your yard or build the pond so it looks as if it disappears underneath a deck.

Small yards can easily hold a water garden made from nothing more than a large pot or container set into the ground, either partially or completely beneath the soil line. A 2-foot-round hole overlayed with a flexible liner and filled with moist soil is ideal for a bog garden with a small lotus or a marginal water plant, such as iris or lizard's tail. Such a design provides the perfect opportunity to add water plants to a perennial border when your yard is too small for a full-scale pond.

SCALE: Scale is important when designing a water feature. A large pond can overpower a small landscape. A small water garden in the midst of a large setting can look like a puddle.

There are some tricks that allow you to break the rules of scale. For example, if you would like to build a large pond on a small site, you can create islands, peninsulas, or decks that overhang the pond to break up the visual impact of the water so that it doesn't seem so large. Also, incorporating existing features as part of the overall design can help give the small element more impact.

Although there are no hard-and-fast rules about the relationship of pond size to yard size, you can estimate the effect of scale with a garden hose, white flour, or colored twine. Lay out the hose or twine in the planned configuration of your pond, and experiment until the scale seems right. Leave the trial outline in place for a week or so to help you decide if the placement of the pond will capitalize on the views from the house, patio, and other spots on your property. This trial run will also help you determine if the water garden fits with the natural traffic patterns in your landscape and whether it will leave enough room for outdoor furniture and decorative objects.

EDGING: Make sure to use an edging that complements other hardscape elements in your overall landscape design. Hardscape elements are those features in your yard that are constructed—decks, arbors, patios, walkways, and driveways, for example. If you've laid a certain type of rock on a path through your perennial bed, use that same rock to edge your water garden. Vary the size of the rocks around the pond so they look natural. Using similar materials in the pond and landscape help achieve a unified design.

Using more than one kind of stone in the landscape can be challenging. For instance, if you use mixed fieldstone to edge the perennial bed and flagstone around the pond, either the fieldstone or the flagstone may look out of place. You don't always have to use the same stone, though. A slate patio can be complemented with wood decking or a jagged stone of a similar color. Try to harmonize the elements without making one seem out of place or too dominant.

WATER FEATURES AND CHILD SAFETY

A water feature raises safety concerns, particularly when young children live near it. Plan ahead and provide for safety by following these suggestions:

- Never leave children unsupervised near water.
- If you have a toddler in your family, you might want to delay construction of the water feature. Meanwhile, make a large sandbox and convert it later into a pond or bog garden.
- As alternatives to a pond, consider building a fountain bubbling over stones or a dry creek that will carry water only during wet periods.
- Locate the feature within easy view of the house and the yard.
- Put a fence around your water feature or your property to keep neighborhood children from wandering onto the site. Your insurance coverage may require a fence with a childproof gate.
- Consider building a raised or partially raised pond that affords a measure of security.
- Lay a safety grate over a pond that rests securely a few inches below the water's surface but allows plants to grow through it. Black or blue dye in the water will disguise the grate.
- For added safety, install a motion-sensitive alarm when you construct the feature.
- Ask local authorities about requirements for safety, permits, and inspection.

Hardscape elements, such as brick or other pavers, help to anchor a raised pool in a formal setting. Careful design of edging and paths can help to draw the eye from one garden feature to the next.

POND STYLE AND SHAPE

Use drystack masonry in a large, informal setting to create a waterfall that cascades gently into the pond and connects the feature to the surrounding landscape.

Building a water garden in the middle of a deck is a good weekend project. When you're through, you'll have a small feature within steps of the house as well as a comfortable place to enjoy it.

Ponds can take whatever shape your imagination and site allow. In terms of style, they break down into two basic categories—formal and informal.

FORMAL STYLE

Clean, simple, straight lines and symmetrical mirror-image arrangements characterize formal styles. Formal water gardens have straight edges and geometric shapes. Brickwork makes a functional yet highly decorative border for a formal pond, as do square precast pavers, tile, and even sod.

Formal designs work well with manicured beds of roses and neat, evenly planted perennial borders accented with clipped boxwood hedges. If your landscape design is formal and you're considering a reflecting pool—a water feature with the principal function of reflecting trees, the sky, or plantings at the edge of the flower border—square or rectangular shapes are just what you're looking for. For lushness, add a large display of water lilies with a towering papyrus.

INFORMAL STYLE

Curving, fluid lines and asymmetrical arrangements define informal design. The American cottage garden or the mixed perennial border dotted here and there with bright colors provides the perfect setting for an informal pond. An informal water garden flows seamlessly, without defined edges, into the surrounding landscape.

In contrast to formal designs in which plants are used as ornaments, informal styles feature plants as the heart of the design. Foliage of similar texture and form in both the pond and perennial borders casually links the pond with the rest of the landscape. Water garden edging complements—rather than defines—informal style. Use large, irregular fieldstone, river rock, boulders, logs, or pebbles to help make a pond look as if it has always been part of the landscape.

POND SHAPES

Rectangles and squares are typical formal shapes. Because of their simple lines, they work well when you need to define a space, whether it's the entire garden or part of it.

Oval and circular ponds are difficult to categorize. They may be either formal or informal, depending on their size and edging and the geometry of their plantings. The more a rectangle approaches—but does not become—a circle, the more it will tend to look informal. Soft planted edges accentuate the effect. A long narrow oval pond looks formal because as its length becomes more than three times its width, it begins to take on the character of a rectangle. It is best to complement it with the hard formal edges of cut stone or other formal materials.

Free forms, such as crescents and kidney and pie shapes, are informal because of their asymmetrical edges.

The final shape of your pond is determined by the relationship of its size to its edging. The proportions of plants and edging predominate in a small pond, so these elements influence shape more than the original shape of the hole. You can actually make the right-angled formality of a small rectangular pond disappear by using informal plantings. Larger ponds are harder to blend in. As the size of the excavation increases—to a quarter acre or more, for example—the shape becomes predominant.

INSTALLATION CONSIDERATIONS

Each pond shape requires different quantities of liner and installation time. The more complicated the shape, the more folds you will need to make in the pond liner.

Rectangles are one of the easiest styles to install; you have to make only four folds when using flexible liner, so a rectangle is the most efficient use of flexible materials.

Circular and oval pond shapes, as well as teardrops and ellipses, are often easier to install when using flexible liner. Because circles and ovals have no corners, the liner is easy to fold.

Free-form designs are the most popular but can also be the most difficult—and the most expensive—to execute because so much liner is taken up in folds and overlaps. These shapes have inner and outer arcs. You'll need to buy enough liner to fit all the outer arcs, which means the inner arcs will have too much liner in them and you'll have to take it up. A crescent-shaped pond can require one-third more liner than a rectangular one of equivalent size; a pie-shaped pond requires less liner than a crescent of the same area. In small ponds, this extra amount isn't crucial, but it can be significant in large ponds.

A yard that has no space for a pond will still have room for a wall fountain. Some types can be installed without running pipe through the wall. Disguise the water tubing with vines.

If space doesn't allow for a full-fledged water garden, tuck a small feature among existing plants in a perennial bed or border. Find a large flat stone with natural depressions in it or an unusual object such as this old column support, and add water. Birds and butterflies will become regular visitors.

WHICH STYLE IS FOR YOU?

A formal pool reflects the symmetry of a rectangular patio.

Water features are as individual as the gardeners who create them. Answer the following questions to help you decide which is best for you.

WHAT SIZE?

- Do you have an hour or two (or more) each week to devote to water gardening?
- Is your landscape fairly large?
- Have you installed a water garden before?
- Are you an experienced do-it-yourselfer?
- Do you have friends or family who can help with installation?
- Will your budget let you spend several hundred dollars or more on a water feature?

If you answered no to most of the questions, you should build a small pond.

FORMAL OR INFORMAL?

- Do you like straight lines and symmetry?
- Does your landscape already have a number of formal elements?
- Do you thrive on order?
- Is your lot a geometric shape?
- Do the doors and windows of your house look out on a landscape designed in grids?
- Is your home interior formal?
- Do natural gardens seem disorderly to you?

If you answered yes to most of the questions, you may prefer a formal pool.

An informal pond takes advantage of existing features in the landscape. Rocks and plants are carefully positioned to make this pond appear to have occurred naturally.

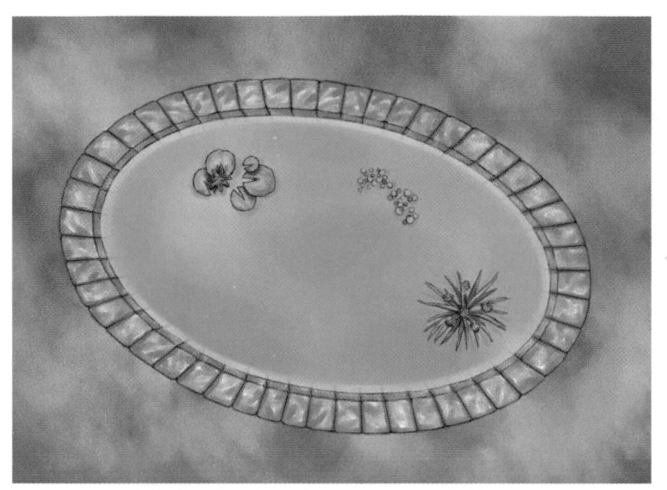

Even a symmetrical pond can have a free-form design. Plantings dramatically alter the appearance of the pond's perimeter. Their form, texture, and placement transform the water surface into any shape desired. You can further change the shape of the pond by using stones in a variety of sizes and shapes. In the long run, a simple pond shaped by plants costs less to build and is easier to maintain than a pond with multiple lobes.

TO DIG, OR NOT TO DIG?

■ Will digging the garden be difficult for you?
■ Would you like the water garden located near a sitting area, and should the water be at eye level when you're seated?
■ Is the water table high in your area?
■ Do you live in a reasonably mild climate?
■ Is your site in a low spot that might flood if the water feature isn't above ground?

The more yes answers, the more an aboveground pool is appropriate for your site; the more no answers, the more an in-ground pool is the better choice.

WHICH FEATURES?

■ Do you want the sound of splashing water?
■ Will you keep fish in the water garden?
■ Do you want to see moving water or watch it course through your landscape?
■ Is your site calm, not buffeted by winds that might disturb a fountain or waterfall?

If you answered yes to most questions, include a fountain, stream, or waterfall in your plans.

DO YOU WANT PLANTS?

■ Will your garden receive four or more hours of sunlight each day?
■ Are you interested in tending new plants?
■ Do you want fish?
■ Are you concerned about keeping the water clear without chemicals?
■ Are you willing to spend extra time to care for plants?

If you answered yes to most questions, add plants to your pond.

SHOULD YOU HAVE FISH IN YOUR GARDEN?

■ Do you live in a mild climate? If not, are you willing to overwinter the fish indoors?
■ Are you willing to provide the extra weekly care that fish require?
■ Do you want to minimize mosquitoes?
■ Is having a self-regulating ecosystem important to you?

If you answered yes to most questions, add fish to your pond.

AMOEBA PONDS

Avoid shapes that exhibit the "amoeba syndrome"—those that have "lobes" extending from the main body of the design. Lobes mean pinches, and pinches mean folds and extra liner. These shapes will be difficult to install with all the extra folding they require. What's more, the lobes create dead zones in the pond where water can't easily circulate. Pond water settles into these dead areas and reduces oxygen levels, which is not good for fish or other fauna. Once the plants in and around the garden mature, the pond loses its artistic, free-form shape. In addition, the pond lobes are difficult to mow around.

WHICH STYLE IS FOR YOU?

continued

IN GROUND VERSUS ABOVE GROUND

In-ground ponds are good projects for beginning water gardeners because their installation generally doesn't require special skills. Aside from digging and hauling soil away, building one is simple—dig it, line it, and fill it. Even when small, an in-ground pond is attractive and can fit into both naturalistic and formal landscapes.

Aboveground pools have advantages, too; however, their installation is not without effort. They're excellent for areas where you want the water close to eye level or situated at just the right height for dangling fingers. Aboveground pools are ideal for those difficult-to-dig locations in clay, compacted soil, or among tree roots. They are suited to mild climates where water doesn't freeze and where footings can be set less thick and deep.

Although some aboveground pools require little digging (others, none at all), they still need sides; depending on the style you choose, constructing them can take skill. The sides can be built from almost any material: brick, stone, concrete, tile, or wood.

PONDS FOR FISH

Some aboveground pools may be large and deep enough to hold a few koi or goldfish. However, if your water garden is designed with fish as a primary focus, you will need to dig an appropriately sized in-ground pond.

A fishpond, by definition, is designed to carry a heavier concentration of fish than a smaller water garden. Your site must allow you to dig the pond with a slope toward center drains that remove settling fish waste. It must also be situated so that you have easy access for pump maintenance and removal of floating debris, which are necessary to reduce the chance of fish infection and increase the quality of the water. A site not too close to permanent utility structures or under dense foliage can make your efforts easier.

To protect water plants from hungry fish, dig two smaller ponds connected by a stream and isolated from each other by a gate valve or waterfall. Design one pond for aquatic plants and the other as a home for goldfish and koi. The planted pond can function as a mini wetland, absorbing waste from the fish and cleaning the water. Both ponds will be healthier and easier for you to maintain.

WATERFALLS AND STREAMS

Waterfalls and streams contribute motion and sound to a landscape. The design of a watercourse determines the emotions it elicits—exciting or calming, energizing or restful. Streams and waterfalls, regardless of their size, add variety to the landscape. What's more, a waterfall or stream may provide a solution for areas otherwise difficult to landscape, such as steep slopes, rocky terrain, or deep shade. A forceful waterfall helps minimize traffic noise. Whatever water feature you choose, it will set your landscape apart from the ordinary.

PLANNING AHEAD

Before designing a waterfall, look for inspiration. Take time to observe some of nature's creations. Notice the water basin or area at the top of the falls, how the water spills over and around the rocks, and how far it falls. Also, look at the land around the top,

This aboveground pond contains the type of lush, natural plantings typically used in an informal, in-ground setting.

In summer, the pond is at its peak. The perennial garden may be waning, but the water garden bursts with blooms. Water lilies and lotuses bask in the warm sun like bathers at the beach.

sides, and bottom of a fall. Visit private or public gardens that have waterfalls, including synthetic ones. Look at photos and artists' renditions of waterfalls. Ask landscape architects or designers to show you installed waterfalls that they created.

Waterfalls look natural when built on a slope. If your property is level, create changes of level in order to make the water feature appear natural. When you excavate for the feature, save the soil and use it to sculpt low walls, shape the watercourse, or create planting areas around the feature.

STYLE AND SUBSTANCE

Once you've gathered ideas, incorporate some into your plans and note others to avoid. The style of your waterfall should be obvious now. A formal design might include geometric elements, such as a straight-sided canal, stair-stepped falls, or a wall that water glides over. Popular building materials for formal designs include cut stone, tile, metal, and acrylic. The landscape could include groundcovers or tailored trees and shrubs.

An informal or naturalistic design typically includes a single spillway surrounded by an outcropping of rocks or a rock garden. Or you might opt for a multiple-cataract waterfall, where more than one stream flows over the spillway. The plumbing for this design utilizes a manifold behind the falls that divides the water pipeline from the pump into two or more lines. Each line has its own valve to regulate how much water flows over each part of the waterfall and through the rock face as it discharges water between rocks at the top of the waterfall.

Watercourses consist of a series of basins or small pools linked by cascades or a tiered stream. As water overflows a pool, it either drops directly into a pond or spills onto rocks and into a stream. When two or more pools are connected by a waterfall or stream, design each lower basin of your watercourse larger than the one above it.

As the water recirculates in a watercourse, it is pumped from the lowest pond to fill the uppermost pool to overflowing. The lowest pond should be large enough that when water is pumped out of it to overflow the pool, the drop in volume won't be noticeable.

If you design a pond with a waterfall, locate the falls on the far side of the main approach to the pond. Plan on a buffer of smooth rocks between a turbulent waterfall and the calm waters where water lilies grow.

SIZE MATTERS

A 10×15-foot pool provides enough water to feed a waterfall about 2 feet high. It's possible to plan for five or six falls over several yards. Falls higher than 3 feet should be reserved for large ponds with extremely powerful pumps.

Limit your waterfall's height to 1 foot to 2 feet to keep it natural looking and to limit water loss as it splashes outside of the waterway. Low falls also allow you to use a less-powerful pump to keep the water flowing. This not only saves money when buying a pump, but can also result in substantial energy savings as the pump operates.

A low waterfall will still provide the appealing view and soothing sounds of flowing water that attract so many people to water gardening.

WHICH STYLE IS FOR YOU?
continued

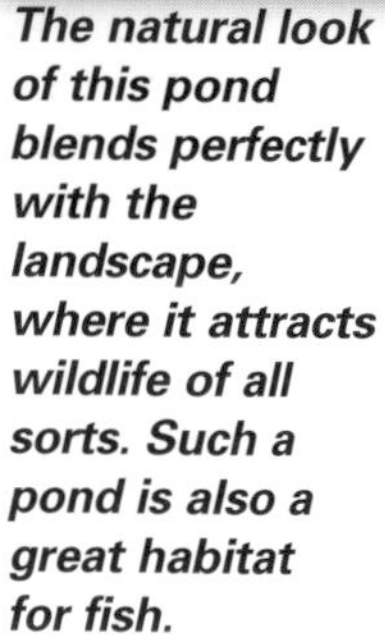

The natural look of this pond blends perfectly with the landscape, where it attracts wildlife of all sorts. Such a pond is also a great habitat for fish.

This small preformed pond catches rainwater to feed a stream that runs to the garden below.

DESIGNING A STREAM AND A BOG

A stream or watercourse typically runs from a waterfall to a pond. However, it can also function independently or be teamed with another element, such as a bog garden.

As with a waterfall, design the stream so it looks as though it occurred naturally. Take as many clues from nature as possible. Check out rocky, gurgling streams in the hills or mountains, and slower, calmer, meandering meadow creeks. Observe how the water flows more quickly where a streambed narrows and slows in wider spots. See how rocks and other obstacles affect current speed and direction. Gather photos of areas that appeal to you. Naturalizing your watercourse with rocks and plants will be essential to making it look as though it is a natural part of your landscape.

WHERE TO BEGIN

If your property has a gentle, natural slope, it should lend itself well to stream construction. Let the stream follow the natural terrain if possible. A streambed approximately level across its width will look natural. If your site provides no natural slope, create one with the soil excavated to make the stream. Design the stream with an occasional dam so that it holds water when the pump isn't operating.

A vertical drop of 1 inch to 2 inches per 10 feet of length provides adequate flow.

If the slope of your proposed stream area drops more steeply, create a series of long pools with vertical drops between them. The higher the vertical drop of water, the larger and deeper the pool under the falls should be to minimize water loss from splashing.

As with any water feature, begin your design with a site plan and sketches depicting the stream's placement and flow direction within your landscape. Keep in mind that a stream is often more interesting if it is not all visible at once. Curves and bends create a natural look—soft, flowing curves rather than quick, sharp turns. Water flows faster on the outside of a curve, and it pushes harder against the outside of the curve than the inside. Avoid long stretches of shallow water because algae will build up if the current is too slow.

Placement of natural rock determines the finished appearance of the stream. Plan to acquire a variety of rock sizes and shapes. Use the larger stones to direct and channel water; use small pebbles to create a ripple effect as water flows over them. Placing rocks on the outside of the curve creates more turbulence there. Rocks may also be used to decrease the width of the stream, making water flow faster. They also enhance the visual effect, and in some cases add delightful sounds as water rushes by or over them.

STREAM LAYOUT

Use your site plan or a sketch as a guide to laying out the stream with a hose or rope. Think about where the piping will go. You'll want a straight, direct-as-possible pipeline from the bottom (source) of the watercourse to its upper end (head). The stream's source might be a waterfall, pond, or plant filter. Or water could appear to arise out of the ground like a spring flowing from a bed of rocks; the end of it is usually a sizable pond. The water could disappear into a bed of rocks, disguising the housing for a pump that returns water to the stream head. However you design it, the catch basin should be large enough to hold all the water when the pump is shut off.

Design one or more places to cross the stream, depending on length and width. Options include bridges and stepping-stones.

Consider adding bog gardens filled with marginal and bog plants adjacent to the stream. Bog gardens create natural transitions from the stream to surrounding dry-garden areas. Bogs look natural when positioned on the outside edges of bends in the stream, where they won't interfere with its flow. The bogs receive water from the stream to replace whatever is lost through evaporation.

Use a water feature to direct garden traffic. This stream and footbridge encourage visitors to stroll into the back part of the landscape, where they might not otherwise go.

BOG GARDEN

Constructing a bog garden puts you on the cutting edge of landscape and garden design. Bog gardens not only mimic a swampy, natural habitat, but they also present an opportunity to turn a poorly draining, soggy area into a beautiful garden teeming with wildlife. For plant lovers, bogs display a vast array of seldom-seen native plants that thrive in wet or moist soil. Known as marginal plants, most grow best with wet roots, but some adapt to periodic dry conditions.

Bogs can be part of a pond or a separate aquatic feature. When incorporated into the edge of a pond with fish, bogs act as a filter, providing an ideal mechanism for enhancing the quality of the water. Fish-waste-polluted water recirculating through the bog carries nutrients to plants and beneficial bacteria growing there. They in turn clean the water and enhance the quality of life in the fishpond. Without filtering, fish die from the toxicity of their own waste.

A swampy or poorly draining area is the perfect spot to create a bog garden with plants that like moist soil.

THE BEAUTY OF CHOICES

Choosing a water feature is like choosing a home: the choice has to suit who you are, how you spend your time, and what you expect from your surroundings. A powerful waterfall gives self-expression and fulfillment to some. For others, nothing is finer than a stream flowing to a bog garden and lily pond. Still others enjoy growing aquatic plants in a deck or patio water garden. The beauty is that the choice is yours.

FEATURES AND ORNAMENTS

INCLUDING A FOUNTAIN

A fountain packs a lot of charm into a small space. Whether traditional or contemporary, it propels a stream of water through the air and creates a cooling effect. It's ideal for up-close viewing, which is why fountains are usually located on or near a porch, patio, or other sitting area.

A fountain can be attached to a wall or stand alone. Some freestanding fountains are designed to rest in—or next to—a pool or pond, while others are water features unto themselves, working well on a deck, patio, or lawn or tucked into a flower bed. Tabletop fountains work well on patios and balconies, taking just minutes to set up.

You can choose from a wide variety of styles, colors, materials, and sizes. However, choose a fountain that is in keeping with the overall style and scale of your garden and home. A classical statuary fountain might look out of place in a simple country garden, for example. A wall fountain fashioned of brick and stone is best set against similarly sturdy masonry and not wood siding.

Most fountains are made of precast concrete. Reconstituted stone and fiberglass have also become popular, simulating the look of stone with amazing realism. Whether concrete or stone look-alike, fountains come in numerous colors and surface finishes. Finding just the right fountain for your garden takes some research. Visit garden centers to scout their offerings. Ask if they offer other fountains that you can special order. Also look at mail-order catalogs. If you want a one-of-a-kind fountain, visit art fairs or ask at art galleries for the names of local artists who might design a fountain for you.

An elaborate concrete fountain in a planted pool presents a focal point for a formal courtyard.

WALL FOUNTAINS

Taking up no floor room, wall fountains are ideal for gardens or seating areas tight on space. Most are powered by a submersible pump that recirculates water from the basin through a delivery pipe up to the spout. Designs are nearly infinite, but most have a jet of water spilling into a trough or basin.

Plumbing some wall fountains can be rather complicated, often requiring piping behind the wall. In other cases, the water lines run on the wall surface and must be disguised with vines or other plants. However, simple-to-install, preformed kits are now available with only an electric cord running from them. Because the ease and cost of installation vary

Install a wall fountain where its basin can overflow into a planted pool below. The trickling water helps to aerate the reflecting pool and adds appealing music to the garden.

widely, consider installation when buying a wall fountain.

Wall fountains attach in several ways. Stone and other heavy fountains attach with mortar and are supported with special T-blocks, decorative braces that act as brackets. Lightweight fountain kits come with mounting hardware.

Freestanding Fountains

Appealing because of the ease of its installation, a freestanding fountain also makes an ideal focal point for a patio, flower bed, or lawn.

In such a fountain, a small submersible pump is housed in the lower pedestal in a hollow base beneath the bowl. Its design should allow easy access to the pump so you can clean and maintain it, usually monthly.

Statuary Fountains

These ornamental fountains can be placed near a pond or pool or in the water feature itself. The decorative statue has a supply pipe projecting from its base. The pipe is connected to the pump with flexible tubing.

Large statues must have firm footing. For a fountain on the side of a pond, make sure its resting place (including any edging) is firm and level. If you want to install the fountain in the pond, you can mount it on a hollow in-pond pedestal created specifically for that purpose or build your own with mortared bricks or stone. If the statue is small, black plastic storage crates make an easy, hard-to-detect base as long as the base of the fountain is slightly under water.

An ornamental fountain can be created from a kit or by drilling through a decorative statue to install water supply pipes. Mount heavy statuary securely on a solid base.

FEATURES AND ORNAMENTS
continued

If you design your water garden for nighttime viewing or entertaining, be sure to install low-voltage lights in strategic spots. They illuminate paths and steps as well as water features.

ADDING ORNAMENTS

Every garden, even the simplest, needs a few accessories to complete the design. After the plants are in place, relax by your water feature and imagine what ornaments might best accent the style of your garden.

Sometimes basic uncomplicated forms are best when it comes to choosing decorative elements for a water garden. Sculptures that imitate wildlife, such as frogs, turtles, or water birds, suit an informal or natural setting. Plaques made of painted metal, tile or wood can highlight specific plants or feature a favorite wild creature.

Not all ornaments must be purchased new. Recycled materials can become treasures in a waterscape. Flat pavers can be reused as stepping-stones in shallow pools. Old pottery bowls and dishes can hold trailing marginals and add bright spots of color to a pond's edge. Leftover chicken wire and cable sheathing can be turned into a one-of-a-kind art object, such as a heron to stand guard in the pond. You can make a whimsical or nostalgic statement with many discarded items that have lost their original usefulness: iron kettles, leaky watering cans, rusted garden tools, even wooden trellises with some pieces missing. No sprucing up is required to make them fit in the design of your garden.

Splashing statuary adds a special music to the garden that draws people outdoors. To emphasize serenity, add the quiet trickle of a recirculating fountain near a seating area. Even a natural depression in a large stone slab

Mortar recycled glass bottles into a stone retaining wall to create an unusual feature. Leave irregular spaces for planting pockets.

can be filled with water to set the scene for quiet contemplation—although you'll likely be joined by birds eager to drink and bathe.

Water gardens lend themselves well to fantasy, too. Fairies and garden sprites are never out of style and blend gracefully with the ephemeral feel of the water. Depending on the pose, place one on a rocky ledge above a stream or waterfall, prop it up on submerged bricks among some water lilies, or tuck it among plants near the edge of the pond for a surprise that will make guests smile. If you have children at home, lighten your idea of what is appropriate decoration, and invite them to be in on the decision making. Unexpected or amusing decorations can help to reflect enjoyment in your hobby.

If most of your pondside hours are after work, consider adding nighttime lighting to your design, in the water as well as on the landscape. Illuminating a water feature adds safety as well as sparkling beauty to the scene.

If your water garden is large, a simple footbridge across some portion of it serves as a link while providing new vantage points to appreciate the view below. Whatever the size and style of your design, be sure to include a chair or bench nearby from which to admire your handiwork.

Use a bridge to span a stream or pond and offer an attractive vantage point for admiring the plants and fish below.

Artfully placed rocks create a natural sculpture that is a water feature in itself. A shallow depression in the top stone holds just enough water to offer a point for quiet reflection. Wildlife will be attracted to this oasis too.

Tuck a small water garden in a flower bed for a charming surprise, such as this natural-looking pond surrounded by mossy rocks and colorful annuals. A surprise sculpture perched at water's edge will bring smiles from your guests—especially children.

FORM, TEXTURE, AND COLOR

Plantings around the pond are just as important as the shape of the pond. Their form gives vertical structure to the water; their texture provides a rich canvas on which to work.

Bushy, upright form: umbrella grass

Upright form: iris

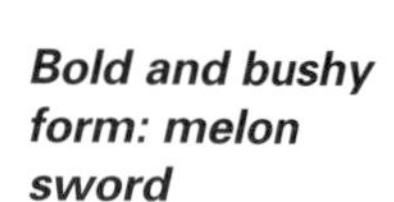

Bold and bushy form: melon sword

Creeping form: moneywort

Plants bring glory to a backyard water feature, transforming a pond from a sterile, flat plane of water into a living, breathing world added to your landscape. It is often the choice of plants more than pool shape and edging that creates the feel and flavor of the water garden. Plants add height, texture, and perspective, making the pond a true garden oasis.

Plant form and texture are two of the primary elements in water garden design. Along with color, they bring balance and mood to the garden that enhance and beautify its hardscape. They are the elements that give the garden dimension.

FORM

Form means the overall shape of the plant. Generally speaking, a plant's form may be upright, mounding (sometimes called bushy), or creeping. Upright plants are tall and columnar. They give vertical thrust to the landscape, as does a fountain or an upright stone. Mounding plants are lower and rounded. Their shape ties the form of upright plants to the landscape, anchoring the vertical plants to the design. Creeping plants lie closer to the ground; in the pond, they float on the surface. Their horizontal habit directs the eye through the aquascape, forward, backward, and side to side.

Well-balanced water garden designs include a harmonious blend of vertical, mounding, and creeping plants. A design that uses only one kind of plant form is one-dimensional and visually uninviting. For example, if you compose your garden solely of upright plants, it may look top-heavy and uninteresting.

Select water plants with form and texture that echo those of plants in the surrounding landscape.

Fine texture: corkscrew rush

A pond that lacks transitions from the taller plants to the ground—one that has no mounding plants—may appear abrupt, as if something is left out.

For example, umbrella grass is an attractive upright plant that gives height to a design. Melon sword *(Echinodorus cordifolius)* is shorter and more rounded in habit. Combining these plants with a creeper, such as water hyssop, makes an attractive, three-tiered planting at the edge of the pond.

TEXTURE

Plant texture is another element of water garden design that will make your garden vibrant. Texture is defined as fine, medium, and coarse, terms that are applied to plant foliage and other elements in the design.

Fine texture is often associated with pine trees and needled evergreens. Fine-textured plants have thin or tiny leaves, about the size of pebbles. The leaves on a medium-textured plant are about the size of a serving spoon or the width of a butter knife. Coarse foliage is large and bold, ranging from the size of a hockey puck to a beach ball; some hardy plants with coarse foliage look almost tropical.

Even the tiniest container pond benefits from a mixture of plant forms and textures. By combining plant texture and form, you'll have a richer palette to work with. Plants on the water surface generally are limited to representing the horizontal aspect of design. It's on the margin of your pond that you have the greatest opportunity for varying plant form and texture.

Your garden will be even more exciting if you rely on elements other than plants to provide some design features. Incorporate forms and textures from the hardscaping. Use edging as the horizontal element along with creeping plants. A large, round boulder can stand in for a bushy plant, a tall stone for an upright plant. Combining stones and hardscape with the plants adds character and depth. Soften a large boulder by planting around it with yellow flag irises and parrot's feather. Pebbles at the edge of the pond take on vibrant character when they serve as the footing for a bold planting of corkscrew rush.

Medium texture: lizard's tail

Medium texture: lobelia

COLOR

The colors of the water garden may be as muted or as loud as those of any perennial border. You can use them to create themes, set moods, or awaken the senses. Because the pond landscape should reflect the sensibilities of the gardener who builds it, choose colors you like or that have meaning for you.

Select all-white flowers contrasted with plants of all-blue foliage to have your own moon garden. White flowers will also light up a shady corner of the pond. Blues and greens create a cool, relaxing atmosphere. Soft pastel shades create a pond reminiscent of a Monet painting.

A simple water garden in a terra-cotta pot is stunning when planted with the bright orange flowers and striking yellow and green foliage of 'Praetoria' canna, complemented by the bright blue flowers and shiny green leaves of lemon bacopa.

Coarse or bold texture: gunnera

Coarse or bold texture: taro

Coarse or bold texture: canna

Plant shapes vary from narrowly upright to arching to rounded to flat. Here, the upright form of the irises draws the eye upward to the cascading ornamental grass in the background.

COLOR AND SEASONAL CHANGES

Just as tulips trumpet the arrival of spring in a perennial garden, so too does the pond have its own harbingers. Even if the water is still cold, the pond can be full of life and color.

The water garden reflects the changing moods of the seasons, just as the perennial border and the rest of the landscape do. Each season—spring through summer and autumn through winter—shows its own distinctive personality in the pond.

SPRING

The water garden's harbinger of spring is the marsh marigold. Its common name speaks to its resemblance to its dryland namesake. This marginal plant has bright yellow waxy flowers and mounds of shiny, rounded, serrated leaves. Marsh marigolds peek their heads above the ice-crusted soil at the edge of the pond in early spring, about the same time that crocuses begin to appear in the perennial border. Like crocus, marsh marigold pays no heed to cold winds or falling snow.

Color in the spring pond is apparent not only in early blooms but also in the new foliage that starts to sprout along the margins of the pond and in bog gardens beside it. Blue flag pushes up its new leaves—pointed swords of green that are streaked with beet red or deep purple at the base. These add important color to the pond when little else in the yard has yet to awake. Blue rushes, with their almost ever-blue foliage, add still more color to the edge of the spring water garden, as do early-rising sweet flags and sedge, which get a jump on the summer color season by two to three months.

On the water surface itself, water hawthorn emerges early, as the ice is leaving the pond, producing fragrant floating white flowers. Water lilies are barely waking up, but white water buttercup *(Ranunculus longirostris)* and floating marsh marigold *(Caltha natans)* will soon be showing their dainty flowers on the water surface. Pink blush tinges the foliage of early-emerging marginals, including 'Flamingo' rainbow water parsley, variegated manna grass, and 'Candy Stripe' reed.

In summer, the pond is at its peak. The perennial garden bursts with blooms around the water's edge.

As summer fades into autumn, marginal plants and deciduous trees that change color as they mature add visual interest to the garden. Some aquatic plants are at their most attractive even after the first frost.

SUMMER

As spring gives way to summer, marsh marigold and hyacinth lose their blush, but color continues to burst forth in the water garden. Irises bloom along the margins, and water lilies and water snowflakes flower on the surface of the water, beginning an early-summer show that lasts until the fall frost.

Just as you would check your perennial border, check your water garden week by week. Note when water lilies are not in bloom and when annuals start to fade, and shop for colorful marginal plants that will flower at varying times throughout the season. If you have any holes or gaps when nothing is in bloom on the water surface, take a look around your local water garden center to see what is in bloom.

Fill in empty spots to keep the design in balance. Tropical marginals, such as cannas and white-topped sedge, can be useful in providing early-summer color. Their vibrant flowers and lush foliage bridge the spring and summer seasons, and they continue to flower right until frost.

July and August are the months when the water garden is truly at its peak. Lotuses begin to flower in July. Pickerel weed is in full flush in summer months, when water lilies also reach their full potential. Even on scorching summer days when the perennial garden looks peaked, the water garden thrives and flourishes in the heat and humidity.

AUTUMN

Once fall arrives, the water garden still has something to offer. Although the foliage of most water plants dies after the first frost or has little autumnal color other than brown, some plants wait for the cooler months to put on their best show. These include sedges and blue rushes, which take on a purple hue after a frost. Colors that were soft and subtle in summer really shine in autumn.

European bugleweed *(Lycopus europaeus)* offers a dazzling display of purple, as does frog fruit *(Phyla lanceolata)*. Star fruit *(Penthorum sedoides)* becomes the burning bush of the pond, with fiery oranges, reds, pinks, and yellows. Tufts-of-gold *(Lysimachia thyrsiflora)* is ablaze with golden-yellow foliage and pinkish-red stems. Cattails, willows, and red-stemmed dogwoods *(Cornus stolonifera* or *C. sericea)* add to the backdrop.

WINTER

Winter, perhaps the bleakest of gardening seasons, can still hold interest. Blue rushes as well as corkscrew rushes are almost evergreen—or ever-blue—even in snow. Water parsnip *(Sium suave)* and water dock *(Rumex hydrolapathum)* stand tall, their seed heads offering birds a welcome treat. Like the catkins of the cattail and the heads of soft rush, they catch the snow as it falls softly to the ground. Their chocolate-brown stems stand out in contrast to the white of the snow, like sentinels keeping watch over the water garden until spring.

Leave aquatic plants with seed heads or catkins standing for winter interest. The birds will be grateful too.

A DESIGN CHECKLIST

SIZE THINGS UP

Take care to build the right size pond. Before you dig, measure carefully to be sure you'll end up with the correct size and depth. A pond that is too small or too shallow or too deep will make it hard to care for aquatic life. Ask other pondkeepers or at a garden center in your area what depth works best for water gardening in your climate.

Make your pond as large as you can for the space you have available. If you must start out small with an in-ground pond, use a flexible liner so you can easily add on later. If you are using a flexible liner, double-check your measurements to be sure you have at least 2 feet of overlap along the edge of the pond. Stones or other edging will hide the excess, while splashing water is kept where it belongs.

Multiply the volume of your pond (surface length × surface width × depth) by 7.5 to determine the number of gallons of water it will hold. It's surprising how many gallons it takes to fill a square foot of space. A half whiskey barrel, for example, holds about 25 gallons of water. A typical backyard pond may hold 250 to 1,000 gallons or more.

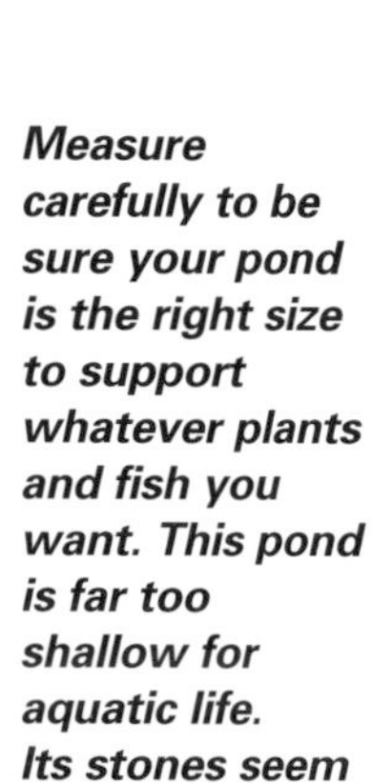

Measure carefully to be sure your pond is the right size to support whatever plants and fish you want. This pond is far too shallow for aquatic life. Its stones seem isolated in the otherwise natural, green setting.

A waterfall too large or too tall for its pond can drain down the water too far when the pump is running.

CHECK YOUR MATH

Make sure your stream or waterfall is in proportion to the main pond. The necessary calculations take some thought but are crucial to making good equipment choices. When the feature is running, it will drain down the pond by the same amount of water it uses; it will fill up the pond by that same amount when it is turned off. For example, a waterfall might move 100 gallons of water per hour for every inch of surface and half inch of depth. Make sure your stream or waterfall is in proportion to the main pond.

Use your calculations to choose the right pump for the features you want to power. Pick one no smaller in size than one-third the total gallons of water in the pond. There are many inexpensive pumps available, but they may have hidden costs, depending on your design. A low-capacity pump may not be powerful enough to run a fountain or may be expensive to use because it isn't energy-efficient. A pump that costs a bit more but comes with a good warranty is a better investment.

KEEP ELEMENTS IN BALANCE

Choose materials and plants that blend well with existing elements in your yard. A water garden should fit in with the rest of your landscape. An isolated pond ringed with nearly identical large stones can look harsh or out of place in an otherwise natural setting. Choose edging materials that match or coordinate with those of your patio or deck. Soften the perimeter with pockets of marginal and companion plants that help to tie the water garden to terrestrial areas of your yard.

Overstocking can cause water quality and fish health problems in a pond. A small feature like this with so many fish will need to have extra filters or a UV clarifier to ensure balance.

Perhaps you can add a bog garden at the edge of the pond nearest a perennial border. Whatever your design, be sure to include enough plants to help balance the pond's ecosystem. Submerged plants will help to control algae growth by adding oxygen to the water, while marginal plants can help by keeping some surface areas shaded and cooler.

A certain amount of algae is unavoidable, no matter how meticulous you are with pond maintenance. When plants and other living things are present, the water will become cloudy, and clarity will change with the season. Both algae and cloudiness are normal, healthy signs of a thriving water garden. Monitor water quality and algae growth to keep them in balance. If you have designed your pond for easy maintenance access, these tasks should be simple.

Fish, too, are an important part of a natural waterscape. They are so much fun to watch and feed that it is easy to overstock a pond. But too many fish can seriously compromise water quality and fish health by depleting oxygen and increasing ammonia, especially during the heat of summer. Most water gardeners recommend no more than one 6-inch fish per 100 gallons of water. If you want more fish, be prepared to install additional filters or ultraviolet clarifiers to ensure good water quality.

Edging made of nearly identical stones calls negative attention to a pond or pool as an isolated feature in an otherwise natural setting. Use asymmetrical rocks and more plants to soften the perimeter.

Water garden construction is easier if you first assemble the materials and equipment you'll need. The basic items are the same for almost every backyard project: a shovel and a spade, a garden hose, a wheelbarrow, a flexible or preformed liner and underlayment, a pump, edging, and aquatic plants. Chances are you'll need someone to help you with a task or two, and if your features are complex, you may want to hire professionals pond installers.

MATERIALS AND EQUIPMENT

Water gardening has been revolutionized by new materials that make it easier than ever to create a feature that's perfect for your landscape. Not too long ago, creating any kind of water feature meant you had to hire professionals to form and reinforce a concrete water course and install complex plumbing and electrical systems. Today, there's an entirely new way to create water gardens.

Flexible and preformed liners have replaced the concrete, and now you can install most water features—in an unending variety of shapes, sizes, and styles—yourself, without professional help.

Pumps install with little effort, use regular household current, and recirculate the water (there's no more need for special plumbing). Fountains attach easily to their supporting structures. Filters (which once had to be installed out of the water) are now often built into the pumps. With simplified techniques and equipment, it's possible to install a small water feature in just a weekend.

Although the materials have been revolutionized, the essential equipment remains the same. A spade, wheelbarrow, carpenter's level, measuring tape, and a pair of heavy leather gloves are the basic tools you'll need to complete your garden pool project.

Make sure all tools are in excellent condition, clean, and in good repair before you begin. Sharpen your spade, tighten the wheelbarrow bolts, and inflate its tire.

Having the proper materials and supplies will help you avoid problems as you easily execute your project to produce professional-looking results.

IN THIS SECTION

CONTAINER GARDENS

Even if you want a big water garden with a waterfall, a stream, and a variety of fish and plants, make a starter garden first. A small-scale project offers experience you'll find helpful when you tackle larger water garden projects later.

A starter garden brings the beauty of water to your landscape in a minimum of time and for much less cost than it takes to develop a large water feature. It is also more manageable when it comes to time, requiring less than an hour of maintenance every few weeks.

You can have an aquascape in little more space than a tabletop. Tucked into a corner of a patio, a water garden will be a pleasant source of sound; incorporated into the landscape, it will be a sparkling focal point.

Large terra-cotta and ceramic pots are perfect for container water gardens that will sit on a patio or other protected porch area. Drill a hole in the bottom if you want to add a pump to run a fountain or other recirculating feature.

CONTAINER WATER GARDENS

A container water garden is perhaps the easiest starter water garden. You can build one in an hour or two with no digging and little expense. And you can locate it in places you may not have considered for a water garden—places unsuitable for any kind of large-scale pond project, such as on a deck.

Virtually any kind of container can be used for a water garden. If it holds water—or can be made to hold water—you can turn it into a water garden. Here are some suggestions: half whiskey barrels, galvanized buckets or livestock troughs (older ones that are no longer shiny; otherwise they can be toxic), oversized dishes or bowls, boulders or rocks with hollows, black plastic tubs designed for water gardens, wooden buckets, iron kettles, and claw-foot bathtubs.

Try using an item you can fully or partially sink into the ground, depending on your location. In-ground locations help

A half whiskey barrel holds about 25 gallons of water, just the right size for a container garden that you can view up close. Whiskey barrels are such popular planters that most garden centers sell preformed liners just for them.

Plug the drain holes in an old claw-foot bathtub to create a brand-new water garden. Tuck the tub among flowers in a perennial bed, fill it with water and a half-dozen aquatic plants, and it's sure to draw smiles from visitors.

HINT

If water becomes cloudy or foul smelling in a small starter water garden, remove 10 percent of the water from the bottom with a siphon hose or water pump. This reduces the buildup of toxic organic wastes. Add fresh water to replace what you removed.

Float one miniature water lily and a trailing plant or two in a shallow bowl that can sit on a tabletop.

minimize summer temperature fluctuations. You especially want to sink unattractive plastic containers, such as buckets and dishpans, into the ground up to their lip; then hide the lip with plants and stones.

If you're planning to have fish or want your garden above ground, locate the container in a spot that receives afternoon shade during the summer. To make sure fish get enough oxygen, keep a thermometer in the water, and never let the temperature rise above 85°F. Keep a small battery-powered aeration pump on hand for emergency aeration.

IS IT WATERPROOF?

After choosing your container, check it for watertightness. Place it on a nonporous, dry surface, such as a sidewalk or driveway; then fill it with water. Let it sit for a day, checking occasionally for leaks. If it leaks, seal minor cracks from the inside with aquarium sealant.

You can make porous containers watertight by painting them with a rubberized sealant available from water garden suppliers or with swimming pool paint, or by installing flexible liner. (Half whiskey barrels must be lined to keep impurities in the wood from killing fish.) If you use flexible liner, tuck it carefully into all recesses inside the container; then staple the liner's edges or glue them with aquarium sealant to the container.

You'll need only the smallest of pumps—a bubbler is a good choice—and it should allow you to adjust the fountain spray to the right size for the container garden.

Use your imagination to create a starter garden from just about any water-worthy container: a discarded galvanized or enamel bucket, a recycled plant stand with a new, watertight liner, even an old tackle box. Close any leaks with aquarium sealant or use flexible liner to keep the water where you want it. Install a damaged container in the ground and disguise it with marginal plants.

HINT

Copper containers are toxic to fish and other aquatic animals. They should not be used for water garden containers unless lined with another material.

LINERS

Flexible liner is so easy to use that one person can install a small water garden with little effort. The time-consuming task is folding and tucking the excess liner.

HINT

To make sure there are no sharp rocks that might puncture the liner, walk barefoot or in socks (carefully) over the bottom of the excavated area.

One of the most important innovations in garden pond technology is flexible liner. Developed in the 1960s to replace poured concrete and other building materials, it allows you to create pools, streams, and waterfalls in just about any shape, length, and style you can imagine.

Flexible liner will help you build water gardens in places not possible before. Line an aboveground brick garden pool, for example, or waterproof a whiskey barrel half. Make an artificial stream with sand, gravel, and stones arranged on the liner. Restore a leaky concrete pond by draining it and laying liner over the damaged concrete.

Flexible liners are made from a variety of materials—polyethylene, polyvinyl chloride (PVC), and ethylene propylene diene monomer (EPDM)—and they vary greatly in thickness, cost, and quality. Heavier liners will generally be more expensive, more durable, and more puncture- and tear-resistant than lighter weight liners. However, new liner developments combine durability with light weight. As a rule, the more you spend, the more the liner will resist the sun's ultraviolet rays.

UV light is the constant enemy of liner material (especially polyethylene). It breaks down the chemical bonds in the liner, making it brittle and prone to ripping. If you're going to build a garden pond with polyethylene flexible liner, remember to keep the pond filled with water and the liner completely covered so none of it is exposed.

Most liner comes in black, a color well-suited to garden pools. Black is natural-looking and blends with the algae that tends to cover it after a few months (and helps the liner resist UV damage). Black also gives a pool the illusion of greater depth.

HOW TO DETERMINE THE LINER SIZE

Purchase a flexible liner by the square foot. Determine the size of your water feature before you purchase a liner for it.

Here's how:

Imagine your pond as a rectangle, even though it may be round or irregular. Make sure the rectangle includes the farthest points of the pond. Then consider how deep the pond will be. The liner size equals the length (l) plus two times the depth (d), plus 2 feet, multiplied by the width (w) plus two times the depth (d), plus 2 feet. This allows a 1-foot margin all the way around the perimeter. Professionals often add only 6 inches around the perimeter, leaving little margin for error. Avoid the risk of having to patch extra on later by leaving a 1-foot margin now.

A pond whose imaginary rectangle measures 15 feet by 10 feet and is 1½ feet deep needs a liner 20 feet (15 + 1½ + 1½ + 2 = 20) by 15 feet (10 + 1½ + 1½ + 2 = 15); 20×15 = a 300-square-foot liner. Make any number of depth and surface configurations, including shelves, with a given-size liner; the same formula applies.

At this point, don't worry about figuring the volume (number of gallons) your water feature will hold. Some suppliers give the maximum gallons possible using their liner (or other product) and assuming a given depth. You will need the volume in order to determine the fish-carrying capacity and to figure the appropriate size of optional features such as a waterfall, pump, mechanical filter, UV clarifier, and water treatments.

Figure the volume of a pond or other feature by multiplying its cubic feet (length × width × depth), then multiplying the number of cubic feet by 7.5 (because each cubic foot contains 7.5 gallons of water).

To size a liner for a finished excavation, measure the length and width of the excavation using a flexible tape. Add 2 feet to each measurement. Unpack a liner only when you're certain it's the right size.

Stock sizes for liners start with 5-foot squares and range up to sections 50×100 feet or more. You can join pieces with liner tape or seam sealer made specifically for this purpose to create streams and other large features.

When buying a liner, make sure it is made for use with plants and fish. Liners for other uses (swimming pools or roofs, for example) will be toxic to living things.

UNDERLAYMENT

All liners require the installation of an underlayment, a cushion layer of material between the liner and the soil that prevents punctures and tears. Sand is a good choice for the pool bottom and other horizontal surfaces but can't be laid vertically. Newspaper is acceptable but deteriorates over time. Old carpet and specially made pond underlayment (which resembles sheets of fiberglass insulation) are ideal.

Some new liners are manufactured with an underlayment already attached. They are extremely puncture-resistant and should be used over coarse gravel or sharp rock, for example, or in locations where punctures from tree roots are likely.

If the liner does tear or puncture, it's no cause for alarm. You can repair it with a patch and solvent cement or special liner adhesive. However, you'll have to drain the pond first, clean the area, and let it dry so the patch will stick to the liner.

Flexible liner conforms to your one-of-a-kind creation. Piece it together as you go. Here, overlapped sections create a streambed flowing into a pond.

Once the flexible liner is in place and the pond partially filled, work the liner into the crevices around the sides.

COMPARING FLEXIBLE LINER MATERIALS

Liner Material	Cost	Advantages	Disadvantages	Comments
Polyethylene	30 cents per square foot and more.	Inexpensive. Most hardware and home supply outlets carry it.	Low-density polyethylene is acceptably durable, but avoid high-density polyethylene. Either can be stiff in cold weather. Polyethylene is difficult to repair.	Purchase black, not transparent. Lasts only about two years in a pond. Will last indefinitely, however, when used in a bog garden where it's not exposed to sun.
PVC (polyvinyl chloride)	35 cents per square foot and more.	Moderately durable; sometimes carries a 10-year warranty. Widely available.	PVC for swimming pools and roofs can be toxic to fish and plants.	20- to 32-mil thicknesses. PVC-E is an improved version for fish and plants.
EPDM (ethylene-propylene-diene-monomer)	45 cents per square foot and more.	Very durable; usually carries a 20-year warranty. Stays flexible even in cold weather. Very resistant to UV light damage.	More expensive.	Look for EPDM-SF, which is not toxic to fish and plants and is available in 45-mil thickness.
Butyl rubber (synthetic rubber)	80 cents per square foot and more.	Very durable, sometimes lasting up to 50 years. Usually carries a 20-year warranty. Is more elastic than PVC and polyethylene. Stays flexible even in cold weather.	Most expensive. Can be difficult to find.	Generally sold in 30- or 60-mil thicknesses.

LINERS

continued

Manufacturers make it easy for water gardeners to match the most appropriate equipment to the design of their water feature. An all-in-one pond kit makes it even easier.

INSTALLING FLEXIBLE LINER

Flexible liner is relatively easy to install. A water gardener can work alone lining a small pool, but spreading liner out evenly in a larger project may require help from several people.

You'll find that flexible liner comes with one drawback that preformed liners don't have: You won't be able to avoid folds and creases. As you fill the pond, you'll have to neatly tuck the liner—especially if it's made of less elastic polyethylene or PVC—into uneven places so the weight of the water won't stress it unevenly and weaken or tear it. This can be difficult to do but will be easier if you let the liner warm in the sun an hour or two before you start work.

FOUNDATION UNDER A BOULDER

Large boulders at the edge of a pond (or in the midst of it) require a concrete support along with extra layers of liner and underlayment to prevent leaks.

Boulder
Layers of flexible liner
3/8- to 1/2-inch steel rebar
4- to 6-inch-thick concrete pad

PREFORMED LINERS

Easy to install and well-suited to small garden ponds, preformed liners (also called rigid liners) are available in many ready-made sizes and styles.

Most preformed liners are constructed of fiberglass or rigid plastic. Fiberglass is more expensive but lasts longer than rigid plastic. A small 6×3-foot fiberglass liner starts at around $300 (compared with $100 for a rigid-plastic liner); large fiberglass liners can cost $900 or more. Properly installed, a fiberglass liner can last as long as 50 years.

Whether fiberglass or plastic, preformed liners are much more durable than flexible liner and are easier to repair if damaged.

Rigid units have another distinct advantage over flexible liners—they make aboveground water gardens easier to install. They're ideal in areas where stony soil or tree roots prevent or hinder excavation. You can place them either entirely above ground or install them at any depth. But don't expect them to support themselves. Aboveground ponds will need a structure built around them.

In-ground preformed liners are especially practical for paved areas where the edges can be supported. Rigid liners are available in many shapes, both formal and informal. And if the wide variety of ready-made shapes doesn't suit you, shop around for a manufacturer to custom make one for you.

Standard preformed liners also come in a variety of depths; some include shallow ledges for marginal plants and deep zones for fish to overwinter. For large water gardens—those more than 12 feet long—you can purchase preformed liners in sections that you bolt together and seal with marine silicone. Such sectional liners can be hard to find, however, and require considerably more work. It's better to shop around until you find an existing shape that's right for your landscape.

Although you can buy preformed units in different colors, black is usually best for the same reasons as it is for flexible liners: It's neutral and creates the illusion that the pond is deeper than it actually is.

Make sure the preformed liner is absolutely level and that you backfill nooks and crevices so the plastic doesn't collapse under the weight of the water. Also, you have to be careful about using heavy edging, such as stone. Some preformed liner edges are convex and the weight of stone will crush them. Other edges are designed to bear weight (check with the supplier), but they must be fully supported with backfill.

Although preformed liners are ideal for formal gardens, they also can be made to look very natural. This one, blended into the surrounding landscape with rock edging and aquatic plants, has a small stream flowing into it.

HINT

A minimum of 2 inches of soil mixed with sand backfilled under and around a preformed pond will help prevent winter cracking and splitting.

Preformed liners come in a variety of shapes and sizes that allow you to design an aquascape to suit most garden styles. You can create a substantial water garden by combining several small liners in multiple layers with cascades or falls in between.

CONCRETE

Concrete or gunite ponds can be costly and challenging to build, but may last a lifetime if designed and constructed well.

If properly constructed, concrete pools last for decades. However, concrete construction is more difficult and costly than the alternatives. Building a concrete pond may require hiring professionals who have the necessary expertise and tools. Ideally, concrete should be embedded with heavy-duty steel wire mesh or reinforcing rods (rebar) for stability and durability. Gunite, concrete sprayed on steel reinforcing rods, efficiently forms a naturalistic pond. Concrete blocks or a combination of concrete and stone, bricks, or decorative tile offer additional building options, particularly for aboveground water features.

Mortar, a form of concrete, is used for building with block or brick and making seals between them as well as for embedding stone, brick, or comparable edging materials. Mortar tends to separate after repeated freezing and thawing. Alternatively, you may use black urethane foam. It forms a lasting seal that helps prevent leaking because it expands when applied and won't deteriorate over time.

Compacted clay-bottom ponds hold water naturally. They are constructed on land with clay-based soil or built with clay that's brought to the site. Their water-holding capacity is sometimes enhanced by adding bentonite, a powdered clay made from volcanic ash.

In sandy soil the digging will be easier, but extra effort is required to be sure the walls are adequately supported. Using both liner and concrete reinforced with wire mesh makes the strongest base, and rebar along the sides anchors the liner and mesh on the wall forms. Be sure to keep some of the excavated soil for backfilling later.

HOW MUCH CONCRETE?

If you want to order enough concrete ready-mix (delivered by a contractor) to make 6-inch-thick walls that withstand a cold climate, use this formula. First, measure the outside dimensions (width × height) of each wall and the pond's bottom; then add the five numbers to determine the total area in square feet. Multiply the total by the thickness of the concrete (6 inches = 0.5 feet) to determine the number of cubic feet. Divide this number by 27 to conclude how many cubic yards of concrete to order. Estimate for a curved or irregular-shape pond by using an imaginary rectangle to figure the area and adding a 10 percent margin of error.

REINFORCED CONCRETE PERIMETER COLLAR

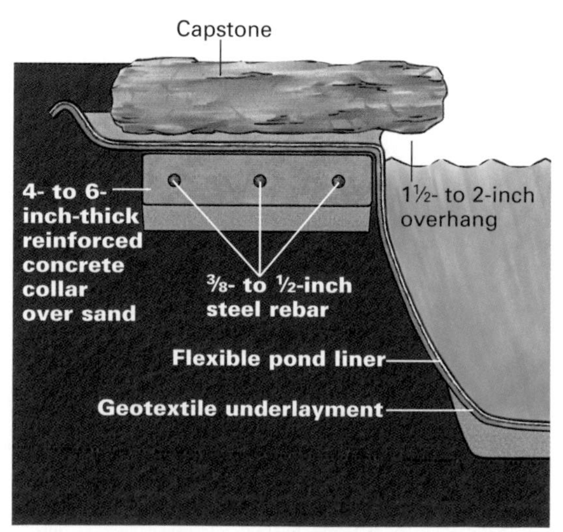

A concrete collar supports the rock edging around a pond and reinforces the edge's stability.

CONCRETE PONDS

Most ponds were made of concrete until the 1960s, when flexible liners presented a less costly, easier-to-install option. Poured concrete and concrete block are classic-looking building materials that can last decades. Conversely, concrete's high cost and challenging construction make it daunting for an inexperienced builder. If improperly installed, a concrete pool will crack, leak, and cause infinite frustration. Avoid using concrete to line a stream. It's expensive and doesn't look natural.

If you prefer, combine the beauty and durability of concrete with a flexible or preformed liner. The liner eliminates the need to neutralize the concrete before adding plants or fish, and if the concrete cracks, it won't leak. Also consider finishing a concrete-lined pond with a handsome exterior framework of brick, treated wood, or tile. Capping concrete walls with brick, stone, or pavers gives a pond a stylish look as well.

POURED CONCRETE OR BLOCKS

A poured-concrete structure requires preparing an excavation and wood forms to shape the walls and hold the concrete while it sets. The base and sides of the excavation should be firmly tamped. Cover the level base with a 4- to 6-inch layer of gravel to help prevent cracking. Sandwich wire mesh or steel rods in between two layers of poured concrete to provide reinforcement and strength. Alternatively, have a professional spray the wire-reinforced form with layers of gunite or shotcrete. Paint the inside of a concrete pool with a waterproof sealant for water gardens if you like.

Concrete blocks offer a simpler way to construct a pond. Stacked hollow blocks, reinforced with metal rods and filled with concrete, make a formidable structure. Build shelves for plants by shaping the excavation to support them or stacking additional blocks along the pond wall. Line the pond with a flexible or preformed liner. Top the edges with mortared block, brick, or stone.

In regions with cold winters and freeze-thaw cycles, the sides of a concrete pool should slope outward by about 20 degrees overall to allow water in the pool to freeze and expand without cracking the concrete.

IN COLD CLIMATES

To ensure its success, build a poured-concrete pond as you would a swimming pool. The walls and base must be at least 6 inches thick. Pour or spray concrete all at once (with no seams) over steel reinforcement until you achieve the required thickness.

Digging a pond in sandy soil is easier than in heavy clay, but you'll need to use both flexible liner and wire-reinforced concrete to support the base. Anchor the walls with rebar.

PUMPS

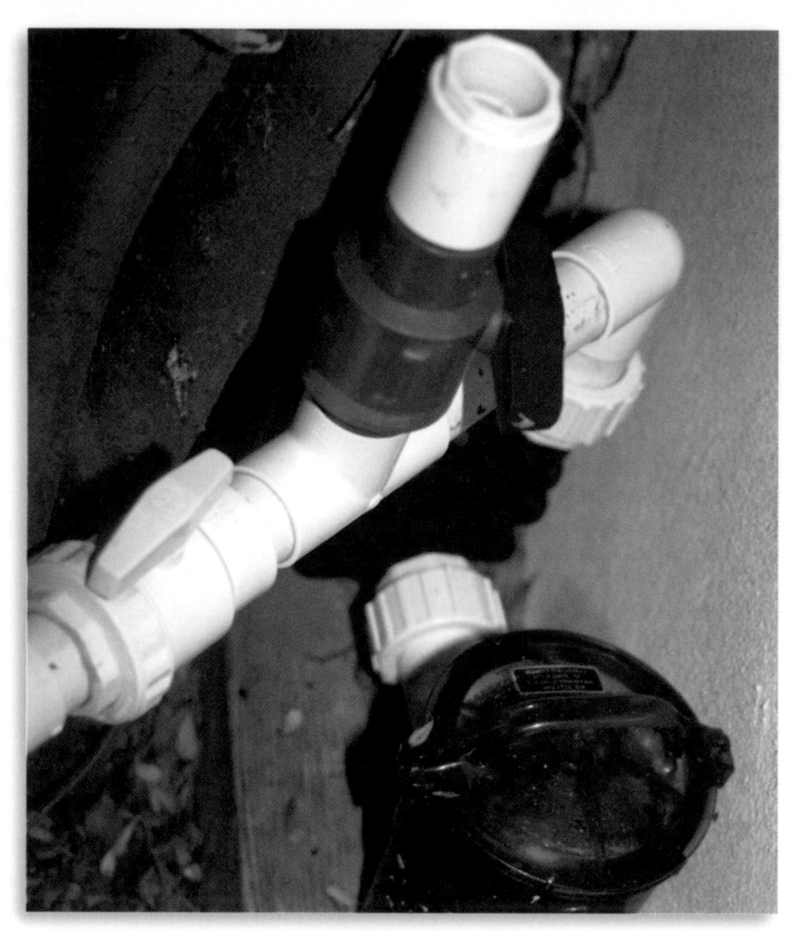

Use an external pump for water features that carry more than 12,000 gph or for waterfalls and fountains that require high lift. Install the pump where it can be kept clean and dry, and choose a location where its noise will not disturb your outdoor activities.

Still water in a garden pool is beautiful in its own right. But moving water is what adds that splash and sparkle to your water garden. For that, you'll need a pump.

Pumps make streams run, fountains spray, ponds drain, and water recirculate so that waterfalls keep falling. Moving water through a water feature once required complicated plumbing. Today, all you need is a pump. Installation isn't complicated, taking just minutes to assemble and set in your pond.

ANATOMY OF A PUMP

Nozzle
Flow adjuster
Impeller
Prefilter

SUBMERSIBLE OR EXTERNAL?

Pumps are available in submersible and external models, and in both the mechanism is simply a set of whirling blades that pressurize the water and force it into motion. Submersible pumps are easier to use than external pumps. They sit directly in the water, and unlike external pumps, which you'll have to locate outside the pond, submersibles are inexpensive. They're easy to install, start without priming, and run quietly. Submersible pumps can be used to power all but the largest water features.

Before buying a pump for your garden pool, check its energy-efficiency rating. Large water features require more pump capacity, so they consume more electric energy.

Look for magnetic-driven pumps, which use less energy than direct-driven pumps. Generally the most efficient pumps are also the most expensive, but they can pay for themselves in energy efficiency.

PUMP SIZE

The most important consideration when choosing which pump to buy is its size. Equipment manufacturers rate electrical power in amps or watts, but the critical measure of pump power is the number of gallons of water it will pump per hour to a specific height, called the head.

To determine the size pump you'll need, first calculate the volume of water in the pond (see the box at right). As a rule, choose a pump that can move half the total volume in an hour. For example, if your pond holds 500 gallons of water, buy a pump that delivers at least 250 gallons an hour (gph).

If your water garden will include a waterfall or stream, it will need a more powerful pump. Pumps have to work harder to move water up a slope or to the head of the stream. (If you're installing a filter as well, you may need to install a separate pump for it.) Figuring how much more power you'll need is somewhat more complicated. In general, the pump should be able to turn over the total volume of water in an hour. To learn more about measuring gph, see page 47.

When in doubt, buy a more powerful pump. You can restrict flow with a valve (either self-contained or one installed expressly for this purpose). Also, when shopping for a pump for a stream or waterfall, make sure its head, or lift, is well above the height you've planned for your falls.

OTHER CONSIDERATIONS

Pumps have varying lengths of cord; check to make sure the cord is long enough to go through the pond and plug in well away from the water. The longer the better, especially since some codes specify that the electrical outlet for a water feature has to be at least 6 feet away from water. Avoid extension cords if possible. If you have to use one, make sure it's made for outdoor use and is plugged into a ground fault circuit interrupter (GFCI), a device that shuts off an outlet immediately if there is an overload.

Some pumps come equipped with prefilters. If you need a filter, you can determine what type by reading pages 52–55.

Be sure to buy a pump that is designed for use in a water garden. Unlike other types of pumps, those for water gardens are made to sustain round-the-clock use.

HINT

Here's an easy way to calculate the volume of your pond after you've dug and lined it. Jot down the reading on your water meter. Then fill the garden pond and note the new reading. Most meters measure the amount of water used in cubic feet. Convert it to gallons by multiplying by 7.5.

FIGURING THE VOLUME OF FIVE DIFFERENT POOL SHAPES

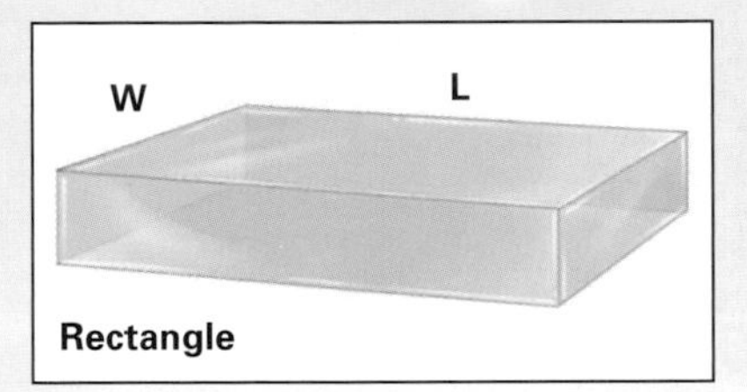

Rectangle

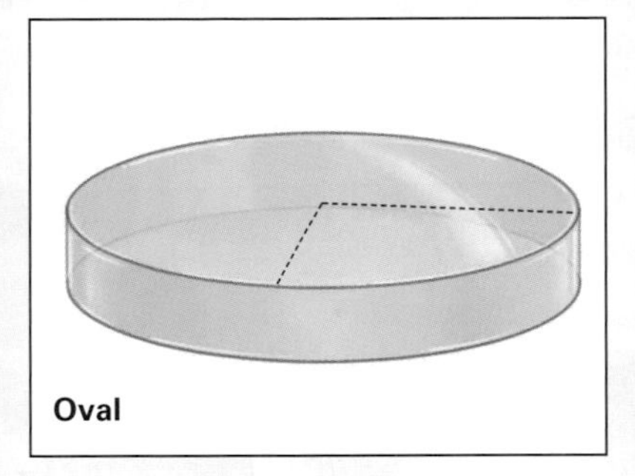
Oval

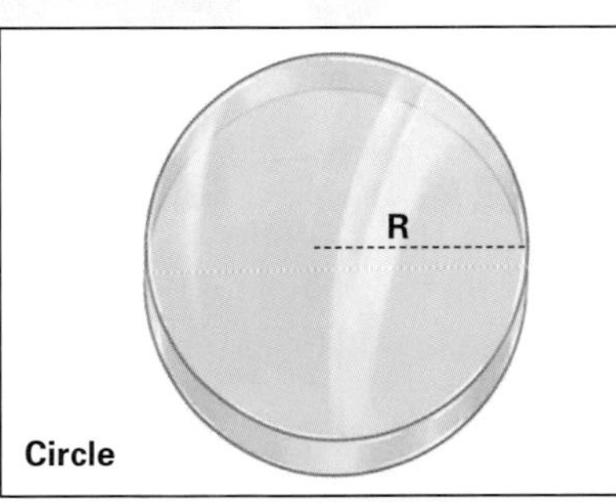

Circle

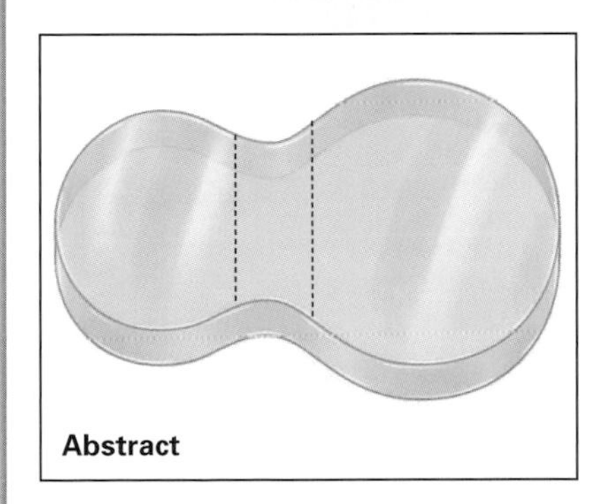
Abstract

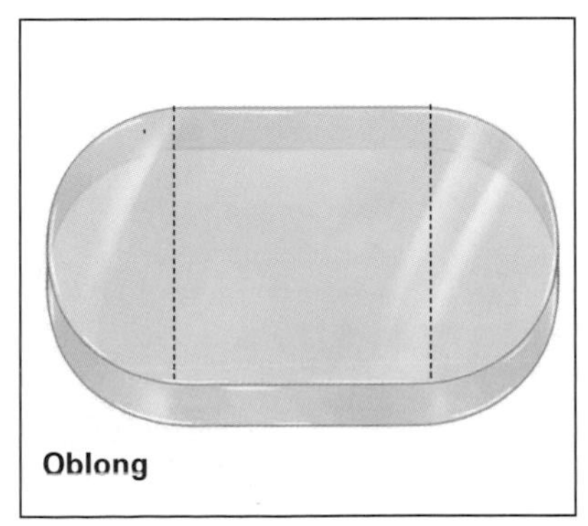
Oblong

For all shapes, the dimensions should be in feet. After calculating the area of the pond, multiply the result by the average depth of the pool. Then multiply that result by 7.5 to get volume in gallons.

RECTANGLE OR SQUARE:

- *Multiply length by width to find area.*

OVAL:

- *Measure from center to most distant edge, then from center to nearest edge. Multiply the first figure by the second and the result by 3.14 to find area.*

CIRCLE:

- *Measure the radius (the length in feet from center to the edge).*
- *Multiply the radius by itself and then by 3.14 to get area.*

ABSTRACT, IRREGULAR, AND OBLONG:

- *Break abstract and irregular shapes into simpler units (here, two circles and a rectangle), then calculate the area of each. If that doesn't work, multiply the maximum length by the maximum width to find the pool's area.*
- *For an oblong, figure the area by breaking it into a square and two half circles. Calculate the area of the square. Then consider the two half circles as one and calculate its area.*

PUMPS
continued

Choose from an array of energy-efficient recirculating pumps to power water features and other equipment.

MAKING THE RIGHT CHOICE

The splashing music of water as it moves and recirculates adds to the appeal of a water feature. It takes the right size pump to move water from a pool through tubing or pipes and other equipment to a waterfall, fountain, or stream. You need to know how you plan to use a pump in order to choose the right type and size for the job as well as how water will flow and how much resistance it will meet along the way.

Ease the selection by answering these questions:

- What kind of water feature do you envision? How will you use the pump? How many gph—gallons per hour—will it require?
- What size is the feature? How much water will flow through the pump? How many gph are needed to operate the feature?
- What else will the pump do? Will it recirculate water through a filter, through a fountain, over a waterfall, or in a stream?
- For features where water returns downhill to the pond, how high above the water surface is the point where water discharges in a waterfall? What is the width of water flowing over the spillway? How thick a sheet of water do you want going over the spillway?
- What are the requirements of the filtering system? How many gph does it take to properly operate the filter?
- Will your feature include fish? If so, how many and what size? A big fish population indicates the need for a biological filter. After deciding on a filter, ask how many gph are needed to operate the biofilter.
- If your design includes a fountain, how

HOW TO INTERPRET PUMP CHARACTERISTICS

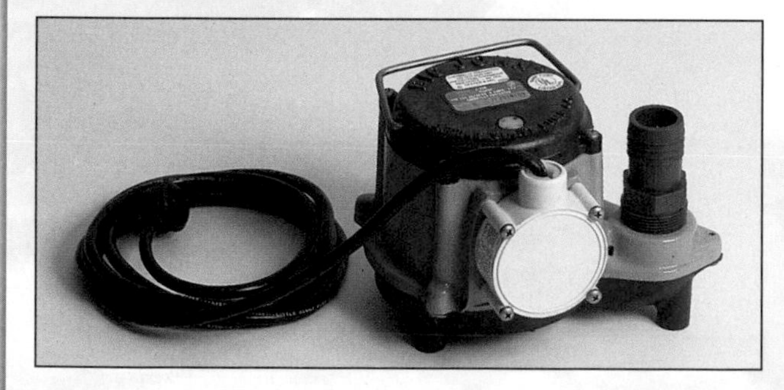

MODEL NUMBER: Identify a pump by the manufacturer's model number. It remains the same from dealer to dealer and helps you with comparison shopping.
GPH: Calculate how many gallons per hour you need, given the horizontal plus vertical distance that recirculating water will flow between the pump and the point where water exits its pipeline. Purchase a pump with a capacity (gph) that's greater than required.
HEAD (LIFT): Head is the vertical distance that the pump forces water in the line. Horizontal distance is converted to equivalent head at the rate of 10 feet of horizontal distance to 1 foot of vertical lift (head).
MAXIMUM HEAD: At the pump's specified maximum head, it no longer recirculates water. Buy a pump with a head height above the total height of the waterfall.
PUMP OUTLET: Water exits the pump and the water line is attached to the pump at the pump outlet. Its diameter determines the diameter of the line that carries water from the pump to its discharge point. When the horizontal distance of the line exceeds 15 feet, use a fitting to increase the discharge connection to the next larger pipe size.
AMPS AND WATTS: Calculate the amount of electricity needed and the approximate cost of running a specific pump based on your local utility rates. Generally, higher numbers translate to higher electrical usage and higher operating expense. Here's a formula: watts × 24 hours (in a day) × 30 days (in a month) ÷ 1,000 = number of kilowatts per month × cost per kilowatt hour = total monthly cost of operating a pump.

many gph are required to operate the type and height of fountain you chose?

When shopping for a pump consider the following characteristics:

- How many gph does it recirculate at the height and horizontal distance required?
- How much electricity does it use?
- How long is it guaranteed to last?
- How much does it cost?

The power consumption of pumps varies so much that an energy-efficient model can save enough electricity to pay for itself in one or two seasons of operation. Compare the amps and wattage of competing pumps to determine relative efficiency of energy consumption. The lower the amps and wattage, the less electricity a pump consumes.

MEASURING GALLONS PER HOUR

As a pump pushes water higher in a vertical pipe, gravity creates increased resistance. Therefore the gph of a pump decreases as the discharge height (known as head or lift) increases. The resistance created by forcing water to flow horizontally 10 feet is roughly equivalent to the effect of lifting the water 1 foot vertically. If your pump forces water 20 feet horizontally, for example, that translates to 2 feet vertically. Knowing this gph at a designated point tells you whether the pump can deliver the quantity of water needed to properly operate a waterfall with the planned spillway's width, depth, and height as well as its distance from the pump.

Manufacturers list how many gph a pump recirculates at 1 foot of lift and at other heights. If the height you need is between two listed heights, estimate what you could reasonably expect. For example, if you need 300 gph released 3 feet above the water's surface, look for a pump rated at least 300 gph at 3 feet of head. That same pump might recirculate only 200 gph at 6 feet of lift. It would not be powerful enough to recirculate 300 gph for a 6-foot-high waterfall.

Measure the water distance vertically from the pump, not from the water's surface, to build in a margin of error. One way or another, avoid skimping on gph. When determining the proper flow rate for a waterfall or stream, figure 150 gph for each inch of spillway width. This rate provides a ½-inch-thick sheet of water over the falls. You'll also need to know how far the water must travel horizontally in the pipeline. Remember that each 10 feet of horizontal distance creates about as much resistance against the pump as 1 foot of head. Consider a pump that must force water 10 feet in a pipe across the pond bottom and then 5 feet up the pipe to the release point in the waterfall. This is equivalent to a 6-foot head.

Although some variation exists from rated gph capacity, pumps do not operate at more than their rated gph capacity for each rated

HOW TO ESTIMATE WATERFALL FLOW

Use a ¾-inch diameter garden hose to test what your new waterfall will look like before investing in a pump for it. This test assumes water pressure at the tap measures 40 to 60 pounds per square inch (normally found in municipal water systems). The hose produces a flow rate of 800 to 900 gph, assuming no nozzle or other restriction. Let the hose discharge at its maximum rate where you plan to have the water line from the pump discharge water. After observing the effect of this rate on your newly constructed waterfall, decide if you want to keep the flow rate at 800 to 900 gph or adjust it higher or lower.

PUMPS
continued

This nonsubmersible pump is designed to handle the requirements of a system with a biological filter and a waterfall.

height. To be safe, purchase a pump with greater capacity than estimated need. While a pump's gph cannot be increased, it is easily reduced using a valve on the pipeline or a restrictor clamp on the flexible tubing that limits the flow of water from the pump to the discharge point. Some pumps come with a built-in valve on the discharge. Any restriction you add should be placed on the water line only after the water exits the pump—never before entering the pump. Pumps easily withstand this restriction. It has the same effect as making the pump push the water higher in the line.

TYPICAL FLOW RATES FOR WATER FEATURES

POND, SMALL: 40 to 400 gph
POND, MEDIUM: 100 to 1,000 gph
POND, LARGE: 400 to 4,000 gph
FOUNTAIN: Varies widely; often 200 to 400 gph. Check the fountain manufacturer's rating.
SPLASHING STATUARY, SMALL: 40 to 150 gph
SPLASHING STATUARY, MEDIUM: 100 to 400 gph
SPLASHING STATUARY, LARGE: 300 to 800 gph
FILTER, BIOLOGICAL: Recirculates 15 to 25 percent of the feature's water volume per hour.
FILTER, MECHANICAL: Recirculates 50 percent of the feature's water volume per hour.
STREAM: Recirculates 50 to 100 percent of the feature's water volume per hour.
WATERFALL: Recirculates 50 to 100 percent of the feature's water volume; 150 gph per inch of spillway width measured at the fall's discharge height.

THE BEST PUMP FOR YOUR WATER FEATURE

Unless you plan to have an extremely large waterfall or stream, use a submersible pump. Residential water features usually employ submersible pumps of less than 4,000 gph. They provide noiseless operation and ease of setup, giving them a distinct advantage over nonsubmersible pumps. Submersible pumps usually feature a screen intake that protects them from clogging. Some models include a built-in filter and work well for most small fountains, waterfalls, and streams.

Buy the highest-quality pump that you can afford. Bronze, brass, and stainless steel models are reliable and will withstand heavy use over the years. Cast iron and aluminum pumps offer moderate prices and quality compared to the least-expensive plastic models. Select a pump with a cord that's long enough to reach the nearest GFCI electrical outlet. If the outlet lacks GFCI protection, use an outdoor extension cord that has a built-in GFCI.

Place a submersible pump on a platform of bricks or flat rocks a few inches above the pond bottom. This keeps the pump above sediment that accumulates on the pond floor and makes it easier to clean the pump.

Choose from oil-filled or magnetically driven submersible pumps. The latter have a longer life than oil-filled pumps and consume substantially less energy per gph than other pumps. Oil-filled pumps are normally required for high head requirements. Beware of the potential of contaminating leaks from oil-filled pumps. Avoid low-priced residential sump pumps, even though they have an attractive gph rating. They typically burn out under continuous operation within a few months.

NONSUBMERSIBLE PUMPS

Use nonsubmersible (external) pumps for large water features using over 12,000 gph or in high-output situations, such as waterfalls, requiring a high lift. Compared to submersible pumps, external models make more noise and are expensive to operate, but they're easier to access for maintenance and cost less. A complex plumbing installation may require a professional's assistance. These units must be kept dry and well-ventilated within a protective housing. Be sure to screen the intake to prevent clogging. Other necessities include locating the pump where water flows to it via gravity or installing a check valve and then priming the pump. Follow the manufacturer's directions for installing and operating your pump.

FOUNTAIN HEADS

The most popular use for a pump is to power a fountain, and there are more choices in fountain spray patterns than ever before—one for just about any garden style.

A fountain head—also called a spray head—is usually sold separately from the pump (although some pumps include them). When choosing a fountain head, first consider the height and width of its spray pattern, although you can often adjust both with a valve on the pump. Second, choose the style that fits the appearance of your water feature. A bubbler, for example, looks natural in a small, informal water garden tucked into a perennial border or among shrubs. A mushroom or bell is striking in a circular formal pool. And a rotating jet adds dazzle to a starkly modern installation.

Fountains, especially geysers or bubblers, also aerate the water for fish—an added benefit. But you may also have to consider the needs of plants. Many, including water lilies, don't like water on their leaves and prefer an undisturbed pond surface.

Fountains with delicate or tall sprays need some shelter; strong winds distort the pattern, increase evaporation, and deplete the pool.

Bell or mushroom

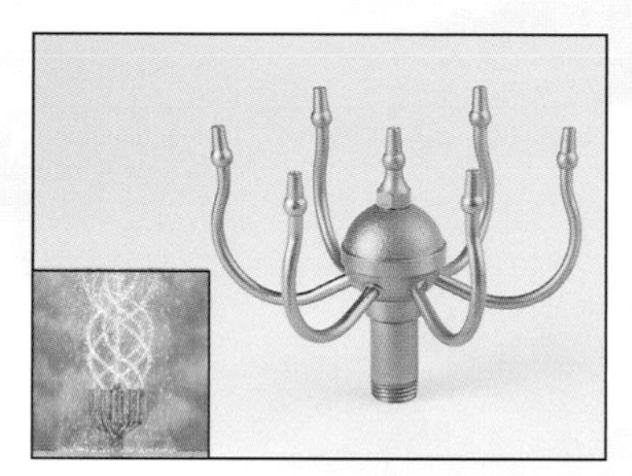

Rotating jet

Bubbler

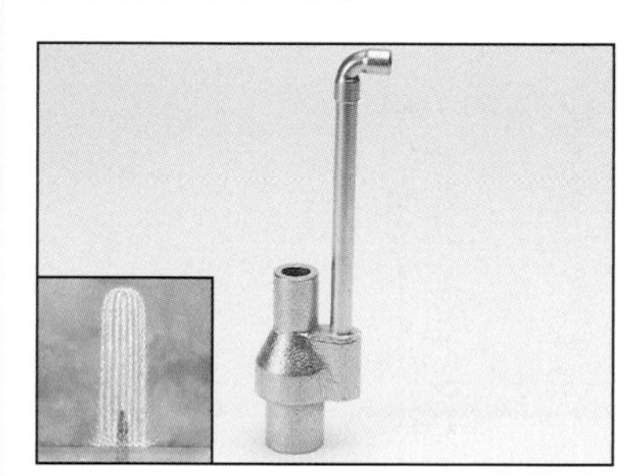

Geyser

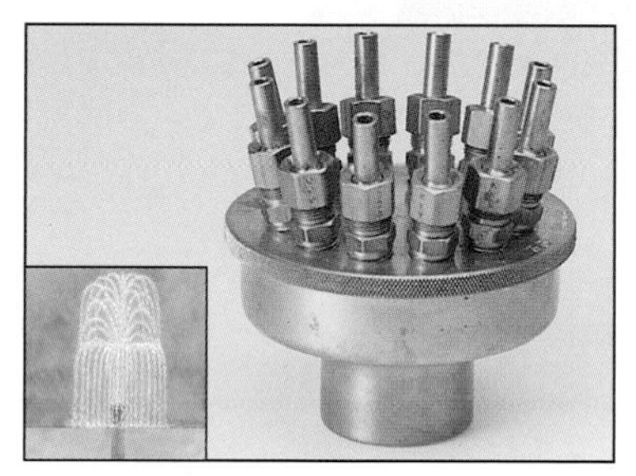

One-tier spray

Multi-tier spray

Flower, tulip, or trumpet spray

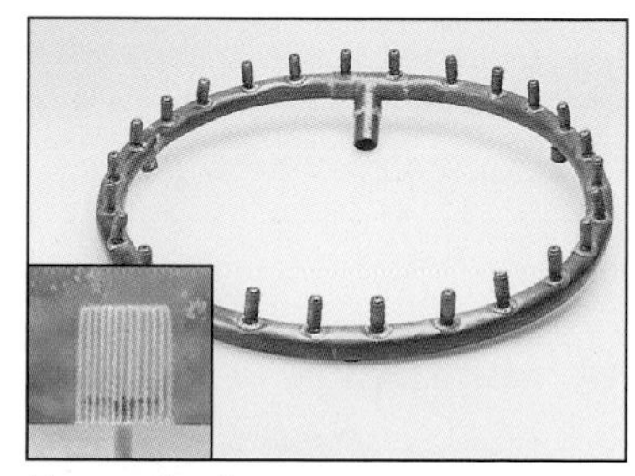

Fountain ring

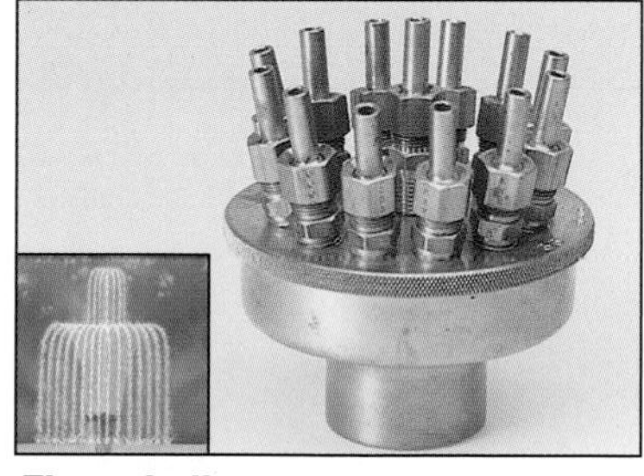

Fleur-de-lis

Straight spray

In-pool fountain head

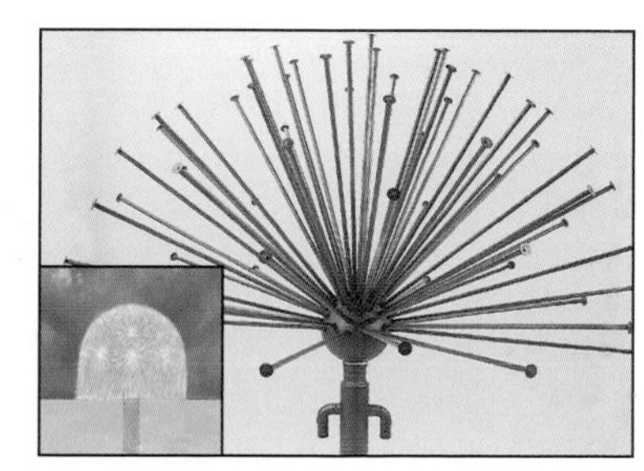

Hemisphere

SKIMMERS AND UV CLARIFIERS

SKIMMER

A skimmer prevents problems associated with leaves and other debris that fall into your water feature and present a hazard to your fish. As leaves decay and sink, they consume oxygen and produce toxic gases that escape harmlessly into the atmosphere. This isn't a problem until winter, when ice forms on the pond, trapping the gases and killing the fish.

A skimmer removes floating matter before it decays and sinks. It helps maintain water quality by increasing the oxygen level as the skimmed water splashes back into the pond.

HOW A SKIMMER WORKS

The skimmer functions as a mechanical filter that sits at the edge of a water feature. A lid on the skimmer top allows access for weekly cleaning. The top of the skimmer typically sits about 1½ inches above the surface of the pond; if the water level in your feature drops too low, the skimmer runs but does not filter, sucking air instead of water.

Netting within the skimmer traps debris. A pump inside the device works constantly to draw the water into it. Water from the skimmer is then pumped to a filter, waterfall, or other location and recirculates back into the pond.

A skimmer works best when installed downwind, allowing prevailing winds to direct leaves and other floating material toward the skimmer. Recirculated water should re-enter the pond at the opposite side from the skimmer.

You can increase the skimmer's efficiency by locating it opposite the waterfall or stream, as the steady current of water entering the pond helps to propel floating debris toward the skimmer.

There are some negatives to using a skimmer. While collecting unwanted floating debris, the skimmer may also draw in floating plants. In addition, it sucks in fish, especially little ones, and traps frogs and tadpoles. Check it daily and rescue any trapped pond denizens.

A skimmer requires extra planning to conceal it, and extra plumbing is required to move water from the skimmer to the far side of the feature, so you'll have to incorporate other equipment, such as a filter or fountain, along the same plumbing path to increase efficiency. A skimmer also increases installation investment and adds to operating expense.

If desired, include an automatic flow valve with a pond skimmer to help maintain the appropriate water level.

SKIMMER AND PLANT FILTER INSTALLATION

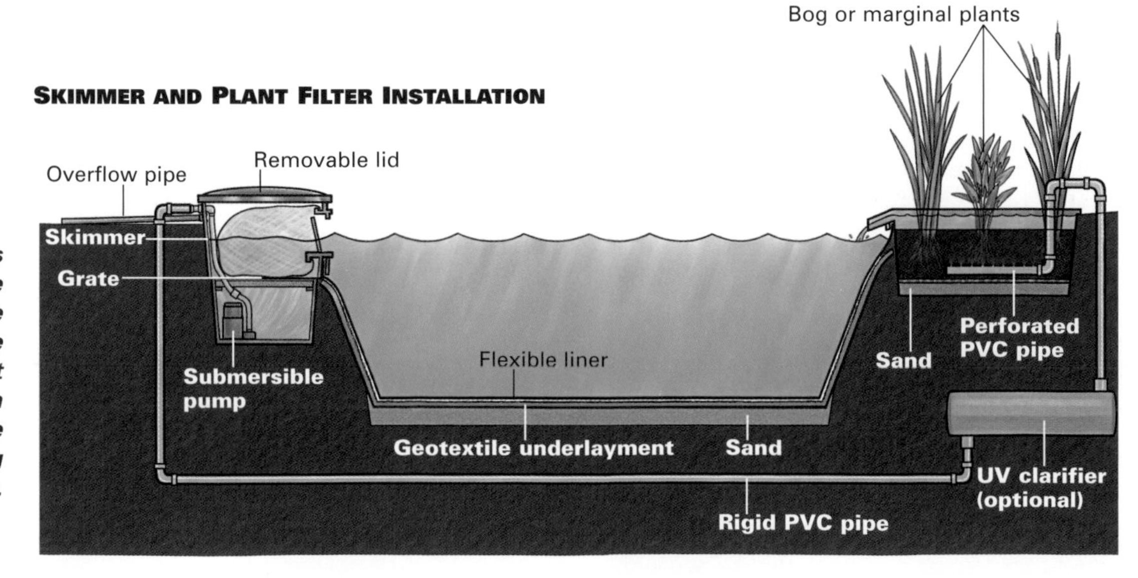

The skimmer's overflow pipe should slope away from the unit to prevent water from entering the skimmer during heavy rains.

UV CLARIFIER

If you are looking for a surefire way to avoid green water due to algae, you'll find it with a UV clarifier. Also known as a UV sterilizer, this device kills suspended algae (planktonic algae), bacteria, and other microorganisms as they flow through the clarifier. A UV clarifier also kills fungi and some parasites that attack goldfish and koi.

A clarifier kills beneficial organisms only if they get into the UV chamber, but it won't affect the beneficial bacteria that colonize inside the biofilter and on the sides and bottom of the pond. Aquatic plants should be included in a plan that uses a UV clarifier. Otherwise, you'll end up with clear water that's full of nitrites, which can be detrimental to fish.

HOW A UV CLARIFIER WORKS

A UV clarifier consists of an ultraviolet bulb inside a quartz-glass tube and PVC housing. A pump forces water through a pipe to the UV unit, which sits outside of the pond. The water is irradiated as it passes between the inside of the housing and the outside of the glass tube. (The light breaks down algae.) The water is then returned directly to the pond or via a biofilter, waterfall, stream, fountain, piped statuary, or bog.

UV clarifiers are labeled according to their wattage, maximum gph, and recommended pond size range. Their strength varies. If the maximum flow rate for the UV clarifier is exceeded, algae will move past the UV light too quickly to be killed. Buy a clarifier with a maximum gph capacity that exceeds the gph of the pump that powers water to it. A higher wattage means that the unit can successfully handle a greater gph.

Because clarifiers kill bacteria, remember to unplug the UV unit when adding beneficial bacteria to a biofilter or directly into the pond. Resume operating it when you want to rid the water of suspended algae. A UV lightbulb is good for a single season, so replace it each spring. Even if the light continues to burn for a new season, its spectrum will no longer be effective.

MAGNETIC ALGAE CONTROLLER

This device works to rid the pond of filamentous algae, the kind that adheres to the walls and bottom of the pond, as well as to objects within the pond. A magnetic algae controller also reduces the lime buildup on the quartz tube of a UV clarifier, which improves its effectiveness. The device works in ponds only when the pH is 7.5 or lower. Filamentous algae require the presence of carbon ions to adhere to pond surfaces. Magnets in the unit alter the nature of the ions so that the algae cannot adhere to pond surfaces. Water passes through the unit with no external power required.

An alternate type requires 120-volt standard household power that is reduced to 12 volts by a step-down transformer. Circulated water passes through piping outside the water feature. Electromagnetic units clamped onto the piping modify the carbon ions.

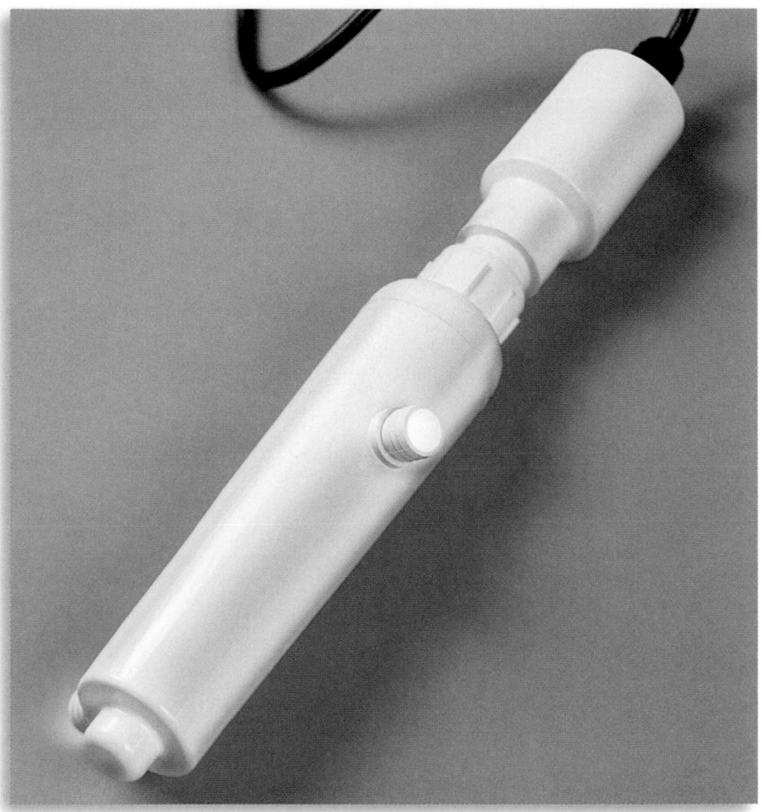

An ultraviolet clarifier kills suspended algae, bacteria, some fungi, and some parasites that kill fish. It will not harm beneficial bacteria outside the UV chamber.

UV CLARIFIER

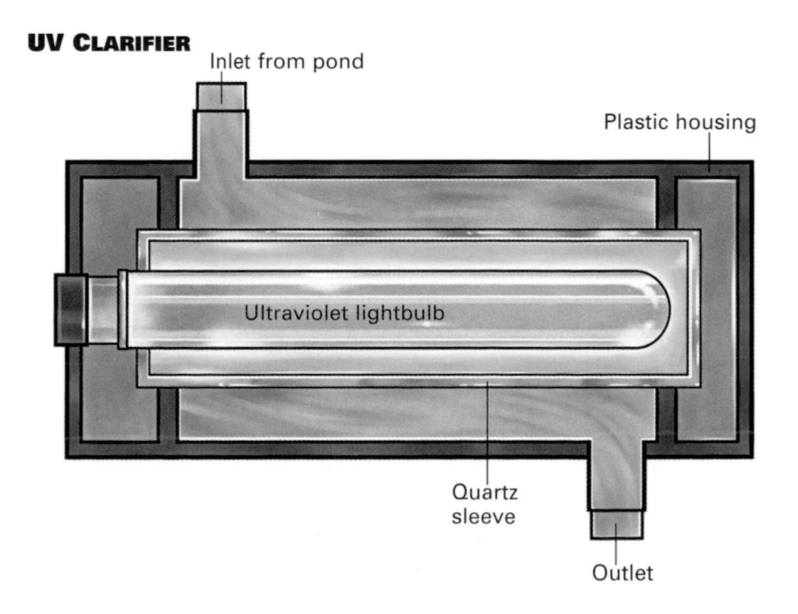

FILTERS

THE NITROGEN CYCLE

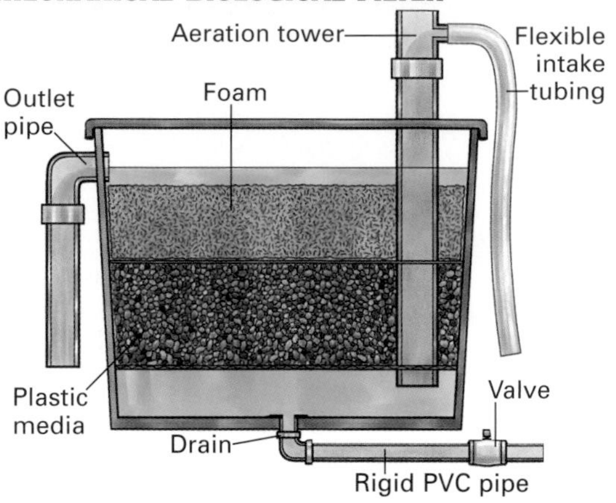

The mechanical part of the filter (foam) strains debris, while the biological part (plastic media) provides a home for beneficial bacteria.

THE NITROGEN CYCLE

The most often asked question about water gardening is how to keep the pond water from turning green. The short answer is to minimize the number and size of fish in the water feature and to maximize the number of plants. A basic understanding that fish waste stimulates algae growth will help you to better manage your pond water.

The healthy balance of life in your water feature depends on a scientific phenomenon called the nitrogen cycle. This process of nature is as fundamental to aquatic life as photosynthesis is to plants. Successful pond owners understand how to harness the cycle for their benefit. Ignoring it leads to toxic water with dead fish and scavengers.

Basically here's how the nitrogen cycle works: Fish eat food they find in the water, digest it, and later excrete it as waste. This waste matter contains nitrogen in the form of ammonia (NH_3). Uneaten fish food and other organic matter (material from plants or animals) likewise contribute nitrogen in the form of ammonia. If left unchecked, the ammonia becomes deadly to fish and scavengers living in the water.

Beneficial bacteria in a biological filter cling to surface areas of plastic, ceramic, or rock media in the unit's chamber and consume suspended matter and nutrients that pass through.

BENEFICIAL NITRIFYING BACTERIA

As ammonia accumulates in the water, beneficial nitrifying bacteria and enzymes break ammonia down into nitrite. These nitrifying critters cling to surface areas all around the pond. They reach significant numbers about the same time the mosslike green algae become noticeable on the sides of the pond. Nitrifying bacteria begin their helpful work as the water temperature rises to 50°F and warmer in spring. They slow down in fall as days grow shorter and the water temperature drops below 50°F.

The action of nitrifying bacteria and enzymes that thrive on nitrite oxidizes nitrite to nitrate, a form of nitrogen generally benign to pond creatures and beneficial to plants. Plants take up the nitrate; fish and scavengers nibble on the greenery and return nitrogen to the water, completing the nitrogen cycle.

AMMONIA

Released into clear, fresh water, healthy fish sometimes lose their appetite and die for no apparent reason. A water test will reveal ammonia in excess of a level safe for fish. That's because during the first four to six weeks of a pond's life, the colony of beneficial bacteria is developing and not yet able to handle the load of fish. Seeding the water with additional beneficial bacteria could have prevented fish kills. So would adding only a few fish at the beginning so that the ammonia level doesn't rise faster than the increasing bacteria population can handle.

Remember that fish food, eaten and uneaten alike, contains nitrogen. The more food you put into the water, the more nitrate results. Algae thrive on nitrate. Unless the water feature grows a sufficient quantity of efficient nitrate users, the algae grow out of control. Limiting the amount of fish food helps reduce the intensity of green water that results from an oversupply of nitrate.

Stop feeding fish when the water temperature drops below 50°F. At this point, the beneficial nitrifying bacteria slack off from their summertime work, and the lower temperatures slow down the decay of organic matter, so the release of toxic ammonia also slows. Overfeeding fish, however, promotes deadly ammonia levels. It's best to allow the pond to reach a natural balance or employ extra help from a biological filter.

People mistakenly believe all green water is bad, but fish thrive in healthy water containing algae. Algae is excessive and needs controlling when you can't see your hand 12 inches beneath the water's surface.

MECHANICAL FILTRATION

When pond water becomes cloudy, filtration offers a solution. Mechanical filtration involves forcing pond water through porous media (usually filter pads) that catch larger particles. Most mechanical filters sit on the bottom of the water feature, but some work outside the pond.

CAPACITY

Do not skimp on the capacity of your mechanical filter. To do so simply wastes money. The pump for a mechanical filter should recirculate the feature's water volume at least once every two hours. A 1,000-gallon water feature needs a pump that can recirculate at least 500 gph through the mechanical filter. Better yet, select a unit designed to function at a slightly higher capacity than you need.

If you choose a mechanical pond filter, make sure it's designed to handle the capacity of your water feature. If you buy a unit with too little capacity or if you fail to clean it regularly, it will be useless. Swimming pool filters become clogged within hours of filtering pond water because they're designed for use with algae-killing chemicals.

The advantages of mechanical filters include their modest cost, ease of setup, and simple maintenance. Disadvantages include frequency of cleaning and lack of ability to eliminate algae.

A mechanical filter with a built-in pump strains particles of dirt and other matter that pass through it and adds oxygen to the water for healthy fish.

FILTERS WITH AN ADDED PUMP

Most mechanical filters come without a built-in pump. If the filter doesn't have its own pump, connect one that's appropriate for the size of the water feature.

Use a pump (with a minimum gph of half the feature's water volume) that can be connected to the filter using flexible vinyl tubing. Attach the filter to the pump's intake (where water is drawn into the pump). Before you attach the tubing to the pump's intake or discharge, remove the pump's screen or prefilter unit, which covers the intake and is designed to prevent clogging of the pump by keeping out leaves, twigs, and such. Do not attempt to take the pump apart—that would void the warranty.

BUBBLE-WASHED BEAD FILTER

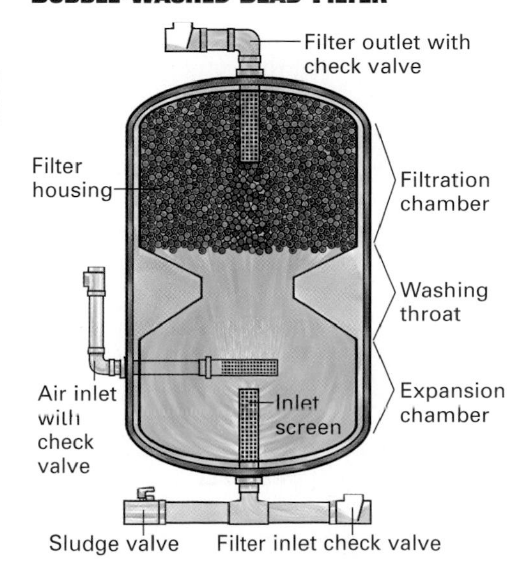

A bead filter clarifies water by trapping debris. It also works as a biofilter: The beads provide a place for beneficial bacteria to flourish.

FILTERS

continued

FILTERS WITH A BUILT-IN PUMP

Mechanical filter units sometimes include recirculating pumps. One type of mechanical filtration unit features a pump built into the bottom half of the filter box. The top half consists of two foam filters, one on top of the other. The bottom filter pad rests on a perforated shelf that allows filtered water into the lower chamber. The pump then discharges the filtered water either directly into the pond or into flexible tubing to power a waterfall or decorative fountain.

Some mechanical filters operate outside the pond, making cleaning easier. In this case, the water goes first to the pump, which forces the water through tubing to the exterior mechanical filter. The newly filtered water then flows under pressure to a waterfall or stream or directly into the pond. Before starting this type of filtration system, attach tubing to the pump's discharge and run it to the intake of the filter unit. Then run tubing from the filter outlet to flow into the pond, stream, or waterfall.

The resistance of the filter reduces the volume of water that the pump recirculates. If for any reason the pump's gph drops too low, the filter's effectiveness is reduced. By the same token, if a filter becomes clogged and a pump's intake is restricted, the pump could become damaged and fail to work.

Aim to recirculate half the water in the pond once per hour or all the water once every two hours. If the pump powers a waterfall 3 feet above the water surface directly above it, the pump should be rated to recirculate at least half the pond water once per hour at the 3-foot head.

FILTER MAINTENANCE

Mechanical filters usually work out of sight, on the pond bottom. But placing the filter in an easy-to-reach location saves time and effort for the busy owner. If the pond is so deep its bottom cannot easily be reached, consider making a platform for the filter using clean bricks or flat rocks.

You will soon learn to recognize when the filter needs cleaning. Reduced water flow indicates that the filter is clogged with debris. Clean the filter daily during warm summer periods. Be sure that clamps hold the tubing tightly to the filter unit and the pump. Efficiency is lost when water leaks at these points, whether the pump is located inside or outside the pond.

BIOLOGICAL FILTRATION

Biological filtration occurs naturally in water features where plants and naturally occurring bacteria maintain water quality without supplemental filtration. Biofilters work to make water clear and healthy for fish. They work partly as mechanical filters, trapping suspended debris from pond water. In addition, nitrifying bacteria and enzymes inside the biofilter remove ammonia and nitrites from the water.

Various biofilters are popular among koi hobbyists and ornamental-fish dealers. Generally, biofilters are efficient and easy to clean. Every month or two, you'll need to rinse off one-fourth to one-third of the elements (more than that interferes with the effectiveness of the nitrifying bacteria). The disadvantages of biofilters include their initial cost, complicated installation, and bulk (which makes them difficult to conceal).

HOW BIOFILTERS WORK

Filter manufacturers search for ways to maximize the number of nitrifying bacteria and enzymes in a filter unit. These beneficial microscopic creatures spend their lives clinging to any stationary aquatic surface, so filter designers employ elements with as much surface area as possible, such as gravel, volcanic rock, and many imaginative configurations of plastic.

Although the bacteria require oxygen to function, water typically comes into the biofilter from near the bottom of the pond where oxygen levels are low. To remedy this deficiency, better-quality biofilters aerate the water before it reaches the nitrifying bacteria. Aeration yields a more dense population of bacteria, which in turn allows a more space-efficient housing for the filter.

Some biofilters include a space for aquatic plants that absorb nitrogen from nitrates and nitrites. When planted, the filter robs algae of the nutrients they need to thrive, thus enhancing water quality.

Use a water test kit to measure the ammonia or nitrite levels. A biological filter is needed if they test too high. Too high a reading results from having a greater fish population than can be handled by the nitrifying bacteria and enzymes naturally found in the pond.

ABOVEGROUND BIOLOGICAL FILTERS

Most biofilters are designed to operate above the ground outside the pond. The pump sends pond water up to the aboveground filter unit. First it is aerated before flowing through the mechanical, debris-removal section. Then it flows through the high-surface section housing the concentrated nitrifying bacteria and enzyme colonies, and they detoxify the water. With some units, the water passes a final sector of aquatic plants where nutrient removal reduces algae growth. The purified water then flows out of the unit.

IN-GROUND BIOLOGICAL FILTERS

Large ponds, especially koi ponds, frequently utilize in-ground biofilters. Often made of high-density polyethylene, they typically feature round chambers and conical bottoms. A typical unit sits in the ground with its top slightly above water level. A nonsubmersible pump draws water through piping from the pond's bottom drain. At the same time, the pump pulls filtered water from the chambers of the biofilter.

Easy-to-clean, pressurized biofilters are available for small ponds. As small, in-ground units, they're accessible and easy to hide with imitation (fiberglass) rocks.

PRESSURIZED BIOLOGICAL FILTERS

Also known as bead filters, these units operate within a pressurized housing. A high-pressure, nonsubmersible pump draws water from the pond, usually through bottom drains. A pressurized vortex at the pump's intake removes heavy suspended matter from the water. The pump forces the pond water into the filter, where nitrifying bacteria and enzymes flourish on beads designed to have high surface area. The filtration media collect suspended matter in the spaces between the beads. The slow water flow over the huge surface area provided by the beads allows excellent colonization of the bacteria and enzymes. Purified water forced out of the pressurized filter housing then goes to a waterfall or into the pond.

A pressure gauge on the intake valve indicates that the filter needs cleaning by showing pressure increases. A decrease in the volume of water coming out of the filter also indicates that the unit needs cleaning. Back flushing for a few minutes does the job. Top-of-the-line units include a propeller to loosen the beads, which sometimes become impacted.

PLANT FILTERS

Plant filters make the nitrogen cycle work to your advantage through a simple concept: Pond water filters through an aquatic plant bed, allowing plants to do the work. If you want to make a plant filter, such as a bog, include it as part of the pond construction. By integrating a plant filter into your water feature, you'll enjoy the plants' ornamental qualities as well as their filtering abilities.

HOW PLANT FILTERS WORK

Nitrifying bacteria and enzymes colonize the gravel bed of the plant filter. Gravel serves as a mechanical filter that removes debris from the pond water. Bacteria and enzymes reduce ammonia in the water to nitrite and then to nitrate. Water-loving marginal or bog plants flourish in the shallow, nitrate-rich water. Most of the suspended matter carried in by the water disintegrates. The gravel filter bed is big enough to function for years without becoming clogged.

TRICKLE TOWER FILTER

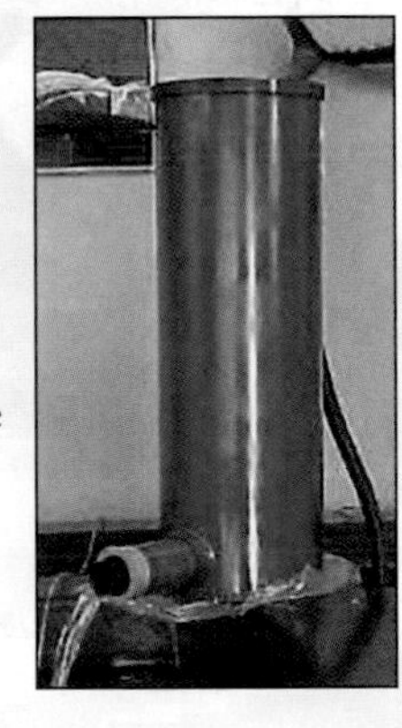

Any pond filter that holds its filtration media above the water is a trickle tower filter. Water flows slowly over the media—typically lava rock or fiberglass—and trickles back down to the pond. Aerobic bacteria in the filter thrive on the oxygen and convert toxic ammonia and nitrite to nitrates, which keeps fish healthy. The cycling process takes only a few days in a trickle tower filter, compared to a few weeks or more in a submerged media filter. Depending on the tower's composition, you may want to add a little calcium volcanite to the water to boost its trace-mineral content.

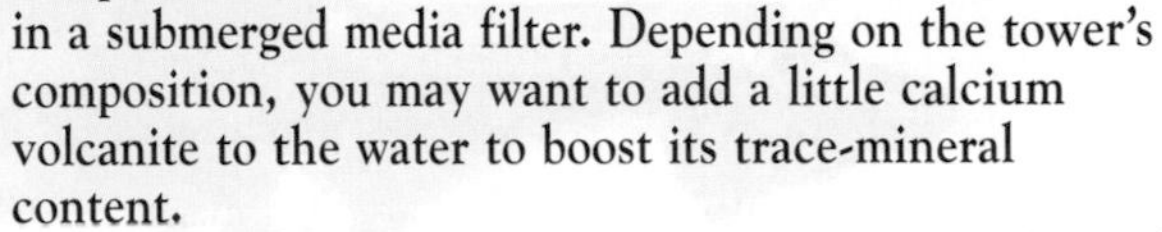

Trickle towers can be made from any material sturdy enough to withstand the water flow but porous enough to encourage bacteria colonization. Commercial models are also available in a variety of sizes and materials.

BOTTOM DRAINS AND BULKHEAD CONNECTORS

BOTTOM DRAIN AND AUTOMATIC FLOW VALVE INSTALLATION

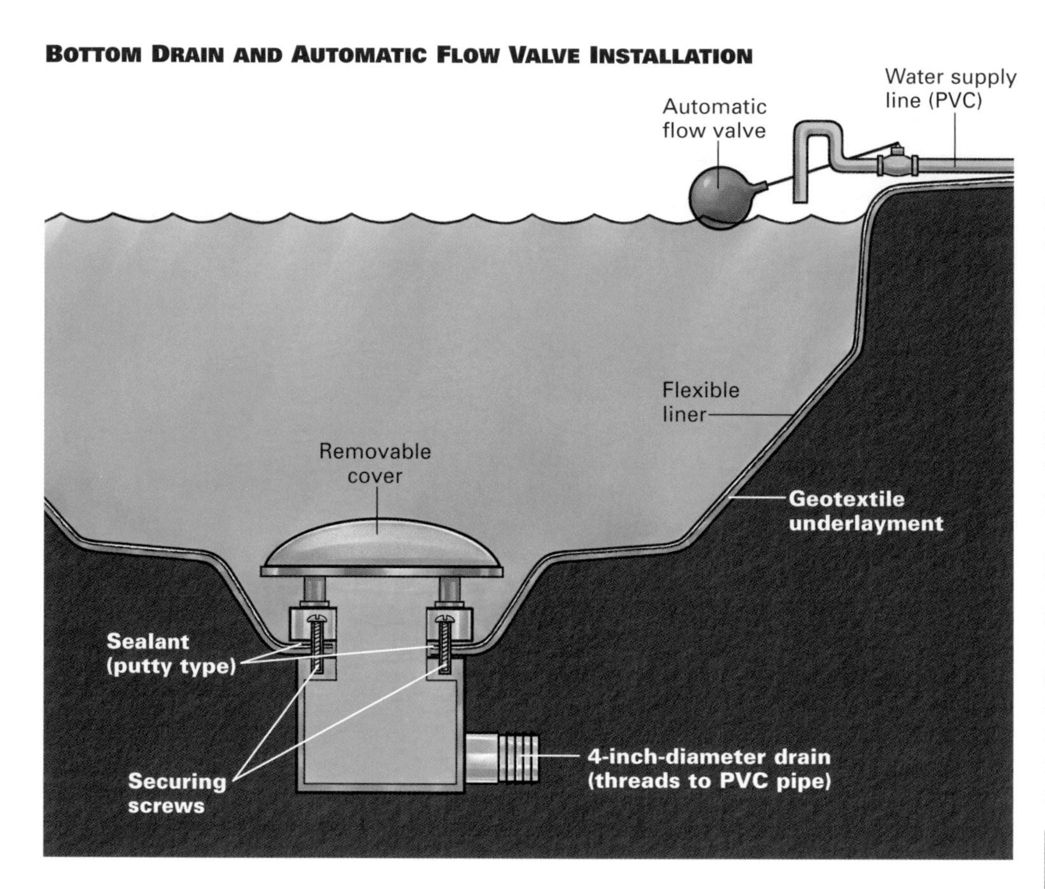

Bottom drains and bulkhead connectors are specialized pipe fittings that allow a watertight passageway for water or power lines to go through a pond liner below the water surface.

A bottom drain allows you to let the water flow out the bottom of your water feature by disconnecting the pump and turning a valve. A bulkhead connection is a specialized fitting on the side of a water feature into which you screw a pipe or pipe fitting. Guard against leaks by following manufacturer's directions carefully when installing a bottom drain or a bulkhead connection.

BOTTOM DRAINS

Ponds stocked heavily with fish, especially koi, often include one or more bottom drains. A bottom drain made for koi ponds works just as successfully in water gardens, particularly if stocked heavily with fish. Koi keepers regularly replace 10 percent or more of their pond water. Drains make this easier to do. Installing a 4-inch-diameter drainpipe greatly reduces the likelihood of clogging.

Bottom drains include a removable cover that minimizes suction created as the water drains. This helps to prevent small fish and large debris from passing through and clogging the bottom drain. The drains also include watertight fittings that clamp against a flexible liner or a rigid shell liner. Bottom drains work well in concrete ponds too.

Swimming pool drains are too fine and quickly become clogged in a fishpond or water-garden environment. Some filter systems are designed to receive water from the pool bottom, thus making a bottom drain necessary for them.

BULKHEAD CONNECTORS

The bulkhead connector is a short length of flanged, externally threaded pipe equipped with a locknut and rubber washer for making a watertight seal. The inside of the pipe is either threaded to accept a variety of pipe fittings or smooth for solvent welding of PVC pipe. The diameter of the pipe that runs through the wall of the feature determines what diameter bulkhead connector you need. Passage for electrical power, overflow water, intake water, or recirculated water for a filter, waterfall, stream, UV clarifier, statuary, or fountainhead are among the uses for a bulkhead connector.

Most water features don't include either a bottom drain or a bulkhead connector. The submersible pump that regularly recirculates the water works well to drain the pond for maintenance. Typically, the water and power lines of a water feature (including many koi ponds) run into the pond between the edging material and the top of the liner, whether the liner is flexible, rigid, or concrete. Cutting a flexible liner or a preformed shell may void the manufacturer's guarantee. What's more, cutting a hole in your liner, even for a bottom drain or bulkhead, increases the chance of a leak.

PIPES AND FITTINGS

Today's professionals and amateurs prefer plastic pipe, tubing, fittings, and valves. Their ease of installation, longevity, noncorrosiveness, and nontoxic properties make plastic piping and other supplies ideal for water features.

Flexible vinyl tubing is the least expensive and quickest to install for a water line. If the size of the line you need exceeds a 1-inch inside dimension (ID), use flexible PVC tubing, which is more expensive but easy to install. For 2-inch lines or larger, use rigid PVC pipe. It costs less than flexible PVC. Rigid PVC resists being squeezed by traffic or the weight of material that is placed over it.

Use galvanized or bronze supplies if you can't find plastic. Avoid copper. It's costly, it deteriorates in acidic soil or water, and it requires a plumber for installation.

FLEXIBLE TUBING AND PIPING

Flexible vinyl tubing has various uses for plumbing water features. Attach one end of the tubing to a pump and attach its other end to the equipment that the pump operates, such as a fountain, waterfall, filter, UV clarifier, or statuary. Or carefully let the line discharge into a waterway basin—the pool of water that overflows at the top of a waterfall. The job might also be more complex. For example, you may attach the line to a UV clarifier and continue with another section of tubing to a filter that empties into a waterfall basin.

Secure a hose clamp around tubing wherever it connects with any equipment to keep it in place and ensure a watertight connection. Match the clamp size to the tubing; use a ½-inch clamp for a ½-inch outside dimension (OD) pipe, for example.

When connected to a submersible pump, flexible tubing makes it easier to lift the pump for inspection or service. Given a choice, thicker tubing resists kinking and squeezing better than thinner-walled tubing. Avoid bending flexible tubing around a corner, burying it underground, or using it in other ways that would restrict the water flowing through it.

Avoid clear vinyl tubing. The growth of algae is encouraged inside the plastic wherever sunlight can reach, and it eventually clogs the tubing. Choose black tubing instead; it blocks light and prevents algae accumulation.

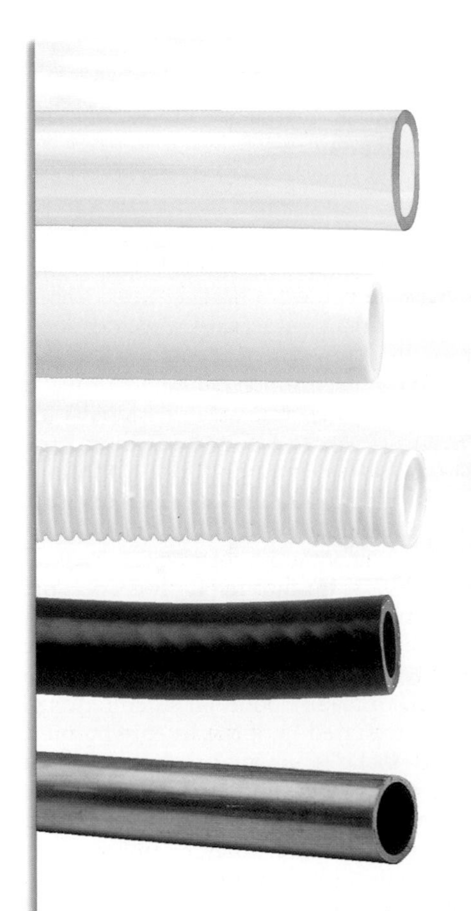

PIPES

Clear vinyl tubing: *Easy to see through but clogs and kinks very quickly; it is best used only where short lengths are needed.*

Rigid PVC: *Use schedule-40 pressure-rated pipe and fittings. It is corrosion resistant, lightweight, and inexpensive, but not flexible. Commonly available in white but can be spray-painted black where it's visible underwater.*

Corrugated plastic: *Extremely flexible, which makes it especially useful for water gardens. Can be expensive and requires barbed fittings with clamps.*

Black plastic: *Many brands and styles. Semiflexible, inexpensive, and requires barbed fittings and clamps. Good pipe to bury underground; and, because it's flexible, requires fewer elbows.*

Metal: *Copper or galvanized steel. Can be toxic to some pond life, such as snails and dragonfly larvae. Expensive and not recommended.*

PIPES AND FITTINGS
continued

Flexible schedule 40 PVC tubing works well for water features. Its flexibility allows the line to run without flow-restricting elbows, yet it's strong enough to resist buckling when covered with soil. Use flexible PVC pipe glue to secure connections.

Nonkinking corrugated vinyl tubing bends around corners without crimping. Like standard corrugated tubing, it has a wavy exterior, but its smooth interior won't slow water flow. Use clamps with foam strips on the inside that correspond to the ridges and valleys of the corrugated material to create a watertight connection to a pump, filter, clarifier, fountain, or other equipment. This tubing can be buried up to 6 inches deep. Use barbed (also called push-in or compression) fittings, which simply push together to link flexible piping; use plastic or stainless steel clamps to secure the connections.

RIGID PIPING

Rigid PVC pipe is corrosion-resistant, lightweight, and inexpensive. Use schedule 40 PVC pipe to avoid the drawbacks of flexible tubing. Rigid PVC resists compression under the weight of soil, rocks, or foot traffic. In addition, algae doesn't grow inside the opaque white pipe. Choose rigid pipe for runs of 15 to 20 feet or longer, for a water volume of 3,000 gph or more, and for situations where the pipe must be buried underground. Elbows, available in 45- and 90-degree turns, allow a change in the direction of PVC pipe and water flow without significantly reducing the flow.

Make a rigid water line by cutting lengths of pipe to match the layout you design. (Lengths of PVC pipe cut easily with a hacksaw.) Then fit and glue the pieces together. Use PVC pipe glue to make a watertight connection. Other connection options include threaded fittings (screw) and compression fittings (push). Use Teflon tape on threaded pipe connections to make them watertight. Carefully inspect and flow-test all connections to make certain they don't leak.

TUBING AND PIPING SIZE

Pipe diameter is determined by the gph necessary to operate the filter, waterfall, or other features. When buying piping or tubing, increase the diameter to the next larger size when the needed length exceeds 15 feet. A larger diameter reduces water friction against the piping, reduces pressure against the pump, and helps to maintain the desired gph. The size of the piping or tubing you use must match the connection piece (either the discharge or intake) on the pump. For example, buy 1-inch ID tubing if the pump volute (outlet) measures 1-inch OD. If you have 1-inch OD tubing for the pump, use a reducer-type fitting to connect the pump and tubing. In the case of a pump that takes a 1-inch PVC pipe that would be more than 15 feet long, use 1¼-inch-diameter piping. Use a reducer connection to make the larger pipe compatible with the pump volume.

ASSORTED FITTINGS

Fittings allow you to regulate, direct, and secure the flow of water through the piping or tubing. Flexible tubing or a hand-tight PVC union makes pump removal quick and easy. If the pump has a threaded female socket and you want to connect it to vinyl tubing, use a polyethylene barb fitting and clamp to do the job. Use standard-socket PVC fittings for PVC pipe and tubing.

BALL VALVE: A fast on-off valve, this water flow regulator operates with a quarter turn of the handle to stop or start the water stream. Inside is a ball with a hole in it. When the hole is aligned with the pipe, water flows through it; when rotated away from the water flow, the ball blocks the water.

GATE VALVE: Where you'll need to make minor flow adjustments, use a gate valve. Turning the handle raises or lowers a barrier (the gate). When raised, water flows freely; when lowered completely, it stops the water flow. You can open or close the gate to any height to adjust water flow.

KNIFE VALVE: Knife valves, also called slide valves, are often used to control water flow to drain lines, filters, and skimmers. Pulling up or pushing down on the handle rapidly shuts off the water for servicing this equipment.

THREE-WAY, OR DIVERTER, VALVE: This water flow regulator has one inlet and two outlets. Changes in the valve-handle position alter the balance of flow between the two outlets. Use it when one pump is operating two features, such as a filter and a fountain.

GLOBE VALVE: The globe valve is too restrictive because it requires a pressure far higher (40 to 60 pounds per square inch) than is generated by water feature pumps.

CHECK VALVE: Check valves permit water to pass in one direction but stop it if it starts to move the opposite way. Install a check valve on the line between the water and a nonsubmersible pump not fed by gravity. Otherwise, when the pump stops, air gets

into the line and the pump loses its prime.
HOSE CLAMP: A hose clamp holds flexible tubing or piping securely to a pump or feature.
HOSE RESTRICTOR CLAMP: A restrictor clamp tightens on flexible tubing to reduce excessive water flow and secure a connection.
BULKHEAD CONNECTOR (FLANGED TANK ADAPTER): A bulkhead connector enables a water line to pass out of the feature below the water's surface while preventing the feature from leaking where the lines penetrate the wall.
T-FITTINGS AND Y-FITTINGS: These divide a stream of water into two lines.
ELBOWS: Elbows make 45- and 90-degree turns in rigid or flexible pipelines.
ADAPTERS: Various kinds of adapters make it possible to join rigid pipe to flexible tubing. Socket weld PVC fittings to male/female threaded connections.
REDUCER: A reducer provides a different diameter at each end to connect piping of differing diameters.
AUTOMATIC FLOW VALVE: Automatic flow valves ensure that, despite evaporation, the water in a pond, stream, or other feature remains at the desired level. It works like the float valve in a toilet. When working properly, the automatic flow valve could mask a leak that might develop in the pond. If the flow valve malfunctions, the feature may overflow with chlorinated tap water, killing the aquatic life in the pond. If it fails to add water while you're away, the water depth could become dangerously low, adversely affecting aquatic life and equipment.

1. ball valve
2. gate valve
3. check valve
4. gate valve
5. diverter valve
6. Y-fitting
7. reducer
8. T-fitting
9. hose clamps
10. restricter clamp
11. adapter

ELECTRICAL POWER

You can successfully operate an ecologically balanced water feature without using electrical power. But most water feature owners prefer to add the visual, aural, and biological benefits that moving, splashing, pump-powered water provides. Other pond accessories require electricity as well. Outdoor lighting enables homeowners to view their gardens in the evening and at night. Fishkeepers in cold regions rely on deicers to safeguard their prized fish during winter.

Solar energy or batteries can power pumps and lights. But solar-powered pumps don't work on cloudy days and at night. A submersible pump quickly consumes the energy stored in a battery. Standard household 120-volt alternating current supplies most of the power for today's water features and their accessories; 120-volt or 12-volt power runs most outdoor lighting systems.

Before starting any electrical installation, learn about your local electrical code from your city or county inspector (department of building inspection). Also check the National Electric Code (NEC), which gives minimum standards for outdoor wiring. Local building codes may have particular requirements, depending on climate and soil conditions. For example, your local code may require underground power lines to be encased in conduit buried at a certain depth.

SAFETY FIRST

Low-voltage systems are easy and safe to install. The potential danger of 120-volt power, however, requires strict attention to safety. Working on electrical lines can be life-threatening if you're not extremely careful, especially around water or moisture. Be certain power is turned off and double-check it with a voltage meter. If you're not completely comfortable about doing electrical work, hire an electrician.

For safety's sake, install a ground fault circuit interrupter in each electrical outlet when you plan to use electricity in or near water. In homes with modern wiring, you'll commonly find GFCI electrical outlets in kitchens and bathrooms. The GFCI senses any electrical contact with water in addition to current overload. If water contact occurs, the GFCI instantly stops the electrical current. If pump wiring, even aboveground,

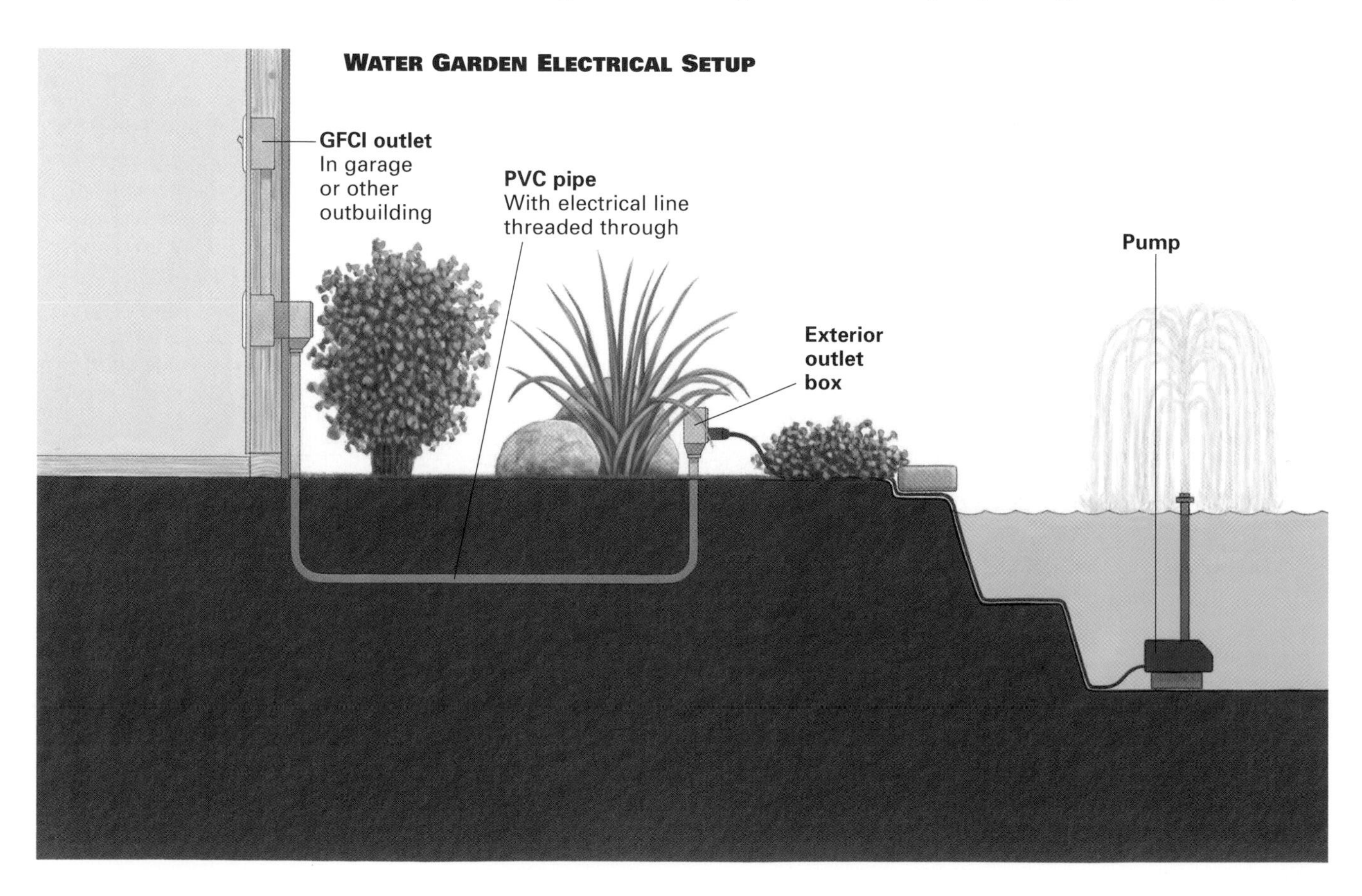

becomes frayed and water touches the power wire, the electricity is cut off. Installing a GFCI outlet requires professional-level skills. A less-expensive alternative would be to install a GFCI near the water feature.

Determine the electrical load needed to operate your planned water feature and all of its components. Pumps and other devices are labeled by the manufacturer as having a certain number of watts or amps. Compare the needed power requirements with the number of amps or watts a circuit can handle. Residential circuit breakers handle 15 or 20 amps per circuit for 1,800 watts to 2,400 watts. Figure amps (current) × volts (potential) = watts (power). For the vast majority of residential water features, a single 20-amp circuit suffices. If your watts are expected to exceed 2,400, and you need 20 amps or more, install a second circuit to your breaker box. A large nonsubmersible pump might require a 220-volt circuit, which calls for its own dedicated power line from the circuit breaker. Leave such an installation to a licensed electrician.

ELECTRICAL LINE INSTALLATION

Remember to call your local phone, gas, cable, and electricity providers and ask them to locate and mark all underground utility lines on your property before you dig. If possible, when laying new electrical lines underground, avoid traversing any area with a septic system, paving, a deck, a patio, or an outbuilding.

Run the power line through a PVC schedule 40 pipe buried at least 18 inches deep. At this depth, the line is less likely to be damaged by digging near it. Consider installing an electrical switch in the house or on a porch with a waterproof outdoor switch to control the lights or other equipment for your water feature.

INSTALLING A POWER BOX OR OUTLET

Ensure the safe and proper installation of a weatherproof GFCI-protected power outlet or a separate box (metal or plastic) by following local building codes. These may specify its location in relation to the water feature as well as the appropriate choice of materials. In addition, determine where the pump and other electrical equipment will be located, because their power cords should reach the outlet without the use of extension cords.

Set the power box or outlet on short lengths of galvanized pipe by screwing the pipes into openings at the bottom of the box or outlet and securing each with a bushing. Dig a trench as deep as code requires from your home's nearest power box to the location of the new outdoor box or outlet. Run the power line from the breaker panel of your home through rigid metal or schedule 40 PVC pipe and into the outlet or box. For long-term support and stability, attach the pipes to a 2×6 pressure-treated post with metal brackets. Prepare an 18-inch-deep hole for the support post; then pour concrete into the hole around the post. To avoid an inadvertent tripping of the circuit by rain, dew, or sprinklers, install a deep box-type outlet cover to shelter the power cords when they're plugged in.

Where power and fixture wires join, a cover allows access while enclosing the junction, keeping it watertight.

LIGHTING

Tinted lenses can be added to lights on land or in water to make the illumination more subtle or to add a glimmer of color at night.

Low-voltage submersible lights provide safe and attractive options for creating dramatic effects, and are practical in or out of the water.

You can create amazing effects with water feature lighting—make a fountain glow, illuminate an entire pond from within, highlight an attractive statue, or heighten the reflection of a beautiful tree.

Water garden lights are available for installation as either in-water or out-of-water lighting. All, however, should be connected to a GFCI outlet for safety, and those used in the water should be made specifically for underwater use.

Before you shop for water garden lights, experiment with different effects from a powerful flashlight or a spotlight on an extension cord (never place either in the water). Aim for restraint and subtlety. Don't get carried away with an effect that's more amusement park than understated elegance.

There are several types of in-water lights, and each creates its own special effect, depending on how you position it (see the box on the opposite page). Most designs call for lights that have dark, subdued casings. Stainless steel or white casings can be obtrusive, especially during daytime.

Fountain lights, either in white or colors, add drama to a spray. Some fountain lights also come equipped with transparent wheels of several colors. Use colored light sparingly, however. Too much can look gaudy.

Many lights include built-in timers that allow you to automatically turn the lights on and off. You can also install an independent timer in the lighting setup. Timers not only save you the trouble of regulating the light, they also save energy costs.

Lighting extends your enjoyment of a water feature. You might choose high-intensity halogen lights that virtually turn night into day, or you may prefer subtle, low-voltage lighting that adds mystery and romance to the evening garden. A hanging light or a wall light draws attention to an otherwise unseen container water garden. Strategically placed spotlights, angled to shine high or low, highlight special features. Soft pathway lights help guide visitors around an area. Edge the perimeter of a water feature with gentle highlights that reflect off the water's surface and dance on the ripples of a waterfall. Use small brightly colored floating lights on the water's surface to create a festive atmosphere for summer parties.

Illuminate a waterfall with an inner glow or add drama to a fountain using submersible lighting. Submersible lights come with their own platform so that they can be moved about the pond floor to satisfy changing requirements. They function best when the water is clear; light dissipates in murky water, accentuating the fact that it's not clear.

After measuring and carefully planning what you want to accomplish with lighting, you have two choices for powering it: low-voltage or line-voltage (120-volt) outdoor lighting. Whatever you choose, always connect any lighting placed in or near the water feature to a GFCI outlet.

WATER GARDEN LIGHTS

FLOATING LIGHTS

Drifting on top of the water, floating lights create a festive atmosphere. Some have smoked glass, which has a more subdued effect. To hold the lights in one place, anchor the cord with smooth-edged brick or stone.

SUBMERGED LIGHTS

Made for underwater use, submerged lights illuminate the pool or draw attention to features outside the pool, such as special plants or statues. They also add drama when installed under fountains or waterfalls. Underwater lighting is available for both floodlighting and spotlighting effects, and their lighting is diffused.

FLOODLIGHT

Use the wide beam of a floodlight to illuminate large areas. Inside a pond or pool, it can make the body of water seem to glow from within. Outside the pool, it's best to restrict lighting to a seating area, such as a deck, because it produces a glare if directed at a sharp angle to the water. If used outside the pool, position it to shoot across the water at a low angle.

SPOTLIGHT

Whether under or out of the water, the tight beam of a spotlight can shine upward to highlight a specific feature. Place it beneath an attractive element, such as a waterfall, and the element will appear to glow. When carefully positioned under the water, a spotlight can create a reflection of the feature it illuminates. Outside the water, aim it to highlight a feature in the water or place it under statues, trees, or large poolside plants.

OUT-OF-WATER LIGHTS

Low-voltage lights that can be installed along a path or at the water's edge include spotlights, floodlights, and decorative light fixtures located outside the water. Use them to increase safety for nighttime strolls or to highlight focal points.

EDGING

Stacked rocks of various sizes disguise the edge of a liner and create a realistic look for a water feature. Flat rocks, adequately secured, provide places to stand or step across.

Edging materials add the finishing touch to a pond, stream, or waterfall. Enhance the aesthetic appeal of a natural-looking feature by concealing the exposed edges of the liner. Use edging to protect the liner from the harsh effects of the sun. A slightly raised edge also protects the pond from water runoff from the surrounding landscape.

Consider the look and function of your water feature when choosing edging material. Formal pond designs usually have geometric shapes, a level capstone, and one type of edging; informal ponds are often irregular in shape and include more than one type of edging. Edging gives birds and other wildlife access to your pond or stream. Even if you don't anticipate people standing near the water, construct the edging with safety in mind. Ensure the edging can withstand your weight combined with that of a visitor or two.

Edging a preformed water feature is more difficult than concealing a flexible liner. Unless the surrounding area is paved, take extra steps to disguise the rim. If you use heavy rocks or pavers as edging, support them with a foundation of concrete blocks or a layer of crushed stone topped with sand buried around the perimeter of the liner to support the lip. Make sure that the edging stones overhang the edge by 2 inches, or enough to conceal it.

NATURAL-LOOKING PONDS AND STREAMS

A concrete edge along a stream doesn't look natural. Instead, consider hiding the liner edge under a ledge of soil topped with a combination of rocks and plants for the most natural look. Placing large flat-topped rocks at strategic points along the stream provides steps as well as seating. A grouping of various-size rocks looks natural. If you have a large pond with a flexible liner, try creating a gently sloping pebble beach along one side, which allows wildlife to wade and bathe or, as raccoons do, wash their food in the shallow water.

ROCK AND STONE: These popular edging materials provide a look that's as natural as the ponds and streams they border. Choose rocks indigenous to your area; if there are no rocks in the native landscape, buy rocks that blend naturally with the local terrain. Granite and slate are hard and long-lasting. Their strata, or layers, when exposed, add a rugged beauty to the water's edge. They're well-suited to waterfalls because running water won't wear away the stone. Sedimentary rocks, including sandstone and limestone, are readily available and reasonably priced edging materials. These soft rocks will deteriorate over time.

Avoid rocks that present a hazard to pond inhabitants. Fresh-cut limestone can make the water toxic to fish, and rainwater leaches the toxins into the pond even when the rocks are set beyond the water level. Stabilize rocks or stones with mortar and reinforcing materials so that overhanging rocks are less likely to fall into the water or shift under the weight of a visitor. One or more large boulders at the pond's edge create a dramatic effect, but plan for extra concrete reinforcement to support the weight of the boulders. To create a visual transition, surround boulders with smaller rocks of the same type. Also consider placing some stones partly submerged in the water.

PLANTS: Create a naturally soft, pleasing look by alternating plants between areas of rocks; avoid encircling the water feature with a necklace of rocks. Low-growing evergreens work well along the perimeter of most water features. Add plants after completing pond construction and installing edging.

TURF: Grass growing to the edge of the water feature looks neat and natural. It provides a good surface to reach the water to do maintenance or to observe fish. Skim grass clippings out of the water after mowing. Algae growth results as the high nitrogen

When skillfully designed and surrounded by stone, an above-ground pool blends beautifully into the landscape.

After you've edged it with bricks and concrete pavers, complete a pond's natural surroundings with a variety of plants.

in grass disturbs the ecological balance of the pond. Avoid using lawn chemicals, such as herbicides and fertilizers, which might run into your pond or stream when it rains and wreak havoc with the pond life.

FORMAL PONDS

Cut stone, decorative tiles, cast concrete pieces, or bricks typically edge formal water gardens. Arrange them in the geometric pattern of your choice; combine two or more types for an unusual, decorative look. Experiment by combining stones and colors at the water's edge to make sure you will be happy with the results. If your pond has curved edges, consider using retaining-wall blocks with a trapezoidal shape.

Set edging on a concrete collar or a 3-inch-deep bed of leveled crushed stone; use mortar to hold the stone, tile, or block in place. Bricks and some sedimentary rocks could raise the pH level of the water and possibly harm fish. Test the water regularly and adjust the pH level accordingly.

WOOD EDGING AND DECKING

Wood looks handsome when combined with turf and other edging materials or as the surface for a deck or walkway. However, do not use treated lumber. It can leach chemicals into a water feature and pose a toxic threat to plants and fish. Use rot-resistant woods, such as cedar or redwood, or manufactured composite woods. If you select redwood, let it age for a year until it turns gray. Fresh redwood contains tannins toxic to aquatic life.

If you like the look of wood edging, consider setting treated timbers, cut pier-style and positioned upright, in a bed of concrete around the pool's perimeter. Alternatively, build a deck over the edge of the water or along the perimeter of the water feature. An overhanging deck offers a place to sit, feed fish, or just watch the water.

Sharp, straight edges and geometric shapes define formal style. Even wood plank edging can seem formal.

Proper building techniques make the difference between a properly functioning water garden and one with chronic problems.

INSTALLING A WATER GARDEN

Building a water garden is not a particularly difficult task, even for a beginner. All you need are a few simple tools. With two exceptions—electrical work and large excavations—you probably won't need to hire an outside contractor. For small jobs with straightforward electrical work, you may be able to wire the pond yourself, if such work is allowed in your community.

Excavation of even a small installation is often the most taxing part. The key to whether it's fun or frustrating lies in how much you can do by yourself without overdoing it. For an extra-large project, you're probably better served to contract out the work to someone with a backhoe. (Or rent one, if you have the skill to operate it.)

Water garden installation, like most home improvement projects, is easier to accomplish if you have a helper. Whether you are digging dirt, hauling rocks, installing liner, laying bricks, or just in need of a second opinion, a companion greatly speeds up the project.

As you launch into building your pond, allow plenty of time for each step. Many homeowners are overly optimistic with their estimate of the time it will take to complete a project. Anticipate unexpected complications, trips to the hardware store, and other time-consuming tasks. Take your time, and the installation can be almost as enjoyable as the finished product.

Use a carpenter's level resting on a long, straight board to check that the edge of the pool is level along its entire perimeter. If one edge is higher than another, add and tamp soil until the sides are even.

IN THIS SECTION

DIGGING

The most daunting part of creating a large garden pond is the digging. But with some advance planning—and when done properly—digging can be downright fun.

ADVANCE PLANNING

When planning your garden pond, take into consideration how much digging you can do and adjust either the size of the water garden or the amount you do alone. Digging even a small pool is not a job for a person with a history of back pain or heart problems.

GETTING HELP: If you can't dig it yourself, consider hiring a neighborhood teen, or get friends and relatives to assist. For very large projects, you may want to hire professional help. As a rule, water gardens with a surface area of less than 250 square feet are most economically built by hand; larger projects are best done with a backhoe, rented or hired.

DIGGING A POOL

1. Mark the outline of the pond with a garden hose, rope, or sprinkled line of flour, fine soil, or garden lime. Live with the outline for a week or so to discover how well the new feature fits into the landscape and how it will affect traffic patterns.

2. Remove turf. Use it to fill bare spots in the lawn or set it aside in a pile of its own to compost. If you have a large quantity, use it as the base of a berm or a raised bed. Stack it in the spot for the berm; then cover with several inches of topsoil.

3. As you dig, keep the pond edge level. If it is not level, the liner will show. Check by resting a carpenter's level on a straight board laid across the pond. Work all around the pond, checking every shelf and side of the pool so that there are no surprises.

4. Create a spot to overwinter plants and fish. In cold areas, you'll need a zone in the pool that won't freeze. It should be up to 3 feet deep and as wide as it is deep. Be sure this deep zone isn't in the same spot you want to place a pump or fountain.

5. Dig the shelf for the marginal plants about 8 to 12 inches deep. Position the shelf so that the plants frame your view of the water garden. Then dig a ledge for the edging as deep as the edging material and slightly less wide.

6. Toss the soil into a wheelbarrow or onto a tarp to protect your lawn. If it's in good condition, use it to fill in low spots in the landscape or to build a slope for a waterfall, or haul it to a construction site that needs fill dirt.

TIME: Allow plenty of time for digging, considering both pool size and soil type. An 18-inch-deep, 3×5-foot pool in sandy soil may take only an hour or so, while a 24-inch-deep, 6×10-foot pool in clay can take a day or more. Pace yourself. Even if you're in good physical shape, divide larger projects into one-hour increments with a half-hour rest in between so you don't strain your back.

TOOLS: Make sure your tools are in excellent condition and well-suited to the task. Start with a sharp spade with a pointed blade. You'll also need a wheelbarrow for hauling dirt and possibly a truck to haul away soil.

It's best to dig when the soil is moist but not wet. That allows the spade to cut through the soil neatly, and the soil isn't overly heavy. If the weather has been dry, you can moisten the top foot or so of soil by soaking it with water from a hose. Let the soil drain before you start digging.

DIGGING IN

Start by marking the site with a garden hose, rope, or garden lime. Then fine-tune the outline with stakes (every foot or so) and twine. Cut along the outline with a spade; then remove the top layer of sod. If you're going to use turf as edging, cut the sod approximately 4 inches in from the outline of the pond. Remove the sod inside the outline and peel back the 4-inch strip. After installing the liner, flip the sod back over it.

To edge with stones or other material, dig an outwardly sloping shelf (6 to 8 inches wide by 2 inches deep) for the liner and the edging. The trench should be deep enough for the edging stones to sit flush with the ground or 3 to 4 inches deep for a concrete footing for edges that will get heavy traffic.

With the sod removed, mark the outlines for marginal shelves; then begin digging from the center outward. Dig 2 inches deeper than the pool depth to allow for an underlayment of sand (less for other materials).

As you dig, angle the sides slightly, about 20 degrees, and make sure the edges of the pond are level, or the liner will show. With a small project, you can place a carpenter's level on a straight piece of 2×4 to check all around the pond.

For a large project, put a stake in the center of the pond with its top at the planned water level. Rest one end of a long straight board on the stake and the other end on the edge of the pool. Check the level. Rotate the board a few feet, again noting the level. Repeat until you return to the starting point.

Use the removed sod to patch bare spots in the yard or add it to a compost pile. If the topsoil is in reasonably good condition, add it to the vegetable garden, spread it on flower beds, or create new beds and berms. If you're installing a rigid liner, set aside the soil to backfill around the liner. Put the soil in a wheelbarrow or on a large tarp or piece of plastic to protect the lawn. Discard clay-laden subsoil or use it to build up a slope for a waterfall. Dump larger amounts at a landfill.

HINT

Keep good-quality topsoil, which you can reuse, and poor-quality subsoil, which you should discard, separate by tossing them into different wheelbarrows or onto different pieces of plastic or tarp.

PROPER DIGGING TECHNIQUE

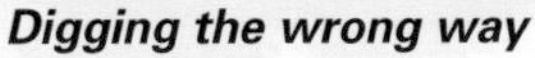

Digging the wrong way

Digging the right way

Digging your garden pond correctly will save you a lot of minor aches and pains as well as possible serious injury.

Wear the proper clothes. A good pair of heavy boots helps you plant your feet, keeps you from slipping, and lets you work more efficiently, reducing fatigue. While digging, be sure to keep a straight back and good posture. Don't stoop or let your shoulders slump. Also keep your knees bent at all times. This distributes weight to your legs. Lift with your legs, not with your back.

Work when the soil is reasonably moist—but not wet—to minimize the effort of cutting into the earth without adding much weight to the soil. Scoop up small amounts of soil at a time. Keep loads on the spade reasonably small to prevent strain. Grip the spade close to the blade to give yourself better control.

When carrying soil away from the pond to the place where you'll dump it, walk with your knees slightly bent. Don't stretch out your body to toss the soil in a pile far away; this will overextend your back. As soon as the hole is large enough, step in and work from inside it.

INSTALLING A FLEXIBLE LINER

To fit a two-dimensional liner into a three-dimensional excavation, you must tuck and fold the liner. Wear sneakers or soft-soled shoes to walk across the liner without causing punctures.

UNDERNEATH THE LINER

Lay a protective 2-inch base of damp sand on the bottom of the pond. Use the sand base to fine-tune the gentle bottom slope. On the pond walls, install an underlayment of geotextile fabric, newspapers, or old carpet. Extend the underlayment to cover the sand bottom for extra protection. Set preformed concrete pads in the bottom of the pond to support objects heavier than 200 pounds that will be placed in the pond, such as statuary, boulders, and bridge piers. Cover the concrete pads with carpeting before installing the pond liner. Once the liner is installed, place three or four layers of scrap pond liner on top of the pond liner over the concrete pad. Lower the heavy object slowly and carefully onto the prepared area.

Upon completing the installation of the protective underlayment, carefully recheck the measurements of the excavation using a flexible measuring tape. Measure the length of the excavation by starting at the edge; lay the tape down the sidewall, across the bottom, and up the opposite sidewall to the edge. Add 2 feet to this measurement to determine the minimum length of the pond liner. On a line perpendicular to the length, measure the width. As with the length, begin measuring down the sidewall, across the bottom, and up the opposite sidewall. Add 2 feet to the measured width. Compare the measured results with the dimensions of the pond liner before opening the carton (you may need to exchange the liner for a different size). See page 38 for more details about measuring for a liner.

UNFOLDING THE POND LINER

Carry the liner into the excavation with assistance if needed. Dragging could harm the liner and might pull damaging objects on top of the protective underlayment. Cold liners, especially those made of PVC, may require several hours in the sun to become pliable. Leaving it in place too long—such as for several days—could kill the grass beneath it.

Starting at the center of the pond, unfold the liner outward toward the sides. Center the liner over the excavation. Wear soft-soled shoes or go barefoot when walking on the liner to protect it. The liner will bunch up at curves and corners; folds are an inevitable result of forming a two-dimensional piece of material into a three-dimensional shape. Create a few large folds in order to eliminate most of the smaller ones. Let one person pull

***1. Cushion the hole with underlayment.** Use moist sand (horizontal surfaces only), old carpet, underlayment made for water gardens, or other materials. Cover both the bottom and the sides. At corners and curves, cut triangles in the underlayment to help fit contours.*

***2. Position the liner.** Drape it loosely in the hole, arranging and pleating as needed. (This job may be accomplished faster and more easily with two or more people.) Anchor the sides with bricks or stones, taking care not to stretch the liner.*

the liner from the top edge while another person works inside the excavation, making adjustments and ensuring that the liner remains centered in the excavation. Place smooth stones or bricks on the perimeter of the liner to prevent it from blowing into the pond.

***3. Adjust the liner.** Add a few inches of water to the pond to settle the liner. Pleat and tuck the liner as necessary to make it fit the contours and corners of the pond.*

***4. Prepare for edging.** Fill the pond with a few more inches of water. Adjust the liner, then fill to just below the edging shelf. Trim the liner at the edge.*

Tucking and Folding

Informal pools will have random folds along the sides. Rectangular formal pools should have one large fold at each corner. Form each fold as a large triangle; secure it with double-sided seaming tape. Allow the seaming tape to cure for 24 hours (or as directed) before adding water. Sealing not only makes the fold less obvious, but also keeps out debris and prevents small fish from becoming trapped behind the liner.

The time spent folding the pond liner should be minimal, less than 20 minutes for a 10×10-foot pool. Usually, the person most concerned about folds and tucks is the pond owner; few viewers ever take note of them. If debris falls into the lined pond, sweep the material into a plastic dustpan. When ready, fill the pond with 2 inches of water before making final adjustments to the liner by smoothing out some of the wrinkles. Finish filling the pond before edging it. After the pond is filled, check for low spots around the edge. If water doesn't cover the liner evenly to the top or spills over the edge in places, lift the liner and build up the soil in those places.

If you exercise care during the liner installation, no damage should occur. However, if you do puncture the liner, it is easily repaired with special adhesive tape or other sealants designed for this purpose.

INSTALLING A PREFORMED LINER

Preformed liners take much of the guesswork out of digging and lining a pool or pond.

Choose the largest liner possible that suits your site and your pocketbook. Preformed units appear smaller once installed, filled with water, and edged. If you want to keep koi or goldfish, the pond should be deep enough to accommodate them; if it has plant shelves, they should be wide enough to hold the pots you will use for planting.

After determining where you want to install your pond, carry the preformed unit to the site. Orient the liner, topside up, on the spot where you want to install it. Use a carpenter's level and plumb bob or a weighted string to establish the outer edge of the pond. You can't simply mark the outline of the form's bottom on the ground and start digging. Preformed rigid pond walls slope slightly inward (from top to bottom), making the top perimeter larger than the bottom perimeter. The plumb bob drops straight down from the top perimeter, enabling you to outline the perimeter on the ground directly below it. Mark the perimeter using a rope or a hose. Enlarge the entire perimeter by 2 inches to allow working room within the excavation. The extra space will be filled later with sifted soil or sand. Finalize the outline by marking it with spray paint, flour, or sand.

Before digging, place the prefabricated pool upright where it will be located, then map the outline using a garden hose or rope.

EXCAVATING THE SITE

The liner must have firm support under the shelves, bottom, and sides in order to be stable and resist buckling. See page 68 for general excavation directions. Set aside the preformed pool while you excavate. If the pond has no shelves, dig straight down (or at a slight angle no greater than the inward slope of the preformed unit) to the bottom. The depth should match the depth of the pond form plus 2 inches. If the pond includes shelves, measure carefully to make the excavation conform to their depth and width. The shelves need to be supported by soil in order to sustain the weight of water when the pond is filled. Leave room to add 2 inches of damp sand under the shelves once the excavation is complete. Damp sand stays in place, whereas dry sand tends to shift off the edges of shelf areas during installation. If you want the top of the preformed liner to be 1 inch above ground level to protect the pond from surface runoff, then measure and dig out only 1 inch extra; the 2 inches of added sand will put the pond top 1 inch above ground level.

Avoid overdigging the shelf areas. Backfilling an excavated space under a shelf could cause the shelf to settle while the

Use a carpenter's level to check that the bottom and shelves of the excavation are completely level.

Comb the sand with a straight board to ensure that it is smooth.

OUTLINING THE FORM

Outline the perimeter of the excavation for a symmetrically shaped pond the easy way by turning the preformed liner upside down on the proposed site and spray-painting around its edges. This method works well for squares, rectangles, circles, and ovals but not for abstract or irregular shapes.

remainder of the pond remains stable. This would make the top uneven and allow water to overflow the edge around the plant shelf.

Decide in advance what to do with the soil removed during excavation. You may use it to build up an area planned for a waterfall or to change the contour of the land somewhere else on your property. Offer it to friends or neighbors if they need the soil. Or look for a place wanting clean fill dirt.

PREPARING THE EXCAVATION

Spread 2 inches of damp sand across the bottom of the excavation on the shelf surfaces. Use a board or the straight edge of a garden rake to spread the sand evenly over the entire bottom and the shelves. Place the liner into the excavation; use a carpenter's level to verify that the pond is level. If it needs leveling, remove the preformed liner and rework the sand. The pond's contact marks on the sand indicate where to remove high sand and where fill-in sand is needed. Continue working the sand until the pond comes within ¼ inch of level. Add the edging.

Perhaps you plan to have a raised pond or one that is partially in the ground and partially above the ground. If it is to be partially in the ground, dig down as already described, but only far enough so that the top of the pond will be at the height desired. Remember to account for the 2 inches of sand added to the excavation. For an aboveground pond, remove the top 2 inches of soil and replace it with sand. Rake and work the sand so that the top of the pond sits level.

BACKFILLING

Despite being made of rigid fiberglass and high-density polyethylene, preformed ponds have a bit of flexibility. Units built of these materials typically possess sufficient structural integrity to hold water without outside support. But because they are somewhat flexible, they may become distorted when filled if the sidewalls are not supported. Prevent the distortion by filling the space between the sidewalls and the excavation with sifted soil or sand as you fill the pond with water. Avoid using vacuum-formed pools, such as children's wading pools, because they easily change shape in undesirable and unpredictable ways, and they're difficult to install and maintain.

As the first few gallons of water spread evenly across the bottom of the liner, it's likely that the form will sit level in the ground, but the weight of added water might cause a slight shift. As the pond fills, backfill around the form. Adjust the water flow so that the pond fills to roughly the same level at which you are working the soil on the outside of the liner. Periodically check the level in all directions three or more times while the pond is filling with water. If it's out of level by more than ¼ inch, remove the water and soil, make adjustments, and start over. Add the edging to complete the installation.

Lift the shell and lower it into the excavation. You may need to remove it several times to make adjustments.

Fill the unit with 4 inches of water. Begin backfilling around it with sand, tamping the sand as you work. Gradually add more water as you backfill, keeping the levels of sand and water comparable.

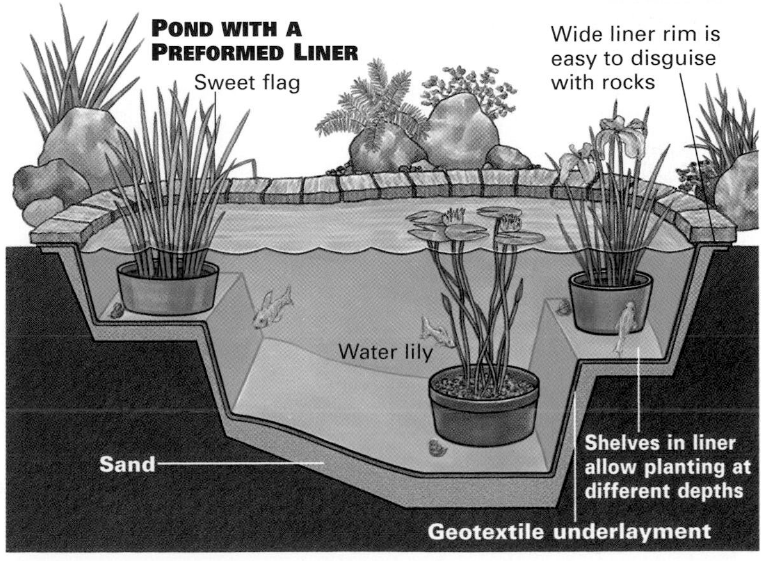

CONSTRUCTING A CONCRETE POND

Sturdy rebar makes any concrete water feature better able to withstand the damaging effects of seasonal freezing and thawing as well as mild earth tremors.

Begin with an excavation that allows for a bottom at least 6 inches thick (4 inches in frost-free, earthquake-free areas) plus an additional 4 to 6 inches of gravel. The walls should be equally thick. The top of the concrete should extend 1 inch above the surrounding ground to keep surface runoff out of the pond.

For large or irregular-shaped ponds, hire a contractor to apply gunite or other sprayed concrete to an excavation lined with reinforced wire mesh. Otherwise, build wood forms that will shape the concrete into the desired design. The walls of the form must be put together carefully because the concrete walls will be an exact impression of the form. Make sure that the tops of the form are level; the level of the walls cannot be altered once they are installed.

In cold climates, consider making the walls 1 inch to 2 inches thicker at the bottom than at the top and angled slightly outward from bottom to top. The angle helps the walls to withstand the pressure of ice.

THE POND BOTTOM

In areas subject to winter freezing, reinforce the bottom and walls with rebar or wire mesh. Add a 6-inch-deep layer of gravel to make a solid base that reduces the risk that the concrete will settle and crack.

When pouring the concrete for the pond bottom, make a saucerlike depression approximately 4 inches deep where you can place the pump when you want to empty the pond. The pond floor should slope toward the depression at the rate of 1 inch per 10 feet of bottom. This eliminates the need to install a drain (and prevents clogged drain problems) in the water garden.

POURING THE POND

For best results, pour the concrete in one day—ideally on a cool, cloudy day. If pouring during hot weather, cover the poured construction with opaque plastic sheeting to allow the concrete to cure slowly. The entire pond should be poured in a continuous process—first the floor, then the walls—to make a seamless form. The pond floor should be carefully smoothed, beginning at one end and working backward toward the opposite end and maintaining a slight slope toward the center, where the drain will sit.

EXTRA SECURITY

It might take a decade or so, but concrete ponds eventually develop hairline cracks and begin to leak. Postpone the leaking by using a flexible pond liner around the exterior of a concrete pond. Lay a base for the liner with 2 inches of gravel topped with 2 inches of sand. Place an underlayment of old carpeting or geotextile fabric over the sand and install the flexible liner over that. Pour the concrete floor over the liner; then pour the walls. After removing the wall forms, wrap the excess liner and underlayment over the exterior and top of the pond walls and backfill the space between the underlayment and the excavation walls with sand or sifted soil.

For best results, the concrete portion of the job should be completed within a day in a continuous process that leaves no seams.

INSTALLING ABOVE GROUND

Rigid liner works well for creating an aboveground pond with stone sides.

Set each successive course slightly closer to the liner; then backfill.

Backfill under the liner lip and conceal the edge with overhanging stones.

Aboveground pools and ponds are good options where digging would be difficult, and they're also appealing because they bring the water up close, which is especially enjoyable near a patio or other sitting area.

Raised water features tend to take longer than sunken ponds to build and usually cost more. However, they're less likely to become cluttered with blowing debris or eroding soil.

TYPES: Aboveground pools must be built from materials sturdy enough to withstand the outward pressure of water. Raised water features are often made of brick, an excellent material in formal gardens or in landscapes that already contain brick. Concrete block—veneered with stucco, brick, tile, or stone—is another option. Wood timbers stacked upon one another or logs stacked on end in a row are other possibilities. Cut or natural stone is another popular choice.

HEIGHT: The height of an aboveground pool can vary from 1 foot to much higher. For a pool that's completely above ground, the ideal height is between 24 and 30 inches, especially if you want visitors to see the fish or to be able to sit on the edge.

The pool should be a minimum of 18 inches deep. For a pool that rises above ground less than that height, partially excavate the pool to make it 18 inches deep. By doing this, you ensure the feature will also be better insulated from the elements.

FOOTINGS: A masonry aboveground pool will need a concrete footing around the perimeter of its base. The depth of the footing depends on your climate, but it may need to be more than 2 feet deep in northern regions. Check local codes for proper depth. You can pour the footing directly into a trench; in soft soil you may need to build wooden forms for the footing. Either way, make sure the footing is perfectly level from one side to the other.

MATERIALS: Wooden raised pools are simple to make; masonry projects require more time and skill. Structures made of wood are most successful when constructed from pressure-treated lumber or aged redwood to prevent rot. The wood should be relatively smooth to prevent flexible liner from ripping during installation.

No matter what material you use for the sides of your raised feature, the pool will need to be underlayed and lined. Rigid liner works well for raised gardens, but flexible liner offers more options for style and shape. Staple the liner to the edges of wooden structures or glue it to them with silicone sealant. In masonry projects, sandwich the liner between the last course of brick and the cap.

Bury the bottom ties for stability. Secure wood ties with threaded steel rods at 8- to 10-inch intervals.

Add a 2-inch layer of sand on the bottom, then cover all surfaces with an underlayment for protection.

Position the liner and pleat carefully. Fill the pool halfway, then staple the liner into place and conceal the edge.

MAKING A BOG

Make a bog garden as an independent unit or as a part of one or more other water features—a pond, a stream, or a waterfall. The bog can absorb water that overflows from your water feature after heavy rains. And when you integrate a bog with other features, it takes little extra work to make it function as a plant filter that absorbs pollutants and silt.

In nature, streams and ponds have wet, boggy areas along their edges. In garden settings, a bog imitates a marshy place where plants grow in standing water or wet, spongy ground. Water-loving plants thrive because the soil doesn't dry out. Depending on the size and location of your bog, make a freestanding garden, as described here, or install bog plants in the moist margins of a stream or pond to blend the boundaries of water and land.

MAKING A BOG

Bog garden construction differs from pond construction mainly in terms of depth. Excavate a bog 12 to 16 inches deep with sloping sides, saving the soil to refill the bog later. Spread a 2-inch layer of sand and top it with a piece of flexible liner. If the site is normally moist, no underlayment is necessary. Perforate the bottom of the liner every 3 feet to allow slow drainage and prevent the standing water from becoming foul.

Build a rim of soil and extend the bog's liner an inch above the surrounding ground to keep water from running off. Use rocks, soil, and plants around the perimeter to disguise the liner's edge and give the bog a natural look.

PLANTING THE BOG

Many bog plants spread easily, quickly overrunning slower-growing species. Keep this in mind when you create a planting scheme, determine where to locate plants, and decide if you will plant in containers. Use plastic nursery pots or water garden baskets to contain invasive plants. Otherwise, plant directly in the soil. Saturate the soil, using a leaky hose laid on or under the soil surface.

ADDING A BOG GARDEN

Build a bog adjacent to a lined pond or stream by extending the liner of the water feature into the bog excavation. The boundary between the pond or stream and the bog must be semipermeable, meaning it will allow water to seep into the bog and saturate its soil. Where the two features meet, the soil should be bermed and hard-packed. After you extend the liner over this berm and into the bog, stack rocks or concrete blocks on the bermed area to keep the soil out of the pond but allow water to seep through.

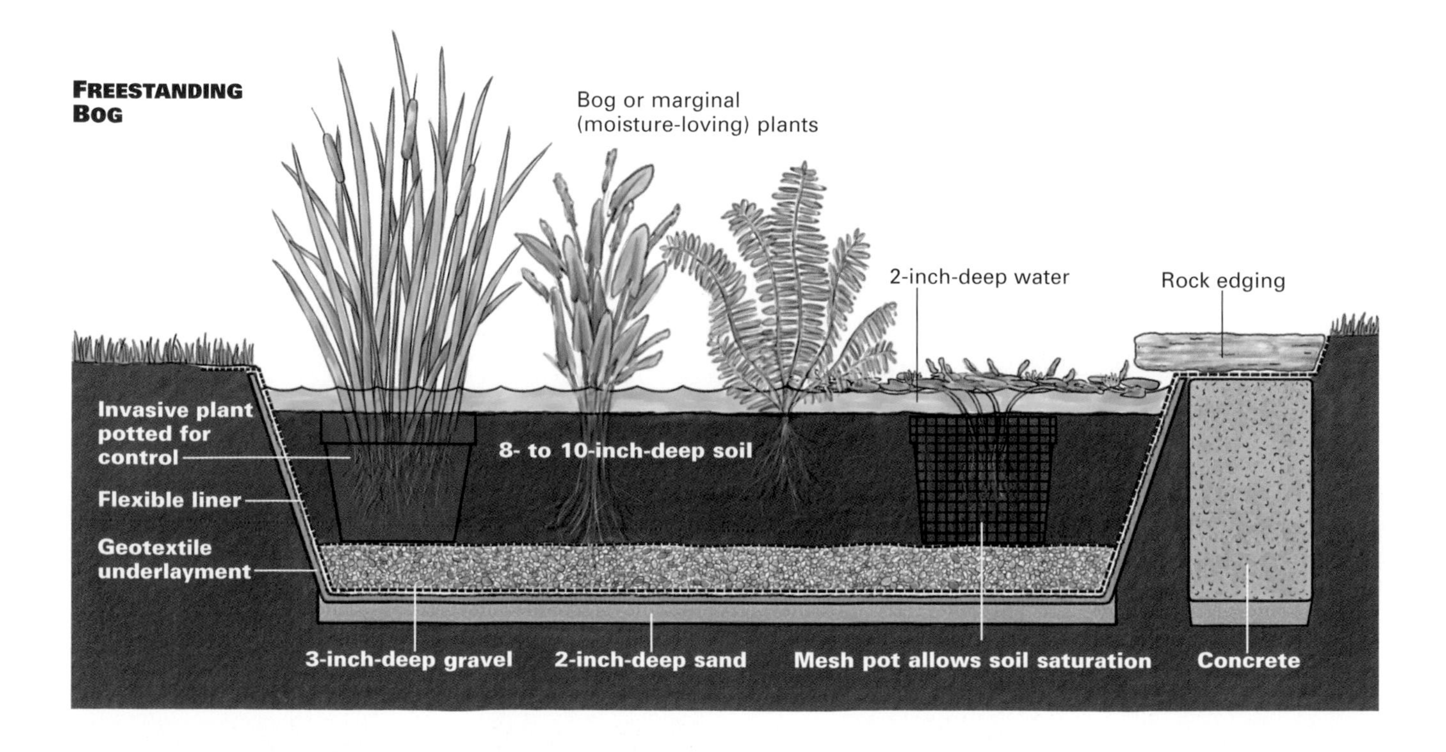

CONSTRUCTING A STREAM

Construct a stream much as you would make a waterfall, with a series of small, shallow pools and cascades along a gently sloping course. The longer the stream, the more likely it will meander as it follows the lay of the land. You can locate a stream just about anywhere. Study the contours of your landscape. If your yard has a slope, it will be easy to turn it into a watercourse. But even if your yard is flat, you can create a slope with infill soil or soil left over from excavation. Miniature bogs along the water's edge will add to the impression that the stream was formed by nature.

1. Mark out the watercourse with stakes or twine, and build up a berm if necessary to create a slope. Then begin digging, creating pools first and spillways next.

2. Install sand or underlayment to prevent tears in the flexible liner. Spread the liner and fold it as needed. Overlap higher sections onto lower ones, check their positions, and seal the seams.

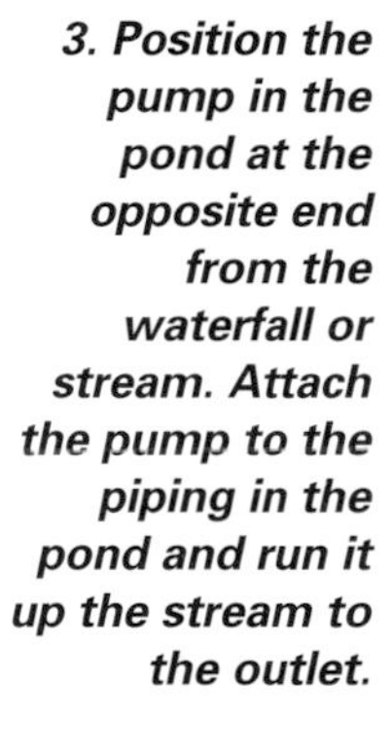

3. Position the pump in the pond at the opposite end from the waterfall or stream. Attach the pump to the piping in the pond and run it up the stream to the outlet.

4. Turn on the pump and check to see how the water flows. Make adjustments by adding or removing soil under the liner.

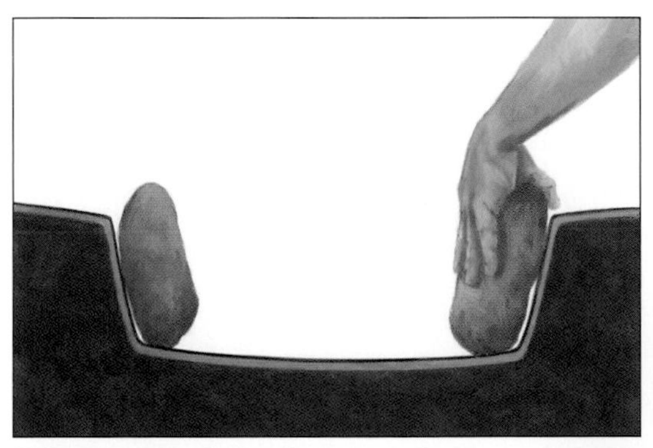

5. Lay a row of rough stones along the stream edges. Mortar them to prevent water from flowing under them and being wasted. Then trim the liner edges.

6. Disguise the liner edges with pebbles or stones in the streambed. Scatter some among the edging stones too. Avoid gravel, as it tends to collect algae.

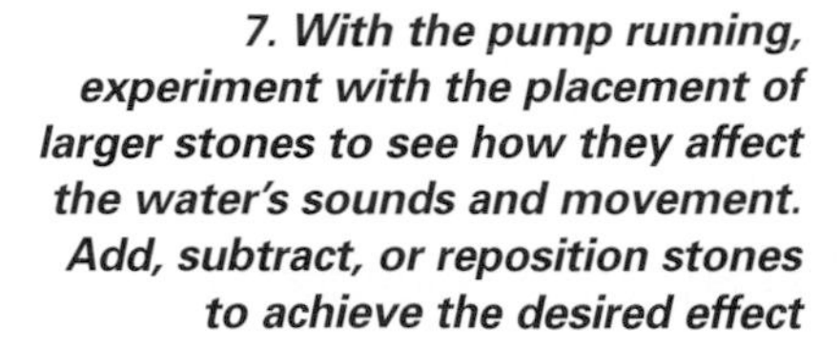

7. With the pump running, experiment with the placement of larger stones to see how they affect the water's sounds and movement. Add, subtract, or reposition stones to achieve the desired effect

INSTALLING A WATERFALL

Preformed waterfalls allow for simple do-it-yourself installation. Most preformed units are made of fiberglass or plastic; many can look natural. Sizes range from a foot high to 6 feet or higher. You may choose among units that include a built-in hidden filter. Use the manufacturer's guidelines for installation and its suggested range of gph to help you choose. Keep the falls within the recommended gph because too much flow can cause water loss and too little flow can result in a loss of visual and aural impact.

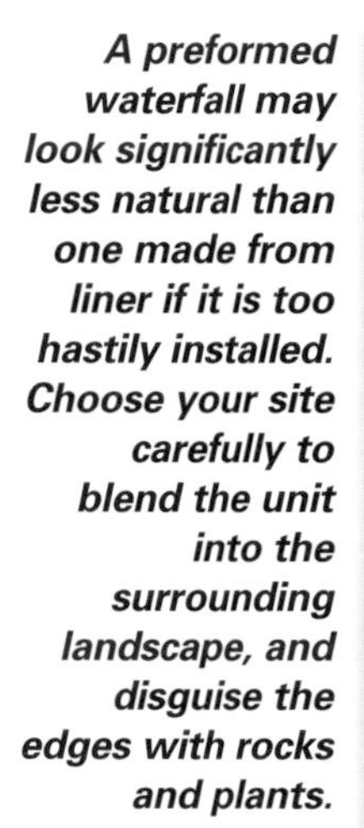

A preformed waterfall may look significantly less natural than one made from liner if it is too hastily installed. Choose your site carefully to blend the unit into the surrounding landscape, and disguise the edges with rocks and plants.

FIBERGLASS AND FOAM WATERFALLS

Experienced water gardeners recommend a small preformed portable waterfall installation for the first-timer. First, determine the size of the submerged pump you will use. Then select a site for the waterfall and place it there. Observe the setup for several days and decide whether to proceed with this site or try another one. Prepare the permanent site by making it level; tamp the ground to make it more stable.

Run tubing from the submerged pump to the connector piece of the waterfall. Use clamps to ensure a watertight connection at both ends. Adjust the position of the waterfall to the exact spot you want, and plug the pump into the power line to commence operation. Camouflage the unit with rocks and plants to blend it with the surroundings.

POLYETHYLENE UNIT WITH BUILT-IN FILTER

Choose a waterfall that corresponds with your desired design. The filter capacity should

CROSS-SECTION OF INTERLOCKING ISSUING BASIN AND CASCADE WATERFALL UNIT

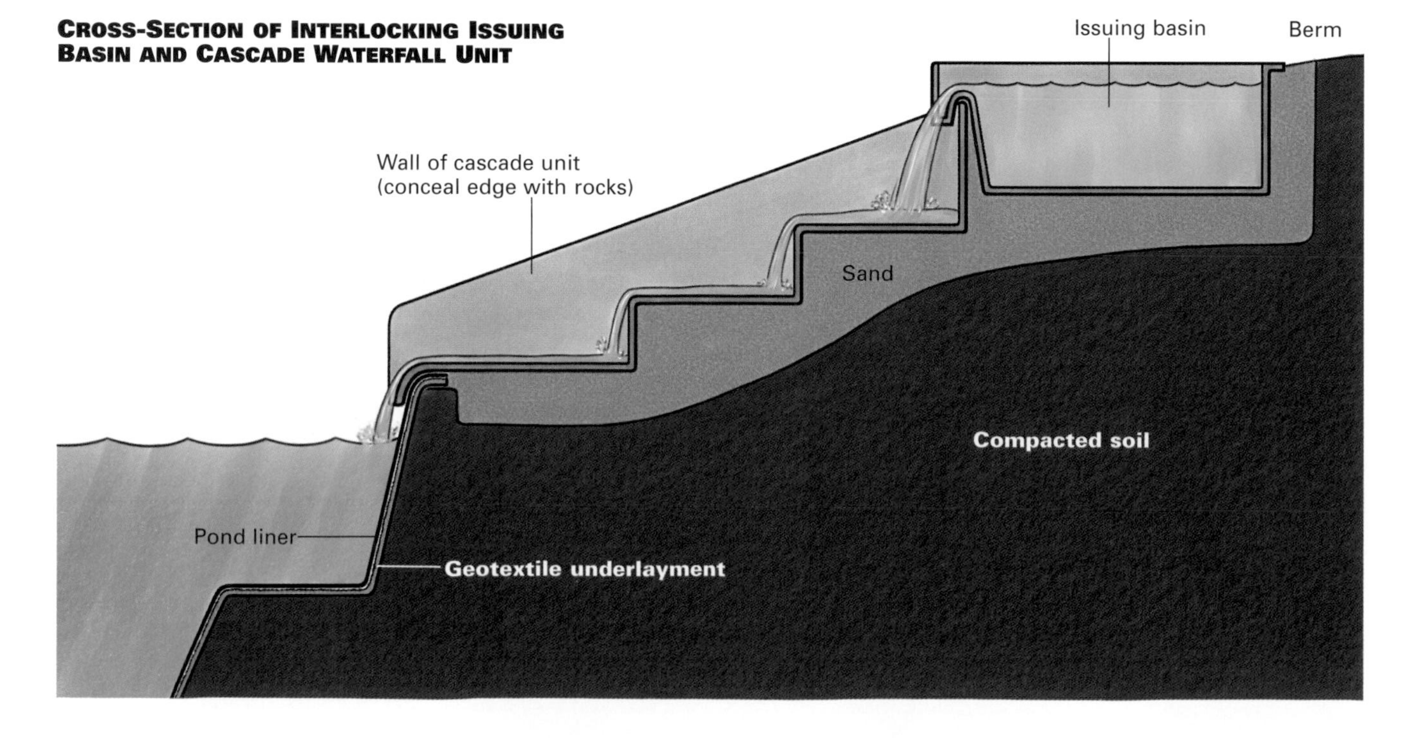

match the size of your pond. Find out what capacity pump it takes to properly operate the waterfall/filter unit. Select a site adjacent to the pond where you plan to install the waterfall. Excavate the site as necessary to accommodate the unit. Tamp the soil firmly; cover the excavation with a 2-inch base of sand. Set the preformed unit in place. Make sure the unit overlaps the pond enough to help prevent water loss. Run tubing or flexible PVC pipe from the submersible pump to the unit, using clamps at both ends.

Attach the waterfall to the flexible pond liner using screws and silicone sealant as detailed in the manufacturer's directions. Check to make sure the unit is level. If necessary, adjust the soil along the edge of the sand base to make it level. Install flat spillway rock for the water's return to the pond. Backfill around the unit using soil or sand. Integrate the spillway rocks with the surroundings using decorative rocks and moisture-loving plants.

ELEVATION VIEW OF INTERLOCKING BASIN AND CASCADE WATERFALL

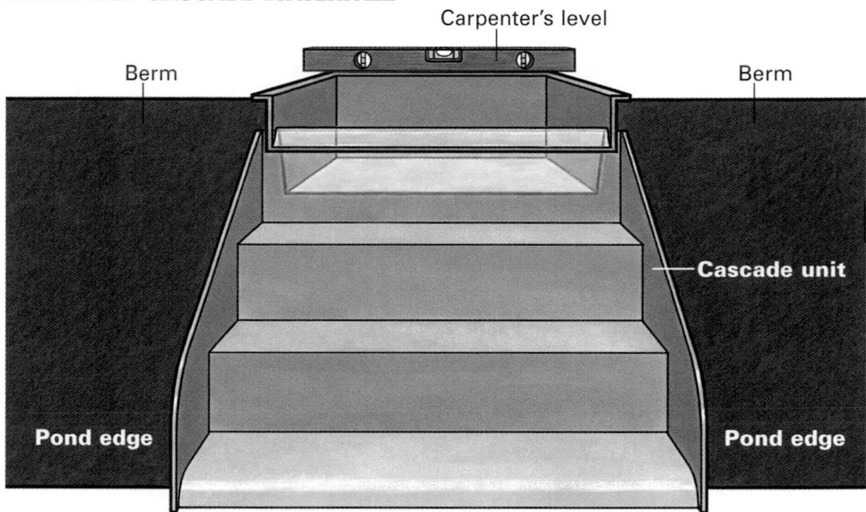

INSTALLATION OF PREFORMED BASIN AND CASCADE

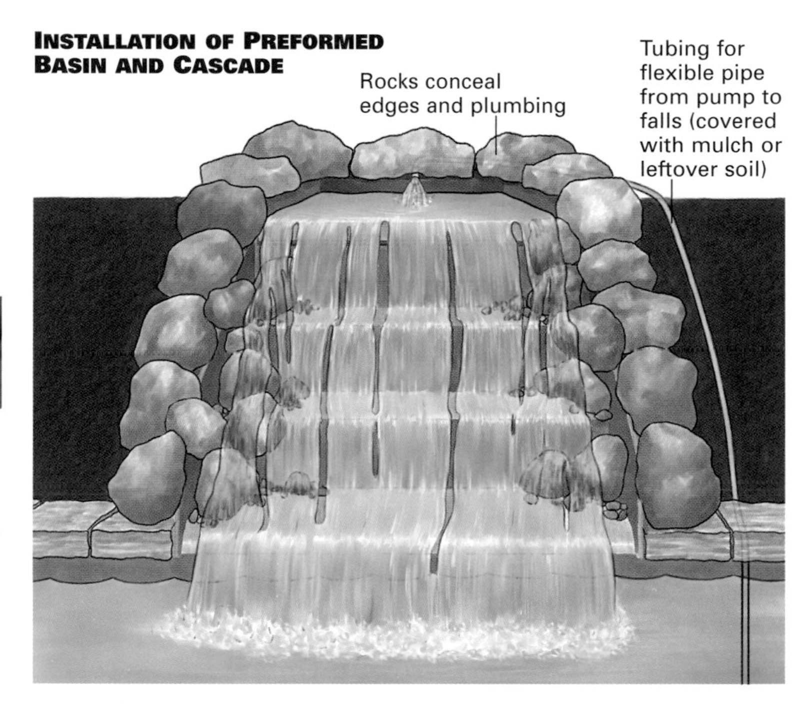

HIGH-DENSITY POLYETHYLENE AND FIBERGLASS CASCADE UNITS

Combine a series of cascade units that, when put together and overlapped, form a watercourse. Use brown or gray forms that match rocks indigenous to your area. Set each unit in its potential position. Change the configuration or placement as you wish. After you are satisfied with the layout, mark the perimeter of the units with stakes, sand, flour, or powdered limestone.

Excavate to support the units, allowing an additional 2 inches for a sand base. Tamp the sand and check that it is level, using a carpenter's level in all directions across the basin. If the basin is not level, water will be lost over the edges.

Place the lowest basin and cascade first. When installed, each unit's outside edges should rise 1 inch or more above the adjacent ground to protect the water feature from runoff. Backfill around the unit and under the edges, using soil or sand, and check that the unit is level.

Temporarily connect tubing or pipe from the submerged pump to the top of the cascade unit. Make a test run of the unit, watching to ensure that the water in each unit stays at least 1 inch below the top edge of the unit. If not, empty the unit and adjust its placement accordingly. Repeat the installation for subsequent cascade units, running a water test following each installation.

Following the successful testing of the final cascade, install the permanent tubing or a pipeline alongside the watercourse, making watertight connections at both ends. The line should maintain its original shape even when buried or walked on.

If the top cascade unit lacks a pipe fitting connection, run the water line over the top end of the cascade unit to discharge the water into the basin. Diffuse the flow of water by placing rocks at the point of discharge or by perforating the water line at the top of the cascade unit.

Camouflage the edges of your watercourse and help blend it with the surroundings by placing rocks and plants around its edge.

INSTALLING A WATERFALL
continued

Create a mini waterfall by laying stones in a pile. Position one rock, such as a large flat stone, to serve as the lip. Add rocks on top to hide the tubing to the pump.

Set more rocks on the lip to hold it in place and form a natural-appearing outcropping. Run flexible tubing attached to a submersible pump in the pond up through the rocks. Adjust the flow to get the right effect.

CONSTRUCTING A NATURALISTIC WATERFALL

Your primary concern in constructing a natural-looking rock- and plant-lined waterfall will be to waterproof it. Most watercourses involve a flow of water between an upper basin, or header pool, and a lower, larger reservoir. It's possible to add a waterfall or watercourse to an existing pond.

Start by preparing an inclined site for the size and shape of the planned waterfall by berming or terracing it. The site should be gently sloping and wide enough to accommodate the waterfall as well as the surrounding rocks and plants. Carefully level, line, and edge the watercourse to prevent water loss.

MULTIPLE CASCADES

Multiple-cascade waterfalls (a series of waterfalls in a stream) should have a reservoir, or basin of water, to supply each cascade, starting with the smallest basin at the top and ending with the largest pool. Picture the watercourse as a staircase, its shape dictated by the site. A gently inclining watercourse will have long steps (the basins) with short risers; steep waterfalls will have shorter steps with tall risers. Vary the length and height of the steps to make the watercourse more natural looking.

Make each basin level across its width; make the overflow area (spillway) 1 to 2 inches lower than the top edge. Thoroughly tamp the excavation. If the ground were to settle, the basin's edge and liner could become uneven and cause water loss. Make a ledge of earth around the perimeter of the excavation, elevated slightly to avoid water loss and to keep out unwanted surface runoff.

Cover the entire excavation with 2 inches of sand. Position a flexible pond liner over the excavation. This liner could be part of the main pond liner or a separate liner that overlaps it. If you use a separate piece, overlap it at least 12 inches over the main pond liner, and use a special adhesive tape made for liners (available from the liner supplier) to seal the pieces together.

ROCKWORK

If your plans call for heavy rockwork (rocks over 200 pounds), prepare for it before installing the liner. Determine the location of these large rocks, and set concrete slabs or poured-concrete footings to support their weight. Cover these foundations with geotextile material or carpet remnants. Use at least two layers of scrap flexible liner between the heavy rocks and the liner. Place the liner over the area after the foundation sets.

Begin placing the rocks for the primary, or lowest, waterfall. Select and place each rock before you use mortar or black urethane foam to seal the rockwork and prevent water from going under or around the rocks. Then choose a large flat rock for the spillway. Place this rock so it projects 2 to 3 inches beyond the rockwork below it. Use sealant as necessary to prevent water from going under or around the spillway rock. Repeat these steps as you continue construction to the upper cascades. Arrange rocks around the edge of the falls and pools to conceal the liner and direct the water flow; the rocks flanking the falls should be higher than the spillway to help keep water in the channel.

Set rocks in mortar, if you prefer, although mortar doesn't survive freezing winters for long. For a better choice, spray expandable urethane foam into openings and crevices in the rockwork. Apply sealant discreetly to the back side of the rockwork; you don't want sealant to show on the front of the falls.

After finishing the liner and rockwork, install the piping, beginning at the bottom reservoir and working up alongside the watercourse to the top falls. Allow at least two days for settling and curing before turning on the water to test the falls. Adjust the rock work to alter the water flow over the falls as necessary. Place small rocks in strategic spots to alter the flow patterns as desired.

DISCHARGE POINTS

Modify the construction somewhat if the waterfall design includes multiple cataracts or points where water emanates or discharges along the face of the falls. After installing the flexible liner, place rocks where you want them, but do not use any sealant yet. Study the rockwork to determine the desired water discharge points along the face. Next, disassemble the falls, carefully keeping track of which stones go where. Disassembly enables you to install pipes (rigid or flexible PVC) directed to each cataract. Construct piping to match the location of the water-issue points. Use a ball valve for each discharge point. These valves must be accessible yet hidden from view. Reassemble the rockwork, sealing each layer with mortar or urethane foam.

When you finish installing the piping, connect it to the pump. Wait two days before turning water on to test the falls. Adjust the valve for each cataract to create the desired look across the face of the falls.

A FINISHING TOUCH

Use plants along the edges of the waterfall to conceal parts of the installation and give it a more natural appearance.

This multiple waterfall employs a natural, cascading design. Flat stones overhang each pool to create an attractive watercourse.

INSTALLING FOUNTAINS

Besides being visually appealing, fountains and piped statuary fill a garden with the music of moving water. Fountainhead designers use their creative skills to provide pond owners with a wide variety of spray patterns, from gentle bubblers and thin columns to spinners and geysers. Statuary choices range from imitations of classical subjects to abstract modern forms. The sight and sound of these water movers greatly enhance the already compelling nature of any water feature. Whatever the landscape style, formal or informal, you can install a fountain or statuary that blends pleasingly with it.

A fountain works as water is forced through the air and falls into a pool or other basin. A fountain head, situated on the end of a pipe, creates a spray pattern. Fountain head kits are available in packages that include a pump, connecting piping, and head.

PUMPS AND FOUNTAIN HEADS

Follow the manufacturer's recommendation when choosing an appropriate pump for your fountain. Match the gph range of the pump with the requirement of the fountain head; also determine the fountain head's spray height. Take into account that the gph of a pump diminishes if it is located at a distance away from the fountain head. The distance between the fountain head and the nearest edge of the water feature represents the maximum desired height of the spray. Beyond being an issue of proportion, this rule has the practical effect of reducing the spray splashing out of the pond onto nearby areas, especially on windy days. The higher the spray, the greater likelihood of making adjacent walkways dangerously slippery or of draining the pool accidentally.

Fountain heads usually connect to a submersible pump, a diverter valve, or a pipe that connects to the pump. If your pump does not discharge water vertically, attach an elbow fitting to send the stream of water skyward so it rises above the water surface. A valve may be used to adjust the height of the spray. Use a diverter valve to allow water from the pump to go elsewhere if the pump powers other features. Even if you intend to operate just one fountain head with the pump, a diverter valve will allow you to easily fine-tune the spray pattern. This frees the pump for another purpose in the future, assuming the pump is strong enough.

Affix the fountain head to the pipe or diverter valve. Set the fountain jets and the decorative parts (if any) above the water's surface. If the setup wobbles, steady it with clean clay bricks stacked against the piping.

Keep water lilies and other aquatic plants in mind when planning a fountain. Rippling water from a vigorous fountain head may retard or even kill water lilies and other aquatics. The spray patterns of some fountain heads, such as a multitier spray, make waves; others, such as the mushroom or bell fountain head, return the water gently in a thin, transparent stream with virtually no surface disturbance.

The fine jets of fountain heads clog easily and the fountain's spray symmetry may be lost. Prevent

PIPING FOR A WATERFALL AND SPOUTING STATUARY

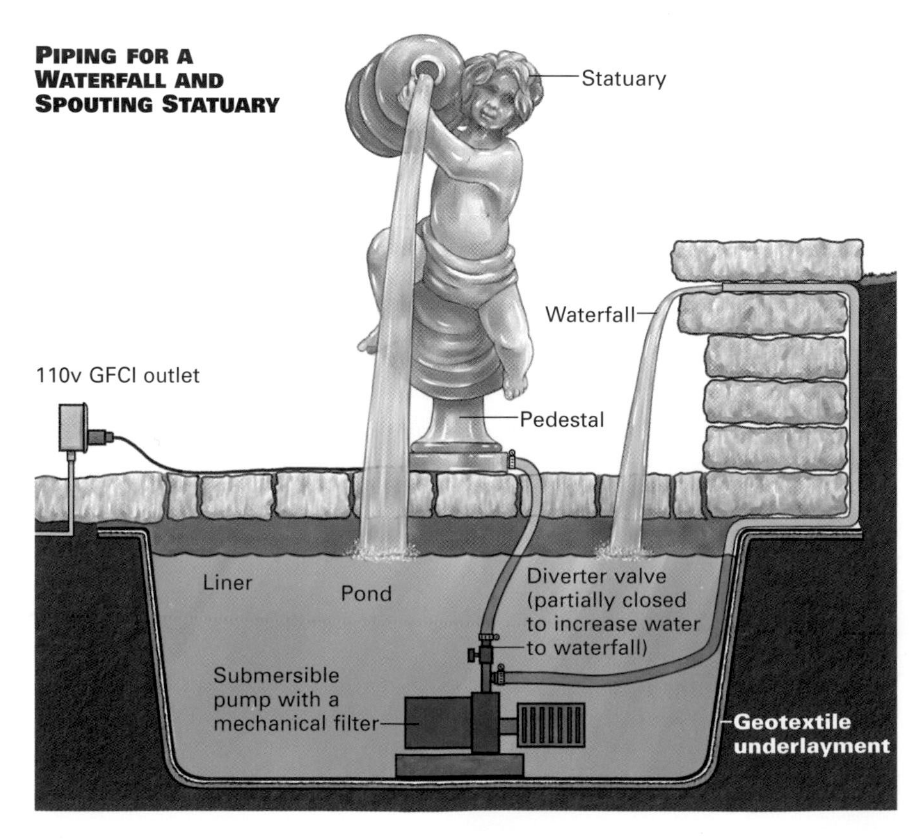

With the right-size pump, you can run more than one water-moving feature, such as a waterfall and spouting statuary.

clogging by installing a mechanical filter that removes particles before they enter the pump. Alternatively, use a foam pump protector or a foam prefilter, and clean it whenever you notice any lessening of water flow.

Enjoy the pleasure of a fountain even if you don't have electrical power available for your water feature. If you use a solar pump to power the fountain, keep in mind that it will function only when the sun shines. Night, as well as shadows from visitors, clouds, and trees, will prevent the pump from working.

FREESTANDING FOUNTAINS

Most freestanding fountains come preplumbed and installation is simple. Check the level of the site on which the fountain will rest and make necessary adjustments to even it up. Use sand, soil, or stone as needed to make the site level.

Fill the fountain with water and plug it in to a GFCI outlet. If the cord doesn't reach the outlet, you can use one length of extension cord designed specifically for outdoor use. You can bury the cord just under the soil surface, but do not bury the connection. Instead, leave it above ground, wrap it with waterproof tape, and disguise it with stone or by setting it among plants.

OUT-OF-POND FOUNTAINS

Out-of-pond fountains are an easy way to add the sound of splashing water to your backyard in a way that ties your aquascape to the rest of the garden.

Small out-of-pond statuary fountains can rest on stones on the edge of the pool or stream. Larger fountains need a more substantial base, such as a perfectly level stone or concrete pad. With either, a pump rests in the pond, recirculating water through a flexible tube. Disguise the tubing and the electrical cord with stones, plants, or soil.

Test the fountain's spray by hooking up the pump and plugging in the fountain. The spray will vary with the design of the fountain but can be made stronger or weaker by turning the flow adjuster valve on the pump.

LIFT PROPERLY

You'll damage a pump attached to a fountain head if you lift the pump by the fountain head. Disconnect the fountain head from the pump before you attempt to lift the pump.

IN-POND FOUNTAINS

In-pond statuary fountains are usually larger than out-of-pond models. For that reason, they must have a solid foundation on which to rest.

Set small fountains weighing less than 30 pounds on a stack of bricks. For larger fountains, either build a substantial base from mortared brick or stone, or install a precast concrete pedestal for the foundation. If you're building your own base, be sure to allow a core for any piping that will be connected to the pump, as most larger fountains are run by an external pump.

HINT

Before you install a pedestal in your pond, put an extra layer of liner under the pedestal base to prevent tears and leaks.

FREESTANDING FOUNTAIN

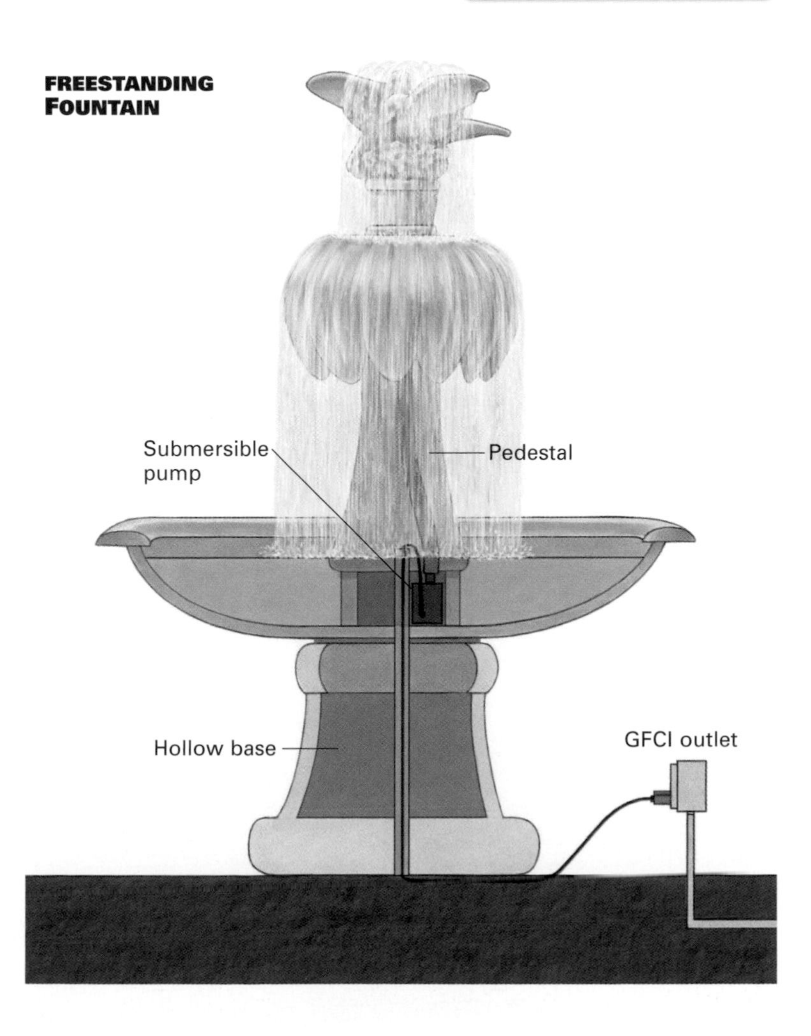

INSTALLING FOUNTAINS
continued

Position a fountain where it will spray into the pond or water feature with minimal water loss to the surrounding terrain. Adjust the flow valve on the pump to get the desired force and trajectory.

Vigorous spray from a fountain can damage water lilies and interfere with aquatic plant growth. Install piped statuary so that the water returns gently into the recirculating basin below.

PIPED STATUARY

Although concrete piped statuary is popular, you may choose from other materials, including metal, plastic, fiberglass, and lightweight resin. Purchase a ready-made pedestal for your statue, or make a firm platform out of bricks or weathered concrete blocks. Place the statuary where it will spout into the water feature without spilling over the edge onto the ground. Setting the statue within the perimeter of the water feature eliminates the risk of water loss if a leak occurs.

Use flexible tubing to connect the statuary to its submersible pump and clamp the tubing securely at each end. If the pump discharge has a diameter different from the piping in the statue, buy fittings to make the transition complete. Small statuary, less than 12 inches tall, usually operate with a 125-gph pump; larger statues, more than 100 pounds and 24 inches tall, may require a 250-gph pump for optimal function. Enlist help to move large pieces of statuary to avoid the risk of injury to yourself and damage to the statue.

New unweathered concrete statuary, as well as concrete blocks used to support statuary, require treatment before they're placed in a fishpond because the concrete can cause an unhealthy rise in the water's pH. Prevent problems by scrubbing the concrete with a stiff brush and a mixture of one part vinegar to two parts water. Rinse thoroughly and repeat twice. Monitor the pond's water daily. If its pH exceeds 8.0, add a pH-lowering treatment according to the label directions.

WALL FOUNTAINS

Your wall must be sturdy enough to hold the fountain, its basin, and the water it contains. Most wood-sided walls are not strong enough, but many stucco and brick walls are. You may need to include a decorative T-block fitted to the wall as a bracket to support the basin.

Drill holes with a power drill (use a masonry bit for stone walls) if the plumbing is to be installed through a wall. Drill one hole just below eye level for the water outlet and one lower for the water intake. Insert pipes through each hole and join them behind the wall with two elbow joints and a piece of flexible pipe.

Attach the fountain to the wall, usually with a combination of mortar and wall plugs.

Connect the pump to the intake pipe and plug it into a GFCI outlet.

If you cannot install pipe through the wall, attach the fountain to the surface with decorative hardware. Use rigid pipe attached to the wall with clamps, and disguise the plumbing lines with vines or other plants.

Most brick walls are strong enough to support a wall fountain's components. A tiered feature like this one combines the beauty of a wall fountain with the simplicity of a formal pool, through which the water recirculates.

WALL FOUNTAIN

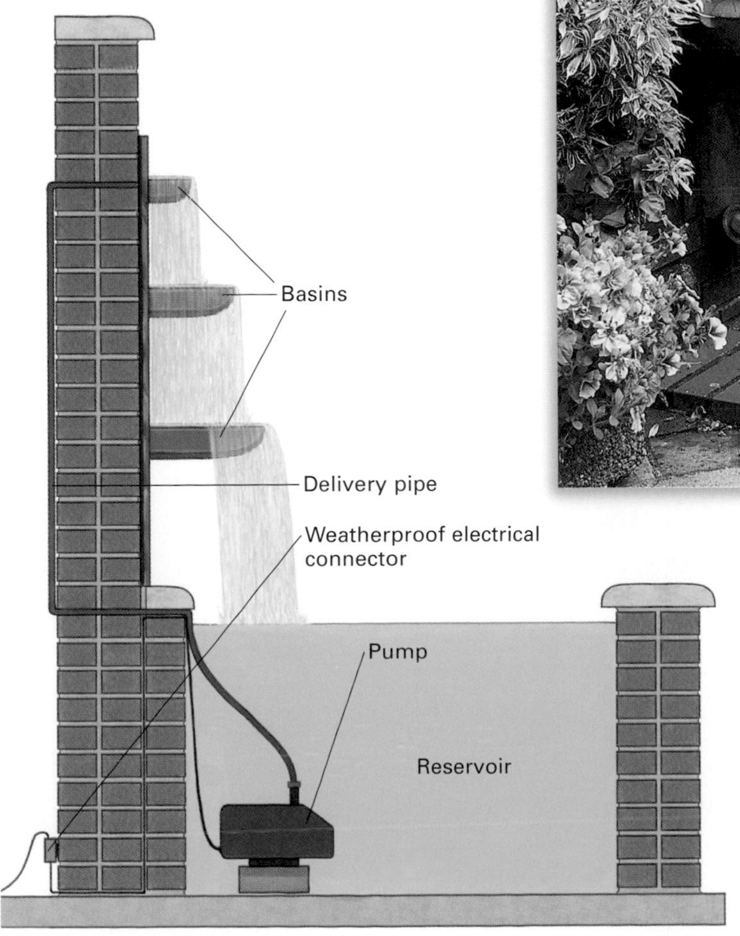

INSTALLING PLUMBING

PUMP LOCATION

Placing the pump far from the waterfall promotes better distribution of the freshly oxygenated water by maximizing circulation across the pond. Locating the pump under a waterfall, however, offers greater efficiency by allowing it to recirculate more water with less effort than if placed away from the waterfall.

Set a submersible pump on clay bricks or another stationary platform to keep it a few inches above potentially pump-clogging debris that may accumulate on the bottom of the pond. Install a ball valve on the pump outlet, if you wish, to control the water flow. Use a diverter (three-way) valve to control two features operated by the same pump.

Use a bulkhead connector through the liner wall to provide a flooded intake for a nonsubmersible pump. If the pump is not self-priming and is located above the pond's water level, install a foot valve (check valve) and a strainer on the intake pipe. Make a housing for the pump to lessen its noise.

KEEP CURRENT

Instructions given here apply to most filter units on the market when this book went to press. Consult the manufacturer's directions for the unit you purchase.

WATER LINES

Rocks and foot traffic can collapse thin vinyl walls, restricting water flow. Conceal and protect vinyl tubing with mulch or a thin layer of gravel. Generally use tubing with a diameter that fits the pump's discharge. But choose tubing of the next larger size when running a water line more than 10 feet horizontally.

Use flexible tubing or a hand-tight union connection to your pump. This allows easy access to the pump for servicing or removal. Clamp all other connections—especially any out-of-pond ones—to be watertight.

Position the line that feeds an issuing basin at the head of a waterfall or stream to release its flow under the water surface. Within the basin, consider using perforated tubing with an end cap. The line can enter the basin between the edging and the liner.

MECHANICAL FILTER HOOKUP

Most mechanical filtration units work with water passing first through the filter and then through the pump. Make certain your pump and filter unit are compatible. Find the pump's intake by removing the intake screen. Screw a threaded male hose barb fitting into the pump's intake. Install a short length of flexible vinyl tubing between the pump and the filter. Secure both ends of the tubing with clamps. Some mechanical filters come with a built-in pump assembled, saving you the task.

NONPRESSURIZED BIOFILTERS

Nearly all biological filters work outside of the pond without pressure. Because water discharged from one must flow by gravity, consider the site for it carefully. Locate a nonpressurized biofilter where its discharge is higher than the level where the filtered water returns to the feature. Possible return points include under the edging of a pond, stream, or bog garden or at the top of a waterfall. Allow easy access to it for servicing.

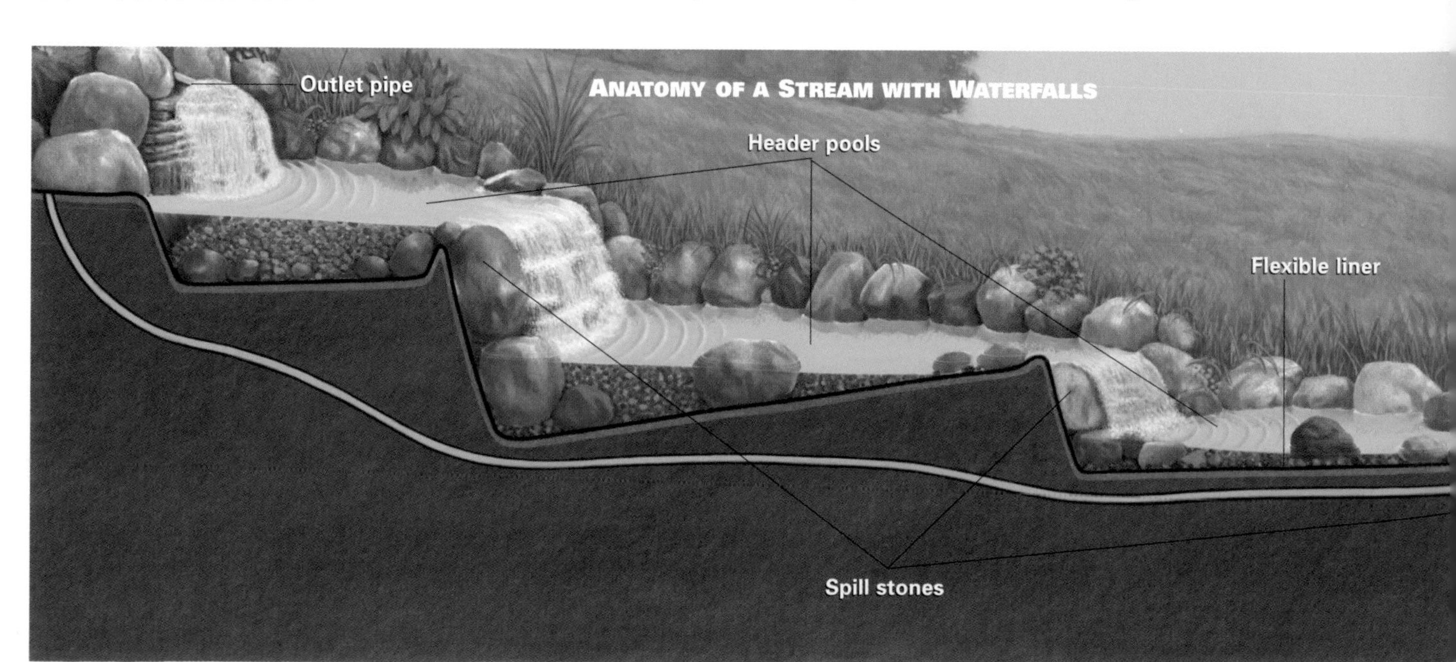

Make sure the biofilter sits securely on a level base. Connect flexible vinyl tubing or PVC or rigid PVC pipe (as appropriate) for inflow and discharge lines. These conduct water from the pump into the biofilter and from the biofilter to the discharge point. Operate the pump to verify that the connections are watertight.

PRESSURIZED BIOFILTER HOOKUP

A pressurized biofilter can be located almost anywhere and is easily concealed in a garage, under the deck, or in a buried vault. Smaller models operate with submersible pumps. These small pressurized units are often buried adjacent to the pond with only their top cap exposed for servicing. Larger pressurized filters utilize more powerful nonsubmersible pumps.

Connect the pond's bottom drain to the filter intake, and connect the filter outlet to a nonsubmersible, flooded-suction pump or self-priming pump. Pipe the pump's discharge to the filter's back-flush valve. Connect the discharge on the back-flush valve to a water line for release of the filtered water back to a waterfall, stream, or pond. Pipe the waste connection on the back-flush valve to a drain or any suitable discharge area for release of the nutrient-rich back-flush water. Start the pump and check the operation of the filter.

IN-GROUND FILTER HOOKUP

Make careful measurements to ensure that when you set the unit in the excavation, its top is slightly above the pond's water level.

Install a level, tamped sand base, concrete slab, or poured concrete footing on which the filter can rest. Make the installation in tandem with the pond construction. Water will exit the pond through one or more bottom drains. A nonsubmersible pump at the end of the filter train sucks water through the system. The water level in the filter will match the pond's water level.

Filtered water travels from the filter through piping to the nonsubmersible pump. The pump draws water from the filter and forces it through piping to a waterfall, stream, bog garden, or pond. Install drain lines equipped with knife valves at the bottom of each filter chamber. Combine multiple drain lines into a single line to direct filtered water to a lower point or a sump pump. Create access from the ground's surface to the buried knife valve handles with vertically aligned piping.

Recheck the level of the components and backfill around the filter. Let the filter fill with water; then start the pump for a trial run.

AERATION WITHOUT A FOUNTAIN

If you'd like a bubbly fountain effect without buying and installing a fountain, place the discharge pipe of your submersible pump an inch or so below the water's surface. Adjust the discharge closer to the surface for a livelier effect; lower it for more subdued results.

INSTALLING LIGHTS

When installing lighting in your water garden, leave the cords long enough to pull the lights out of the pond for easy maintenance access. Coil up the excess cords and hide them under rocks.

One rule in placing lights is never to let them shine directly on the water because they will create a harsh glare. In-pond lights need fairly clear water to be effective. Murky water blocks too much light and considerably diminishes the light's effectiveness. If you have fish in your water garden, leave dark areas where they can retreat from the light. Fish need plenty of crevices for refuge. Never light up the entire pond for nighttime viewing.

Whenever possible, position out-of-water lights to conceal their housings and cords: underneath a deck, behind a rock, or tucked into the foliage of a shrub.

Whatever type of lighting you choose, be sensitive to its effect on the neighbors. Don't let the lights shine in their windows.

LOW-VOLTAGE OUTDOOR LIGHTING

Low-voltage lights offer many advantages. They are easy to install and change, use less energy than 120-volt lighting, don't require complicated precautions or configurations, give you more flexibility in your lighting options, and are intrinsically safe. Their initial cost is modest compared to the alternatives. Installation of a low-voltage lighting system does not require the services of a licensed electrician; it's a simple do-it-yourself project. Often used with residential water features, low-voltage lights require an electrical transformer that converts regular household 120-volt current into safer 12-volt power. The lights and transformer are sold together in kits along with additional modular pieces. Here's what you'll need: a transformer, a power cable, stakes for placement in the ground or holders for placement in water, a set of lights, a set of 12-volt bulbs, and optional colored lenses. Some kits include a timer that turns the lights on and off. Check the wattage of the transformer to determine the maximum number of lights it can support. You may want to add more lights later without having to buy another transformer.

Consider your options; then decide the location of each light. Measure carefully so that you can determine which components or kit you need. Follow the instructions

HINT

For the best effect when positioning anin-water light to illuminate moving water, make sure the beam shines in the same direction as the water flows.

INSTALLING LOW-VOLTAGE LIGHTING

Unlike regular 120-volt lights, installation of low-voltage landscape lights is a snap, even for beginners. And they're fairly safe because of their low voltage. Many low-voltage lighting systems are sold as kits, complete with instructions.

Hooking up a low-voltage system starts with installing a transformer, which reduces household current from 120 volts to 12 volts. Install the transformer near the GFCI receptacle closest to the water feature, following the manufacturer's instructions. Even 12-volt systems should use a GFCI unit to prevent shocks. Most transformers are mounted next to an outlet and plugged into it.

Run exterior electrical cable from the transformer to the lights. It's important to choose a cable that has the right size wire for the total wattage of the bulbs in the system (add the total watts of each bulb supplied by the cable): 14-gauge wire can handle up to 144 watts, 12-gauge up to 192 watts, and 10-gauge up to 288 watts.

Bury the cable several inches underground, running it through a length of PVC pipe if you want extra protection from tillers and spades.

Then attach the lights to the cable. Some lights attach with clips; others must be wired into the system. Be sure to refer to the instructions that come with the lights.

Well-positioned submersible lights offer an extra dimension for nighttime enjoyment of your water feature, especially when you maintain water clarity.

that come with the kit or lighting pieces. Setup usually involves attaching a low-voltage cable to the transformer, laying the cable, and attaching lights along the cable where desired. Plug the transformer into a GFCI outlet when you want to turn on the lights. For wiring simplicity, install a transformer with a built-in timer.

LINE-VOLTAGE LIGHTING

Large deep pools generally require the more intense light that comes from line-voltage (120-volt) lighting. Although it has the power to provide brilliant lighting, line-voltage lighting can be used for the same purposes as low-voltage lighting. Enlist an electrical contractor or swimming pool contractor to install submersible lights into the walls of a concrete pool.

Remember to include lighting needs when planning power requirements for your water feature. Local regulations often require the services of a licensed electrician to install any 120-volt power line and fixtures connected directly into it. Use only equipment designed for outdoor or underwater use. Fixtures, wire, and other components approved by the Underwriters Laboratories carry the UL seal, indicating that they meet safety standards and can be used in or near a water feature.

HINT

When planning your water features, consider installing a remote switch inside the house. You'll be able to turn on the falls, fountains, and lights without going outside.

TIPS FOR SUCCESSFUL LIGHTING

1. Install underwater lights directly below a waterfall or fountain. Aim light in the same direction as the water's motion to highlight it.
2. Install ground lighting so that it shines away from the observer. Pathway lights should focus on the ground or nearby plants or ornaments and present no visual glare.
3. Low-voltage underwater bulbs are typically 20 watts; low-voltage garden lightbulbs are usually 10 or 12 watts. Underwater and garden bulbs may be used interchangeably. However, if you are using a low-voltage garden light set that powers six ground lights and decide to add one underwater light, you will have to cut back to only four of the ground lights to avoid overloading the circuit.
4. Avoid directing lights to shine on the water's surface—this creates glare. Use the water as a reflecting pool by leaving the surface dark and lighting the surrounding landscaping instead.
5. Periodic cleaning of submersible light lenses keeps them performing at their best.
6. Install lighting around your water feature before you finish landscaping, such as laying sod or adding mulch or gravel.
7. Spotlighting an unusual specimen such as a night-blooming tropical water lily shows off its special attraction. Avoid spotlighting a night bloomer from below; more subtle side lighting works better.
8. If a low-voltage light fails to work when you test the set, check to be certain that there is contact with the power cable.
9. Mount the transformer to a vertical stake that is set in concrete for stability.
10. Low-voltage lighting works best in small gardens because each lamp lights a small area. Standard-voltage systems prove more valuable in areas where brilliant illumination is required for safety or security.

INSTALLING EDGING

Whether you choose some form of rock, wood, or plants for edging depends on the style and function of your water feature. Rock and stone are the most common and natural edging materials. Review the edging options described on pages 64 and 65, and consider the functional aspects of standing or sitting on edging to view, maintain, or otherwise access the water feature.

ROCK AND STONE

When edging a pond with a preformed liner or using heavy stonework on a flexible liner, build a masonry collar under the edge for adequate support. On a 2-inch layer of gravel, set a collar of concrete block or flat rock in a 1-inch layer of mortar. Extend the liner over the collar; then spread underlayment on top of it before setting the rock edging in place. Scatter smaller stones in between and behind the rocks to create a natural look. Set larger partially buried rocks behind the edging here and there to complete the effect.

Place heavy edging rocks (weighing more than 150 pounds) on the ground around the perimeter of the water feature. Mortar or concrete isn't necessary as long as the rocks are situated in stable positions. Create a firm foundation for lighter-weight stonework edging by spreading a 3-inch layer of crushed rock. Top that with a 1-inch layer of concrete or mortar before setting the stones in place.

Rock edging such as this drystack masonry is the most common choice of hardscape materials for hiding the liner of an informal water garden. The stones create a natural transition to the surrounding landscape and are easy to move if needed.

EDGING TIP

Here's a good way to prevent the liner from showing. Dig the edging shelf deep enough for a double layer of flagstones, cut stones, bricks, or other edging. Lay the first layer of edging, then wrap the liner over the first layer as shown and top with the second. Water can now be filled to the middle of the first layer of edging. With one layer of edging, the water can be filled only a little below the bottom of the edging.

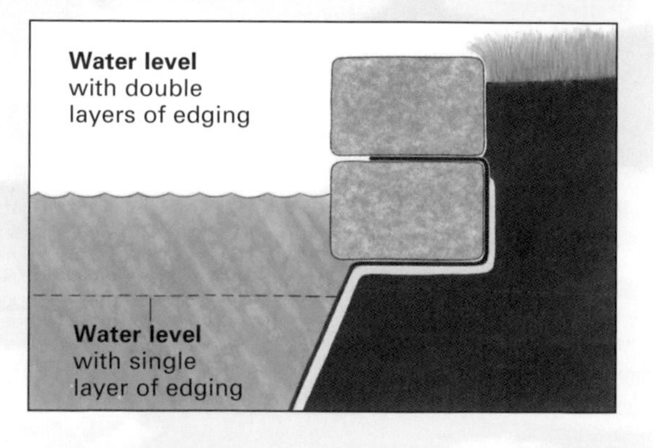

CONCRETE, MORTAR, AND PH

Mortar or concrete used for stabilizing edging is alkaline. If left this way, pond water and rain that splash the material wash lime into the water and the pH rises to levels dangerous or even fatal to fish. You can neutralize the concrete or mortar by scrubbing it with a stiff brush and diluted vinegar. Scrub and rinse the neutralized areas several times using water from a garden hose and then pump the water out of the pond.

BRICK

Before laying a brick edge, make sure the perimeter of the water feature is level. A single layer of brick requires a 3-inch-thick foundation of crushed rock. Use paver bricks —the solid ones, not the ones with holes— as edging to minimize the invasion of weeds and grass among the edgers. Apply mortar under and between the bricks to make a sturdy edge.

WOOD

Set wood posts or logs vertically in concrete to form a pier-type edging. Use water-resistant wood planks or recycled-plastic "lumber" to build a deck or walkway along the water feature or jutting into it. Set the construction on concrete footings.

TURF AND PLANTS

Turf makes a neat edging, but it could get messy if soil washes out of the lawn into the water feature or grass clippings blow into the water when you mow. Prepare the edge for a lawn by excavating a shallow trench around the perimeter of the water feature and letting the liner extend into it. Cover the liner with a ledge of brick or flat rock set in mortar. Lay sod over the ledge to finish the edge.

Intersperse plantings with rocks and stones to create a natural-looking edge; avoid ringing the water feature with a single strand of rocks like a necklace. Choose easy-care plants, such as low-growing evergreens, irises, and hostas. Groundcovers and small beds of wildflowers also make excellent edgers. Choose plants suited to your climate as well as to your garden's conditions, including sunlight, soil, and moisture level. Stagger three, five, or seven plants around in clusters for effective results. Place tall plants on the far side of the water feature where they won't obstruct your view of it. Keep plantings simple: Too many different kinds of plants can create a busy, confusing scene.

CONCEALED EDGE CONSTRUCTION

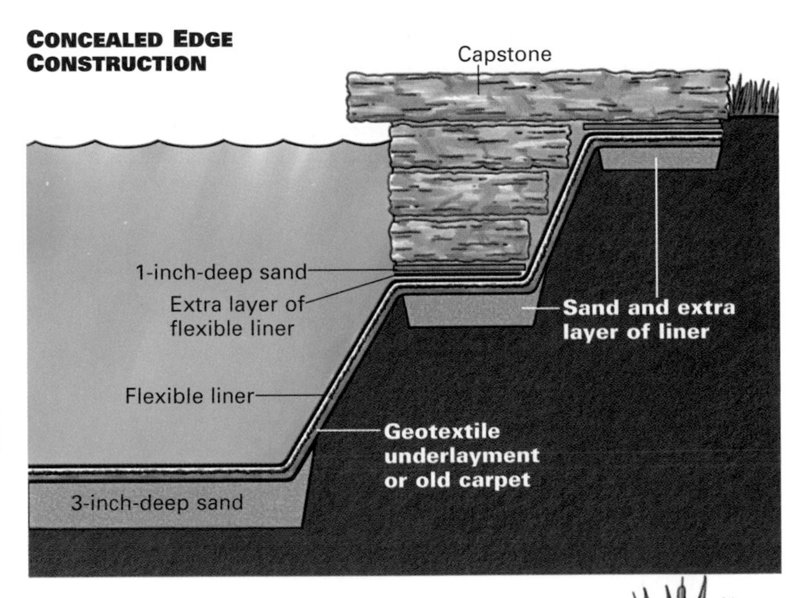

POND WITH BOG EDGE

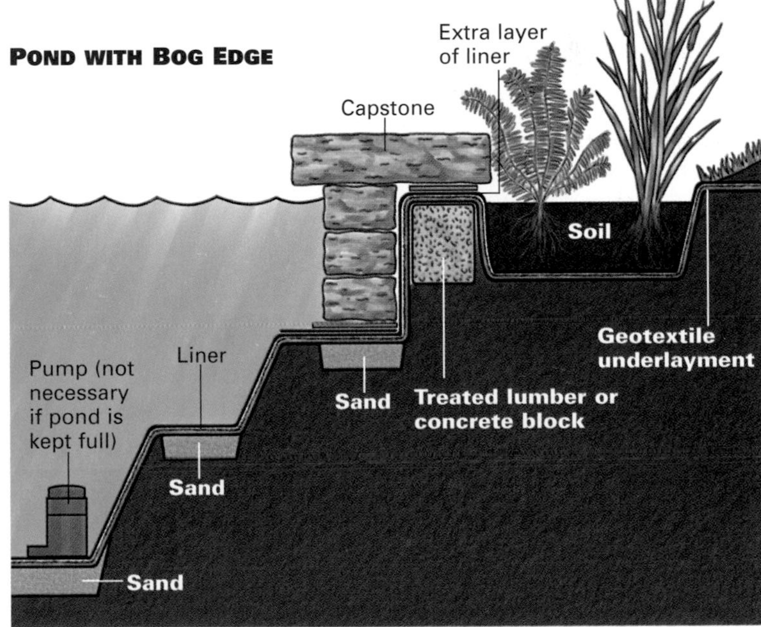

Brick or concrete edging echoes the geometric perimeter of a formal raised pool and may also match other hardscaping around the house or garden. Bricks can raise the pH level of the water; if you have fish, be sure to test the water regularly.

Cleaning a pond is a chore you'll need to perform only once in a while, but it helps keep an aquascape in healthy balance. Cleaning reduces certain kinds of algae and other pond problems.

MAINTENANCE

A well-designed water garden should take minimal time to maintain. Unless you have a very large water feature or a fish-only pond, you'll spend about an hour or less each week feeding fish, grooming plants, and monitoring water quality. When estimating the amount of time to budget for maintenance, plan on about 10 minutes per thousand gallons of water per week.

Completely emptying and cleaning the water feature on a regular basis isn't necessary, nor is it advisable. In fact, frequent emptying and cleaning can cause more harm than good. It can injure your fish as they try to adjust to varying water temperatures and conditions. It can destroy and wash away beneficial bacteria, which can take days, even weeks, to re-establish. Unless the pond is very dirty from too many fish or too many decaying leaves in the water, it will need to be drained, cleaned, and refilled only once every few years.

Fishponds require quite a bit of care to keep fish wastes from fouling the water and to maintain fish health. Plan on spending extra time cleaning filters (which remove the wastes), skimming debris from the surface, and making sure the pumps that aerate and recirculate water are working.

If your water garden takes too much time to maintain, it may have a fundamental problem in its design or construction or in the ratio of plants, fish, and water. It's better to correct the basic problem instead of spending hours each week fixing its side effects. In the long run, you'll save time and money. If you can't determine the source of the problem, consult a professional water garden specialist.

As long as the pond has no problems, you'll have a burst of chores in spring—dividing plants and returning them to their spots in the pond, removing dead foliage, and so on—and in fall—readying the pond for winter—and just a little grooming each week in between. The few extra hours in spring and fall will save many hours of headaches throughout the summer. Your water will stay clear, your fish healthy, and your plants green and floriferous.

A well-designed pond with the right number of fish for the amount of water and enough plants to support them requires little care. If you would like water gardening to be a more intense hobby, try a koi pond. Not only can you compete with other fanciers for the showiest koi, but raising them also offers plenty of opportunities to "primp" the pond.

IN THIS SECTION

FUNDAMENTALS

Water splashing from a fountain aerates the pond, keeping it fresh and free of anaerobic bacteria, which thrive in oxygen-depleted environments and produce rank odors.

Ponds in nature contain a complex network of checks and balances that generally maintain pond health without help. Garden ponds have the same network but, being artificial, require your assistance. If your pond is out of balance, it will give you signals: bad odors, fish dying or gasping for breath at the surface, dark or murky green water, and stunted and diseased plants. Here's how to help keep your garden pond healthy.

USE ALL THE ELEMENTS: Plants and other pond life work together. Fish are not required in the water garden, but they do consume mosquito larvae and add lively interest to the pond. Floating plants provide shade, and they cool and filter the water and control algae. Submerged plants are also filters, and they feed fish as well as create shelter and spawning areas for them. Use one bunch of submerged plants for every 2 square feet of pond surface. Also stock the pond with snails, which feed on the algae.

Spreading bird netting over the pond in autumn is a simple way to catch leaves and make cleanup easier. Hold the netting in place with bricks or stones.

KNOW YOUR WATER: Invest in a kit for testing pond water. They're inexpensive, and a number of types are available. Test for ammonia and nitrite levels when you first fill your pond and then periodically thereafter, particularly if fish look stressed or are dying. If the pond develops a chemical problem, a partial water change, described below, will help lower ammonia and nitrite levels.

KEEP THE POND FILLED: Don't let the pond evaporate—a drop of an inch or more below the normal water level starts to create unhealthy concentrations of salts and minerals and exposes the liner to deteriorating UV rays.

When you add water, fill the pond with just a trickle from the hose (place it at the bottom of the pond) to allow fish and other pond life to adapt to the gradual changes in temperature and pH. Add no more than 10 to 20 percent of the total volume at any one time or the fish could go into shock. If using municipal water, add chlorine remover to the pond whenever you top it off.

Partially change the water when needed. Although it's best to keep the pond filled, over time—even with refills—salt and waste materials build up in the water. To freshen the pond, drain it by about 10 percent of its capacity, preferably by drawing water from the bottom, where concentrations of harmful substances are highest. Then refill it as described. It's best to do this right before a rain, so rainfall can replace at least some of the water.

PROVIDE AERATION: Whether from a fountain or waterfall, splashing water keeps the pond well-oxygenated, which is essential for supporting fish. Oxygenated water also stays fresh, warding off foul-smelling bacteria that thrive in a low-oxygen environment.

REMOVE LEAVES AND DEBRIS: Debris decomposes and fouls water if not removed. Skim leaves, fallen petals, and other floating plant matter from the bottom and surface of the pond with a net or by hand.

Pinch off yellowing and dying leaves. In autumn, put netting over the pond to catch falling leaves, or make skimming the pond a daily routine. In late fall, when you remove the pump for the winter, make sure the water is free of debris before the pond ices over.

KEEP IT UNDER CONTROL: If populations overflourish, give some fish away. Regularly thin aggressive plants, and divide overgrown plants so no one element takes over.

CONSIDER A FILTER: If the garden pond has continuing problems with debris, too much light, or excessive fish wastes, consider adding a biological filter to the pond setup.

PREVENT RUNOFF: When fertilizing or applying other chemicals to the lawn and plants surrounding your garden pond, avoid letting the materials run off or trickle into the water. They can be toxic to fish and may promote algae growth in the water.

FEED FISH PROPERLY: Feeding too much or too often fouls the water and necessitates a larger filter. Feed fish only when they are ravenous; then give them only as much as they can eat in about 10 minutes.

CLARIFIERS

Flocculating clarifiers are designed to eliminate cloudy water created by algae and dirt. These products cause detritus suspended in the water, including algae, to clump together and fall to the bottom of the water feature, where they decay. Lighter-weight particles float; mechanical filtration, vacuuming, and skimming easily remove the heavier particles. Results of this treatment show quickly, often within 24 hours. Dense algae growth requires an additional treatment or two, spaced one week apart. Potent for only a day, the liquid clarifier destroys only algae growing on the day of application. Apply it again when algae reappear.

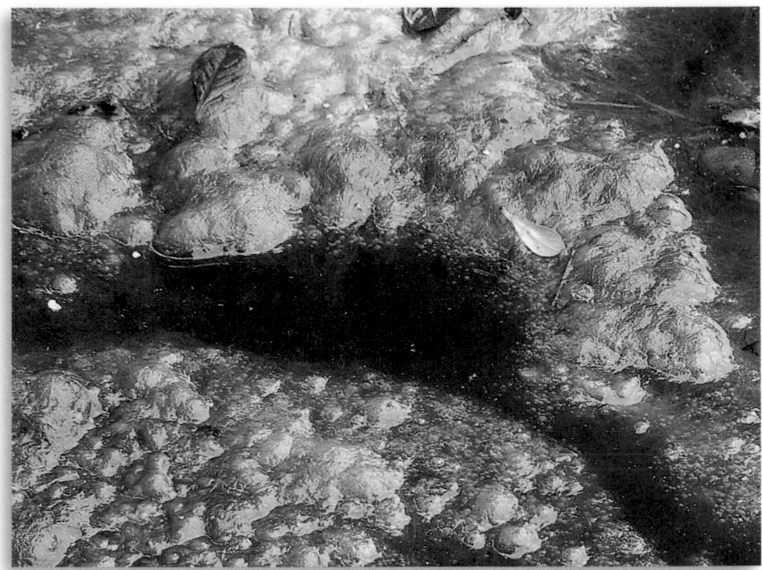

Fish food and other wastes result in nitrates, which algae thrive upon. Tame out-of-control algae with filters or a UV clarifier.

BARLEY STRAW

Barley straw placed in a pond or stream prevents algae growth when introduced in the spring before algae appear. As the straw decomposes, it releases substances that, when exposed to oxygen and sunlight, convert to hydrogen peroxide. Peroxide inhibits algae growth but evaporates quickly; barley straw in the water produces a continuous supply of peroxide for up to six months. It is safe for plants and fish.

Use about three-tenths of an ounce of barley straw for each square yard of water surface. Bundle it loosely in net bags or nylon stockings, and attach corks or plastic floats to keep the bundles from sinking. Barley straw works its magic near the surface where there is more oxygen.

String algae can help keep water crystal clear but may quickly take over if too many nutrients are present. Remove excess string algae with a toilet bowl brush tied to a pole.

WATER TREATMENTS

Think of water treatments as you would prescription drugs. Avoid them if possible, but when necessary, use them as directed. Use only treatments designed for water gardens if you raise aquatic plants, ornamental fish, scavengers, and unseen-yet-beneficial nitrifying bacteria. Algae control treatments and water test kits for swimming pools work well in swimming pools, but the treatments kill all water garden life and the pool test kits aren't designed to show what a pond-keeper needs to know.

CHLORINE AND CHLORAMINE REMOVAL

Check with your local utility to learn what chemicals are used to treat public water. Chlorine or chloramine (chlorine combined with ammonia) are both commonly used, and both kill fish. Fortunately, chlorine and chloramine removal treatments work almost instantly. Follow label instructions. Chlorine naturally escapes when exposed to the atmosphere, making pond water fish-safe two to three days after the water is drawn. If you're adding less than 10 percent to the volume of water already in the pond, there is no need to dechlorinate. However, if you're increasing the volume of water by more than 10 percent, add dechlorination treatment to neutralize the chlorine.

Chloramine, a powerful antibacterial agent, remains in water for months, making treatment mandatory if fish are to survive. Chloramine shows up on the ammonia test in a pond water test kit. Weekly monitoring for ammonia could keep your fish healthy. Add chloramine treatment (which also removes chlorine) each time you top off the pond. If you add about 5 percent of the water volume, treat the pond with 5 percent of the quantity needed to treat the entire pond.

Fish-keepers who use public water need to maintain a sufficient supply of antichlorine or antichloramine treatment for a complete water change. Discovery of toxic matter in the water, a massive leak, or an accidental overflow of water call for the immediate use of these water-quality treatments.

BENEFICIAL BACTERIA

Beneficial nitrifying bacteria remove ammonia and nitrite from the water. They colonize around whatever surface areas they find in the pond. To get their work off to a good start, add concentrated bacteria to the biological filter and around the pond itself. These bacteria are sold in dry and liquid forms. The liquid form acts more quickly but has a shorter shelf life and costs more. You can confirm that the bacteria in liquid form are alive by their strong barnyard odor. Once in the pond or biofilter, they produce no noticeable smell.

WATER-QUALITY TEST KITS: A LIFE-AND-DEATH MATTER

When water quality becomes compromised, fish may die. Test kits enable you to check pond water for unsafe levels of certain chemicals. When ammonia and nitrate reach toxic levels, for instance, fish become listless, uninterested in eating, and vulnerable to disease and parasite attack. Chlorine and chloramine must be absent. Ammonia and

Fish will let you know if your pond is out of balance. They will become listless or gasp for air at the surface if the pond water loses too much oxygen. Always keep a water test kit on hand.

Splashing or spraying water from a fountain or waterfall adds oxygen to the water, which is necessary to support fish life. To refresh a stagnant pond, pump out about 10 percent of the water from the bottom of the pond. Refill with spray from a hose or fountain.

nitrite levels must be low. Stress becomes a threat if pH is under 6.5 or over 8.5. As pH increases, ammonia becomes much more potent and more likely to kill fish. Check the levels daily in midmorning when establishing a fishpond.

Using a test kit is usually simple: you add a reactive chemical agent to a pond-water sample or dip treated paper strips into the water and compare the results with a chart.

Most test kits don't measure the level of dissolved oxygen in the water. If oxygen is low, however, the fish tell you by gasping at the surface. Other water-quality deficiencies may also cause them to gasp. Once you become comfortable with the daily readings from a water-quality test kit, weekly checks will suffice. Also, as you learn to recognize behavior patterns of the fish, you'll be able to read their signs too.

When Applying Algae Control

When you use an algae-control agent, your pond water loses oxygen as it is absorbed by the killed, decaying algae. The decaying algae may consume so much oxygen that the fish become stressed or possibly suffocate. Monitor fish for signs of stress, such as gasping at the surface or listlessness. Aerating the water with a waterfall, a fountain, air stones, or water sprayed through the air from a garden hose into the pond makes up for the oxygen depletion. Be especially alert to this potential situation when the water temperature is over 80°F. As the temperature rises, fish consume more oxygen but the water holds less.

Bundle loose barley straw or pellets in net bags and float them on the pond. The decomposing barley produces peroxide, which inhibits algae growth. The barley may last up to six months in the pond.

KEEPING THE POND CLEAN

Signs that your pond should be cleaned include overgrown plants and a several-inch-thick layer of decomposing debris on the bottom. Remember, this should occur only every three to four years.

Late summer to early fall is the best time to clean ponds. If the pond has fish, do the work on a cool day, which is easier on fish, at least a month before winter sets in to give the fish enough time to recover. In warm climates, wait until plants go dormant and the water temperature is around 60°F.

First, begin draining the pond. You can bail the water, or if you have a submersible pump, replace the output piping with a hose. Run the hose out of the pond and siphon the water. While you wait for the level to drop, clean the filters.

A partially empty pond makes it easier to catch fish. Net them when the water is drained to 6 inches and place them in a bucket of pond water. After catching a few, transfer them to a 30-gallon trash can or an untreated (for algae) child's wading pool in the shade. This holding pen should be filled the day before with half pond and half fresh water, treated to remove chlorine and chloramine. Cover the holding pen with netting so the fish won't jump out. Don't feed the fish at this time. If they are going to be held for more than an hour, put an aerator in the container.

Continue to remove water until only several inches remain in the bottom of the pond. Then stop pumping and check the muck for small fish and frogs, tadpoles, and other animals. Put these in the bucket also.

Next, remove the plants. Take care that their foliage remains wet or at least damp, so they survive their out-of-water experience. You can wrap foliage and pots in wet newspaper and set plants in the shade, or submerge them in the wading pool or in buckets of water.

Bail the remaining water and pour it onto flower beds and the rest of the landscape. Don't pour it down a drain; it will clog the plumbing. Scoop mud from the pond bottom, taking care not to damage the liner. Dump the mud on the compost pile.

Once the pond is empty, hose it down. Use a soft brush to clean the sides of the liner. Scrubbing also removes beneficial bacteria and helpful algae, so don't scrub too thoroughly. After hosing down the pond, remove the dirty water. Make any necessary repairs, especially if you have detected a leak. Divide and re-pot any root-bound plants.

Next, fill the pond about halfway and add the plants. Then continue filling the pond, preparing the water in the same way as for the pool's first stocking, with chlorine and chloramine removers, if necessary. Return frogs and scavengers to the pond. Check the fish for disease, and treat them if necessary. Then gently place them in plastic bags, inflating and sealing the bags. Float the bags on the surface until the water temperature inside the bags is close to the pond temperature. Another method is to gradually add fresh pond water to the temporary holding pen. Either way, when a container's water temperature is within 2°F of the pond's, it's safe to release the fish. It's okay to return some of the water from the bucket and holding pen to the pond; it contains beneficial microorganisms.

Use a soft brush to gently clean the surface of the liner. Hose down the liner and remove the dirty water before refilling the pond.

SPRING MAINTENANCE

FISH

Spring heralds renewed water-garden life. Plants bloom, fish spawn, and frogs croak.

■ As water begins to warm and fish resume activity, begin feeding them minimally with a spring/fall high-carbohydrate food.
■ Inspect fish closely, looking for signs of sores, parasites, or lethargic behavior. If you have never added salt to your pond, add 1 pound (solar, sea, or kosher; none with iodine) per 100 gallons of water over a two- to four-day period. If you see symptoms of a fish disease or parasite, use a remedy formulated to eliminate it.
■ Test for ammonia and nitrite weekly. If levels are high, decrease feeding the fish until the biofilter takes effect and the ammonia and nitrite levels drop. If levels continue rising, use an ammonia-absorbing zeolite package in the waterfall-issuing basin or filter.
■ Add nitrifying bacteria to guard against potentially toxic buildup of ammonia from fish wastes.

PLANTS

■ Clean up, weed, and mulch peripheral beds.
■ Return hardy aquatic plants to the pond if you removed them for the winter. Or if you put them in the deepest part of the pond, relocate them for the growing season. Some water gardeners elevate hardy water lilies 3 to 4 inches below the water surface, where the warmer layer of surface water stimulates them to a faster start. After a water lily produces six pads, lower it to its normal growing range of 6 to 18 inches of water cover.
■ Add new marginal, submerged, and floating plants.
■ Divide root-bound plants and re-pot the divisions; give excess plants to friends or take them to a plant swap.

THE POND

■ Clean out any debris that accumulated over winter.
■ Vacuum or sweep the pond bottom if there is a significant accumulation of leaves and other detritus. Otherwise, drain the pond while removing its denizens, clean out the accumulation, and rinse—don't wash—the pond before carefully restocking it, following the directions on page 98.
■ If a cloud of algae blooms, don't panic. This seasonal adjustment of the ecosystem is a natural occurrence.
■ Collect and add rainwater to top off the pond. Rainwater contains fewer chemicals than tap water.

EQUIPMENT

■ Reconnect the pump and filter if stored over the winter.
■ Check lights and electrical connections; make any necessary repairs or hire an electrician.
■ Inspect the liner for tears or punctures and make repairs.
■ Start a biological filter by adding beneficial nitrifying bacteria. They're available in dry (less expensive) or liquid (faster-acting) forms from your water garden dealer. A biological filter begins to function when the pond water temperature reaches the 55°F.
■ Reinstall the UV clarifier with a new bulb.

CLEANING HINT

Fall is the best time of year for cleaning the pond. Removing fallen leaves before they foul the water benefits fish all winter. Mild autumn temperatures and end-of-season robust health make it easier for the fish to withstand the stress associated with being handled.

SUMMER MAINTENANCE

Spend the summer relaxing near your water garden. It won't need weeding, hoeing, raking, or mowing.

FISH

■ As the water temperature rises above 60°F, switch from high-carbohydrate fish food to a high-protein product. If you have a light load of fish and plenty of beneficial nitrifying bacteria and submerged plants, you can feed your fish more. But if you have a full load of fish and few nitrifying bacteria and submerged plants, even this level of feeding could prove disastrous. These guidelines apply especially when a high fish population is combined with low oxygen levels and high summer temperatures.

■ Test the water weekly, checking the levels of pH, ammonia, and nitrite. If the pH rises above 8.0 or falls below 6.8, follow directions carefully when adding a pond remedy designed to change pH. Adjust pH by 0.1 point per day to reach the normal range of 6.8 to 8.0. If your fish have adapted to a pH of 8.0, you could postpone treatment unless and until the pH rises above 8.0. Check the pH at the same time daily.

■ Fish gasping at the surface of the water may indicate poor water quality (usually low oxygen content). It can also indicate other problems, such as improper pH or the presence of toxic matter. It may also suggest a gill problem. First, do what you can to increase oxygen. Keep the waterfall or fountain running 24 hours. Alleviate a moderate level of toxicity by removing one-third of the water. Replace it with water sprayed through the air from a garden hose (to release chlorine and absorb oxygen). If you use public water, add antichlorine or antichloramine treatment to the pond and replace no more than one-third of the pond's volume at a time.

■ Be vigilant about predators that may occasionally visit your pond. Netting, electric fencing, scarecrows, plastic snakes and owls, and motion detectors connected to impulse sprinklers help deter predators. A watchful dog works most effectively.

THE POND

■ Be alert to any change in the rate of water flowing from a waterfall, fountain, statuary, or filter. This indicates an impediment, such as a clog in a pump intake or filter, kinked tubing, or a blocked water line. Keep water recirculating 24 hours a day through a biological filter. The more fish you have and the hotter the weather, the more vital recirculating water and increased oxygen in the water become.

■ Summer evaporation accounts for the loss of up to an inch of water per week. If your pond consistently loses more than this, look for a leak. Begin by checking the waterfall or any other feature outside the pond walls, where about 90 percent of leaks appear. Otherwise, check the pond walls and bottom for leaks. If there are none, add water sprayed through the air from a garden hose.

■ Control algae naturally using submerged plants and floating plants. Anacharis and cabomba, for example, along with water hyacinth and water lettuce, work by absorbing nutrients from the water so effectively that they starve algae to death. A properly sized UV clarifier turns green water clear within a day. Use a rake to remove filamentous algae.

PLANTS

■ Remove spent flowers, yellowing foliage, and excess plant growth.

■ Fertilize water lilies, lotuses, and other nonsubmerged water garden plants with aquatic plant food. Follow the directions on the package.

■ Plant tropical water lilies and other tropical plants when the water temperature stays above 70°F.

■ Early in the season, divide overgrown water lilies and other aquatic plants that produce lots of leaves but few flowers. Lift the plants out of the water and split them into smaller plants. Re-pot and replace them in the water.

■ Introduce new plants to the water feature.

■ Remove weeds regularly.

■ Rake off overexuberant floating plants, especially if they cover more than 60 percent of the water's surface or cover the crowns of marginal plants.

■ If insect pests appear on plants, avoid using insecticides. Pick off pests or blast them off plants with water from the garden hose. Remove and dispose of thoroughly infested or diseased plants.

EQUIPMENT

■ Clean the pump intake weekly; clean the filter, skimmer, and light lenses regularly, as needed for efficient operation.

AUTUMN MAINTENANCE

Autumn brings a spectacular look, as well as many seasonal activities, to the water garden.

■ In cold climates, autumn marks the slowing down of fish and plant activity and the preparation for winter. When the water temperature drops below 60°F, switch from summer's high-protein fish food to the high-carbohydrate spring and autumn food. Cut back on feeding to every third day; gradually stop feeding fish until spring.

PLANTS

■ Remove floating and tropical plants once frost makes them unsightly.
■ Save tropical lilies in a greenhouse pool.
■ Move tropical marginal plants indoors and enjoy them as houseplants over winter.
■ Once hardy water plants display frost damage, remove their foliage. Cut upright plant stalks 1 inch to 2 inches above the water surface (wait until spring to cut cattails and grasses). Cut submerged plants to within 6 inches of their containers. The greater volume of fish that reside in the pond, the greater the need to remove decaying (oxygen-consuming, sulfur-dioxide-releasing) foliage.
■ Transfer hardy water lilies to deeper water, where they won't freeze. Or remove foliage, wrap plants in moist newspaper and then loosely in plastic bags, and store in a cool, dark area, such as a root cellar or an old working refrigerator.

EQUIPMENT

■ Before leaves fall, install netting over the pond to prevent them from landing and decaying in the water. Support the netting with 2×4s or beach balls. Or use the type of tentlike netting that causes fallen leaves to slide down to the pond edges.
■ If you don't install netting, use a hand skimmer daily to remove leaves. Use a vacuum or leaf sweeper to remove leaves from the pond bottom. If you use a pond sweeper that's powered by a garden hose, add dechlorinator to the water before sweeping. If an inch or more of sediment has accumulated on the bottom, clean the pond before the weather makes it too cold to do the job.
■ When the water temperature drops below 50°F, remove, clean, and store your mechanical filter and pump, as well as the biofilter and pump. Install a thermostatically controlled floating pond heater in the final compartment of a large in-ground biofilter, if you have one, and change the water source from bottom drain to skimmer.
■ Drain pipes to prevent them from freezing and cracking. Turn off the water supply.

WINTER MAINTENANCE

In winter, your water feature can be just as attractive as in other seasons. But run your pump in winter only if you line in a mild climate where ice is rare.

FISH

■ Discontinue feeding fish when the water temperature drops below 45°F. Resist the temptation to feed them during any midwinter warm spells. Cold quickly returns, making the fish too cold to digest food. The undigested food spoils in the fish's guts, a sometimes fatal situation.

PLANTS

■ Leave the dead foliage of grasses and other perennials to stand at the edge of the water feature. This not only helps the plants survive winter, but it also offers an element of interest, as well as occasional protection for birds.

■ After the ground freezes, mulch around plants at the edge of a water feature. Spread a 4-inch layer of compost or shredded leaves on the ground to help preserve soil moisture and protect plants from the damage of winter's freeze–thaw cycle.

■ At least once a month, verify that your stored hardy water lily rootstock remains moist. Remoisten the newspapers if necessary.

■ Order new plants for spring arrival. Restock your water test kit and any other needed supplies at the same time.

EQUIPMENT

■ Remove the leaf netting to avoid snow buildup on it.

■ Try to prevent the pond from freezing solid if it contains fish and plants. Either remove the inhabitants and partially drain the feature or install a pond deicer.

■ Avoid smashing the ice; it can harm the fish. Use an electric or solar deicer to keep a spot on the surface open for oxygen exchange.

■ Avoid operating the pump during freezing weather; it can damage the pump, the pipes, and the fish. Allow the pump to continue working only if you live in a mild climate where ice is a temporary occurrence.

■ Despite risks of freezing weather that damages pipes, some waterfall owners keep their water feature running over the winter. In cold climates, waterfalls should be shut down and the pump disconnected and stored until spring.

■ Protect a raised pond from ice damage by draining it to ground level.

Repairing a Leak

Is the water level in your pool or pond dropping faster than you think it should? Before draining the water to locate a leak, make sure the loss is not due to normal evaporation. If the pond is near a building that reflects heat, is located in full sun, or has a large fountain or falls, evaporation may be the cause. Water levels also drop more quickly on hot or windy days. Aquatic plants increase evaporation too. Put a bucket filled with water near your water garden and watch the level for a day or two to make an informal measurement of normal evaporation.

Leak Detection

If the water level in your feature drops more than 1 inch to 1½ inches per week, you have a leak. Waterfalls and streams account for leaks 9 out of 10 times. Shut off the waterfall or stream so that you can isolate a leak. Top off the pond. Wait 24 hours, then check the water level. If you find that the pond is full, then the leak is in the waterfall or stream.

If the pond loses water while the waterfall and stream are turned off, look for the leak by adding a trace of food coloring to the water. Sometimes, as a slow steady leak draws water, the dye makes it visible. Another method involves allowing the water level to drop until it stops. At that point, examine the liner's perimeter, marking the water level using a crayon or chalk on the liner.

Pump out another few inches of water if the reduced water pressure results in a slower leak. This also permits closer scrutiny of the suspected area. Monitor the dropping water level and relocate pond inhabitants to temporary quarters before they suffer from insufficient water depth. The water level will sink to the bottom if that's where the leak exists. You might find the leak on the bottom even if the water drop stops a few inches above it. Wherever the leak is, clean the area before examining it.

Flexible Liner Leaks

Before making repairs, try to determine what caused a puncture. Remove any sharp objects under the liner and add fresh sand there if necessary. Clean the area surrounding the leak with a plastic abrasive pad or steel wool (to promote a better bond between patching materials), and allow it to dry. Use a scrap of liner to make a patch.

Puncture Repair

Apply a thin coat of PVC glue (made for flexible, not rigid, PVC) to the patch for a PVC or PVC-E pond liner. Center the patch over the tear and apply uniform pressure on the patch with a wallpaper roller or a rolling pin. After 12 hours, refill the pond. For a punctured EPDM, butyl, or Xavan flexible liner, use a liner repair kit with adhesive-faced patches. If possible, insert a board behind the area being repaired. Remove the protective paper from the adhesive face and apply the patch over the hole. Apply uniform pressure over the face of the patch with a wallpaper roller, rolling pin, or burnishing tool.

Tear Repair

If a tear has caused a leak, apply two-sided liner sealing tape in a rectangular shape around the tear. Apply a patch of liner material of the same rectangular size. Roll over the patch to secure it (as described above). Apply single-sided liner seaming tape over the edges of the patch.

Waterfall and Stream Leaks

Settling under a waterfall or stream liner causes water loss as the water sprays outside of the area covered by the liner. In this case, disassemble the feature and rebuild it accordingly. Rodents might chew a hole in the liner, or maturing plants may cause water to rise higher than what the liner can control. Look for moist soil along the outside edge of the liner and repair as needed.

Preformed Liner Leaks

Repair a crack or puncture in a fiberglass unit using a fiberglass repair kit. Look for the cause of the damage, and repair it to prevent a recurring leak. Roughen the area around the leak with sandpaper. Apply a resin-soaked mesh patch according to the repair-kit instructions. If your water garden supplier doesn't stock the repair kit, check with a boat or auto supply store.

Repairing Concrete Cracks

Temporarily remedy the cracks in concrete that appear over time as a result of settling, flaws in construction, freeze-thaw cycles, or aggressive tree roots, by applying quick-setting concrete sealer. Apply the sealer to a clean, dry surface.

If cracking is severe, line the entire pool with a flexible or preformed liner. Camouflage the edge of the liner as necessary. Or if faced with many hairline cracks, consider applying a liquid neoprene coating over the entire surface of the concrete.

MAINTENANCE EQUIPMENT

Autumn leaves drifting on the water surface may look attractive, but they foul the water and threaten the health of your fish. A leaf skimmer is a flat, netlike device that you sweep across the water to collect fallen, floating leaves. Ideally, its handle reaches halfway across your pond. Some skimmers come with a handle; others require that you add one. The same handle (either fixed length or telescopic) that you buy separately for the skimmer can be used with a pond vacuum and a fishnet.

FISHNETS

Fishnets typically are made of long-lasting nylon or cotton, which is softer and thus gentler for fish, with 1/8- to 1/16-inch openings. The fishnet should be at least as wide as the longest fish in your pond. A deep net gives you better control than a shallow one when catching fish.

Healthy fish easily evade most overt attempts to net them out of a pond. Experienced fish-keepers slowly maneuver the net under the fish as the fish eagerly eat floating fish food, catching them unaware. Koi-keepers use a net to guide a fish into a plastic pan, then carry the fish in the pan to its next location. This procedure minimizes loss of the fish's protective body slime.

LEAF NETTING

A sheet of lightweight plastic leaf netting prevents pond pollution caused by fallen leaves. In autumn, before leaves begin falling, stretch leaf netting over the pond. Select netting with openings in the mesh that are small enough to catch most of the leaves that would fall into your pond. Support the net above the water using 2×4s or beach balls; secure edges with stakes or bricks. Deluxe netting kits include poles for creating a tent effect that allows leaves to roll off toward the pond edges.

Fishnets and leaf skimmers have telescoping handles that extend your reach. Pond netting thwarts predators.

POND VACUUMS

Pond vacuums suck up debris from the pond bottom. The simplest type consists of an empty cylinder on an extended handle. It works like a siphon as debris-laden bottom water replaces air in the cylinder. A garden hose powers the venturi-type vacuum. It collects debris in a fine-mesh bag attached to its sweep head. As with a home vacuum cleaner, you can change sweep heads; use a small one for fine debris or a large head to collect leaves. To remove debris covering the bottom of a drained pond, use a wet-dry shop vacuum.

POND DEICERS

A floating deicer maintains a hole in the ice that forms on a pond in cold-winter regions, allowing oxygen to reach the water and the toxic gases that arise from decaying material to escape. Both actions are vital to the well-being and survival of your plants and fish.

Basically, an electric deicer is a heating element attached to a float. It's plugged into a 120-volt outdoor outlet with a GFCI. The deicer's thermostat turns on the heating element as the water temperature approaches freezing and turns it off as the surface water temperature rises above freezing, heating a small volume of water in its vicinity. Most deicers are 1,000 or 1,500 watts, the equivalent of 10 or 15 lightbulbs of 100 watts. Hang a 50-watt deicer on the side of an in-ground container garden of 50 gallons or less.

DEICER NOTES

Operating a pump or air stone (an aeration device that releases air bubbles through the water) when using a deicer causes currents, which move the warmed water away from the deicer, making it consume extra amounts of power to warm colder water. In addition, deicers emit a small, harmless charge into the water that might trip the circuit breaker if it's connected to a sensitive GFCI. In this event consult an electrician to determine whether the GFCI outlet can be replaced with a less sensitive one.

POND EMERGENCY KIT

Even the most meticulously maintained water garden will experience a crisis once in a while. Being able to diagnose and correct problems quickly when they arise can turn a potential disaster into a minor inconvenience. Having a few basic items stored together in a convenient spot can be a big help when an emergency does occur.

Be prepared to deal with emergencies when they arise. Keep a few basic supplies on hand: a water test kit, a small backup pump, a liner patch kit, chlorine and ammonia removers, and a kiddie pool or other temporary holding pen.

WATER-QUALITY TEST KIT

Buy the best kit you can; it's worth it. There's no other reliable way to tell if chemicals in your water have reached toxic levels. If you take readings as part of your regular maintenance schedule, it will be easy for you to detect a change that indicates a problem. If something seems to be wrong in your pond, a quick test of the water is your first step toward diagnosis.

WATER TREATMENTS

Most common water quality problems are caused by too much chlorine or ammonia. If you use public tap water to fill your pond, be sure to have chlorine remover on hand. An accidental tap water overfill can increase the chlorine in the water to a fatal level for fish. Too much ammonia in the water is a more complicated issue. Ammonia can build up in a pond for many reasons—the weather is hot, the filters aren't functioning, the pump is broken—that ultimately require long-term solutions. To reduce ammonia levels in an emergency, use commercially available tabs or "rocks."

BACKUP PUMP OR AERATOR

There's nothing more important to your aquatic ecosystem than oxygen. When the pump shuts down, oxygen is quickly depleted from the water and the fish come to the surface to gasp for air. A small backup pump, air stone, or even a fine mist from the garden hose will keep the water oxygenated until you can repair your main pump.

LINER PATCH KIT

If you've made sure a dramatic drop in water level has not been caused by evaporation, it's time to locate the leak and affix a patch with glue or tape, available from water garden suppliers. As you wait for the water to drain completely so you can hunt for the crack or puncture, prepare a temporary holding container for fish.

PLASTIC WADING POOL

If the quick fixes don't work and you must empty your pond to correct a problem, you'll need one or more temporary holding pens for fish and plants. Buckets work but they don't hold much; garbage cans are too deep. A child's shallow plastic wading pool is a more effective solution because it can be filled and dechlorinated quickly.

If you must drain the pond to fix a problem, move plants and fish to shallow plastic buckets or wading pools in a shady area.

TROUBLESHOOTING

To cover the exposed edges of a flexible liner, you may need to place additional rocks or adjust the existing ones.

THE LINER SHOWS

PROBLEM: The pond is finished, but the liner sticks out along the edges.
SOLUTION: First, make sure the pond is full. If that doesn't solve the problem, and if practical, disassemble the edging and re-lay it to make it level with the water surface. Dig soil out from underneath the edge of flexible liner to lower the edging. If necessary, add additional edging material or stone, making sure it overlaps the edging and disguises the exposed liner.

Consider planting evergreens or other sprawling plants alongside the edge to help conceal the liner. The plants will provide a cosmetic fix as well as protect the liner from UV rays.

THE FISH ARE DYING

PROBLEM: The pond has a lot of fish now, and some of them are dying.
SOLUTION: Make sure your pond isn't overstocked. There should be 5 to 10 gallons of water per inch of fish.

If fish have been gulping at the surface, they are suffering from lack of oxygen. Install a pump with an air stone or aerator, or add a trickle of cool (75°F) water from the hose.

Disease may also be the culprit. Observe the fish, removing them to a bucket of pond water if necessary. If signs of disease are present, take the fish to a veterinarian or fish supplier for further diagnosis and treatment.
PROBLEM: Fish added to a small, container-sized water garden with a fountain die within a couple of weeks.
SOLUTION: It may be that there's too much current in the water. Especially in container and other very small water gardens, there should be an area with no current so that fish don't become stressed. Reduce the current by turning the flow adjuster. If the fountain's nozzle is supposed to be underwater, make sure it is indeed just under or as much as an inch below the surface.

THE WATER LOOKS OR SMELLS FUNNY

PROBLEM: City tap water has chlorine and various minerals in it. Can it be used in a water garden or is a special source required?
SOLUTION: Chlorine dissipates from tap water in just a few days, or you can add a dechlorinator. After filling your water garden, let it sit for five to seven days before adding plants and fish. The minerals in the water will not harm aquatic life.

More of a concern to water gardeners are chloramines, powerful antibacterial agents that are added to (or occur naturally in) many local water supplies. Call the water supplier to ask if chloramines are present. If they are, treat your water with a special chloramine remover before adding fish. The treatment also removes chlorine.
PROBLEM: Muddy water remains for several hours or even all day after a heavy rain.
SOLUTION: Muddy water, in itself, is usually not a problem, especially if the silt settles within a few hours. The problem, however, could be caused by soil erosion or mud splashed into the pond by heavy rain. Check around the water feature, especially at its edging. Spread any eroding soil with gravel or organic mulch, or plant a groundcover.
PROBLEM: The water has a foul smell.
SOLUTION: Bad smells from your pond mean that anaerobic bacteria (those that don't use oxygen) have gotten out of hand. A buildup of anaerobic bacteria could be caused by poor aeration, a dead animal in the water, or an excess of uneaten fish food.

Add a waterfall or a pump (or increase pump volume) to increase aeration. Promptly remove dead or decaying plant matter and dead fish. Minimize fish feeding, and don't feed at all during hot weather. Keep the water feature topped off in warm weather so the water doesn't get murky. Finally, reevaluate your ecosystem—adding filtering plants may help. In severe cases, a biological water filter may be the solution.

The Pond Is Leaking

PROBLEM: The water level drops and the pond leaks.
SOLUTION: Pool repair kits are readily available. To repair a pond, drain it with a pump or siphon and locate the leak. Remove anything that might have punctured the liner, such as stones or sticks. Back the puncture or tear, if possible, with damp sand or pond underlayment. Then clean and dry the surface area completely. Using a pond liner adhesive and following repair kit instructions, spread a generously sized patch (at least 2 inches longer and wider than the leak) with adhesive and attach it. Let the patch dry before refilling the pond.

The Pump Stopped

PROBLEM: A new submersible pump quit operating after just a few months.
SOLUTION: With proper care, a good-quality water garden pump should last for several years. For longest life, make sure debris and algae don't tax its motor. Clean the prefilter or intake filter at least once a week during the spring and up to three times a week in summer and fall. Make sure the pump isn't sitting directly on the pond bottom, where it will take in more silt. Set it on a brick or flat stone. If algae clogs the pump, clean the pump and make an additional filter by wrapping the pump in a large piece of fiberglass window screen; then place it inside a black plastic basket. Never run the pump without water. It will burn out the motor.

The Pond Is Full of Muck

PROBLEM: In autumn, fallen leaves and other plant detritus fill the pond.
SOLUTION: Fallen leaves need to be removed almost daily so they don't have a chance to decay and pollute the water. If your pool or pond is located under a tree or regularly collects fallen leaves, consider stretching netting over the pond to catch the leaves. Anchor the netting on the sides with bricks or stakes driven into the soil. Be sure to remove these netted leaves regularly so they don't shade the water.

If the leaves have sunk to the bottom, they can be removed with your hand or with a lightweight plastic rake. For larger pools, especially those without many plants or fish, consider investing in a pool sweep, which attaches to a garden hose and uses water pressure to remove debris and silt from the pond bottom. A spa vacuum will also work. Both are available from swimming pool and water garden suppliers.

Water Quality Checklist

All local water supplies contain some form of chemical disinfectant, usually chlorine or chloramines. (Chloramines also occur in water naturally.) These disinfectants may be present alone or in combination.

Technically, plants will not be harmed by these chemicals, but attendant wildlife (snails and frogs, for example) will. It's best to remove the disinfectants in a new pond, even if you don't plan to stock fish.

Before you introduce fish or plants to your garden pond, check with your local water supplier to see which disinfectants are present in your water. Then take the following steps to remove them.

- Use a dechlorinator to remove chlorine, or let the water in your pond stand for five to seven days (the chlorine will dissipate in this period).
- Chloramines will need to be eliminated with a chloramine remover, which also takes out any chlorine present. You can purchase chloramine remover at a water garden supply house. The action of both dechlorinators and chloramine removers is almost immediate—you can introduce fish into the pool shortly after using either one.

Follow the above steps when stocking new ponds and when refilling the pond with more than 10 to 20 percent of the water volume.

When topping off the pond (to replace evaporation, for example), you don't need to treat tap water. However, you do need to follow these steps:

- Run the hose into the bottom of the pond.
- Add the water slowly, in a trickle, to avoid shocking the fish and to prevent them from being attracted to the activity of the water bubbles. (Do not use the hose to aerate ponds containing fish.)
- Replace no more than 10 to 20 percent of the water at a time; set a timer if necessary.

AQUATIC LIFE

PLANTS FOR THE WATER GARDEN

IN THIS SECTION

A landscape feature with rocks, fountains, and clear, sparkling water dresses up any yard. Without plants, though, it may look like a glorified swimming pool. Add aquatic and companion plants to the garden design, however, and you will witness a complete transformation.

Plants soften the water garden and tie the pond to the rest of the landscape by providing a colorful and textured transition. Large pots brimming with plants conceal the hard edge of a preformed pond, blending it with its natural surroundings. Plants growing in and around the water provide a safe haven for frogs, toads, and other creatures. In the water, plants supply cover and shade for koi and goldfish. They aid in the biological stability of the pond, adding oxygen to the water and consuming harmful or algae-feeding nutrients in the water. Marginal plants attract birds and butterflies, even hummingbirds.

A WEALTH OF PLANT CHOICES

There are water plants to fit every need and every budget. Just one water lily will produce flowers from the time the water warms until frost, adding color and charm to even a small container pond.

Some plants thrive beneath the water and some float along its surface. Others hold their blooms well above the water. Yet others prefer to grow nearby with just their roots moist.

Water-loving plants are easy to care for and are not usually bothered by pests or diseases. They grow readily in average garden soil and need only a monthly dose of fertilizer in spring and summer. Those that are winter-hardy may be left in the pond during the cold months. Frost-tender selections can be brought indoors to overwinter as houseplants with their pots in saucers of water.
The following pages guide you through some of the many choices available.

Some water gardens are created as habitats to attract birds and other wildlife, while others are designed to showcase a specific element, such as a favorite fish variety or special lotus cultivar. Whatever you choose, you'll want to include some moisture-loving plants in your aquascape.

WHAT ARE WATER PLANTS?

Water plants come in all shapes and sizes. Some grow completely underwater; others only want their roots wet. Depending on how and where they grow in the pond, water garden plants fall into six categories. You'll find general descriptions of each category here and information about specific species, varieties, and cultivars on the pages that follow.

Each description offers planting tips, including the amount of sunlight and shade needed, the hardiness of the plant, its stem length and spread, and water depth (the distance from the water surface to the crown of the plant). By way of explanation, "part shade" means four to six hours of sunlight daily or constant dappled shade. Also, a "running" plant grows in one or two directions, like a vine; a plant with a "creeping" habit grows equally in all directions.

Anacharis, with its easy-to-care-for, bright green leaves, is one of the most popular submerged plants.

Nymphoides peltata ***(water fringe, or yellow floating heart), is a water-lily-like plant that looks and grows much like a true water lily. Its miniature size is ideal for small ponds and containers.***

In each of the six categories are plants called filtrators. Filtrators absorb large amounts of nutrients, readily soaking them up from the water and thus depriving algae of nutrients. They reduce nitrogen levels in the water, which is conducive to healthy fish life.

SUBMERGED PLANTS AND OXYGENATORS

Aquatics with foliage that grows underwater are called submerged water plants. Just because their leaves don't rise above the surface of the water doesn't mean they're not beautiful. Many submerged plants have colorful foliage that glistens underwater, and several even have attractive flowers that float on or rise just above the water surface during the summer.

Although most plants add a small amount of oxygen to the water, submerged plants do so more effectively. If you look closely, you can see bubbles forming on their leaves. In addition, submerged plants remove nutrients from water, which helps to contain algae growth. Most submerged plants thrive in water depths of up to 10 feet, but some varieties need only a little light and grow at depths of 15 to 30 feet.

FLOATING WATER PLANTS

Plants that sit on the water surface with no need of pot or soil are called floating water plants. Their roots dangle in the water, drawing from the pond nitrogen and phosphates that could otherwise cause an algae bloom.

Floaters are extremely easy to grow—you can even grow them in a watertight pot on your deck or patio. Some flower with bright blue blooms that start when the weather warms and continue until fall.

Although some floating plants are winter-hardy, most are not. But they are among the cheapest of all water plants, so treat them as annuals and buy them fresh each year. In winter, simply pull them out of the pond and add them to the compost pile. Because of their high nitrogen content, they'll add nutrients to the pile.

WATER-LILY-LIKE PLANTS

These plants grow in soil from 1 inch to 2 feet below the water surface; like water lilies, they hold their leaves and flowers on top of the water. Although they grow like water lilies, botanically they are not the same, and so they are classified in a separate group. Some, such as water hawthorn, are winter-hardy. (Water hawthorn prefers the cool waters of spring and autumn to summer's heat and may go dormant in hot weather.)

The small form and plentiful blooming of water-lily-like plants make them an excellent choice for container gardens and provide delicate contrast to other pond plants.

WATER LILIES

Like marginals, water lilies grow with their roots and stems in soil below the water surface, but their foliage—round leaves that look like green platters—floats on the water. Some cultivars also have floating flowers; others hold their blooms on stems several inches out of the water. Most water lilies grow in 3- to 4-foot depths, some in depths of up to 8 feet, but they do quite well in ponds with only 6 to 18 inches of water over their roots. They provide shade and cover for fish, as well as an egg-laying platform for certain species of dragonflies whose larvae feed on insects.

Water lilies are classified into two broad groups. Hardy water lilies survive winters in cold climates. Tropical water lilies cannot withstand a winter freeze and need special care during cold months. To tell if a water lily is hardy or tropical, look at the edge of its rounded leaves. If the edge is smooth, the lily is hardy. If the edge is crinkled, wavy, or toothed, the lily is tropical.

HARDY WATER LILIES: These flowers come in many colors, and some even change their color each day of their three-day bloom life. Hardy water lilies flower during the day, with blossoms opening around 9 a.m. and closing around 4 p.m.

TROPICAL WATER LILIES: There are day-blooming cultivars and night-bloomers. Like their hardy counterparts, the flowers of the day-bloomers open around 9 a.m. and close about 4 p.m. Night-blooming tropicals open after the sun sets and stay open until between 10 a.m. and noon the next day.

Tropical water lilies have a distinct, enticing fragrance that floats on the wind, often announcing from several feet away that the flowers are open. Most hardy water lilies are not nearly as fragrant.

Golden club (Orontium aquaticum) *is a marginal plant with silvery foliage and yellow spadix-like flowers borne on white stalks.*

Water plants fall into six categories, and this scene showcases four of them: lotuses, marginals (sedge and thalia), water lilies, and oxygenators.

LOTUSES

Lotuses are similar to water lilies, growing in wet soil in water up to 3 feet deep, but unlike water lilies, they hold some of their leaves and all of their flowers well above the water. In modern cultivars, the blooms rise well above the leaves. Lotus leaves are round and either float or stand out of the water like inverted parasols. They have a waxy covering that makes raindrops roll around like little balls of mercury. Lotuses provide cover for fish and aquatic animals and food for nectar-seeking insects.

Lotus cultivars grow from 6 inches to 6 feet in height. Smaller selections, called bowl lotuses, can live happily in containers less than a foot wide and in just a few inches of soil and water. Lotus plants also grow well in bog gardens with just a few inches of water.

MARGINALS

At the edge, or margin, of the pond, where the soil is moist or the water shallow, grow the marginals. Some grow in moist or wet soil; others grow in submerged soil—from a few inches to about 2 feet. Many marginals will also adapt to the perennial garden. This adaptability makes them ideal as transitional plants that link the pond with other gardens.

Marginals can be taller than 6 feet or less than 2 inches. Some are clump-forming, such as hosta, and stay where they're put. Others are rambling types that traverse the pond edge. Marginals' chief function is decorative, adding color, texture, and form to the design. They're also an important transitional element in the landscape.

Lotuses, planted here among blue pickerel weed, grow well in containers or at the boggy edge of a pond.

SUBMERGED PLANTS

Important to water quality as well as clarity, the underwater foliage of submerged plants (also called oxygenators) filters unwanted nutrients. During the day, the plants add oxygen to the water, and at night they remove it. Too many submerged plants, however, can cause wide pH swings, so in a pond with fish, keep their area to about half the size of the pond. The time to plant most oxygenators is when water temperatures reach 55° to 60°F.

Clockwise from left: anacharis, pondweed, and fanwort

CABOMBA CAROLINIANA

Fanwort

- Sun to shade
- Zones 5 to 11
- Stem length: to 6 feet
- Spread: 1 foot
- Water depth: 1 foot to 10 feet

A submerged aquatic with delicate, finely cut foliage (dark green on top, deep purple underneath), fanwort is winter-hardy, even in cold regions where ice forms on the pond.

In summer it grows long stems that reach to the water surface and sprout a multitude of small white flowers with bright yellow centers. An attractive aquatic in the pond, it has a fluffy structure that is excellent for goldfish spawning.

Water starwort

CALLITRICHE HERMAPHRODITICA

Water Starwort

- Full sun
- Zones 6 to 10
- Stem length: 18 to 36 inches
- Spread: 12 inches
- Water depth: to 20 inches

A good choice for ponds that receive sun all day, water starwort's finely cut foliage grows rapidly from single crowns. A U.S. native found mostly in Western states, it works as well in still pools as it does in moving water. Like all submerged oxygenators, it will need attention so that it does not become invasive.

CERATOPHYLLUM DEMERSUM

Hornwort

- Sun to part shade
- Zones 5 to 11
- Stem length: to 10 feet
- Spread: 1 foot or more
- Water depth: 1 foot to 10 feet

Hornwort

Looking something like an underwater juniper bush, hornwort is a many-branched oxygenator with thick, dense dark green foliage. It grows in a fluffy mat that floats just below the surface; because it doesn't produce roots, there's no need for a pot or soil—just put it in the pond. If you want to keep it in one location and at a certain depth, secure it to a brick with a rubber band. It makes an excellent spawning ground for fish in spring and is somewhat resistant to koi feeding.

EGERIA DENSA

Anacharis

- Sun to shade
- Zones 8 to 11
- Stem length: to 10 feet
- Spread: 1 foot
- Water depth: 1 foot to 10 feet

Anacharis has shiny, fleshy bright green leaves that radiate from a central stem; it resembles submerged feather dusters. Three-petaled white flowers float on the water surface in summer. To overwinter anacharis in cold climates, bring in stem cuttings and keep them in an aquarium, where they will quickly root and grow.

ELODEA CANADENSIS

Common elodea

Elodea

- Best in full sun
- Zones 3 to 9
- Stem length: to 6 feet
- Spread: 12 inches
- Water depth: 6 inches to 40 feet, as deep as the light is sufficient

This plant likes water that is alkaline and fairly cool (65° to 75°F). It does best in fine sand mixed with a small amount (about 20 percent) of peat moss. Propagate it from stem cuttings. Its dwarf habit and hardiness make it excellent for small ponds in northern regions, and it's a favored food of koi and goldfish. Elodea is rather brittle so it is not suitable for water gardens that have fish a foot or more in length (unless you plant a lot of it). Some studies report that Elodea secretes a chemical compound that reduces mosquito larva populations by 30 percent.

FONTINALIS ANTIPYRETICA

Water moss

- Full shade
- Zones 3 to 11, depending on species
- Height: floating to just below the surface
- Spread: creeping
- Water depth: to 18 inches

This free-floating plant is the ultimate spawning medium—soft and covered with small, scalelike leaves to which eggs easily adhere. Willow moss requires fairly clean, soft, and neutral to slightly acidic water, so if it fails to thrive, your water quality needs attention.

HOTTONIA PALUSTRIS

Water violet

- Sun to shade
- Zones 5 to 9
- Stem length: 18 to 30 inches
- Spread: 12 to 20 inches
- Water depth: to 18 inches

Water violet holds its light green foliage both above and below the water. As with other oxygenators, the floating leaves offer valuable shade while the submerged ones absorb fish wastes. The real beauty of water violet is its flower spikes, which rise above the pond's surface in spring with a profusion of small pale lilac flowers. It is suitable for still or moving water.

HYGROPHILA POLYSPERMA

'Tropic Sunset'

- Full sun
- Zones 5 to 11
- Stem length: to 4 feet tall
- Spread: Creeping
- Water depth: to 5 feet; shallow is best

Hygrophila 'Tropic Sunset'

Popular as an aquarium plant, 'Tropic Sunset' also lends its colorful, variegated foliage and helpful oxygenation to ponds and container gardens. It tolerates a little shade and water up to 5 feet deep, but prefers sun, shallow water, and lots of fertilizer. If crowded by other plants, 'Tropic Sunset' will grow out of the water and set terrestrial leaves. *H. polysperma* is so vigorous and its propagation from stem cuttings is so easy that its sale is banned in southern Florida.

'Tropic Sunset' can be grown successfully in northern ponds during the summer, but must be overwintered in an aquarium indoors. The extra effort is worth the value of the lively color the plant brings to the underwater view.

Water violet

NOTE

Nearly all submerged and floating plants are considered to be invasive weeds in some locales. Individual species may even be banned in certain areas. Check with your state department of natural resources for regulations and guidelines on planting and propagating the ones you want to grow in your pond.

SUBMERGED PLANTS
continued

LYSIMACHIA NUMMULARIA

Moneywort

- Sun or shade
- Zones 3 to 8
- Stem length: 3 feet
- Spread: creeping
- Water depth: up to 2 inches

Also called creeping jenny, this fast-spreading oxygenator offers above-the-water interest in addition to its below-the-surface appeal. Bright yellow flowers bloom an inch or two above the floating leaves from June through August as the plant sends its shoots across the pond. Moneywort can be invasive, especially in smaller ponds, so pull out any excess shoots during routine maintenance.

MYRIOPHYLLUM HETEROPHYLLUM

Foxtail

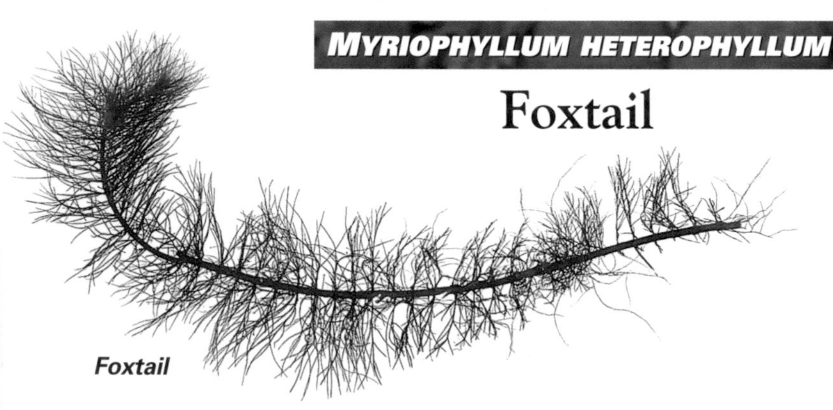

Foxtail

- Sun to shade
- Zones 3 to 11
- Stem length: to 6 feet
- Spread: 1 foot
- Water depth: 1 foot to 10 feet

A very winter-hardy underwater favorite, this plant has thin, wispy leaves that grow from a stout central stem. Foliage is dark reddish brown and fluffy when submerged, somewhat like a fox's tail, from which it derives its common name. There are several similar species including *M. hippuroides*. *M. spicatum*, water milfoil, is often sold, but it is highly invasive and prohibited in some states.

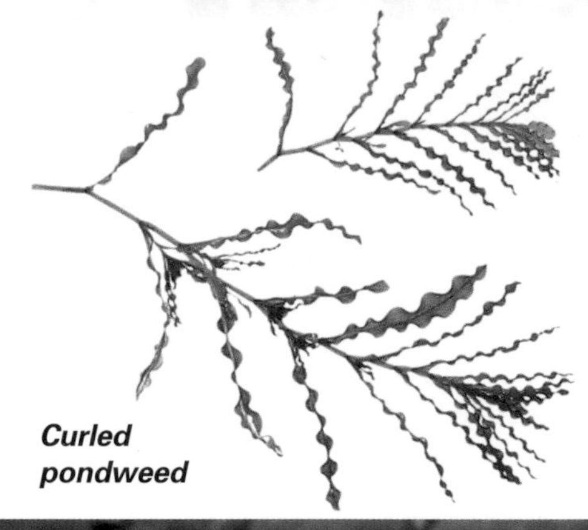

Curled pondweed

POTAMOGETON CRISPUS

Curled pondweed

- Sun to part shade
- Zones 4 to 11
- Stem length: to 3 feet
- Spread: running
- Water depth: 10 feet

One of many species of pondweed native to North America, curled pondweed has leaves that are long and wavy, with edges like crinkly red aluminum foil. This plant is an important source of food for waterfowl, and its submerged leaves make a good spawning ground for fish.

RANUNCULUS LONGIROSTRIS

Water buttercup

- Sun or part shade
- Zones 4 to 11
- Stem length: to 4 feet
- Spread: 1 foot
- Water depth: 1 foot to 6 feet

The leaves of this plant are finely cut, open and airy, and almost threadlike, borne alternately radiating from a central stem. Like fanwort, water buttercup has large white flowers in summer that float on the water surface. It is more brittle than fanwort, and its stems can break easily when handled. In still or slow-moving water (which it prefers), it can form dense stands. It is an excellent early filtrator (plant it in 35°F water) and starts growing early in spring. *R. flabellaris*, also called water crowfoot, has flat leaves, and its June-blooming flowers are yellow.

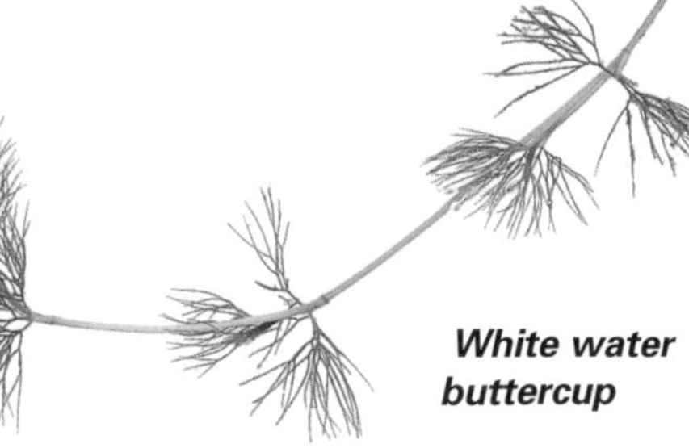

White water buttercup

Dwarf sagittaria (left); normal-sized **S. natans** *(right)*

SAGITTARIA NATANS

Sagittaria

- **Sun to shade**
- **Zones 4 to 11**
- **Stem length: to 3 feet**
- **Spread: 6 inches to creeping**
- **Water depth: 2 to 3 feet for flowering; it will grow deeper but may not flower**

Looking much like eel grass but with thicker leaves, this plant is not as fluid in the water, but it is sturdy enough to hold up to koi and large goldfish. Also called tape grass or arrowhead, it is one of the first plants up in spring, so it is a great aid in removing fish wastes. Displaying the largest blossoms of any of the submerged plants listed here, it has white summer flowers, held on the water surface, which are up to half an inch in diameter. Plants spread by creeping stolons to form sods or colonies.

Dwarf sagittaria (*S. subulata*) forms a submerged, 4- to 6-inch sod and is ideal for small ponds. Plant it in 4 to 12 inches of water, and in summer you will have white flowers floating on the surface. In deeper water, it may never flower, but its extra surface will aid in filtration. In an earth-bottom pond, plant it in a shallow tray topped off with pea gravel so the fish won't dig it up.

UTRICULARIA VULGARIS

Bladderwort

- **Sun to shade**
- **Zones 3 to 11**
- **Stem length: 2 to 24 inches**
- **Spread: 1 inch to 6 inches, depending on species**
- **Water depth: floats just below the surface**

An unusual submerged plant for the pond or the aquarium (it's carnivorous), bladderwort has very fine foliage. Some plants look like soft hornwort. Others are so fine that they look like floating bits of green hairnet or string algae; they provide food and cover for fish. Nestled among the foliage are tiny "bladders," which trap microscopic prey. Leaves and stems grow as floating mats just below the water surface. Their dainty yellow, white, purple, or lavender blossoms stand above the water surface and resemble small snapdragons. Most bladderworts prefer neutral to acidic water conditions. Because they do not produce roots, no soil or potting is necessary.

Bladderwort

VALLISNERIA SPIRALIS

Eel grass

- **Sun to shade**
- **Zones 4 to 11**
- **Stem length: 2 to 3 feet**
- **Spread: running**
- **Water depth: 1 foot to 15 feet**

The plants in this genus of several species of submerged plants have long tapelike leaves. Their foliage often ripples in moving water—excellent near the base of a waterfall or in deep streams. Selections come in a variety of colors and shapes, with both red-leaved and twisted or curled foliage. Plants grow from underground runners to form large colonies in earth-bottom ponds that are ideal for small fish to hide. 'Crystal' eel grass has a green, glassy look. 'Red Jungle' eel grass has broad burgundy foliage.

Clockwise from left: 'Red Jungle', 'Curly', and 'American' eel grass

FLOATING PLANTS

Floating water plants are the ultimate in easy gardening—there's no potting necessary. Just set them in the water. Because they float on the water surface, floaters grow in any depth of water. They are among the best filtrators. They shade fish from sun and protect them from predators. Too many floaters in a pond, however, can reduce oxygen, which harms fish. Don't let floaters completely cover the pond's surface.

Fairy moss

AZOLLA CAROLINIANA

Fairy moss

- Sun to shade
- Zones 9 to 11
- Height: floating
- Spread: running

This fern, its leaves fuzzy and finely toothed, is bright green in summer, red in spring and fall. An excellent cover for fish and other wildlife, it can be planted just after the ice has melted. Fairy moss is light-sensitive and tends to die during the short days of winter. It fixes its own nitrogen, which will enrich the compost pile later on. *A. pinnata*, invasive and prohibited under federal law, has triangular leaves.

Clockwise from upper left: 'Aqua Velvet', 'Ruffles', and regular water lettuce; frogbit (round leaves); salvinia (rectangular leaves); duckweed (light green); water hyacinth; and azolla (dark green in center).

CERATOPTERIS THALICTROIDES

Water Fern

- Part to full shade, does not tolerate sun
- Zones 9 to 11
- Height: 1 foot
- Spread: running

The foliage of this unusual plant looks like big puffy parsley. New plantlets form on the leaves. Water fern grows floating on water and in soil with a few inches of water over its crown. In soil, it looks like curly parsley. The foliage of water fern's relative *C. pteridoides* is slightly coarser in appearance. Plant water fern when water reaches 65°F.

EICHHORNIA CRASSIPES

Water hyacinth

- Sun to part shade
- Zones 9 to 11
- Height: to 1 foot
- Spread: running

Water hyacinth

Known for its lavender flowers and shiny round spongy green foliage, this floater filters water so well that it is sometimes grown to treat sewage.

It does best in warm water, and won't survive freezing weather. Wait until the water is consistently above 65°F before planting. In cold climates, treat it like an annual.

Water hyacinth makes an ideal container plant. Drop it in any pot that holds water and add fertilizer. Creeping or peacock water hyacinth *(E. azurea)* grows from a thick, fleshy stem that spreads across the water surface. Its blue flowers are small and rounded. It is illegal to possess water hyacinth in some states, and federal law prohibits interstate commerce in it.

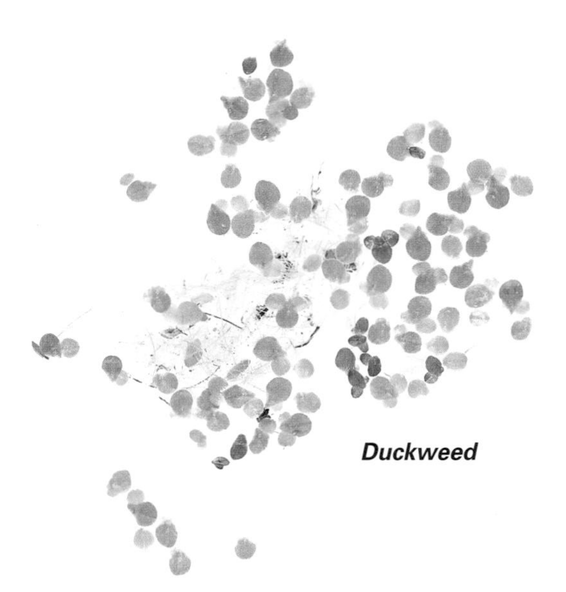

Duckweed

HYDROCHARIS MORSUS-RANAE AND LIMNOBIUM SPONGIA

Frogbit

- **Sun to part shade**
- **Zones 4 to 10**
- **Height: floating to ½ inch tall**
- **Spread: running**

The common name frogbit actually refers to several different plants. *Hydrocharis morsus-ranae* is the prettiest, with small white three-petaled summer flowers like miniature water poppies. The foliage is shiny and heart-shaped. This plant grows well in small ponds and containers. In winter its buds sink to the bottom of the pond, where the plant overwinters until spring. American frogbit *(Limnobium spongia)*, a lookalike with oval leaves, has not-very-showy quarter-inch blossoms. In most climates, you'll find frogbit available for planting in late April.

LEMNA MINOR

Common duckweed

- **Sun to part shade**
- **Zones 3 to 11**
- **Height: floating**
- **Spread: running**

Known as the smallest flowering plant in the world, common duckweed has round or almost-round light green leaves less than ⅛ inch in diameter, with a single root growing from under the leaf. Duckweed is a favorite of goldfish and koi. Use it as a spring and fall fish food, planting just after the ice leaves the pond. Caution: Duckweed can overtake a pond in a single season unless checked by fish or routine thinning.

PISTIA STRATIOTES

Water lettuce

- **Sun to part shade**
- **Zones 9 to 11**
- **Height: 4 to 12 inches**
- **Spread: running (up to 1 foot wide)**

Its spongy, velvety lime-green foliage grows like a rosette from a single crown, resembling a floating head of lettuce. 'Ruffles' (4 to 6 inches in diameter) has smaller leaves with folds obscuring the center. 'Aqua Velvet' (6 to 8 inches wide) has deep blue-green leaves. 'Angio Splash' (6 to 8 inches across) is streaked and blotched in creamy yellow. Plant when the water is 65°F.

Water lettuce

FLOATING AND WATER-LILY-LIKE PLANTS
continued

Left to right: Marsh marigold, water hawthorn, Illinois pondweed, and water clover

SALVINIA OBLONGIFOLIA

Salvinia

- Sun to part shade
- Zones 10 and 11
- Height: floating
- Spread: running

Like fairy moss, salvinia is a true fern. The species has velvety leaves that grow on a long floating chain. *S. oblongifolia*, good food for small fish but aggressive in southern climates, has 1- to 3-inch oval leaves and should be used only in northern areas. It's excellent in containers or small ponds where control is easier. In northern climates it is very cold-sensitive, requiring a minimum water temperature of 40°F before planting. Avoid the round-leaved salvinia species *S. molesta*, which is invasive and prohibited in many southern states.

WATER-LILY-LIKE PLANTS

Water lilies aren't the only plants that grow from a submerged crown with floating leaves and flowers. Other aquatics have adapted to water in the same way, and some are winter-hardy enough to stay in the pond all year. Their small foliage and blossoms provide an unusual accent to water lilies in any size water garden. Keep the tender ones indoors in an aquarium in a sunny window during winter.

APONOGETON DISTACHYUS (SYN. A. DISTACHYOS)

Water hawthorn

- Sun to part shade
- Zones 5 to 11
- Spread: 2 feet
- Water depth: 6 to 24 inches

Ornamental and extremely fragrant, water hawthorn smells like vanilla. Blooms appear when the water is just above freezing, in spring and again in fall. In cold spring-fed waters, it can blossom all year. In warm water, it may go completely dormant in summer. Propagate it whenever the plants produce bulblike seeds. Push the seeds into the soil, just so their tips show.

CALTHA NATANS

Floating marsh marigold

- Sun to part shade
- Zones 2 to 7
- Spread: 1 foot
- Water depth: 2 to 6 inches

Floating marsh marigold is a dainty, spring-flowering plant for container gardens and small ponds. Its white single-petaled blossoms, only as big as a quarter, appear when the ice is off the pond. Its heart-shaped leaves are also very small. Water must be cooler than 65°F.

HYDROCLEYS NYMPHOIDES

Water poppy

- Sun to part shade
- Zones 9 to 11
- Spread: to 6 feet
- Water depth: 4 to 12 inches

Left to right: Water poppy and Peruvian water poppy

This tender aquatic has rounded, slightly inflated leaves and 2-inch creamy yellow flowers with dark red or brown stamens. It starts blooming in 75°F water and keeps going all summer. Giant water poppy *(H. peruviana)* is about half again as large as the standard-sized water poppy but is otherwise the same.

Water poppy sprouts new floating plantlets that flower and grow more leaves and stems across the water surface. It is considered a nuisance in warm climates, where it can quickly take over a pond. Divide it by breaking off the floating stems after they have rooted. You can also grow it from seed when the water temperature reaches 70°F.

Water-lily-like plants bloom prolifically in both container gardens and large ponds. Like water lilies, their small flowers are held upright at or just above the water surface.

NYMPHOIDES SPP.

Water snowflake

- **Sun to part shade**
- **Zones 7 to 11**
- **Spread: running**
- **Water depth: 4 to 24 inches**

Most water-lily-like plants that fall into the snowflake family have dainty white or yellow flowers that often rise from the junction of a leaf on the same stem. *N. aquatica*, also called banana plant, has tubers that in the aquarium look like little bunches of green bananas. In the water garden, it has floating, round leaves and diminutive white star-shaped flowers Painted yellow water snowflake *(N. crenata)* has toothed leaves heavily mottled in dark red. Flowers are yellow, star-shaped, and fringed. Painted white water snowflake *(N. cristata)* has leaves heavily painted in dark burgundy and white, star-shaped, lightly fringed flowers. Yellow water snowflake *(N. geminata* syn. *N. peltata)* has foliage that's an even green, not mottled or variegated; flowers are yellow, star-shaped, and frilly. Free-flowering, fast-growing, and hardy in cold climates, it will overwinter in Zones 5 to 11. White water snowflake *(N. indica)* is like yellow water snowflake except it has white flowers. 'Gigantea' has flowers larger than the species. Orange water snowflake *(N. hydrocharioides)* has fringed orange flowers and slightly mottled leaves. It is otherwise similar to white water snowflake. Plant when the water temperature is above 70°F.

Left to right: Painted white water snowflake, white water snowflake, and yellow water snowflake

POTAMOGETON ILLINOENSIS

Illinois pondweed

- **Sun to shade**
- **Zones 3 to 9**
- **Spread: to 3 feet**
- **Water depth: 1 foot to 15 feet**

Illinois pondweed is one of several species of *Potamogeton*. It has shiny elliptical khaki-green leaves. Its late-summer flowers are clublike and rise a few inches out of the water. You can plant it just after the pond has thawed.

WATER LILIES

Water lilies are often considered the jewels of the pond. We can visualize a pond without marginals or submerged plants, even without fish. Who can imagine one without water lilies?

Water lilies belong to the genus *Nymphaea*, but virtually all the lilies available today are named cultivars that have been hybridized by cross-fertilization. Native species are not the best for the homeowner's pond, because they are not as ornamental and do not perform as reliably as named cultivars.

HARDY WATER LILIES

- **Full sun (some cultivars bloom even in part shade)**
- **Zones 3 to 11**
- **Spread: to 8 feet, depending on cultivar**
- **Height: floating**
- **Water depth: 6 to 36 inches; some cultivars tolerate deeper water, even up to 8 feet**
- **Flowers: when pond water is over 65°F**

Hardy water lilies are day-bloomers. They open around 9 a.m. and close around 4 p.m. On dark, cloudy days, they may not open at all. Generally, their flowers rest on the water surface. Hardy water lily cultivars flower in a wide range of colors, from the darkest reds to the purest whites, with bright pinks and creamy yellows in between. The only colors missing are blues and purples.

PINK, WHITE, AND YELLOW: 'Alba' is an easy-to-grow white lily with colorful leaves. 'Peace Lily' grows well in a wide range of climates, producing pink, white, and yellow flowers. Both are suitable for medium and large ponds. If your pondside time is mostly after work, plant 'Helvola'. Its medium-yellow flowers open later in the day than other hardy lilies and stay open into early evening. A dwarf cultivar, it works well in small ponds and container gardens.

PEACH AND SALMON: Although there has never been a true orange water lily, recent introductions include several peach-flowering hardy water lilies. 'Clyde Ilkins' has large

Giant water lily Nymphaea Victoria amazonica requires a large pond for its 4- to 6-foot-wide leaves. The night-blooming, fragrant flowers change from white to purplish-red as they mature.

The miniature blossoms of N. helvola *'Yellow Pygmy' are perfect for small ponds and container gardens. The lightly scented flowers bloom in early afternoon.*

WILL IT FIT?

Water lilies are often described as being suitable for small, medium, or large ponds. Here are the general guidelines for the different sizes of water gardens discussed in this book.

Container garden	1 foot to 3 feet wide
Small pond	3 to 6 feet wide
Medium pond	6 to 10 feet wide
Large pond	More than 10 feet wide

Natural, or earth-bottom, ponds may be any width but are usually at least 3 feet deep.

Water lilies are sized according to leaf spread. N. odorata *'Minor', a dwarf cultivar, transforms this ceramic pot into a container water garden.*

apricot-colored flowers that rise 6 to 8 inches out of the water. It produces over a long season, from early spring to late fall. 'Colorado' has salmon-colored flowers, with large, pointed petals. 'Cynthia Ann' has small peach blossoms suitable for container gardens or small pools. 'Berit Strawn', for small and medium ponds, will bloom in part shade.

CHANGEABLE COLORS: There is even a "changeable" group of hardy water lilies whose blossoms open one color and then age to a different hue. These are good for the small pond or container that holds only one or two lilies. Several varieties will flower in part shade. 'Comanche' is a medium-sized lily that starts out a creamy yellow-apricot and changes to peach-pink and then deep reddish-orange as the days pass. 'Arc en Ciel', a fragrant cultivar that blooms well in a shaded pond, starts out shell-pink and fades to white. Its leaves are mottled with cream, yellow, or pink. For container water gardens, try 'Indiana', a dwarf lily that changes from apricot to red. Its leaves are showy too.

RED: Many dark red selections are more suitable to northern climates. In warmer areas, red lily petals may "melt" in the afternoon summer sun. However, newer selections have been developed to avoid this. One cultivar, 'Almost Black', has red flowers the color of dark cherry soda. 'Fireball' has double blossoms and is hardy in Zones 3 to 11. Some red lilies will bloom in part shade, such as 'Gloriosa', for small and medium ponds, and 'Rembrandt', for larger ponds.

WATER LILIES
continued

N. odorata *'Texas Dawn' is a hardy, fragrant, day-blooming cultivar suitable for medium to large ponds. It tolerates shade.*

'Gladstone' is among the largest hardy lilies and well-suited for big water gardens and ponds up to 4 feet deep.

The extremely double, deep pink blooms of* N. odorata *'Perry's Fire Opal' are free-flowering if given room.

LEAF SPREAD: Water lilies are often classified by their leaf spread—that is, how much water surface the plant will cover once it is mature. Hardy water lilies can have a spread anywhere from 1 foot to 8 feet in diameter. The largest cultivars, such as 'Gladstone' (also called 'Gladstoniana'), are particularly suitable for large water gardens and earth-bottom ponds and will grow well in water 1 foot to 4 feet deep. The smallest, called miniatures, have flowers only 1 inch to 2 inches wide. The white-flowering pygmy water lily, *N. tetragona*, blooms earliest, in the cool waters of spring. Soon to follow are the pink forms 'Joanne Pring' and 'Rosea Laydekeri'. Last to appear are the bright yellow blossoms of 'Helvola'.

ODORATA AND TUBEROSA: Hardy water lilies also differ with respect to the growth habit of their rootstocks, which can affect how you use the plants, how much attention they need, and how they perform in your pond. Odorata types and tuberosa types grow with

'Escarboucle', a hardy marliac-type lily, has won awards for its large, deep-red flowers that stay open late in the day. They are also fragrant.

Many pondkeepers consider hardy 'Virginalis' to be the most desirable white water lily available. Its large flowers bloom profusely on medium-sized plants.

rhizomes horizontally across the soil surface. Both types can grow wild and unrestrained, requiring more frequent division to contain them in their pots. (Odorata lily rhizomes can be larger than 3 inches in diameter and can spread more than 3 feet in a single year.) Because these types put more energy into tuber and leaf production than into blossoms, they tend not to flower as often as the modern hybrids. The tuberosas are more productive than odoratas.

The fragrant blooms of 'Pink Opal' are held above the water. They are suitable for small and medium ponds, and can be used as cut flowers.

'Marliacea Carnea' is a good choice for deep ponds. Its pale pink petals are nearly white and bloom late in the summer. The plant tolerates some shade.

WATER LILIES
continued

Hardy 'Andreana' is a changeable-type lily, maturing from red to orange to peachy yellow.

'Chromatella' grows well in deep water.

MARLIAC AND MEXICANA: Two other types, marliac and mexicana, exhibit more restrained root growth and better flower and foliage production in a smaller space. Marliac-type water lilies have more compact roots and do not run across the soil as much as odorata and tuberosa types. They are named after Joseph Bory Latour-Marliac of the village Temple sur Lot in France. In the late nineteenth and early twentieth centuries, Marliac hybridized many of the hundreds of hardy water lily cultivars popular today.

Mexicana-type water lilies have upright, nonrunning rhizomes and are named after the semihardy *N. mexicana* water lily, which has this type of rhizome. The rhizome shape is

'Arc-en-ciel' holds its fragrant, changeable blooms above variegated foliage. It tolerates shade.

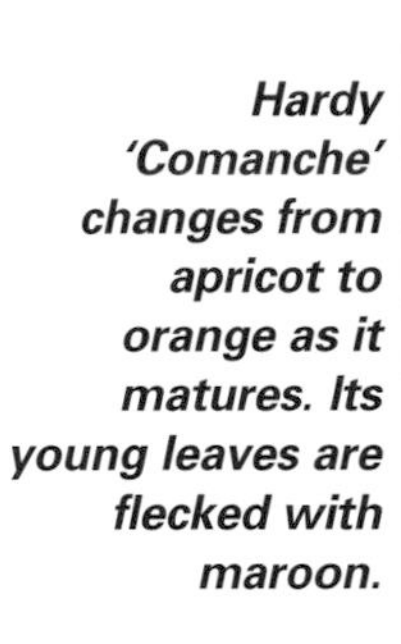

Hardy 'Comanche' changes from apricot to orange as it matures. Its young leaves are flecked with maroon.

similar to a small pineapple, which it is also sometimes called. Many of the changeable water lilies and 'Chromatella' have mexicana hybrid-type rhizomes.

Planting: You can plant hardy water lilies either when they are dormant or when they are actively growing. Plant dormant hardy water lilies when the water temperature is 50°F. Most love locations with full sun, although a few do well in partly shaded spots.

The inner petals of 'Solfatare' start out a yellowish apricot, turn to creamy peach, and then to salmon. Outer petals are darker.

The deep red blooms of* Nymphaea atropurpurea *will fade and wilt in high heat. Keep this plant shaded.

WATER LILIES
continued

Tropical day-blooming lily* N. tuberosa *'Albert Greenberg' flowers yellow, orange, and pink. Its mottled leaves are also dramatic. The plant is a strong grower and a prolific bloomer.

The fragrant blooms of 'Shirley Byrne' add brilliant color to medium and large ponds.

TROPICAL WATER LILIES

Water lilies from tropical climates are the most enchanting of all water garden plants. Their flowers exude an almost intoxicating fragrance. It is no surprise that they are often used in creating perfumes.

Tropical water lilies flower much more than hardy water lilies. The most common color is blue, but they also come in a range of lavender and purple, as well as pink, yellow, and white. Some are small and suitable for container water gardens. Others can grow more than 8 feet in diameter in a single season; one leaf alone may measure more than 2 feet wide. The foliage is often mottled in purple or brown.

The bright burgundy-red flowers of 'Renegade' stand out against its dark pads. 'Star of Siam' has purple-blue flowers with elongated white stamens that are yellow at the base. With a spread of 3 to 5 feet, it is suitable for medium and large ponds. 'Florida Star' has large white star-shaped flowers with yellow stamens. Suitable for larger ponds, it is hardy in Zones 9 to 11. Pygmy cultivars are available for small ponds and container

The highly fragrant rich purple flowers of 'Midnight' open during the day. It is a prolific bloomer suitable for small and medium ponds.

The large scarlet blooms of 'Red Flare' open in the evening, held a foot above mahogany leaves. They are slightly fragrant.

Suitable for ponds or container gardens, free-flowering 'St. Louis Gold' opens late in the day and stays open in the evening.

gardens. 'St. Louis Gold' is lemon-yellow; 'Colorata' is violet with purple stamens; and 'Dauben' is such a delicate shade of pale blue that it can appear to be starry white.

Some tropical water lilies are night-bloomers, opening after the sun sets and staying open until late the next morning. These night-blooming lilies are especially suitable for gardeners who work during the day and come home after four in the afternoon, when the hardy water lilies have already closed. The night-bloomers often flower in red, with rose, pink, or white cultivars also available. Red night-bloomers may have maroon foliage. 'Red Bowl' has large, rose-pink flowers held high above its bronze-green leaves. Add the clear pink blossoms of 'Mrs. George C. Hitchcock' to your pond for their cinnamon scent as well as their beauty.

Plant tropical water lilies when the water temperature reaches 70°F. Most cultivars will require locations with full sun, but a few can tolerate part shade.

LOTUSES

Lotuses should be contained in the largest pot possible or planted in contained bogs; they run freely by underground tubers that can overtake a pond.

LOTUSES

- Sun (a few cultivars bloom even in part shade)
- Hardy in Zones 4 to 11
- Height: miniature, 6 to 10 inches; dwarf, 10 to 12 inches; medium, 2 to 4 feet; large, over 4 feet
- Spread: running; keep potted for best results
- Water depth: moist to 12 inches; some large varieties tolerate water to 3 feet deep
- Flowers: 6 to 8 weeks beginning May or June in the deep South, in July farther north. Lotuses require several weeks of 80°F weather to bloom. In the South, plants may bloom a second time in September.

Lotuses are among the most ancient of plants. Viable lotus seeds have been found dating back more than 2,000 years. Within the lotus genus *Nelumbo,* there are two species. *N. lutea* is the American native lotus, with creamy yellow flowers that are usually single, occasionally semidouble. *N. nucifera,* Asian lotus, usually has white or pink single, semi-double, or very double blossoms.

HYBRIDIZATION

Although few improved varieties of the American native lotus have been selected, one U.S. hybridizer, Perry D. Slocum, has crossed *N. lutea* with *N. nucifera* to make free-flowering hybrids in new rich colors. 'Ben Gibson' is a fully double red-tipped pink lotus. The fragrant single blossoms of 'Charles Thomas' bloom pink and then fade to lavender. 'Sharon' has dark pink, semidouble flowers with yellow in the center. All three hybrids grow 3 to 4 feet tall.

Slocum's additional contribution has been the introduction of lotuses with blossoms that consistently rise above the foliage—an important trait because many forms have flowers that appear among or remain hidden underneath their large parasol leaves.

Much hybridization has been done with Asian lotuses. Because of their exquisite flowers and unusual foliage, these lotuses have been grown and cultivated for hundreds of years, especially in China; at last count, more than 600 varieties have been recorded in China alone.

Gardeners around the world have profited greatly from these efforts. Lotus cultivars are available in a wide range of sizes and colors. Some selections are truly miniature, growing no more than a foot or so in height with flowers no larger than a tennis ball. Others are huge and stately, standing more than 6 feet tall, with leaves more than 2 feet in diameter and flowers as large as basketballs. Fragrance varies from heady and fruity to mild, like baby powder. Colors range from the deepest rosy pink (there is no true red) to the cleanest white. There are also bicolors and tones that blush or fade.

BOWL LOTUSES

Bowl lotuses from China are also available. Often called teacup lotuses, they are like standard lotuses in all respects except

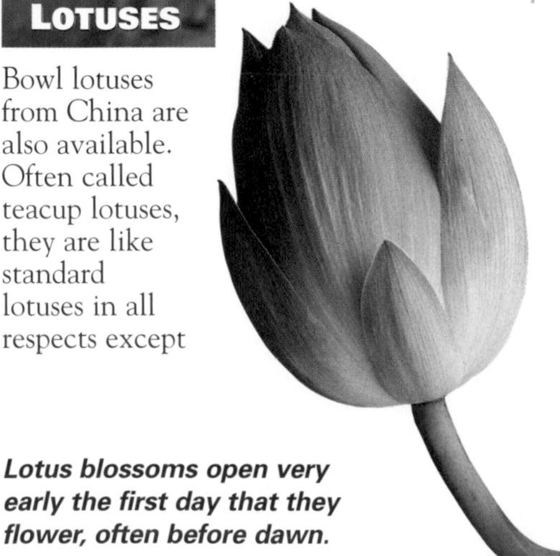

Lotus blossoms open very early the first day that they flower, often before dawn.

their size. They grow to no more than 2 feet in height, some only to 4 inches tall—perfect for tabletop ponds. Some cultivars grow much larger when planted in large pots or container gardens, although they never reach giant size. Some of these change flower size and shape (by adding petals).

Bowl lotuses are popular in China but many selections are becoming available in the United States. 'Chongshuihua' has pinkish-white flowers only 3 inches across. Red-flowering 'Welcoming' and 'Red Ball' and pink cultivar 'Shining Sunglow' grow to a foot or so tall.

When growing bowl lotuses, be especially careful with the amount of fertilizer added during the growing season. Miniature lotuses burn more easily than standard-size plants. They are also more sensitive to pH, so be sure to use distilled water. Hard tap water can quickly burn the leaves. Rainwater may be suitable, depending on its acidity.

SUN AND WARMTH

Lotuses are generally sun-loving plants that require at least 6 hours of sunlight each day. Only a few cultivars, such as white-flowering 'Angel Wings' and 'Perry's Super Star', which blooms a creamy yellow that turns pink, will grow and flower in part shade. Lotuses are not a tropical plant; they simply love hot weather, preferring warm soil and water temperatures. They revel in humid weather, and generally will not start to grow in spring until the pond water reaches 60°F. Consistent water temperatures are the best; temperatures that swing up and down will delay flowering and in extreme instances may send the plants into early dormancy. Lotuses flower several weeks later than water lilies, often not until July and August in some zones. In areas where the days are warm but the nights are cool, lotuses grown in a freestanding pot can be covered with a plastic canopy to retain warmth overnight.

Lotus blossoms are so large and their fragrance so heady that people often compare them to flowering brandy snifters.

FLOWERS

Lotus flowers open at different times during the day and night, depending upon the age of the blossom. First-day flowers usually open at about four or five in the morning, stay open for just three or four hours, then close around eight o'clock. On the second day, flowers begin to open just after midnight. By seven or eight in the morning, flowers will be fully open. Again they stay open for only a few hours, closing around noon that same day. On the third day, flowers open in the dark,

Sun-loving lotuses thrive in hot weather and high humidity. Daytime air temperatures consistently above 80° F and water temperatures above 60° F are necessary for several weeks before lotuses will bloom. All but a few cultivars need at least 6 hours of direct sunlight each day.

LOTUSES
continued

The semidouble, red flowers of* N. rosea plenum *show up easily as they rise above the dark green foliage of a bog garden.

Nelumbo nucifera *'Momo Botan Minima' is called the sacred lotus. A very double, dwarf cultivar, it is suitable for container gardens.*

after midnight. They open fully by 9 o'clock. By noon, they begin to close but not always completely. On the fourth and final day, flowers open during the late morning or afternoon, but they will be faded and tattered and begin to shed their petals.

CARE

Lotuses are hardy water plants that can be overwintered even in cold climates. Cut back the foliage to the water surface after the leaves have died and turned brown. If you cut it while it is still green, fungal or bacterial infections can reach the underground tuber and kill the plant.

Care for lotuses as you would hardy water lilies, keeping the tubers deep enough in the pond that ice and frost will not reach them. In a shallow pond, this can be easier to accomplish with lotuses than it is with hardy water lilies; lotus roots grow at the bottom of the pot, while lily rhizomes are often at the soil surface. In spring bring the pot up to the surface, where the water and the soil will be warmed by the sun. If you do not overwinter lotuses in your pond, put the pot in a trash bag and store it where it will stay cool (but not freezing), dark, and damp.

N. lutea *is a very free-flowering yellow lotus native to North America.*

AMAZING ANCIENT LOTUS

In the years after World War II, Dr. Ichiro Ohga, a Japanese botanist and researcher, attempted in vain to grow ancient lotus seeds excavated from a site near the Namegawa River in Japan. After his first attempts failed, he recalled that ancient lotus seeds had also been discovered at a site near the Kemigawa River. In March 1951 Ohga traveled to the area and enlisted help from local residents to find the lotus seeds. The volunteer crew, aided by children from the local elementary and high schools, dug for almost a month. At last they found the seeds, estimated to be more than 2,000 years old. Ohga set the seeds in water and amazingly they sprouted and grew. The resulting lotus now bears Ohga's name. A full-size lotus, 'Ohga' has stunning dark pink single flowers that look almost red when they first bloom. 'Ohga' is what lotuses must have looked like centuries ago, when they were first prized and revered.

DIVISION AND PROPAGATION

Starting lotuses from seed is not the easiest method of propagation. The seed coats are tough and must be nicked with a file before soaking overnight in warm, chlorine-free water. When the seed coat is soft, remove and discard it. Keep the seed in shallow distilled water until three sets of leaves have emerged, changing the water daily until then to keep it aerated. When the leaves have formed, carefully transfer the seedling to a shallow pot filled with fertile soil. Do not bury the seedling but simply hold it in place on top of the dirt with a small stone or shard of pottery. Keep the plant in a warm, sunny location for the first year and until the plant blooms.

A simpler approach to creating more lotuses is to divide and re-pot them in early spring before they have sprouted leaves. Turn the pot upside down and empty the dirt. Dig in carefully with your fingers; you will find the tubers in the dirt that was near the bottom of the pot. Gently rinse the soil away from the tubers so that you can see the joints where the tuber sections come together, and the growing tips. Each division must include a growing tip with at least one tuber section behind it. Using scissors or a sharp knife, cut the tuber after, and not at, the joint.

Fill a pot with a few inches of soil and place the new division on top. Cover most of the tuber with soil, but leave the growing tip or tips exposed. Then fill the pot with water or place it under water at least a few inches in a warm, sunny spot. New leaf sprouts should appear soon.

For more detailed instructions on how to divide and re-pot lotuses, see pages 164–165.

N. nucifera *hybrids can grow to 4 feet tall. 'Paleface' grows in shallow or deep water.*

The cherry-red blooms of* N. caspicum*, a Russian cultivar, really stand out.

ARRANGING THE LOVELY LOTUS

The flowers, seedpods, and foliage of lotuses look striking in floral arrangements. Lotuses have been used for centuries in Buddhist ceremonies.
In Indonesia, buds are stripped of their outermost sepals and placed among folded lotus foliage; they resemble delicate pink rosebuds. Flowers that have already opened are also highly decorative, with their outermost petals folded to look like pink ribbons. Blossoms are also attractive floating in a bowl of water as their powerful fragrance quickly fills the room. The foliage adds a dramatic flair to any arrangement; the seed heads last for years and work in both fresh and dried arrangements.

N. nucifera *'Charles Thomas' has fragrant single blossoms that bloom pink and then fade to lavender.*

MARGINALS

ACORUS CALAMUS

Sweet flag

Acorus calamus 'Variegatus' grows to 3 feet tall. Japanese sweet flag is a similar, shorter cultivar.

- **Sun to shade**
- **Zones 4 to 11**
- **Height: 8 to 36 inches**
- **Spread: to 18 inches wide, depending on cultivar**
- **Water depth: moist soil to 2 to 6 inches**

Sweet flags are invaluable for their neat, clean appearance. Hardy and foolproof, they add textural interest to a pond. They need constantly moist soil; underwatering burns leaf tips. Most tolerate seasonal flooding; once mature, they can handle several inches of water over the crown. However, Japanese sweet flag can't take water over its crown for more than a few days.

All sweet flags can overwinter in the pond or in a mulched perennial border, but don't let them dry out. Propagate by dividing the rootstock, anytime from spring through fall.

Smaller forms are prone to spider mites. Larger selections may develop a fungus that causes black spots and can kill the foliage. Clean up dead foliage in autumn; remove affected leaves if spots appear.

Sweet flag *(A. calamus)*, green and variegated forms, are tall and upright. They grow from roots that run freely and form small clumps. Graceful 'Ogon' Japanese sweet flag *(A. gramineus)* has light green foliage with bright yellow stripes and is generally evergreen.

ALISMA PLANTAGO-AQUATICA

Water plantain

The large leaves of water plantain stand erect above the water. Flowers appear in late summer through fall.

- **Sun to part shade**
- **Zones 3 to 11**
- **Height: 12 to 36 inches**
- **Spread: to 18 inches**
- **Water depth: moist soil to 3 inches**

Water plantain is an herbaceous perennial with deeply veined spoon- or lance-shaped foliage. The leaves stand erect above the water when growing along the pond edge. Submerged leaves become long and ribbonlike. Blooms are larger at the bottom and taper to a point at the top. The flower, with large pyramid-shaped heads, forms whorling white or pink clouds, appearing in summer and autumn.

Plants are suitable for medium to large ponds. If they are not dead-headed regularly, they self-seed and become invasive in an earth-bottom pond. During a drought, seeds are prone to sprout to the point of being a nuisance along a shoreline.

Overwinter water plantain in the pond. Winter chilling is essential to its growth and flowering in subsequent seasons. Bulblike corms form at the base of the plant, and the leaves and roots wither and die off completely in winter. Don't overlook them and toss them out during spring cleaning. You can propagate the plant in spring by growing seeds in wet soil or by dividing the corms.

ALTERNANTHERA PHILOXEROIDES

Alligator weed

Equally happy in or out of the water, alligator weed blooms in summer.

- **Sun to part shade**
- **Zones 9 to 11**
- **Height: 2 to 6 inches**
- **Spread: floating runners**
- **Water depth: moist soil to 3 inches**

Alligator weed is a low-growing, tropical plant that provides cover and shade for fish. It trails on the water surface and clambers around the base of taller marginals, such as canna or umbrella grass.

Alligator weed leaves are small, rounded, and fleshy, and held on large stems. Small white powder-puff flowers nestle near the leaf base. This species can be a nuisance in warm climates.

Alligator weed grows equally well in or out of the water, but when submerged, it needs crystal clear water or it may rot. It is susceptible to spider mites and aphids.

Plants do not survive below-freezing weather, and overwinter best above 50°F. Grow them from seed or propagate them from stem cuttings, which quickly root in water.

Copperleaf *(A. reineckii)*, a related plant, has purple-red foliage accented by white summer flowers. It has an open habit that works in any size pond. It is best grown as a marginal; although it will tolerate deep water, it has a tendency to let go of the soil and root at the water surface.

BACOPA SPP.

Water hyssop

- Sun to shade
- Zones 6 to 11
- Height: 2 to 4 inches
- Spread: creeping
- Water depth: moist soil to 6 inches

These dainty, low-growing tropicals make excellent groundcovers in bog gardens and near the edge of ponds and trail nicely in a waterfall or a tabletop pond.

Foliage is usually small, rounded, and fleshy. Tiny flowers bloom in summer and range from white to blue, depending on the species. Leaves smell lemony when crushed.

Water hyssop grows year-round in warm climates. In cold areas, cut about 3 inches from several tips of the plant and place them in a cup of water in a warm, sunny room. They will root and grow during the winter. Replant them in a pot outdoors when all chances for freezing weather are past.

Water hyssop (*B. monnieri*), also called water purslane, has tiny, light green leaves and white summer flowers with faint pink stripes in the petals that look like ridges. It grows well submerged in clear water, but it does not produce flowers below the water surface.

Lemon bacopa (*B. caroliniana*) has large blue flowers as does variegated lemon bacopa (*B. lenagera*).

The pink stripes on the white blossoms of water hyssop are almost too faint to see.

BUTOMUS UMBELLATUS

Flowering rush

- Sun to part shade
- Zones 3 to 7
- Height: 3 to 4 feet
- Spread: 1 foot to 2 feet
- Flowers: Umbels 4 to 5 inches
- Water depth: moist soil to 3 inches

Though its foliage is unremarkable, the white, pink, or rose umbels of flowering rush add a bright sparkle to the spring and early-summer water garden. The tall, thin leaves blend in among other marginals, disguised until the flowers bloom.

Once the heat of summer arrives, flowering rush quits blooming or sometimes dies back altogether, but in cooler climates it may bloom again. Divide and re-pot the rhizomes after blooming has stopped. New plant growth will follow soon.

The plants are rampant growers and thus should be kept in pots when used in the pond or bog. Because of its invasive nature, some states prohibit the use of flowering rush in terrestrial gardens. Check with your state department of natural resources to be sure.

Stop fertilizing when the plants go dormant in the fall. Native to Europe and Asia, flowering rush is so cold-hardy that it can be left in the pond over winter.

Flowering rush thrives in damp flower beds as well as by the pond.

CALTHA PALUSTRIS

Marsh marigold

- Sun to part shade
- Zones 4 to 7
- Height: 12 to 18 inches
- Spread: 12 to 18 inches
- Water depth: moist soil to 1 inch

Favored by water gardeners because their bright yellow flowers open in early spring, marsh marigold has giant, lima-bean-shaped leaves that are dark green, glossy, and toothed. Blooms are usually single but sometimes double. Plants grow in mounded clumps in moist to wet boggy conditions. In cool climates they grow from spring through fall. In warm areas they may die back in the hot summer sun.

Overwinter marsh marigolds in cool conditions so they bloom well the following season. Propagate by dividing offsets in early spring or by seed, although seed requires cold, moist stratification before sowing on moist spring soil, and seeded offspring may not grow true to form.

Marsh marigold (*C. palustris*), also called cowslip, is the most widely grown of all the species. The plant has been used medicinally but is poisonous if eaten raw. *C. palustris* var. *palustris* (syn. *C. polypetala*) is more hardy and vigorous, and its flowers may be twice the size. It grows 18 to 24 inches tall with a 12- to 24-inch spread.

Marsh marigolds are among the earliest spring-blooming plants in a water garden.

CANNA SPP.

Water canna

Water cannas add color and vertical interest to the late-summer pond. Bring them indoors for winter.

- **Sun to part shade**
- **Zones 9 to 11**
- **Height: varies with cultivar**
- **Spread: 2 to 3 feet**
- **Water depth: moist soil to 10 to 12 inches**

True water cannas (C. *glauca* and C. *flaccida*) grow well in saturated soil with water over their crowns. They have attractive foliage and yellow blossoms. Other cannas are terrestrial but will adapt to waterlogged soil.

Growing several feet tall in a single season, cannas are topped by colorful flowers that start in midsummer and last until frost. Canna foliage is large, long, and tapered, ranging from bright green to blue-green, dark purple or crimson to striped in yellow, white, or red. Flowers also come in a wide variety of colors, from delicate creams and yellows to brassy oranges and reds with either large, overlapping petals or a more delicate narrow form.

Cannas cannot withstand a freeze. Bring them indoors for the winter; let the rhizomes dry out; then clean and store them. Canna rust may occur if the tubers are not cleaned well before storage.

Aphids and Japanese beetles will eat the foliage in summer. Propagate cannas by division.

CAREX SPP.

Sedge

The V- or M-shaped leaves give sedges a grassy appearance. This is 'Oheme' palm sedge.

- **Sun to shade**
- **Zones 4 to 11**
- **Height: 6 to 12 inches**
- **Spread: 6 to 12 inches**
- **Water depth: moist soil to 1 inch**

Sedges are grasslike plants with mounded tufts of foliage that will ornament any water feature—even a container planting. Several species are truly aquatic, and many prefer moist soil. Stems are triangular; leaves are V- or M-shaped, with a distinctive midrib rising from the clump and arching up and out.

Sedge meadows along the shores of lakes or ponds are an important part of wetland ecology. They fill in gradually as the shoreline recedes, replacing plants that grew when the waters were deeper. Most sedges can be propagated from seed or from rhizome division in early spring.

Blue sedge (C. *flacca*) is a worthy addition to the shade garden, although it also grows well in full sun. It makes a perfect companion to hostas. Inflated tassel sedge (C. *fascicularis*) has large puffy seed heads that resemble spiny cucumbers; they are attractive in dried arrangements. Palm sedge (C. *muskingumensis*) is easy to grow and forms a clump much like a hosta. It tolerates full shade yet also grows in full sun.

COLOCASIA ESCULENTA

Taro

In the pond or at the water's edge, taro produces large, eye-catching foliage in a variety of colors.

- **Sun to part shade**
- **Zones 9 to 11**
- **Height: 2 to 6 feet**
- **Spread: 2 to 4 feet**
- **Water depth: moist soil to 6 inches**

Bold and large-leaved, taro (also called elephant's ear) thrives on fertilizer and hot, humid weather. Ideal for container gardens as well as full-size ponds because of its eye-catching foliage and graceful habit, it produces larger leaves if it is protected from the afternoon sun. The petiole, or leaf stalk, comes in many beautiful colors, so locate the plants to show them off.

Overwinter plants indoors by keeping the pots in saucers of water in a warm, sunny room. Or let the plants dry out; then dig up the corms and store them until spring in coarse vermiculite in a sealed container or in a cool (but frost-free), dark spot. Transplanting every year will keep plants healthy.

Propagate from corms that are divided from the main plant, or from "hulis" (top or side sprouts).

'Black Magic' taro has very dark, black-purple leaves and stems. 'Metallica' is particularly elegant, with deep purple stems and large velvety blue-green leaves. 'Chicago Harlequin' has stems striped in purple and white and large leaves veined in purple.

CYPERUS SPP.

Cyperus

- Sun to part shade
- Zones 7 to 11
- Height: 2 to 12 feet
- Spread: 2 to 5 feet
- Water depth: varies with species

Related to the sedge family, cyperuses are tropical water plants grown for their sprays of ornamental leaf fronds, which resemble small paper umbrellas. The large heads are held high atop triangular stems sprouting from a central clump. "Flowers" are small and green and turn tawny brown as the seeds develop. There's a species of cyperus—from very large to very small—for every pond. Some have open grassy heads with thin wiry leaves. Others are dense, bushy, and full. Cyperuses shade shorter plants at the edge of the pond. Besides having ornamental value, they are excellent filtrators.

All species are heavy feeders, and should be fertilized at least once a month. Only a few species are hardy in cold regions, but plants will overwinter easily in a greenhouse. Although you may grow cyperus from division, umbrella grass is often propagated by cutting off the fronds just below the point where they join the stem. Trim the foliage to an inch and float the head in water. When it sprouts new stems and grows roots, you can plant it in a pot with soil. Cyperus also grows easily from seed sown on moist soil and kept warm until they sprout.

Umbrella grass (*C. alternifolius*) is the most commonly sold species. Its top leaf sprout can grow up to 2 feet in diameter in mature specimens, forming the characteristic umbrella shape for which the plant is named. Individual leaves are about half an inch wide and a foot or more in length. A quick grower, umbrella grass usually requires division every few years to keep the center from becoming woody and empty of foliage. New stems will grow from the outer edge of the base, creating a ring around the corky middle of the plant. Dwarf umbrella grass (*C. alternifolius* 'Nanus') is a compact plant that has long, umbrella-like fronds. It's hardy in Zones 9 to 11 and grows to 2 feet tall. It tolerates moist soil and up to 4 inches of water over its crown.

Papyrus (*C. papyrus*) and Mexican papyrus (*C. giganteus*) are favorites of many water gardeners. Papyrus is stunning, with its 10-inch ball of long green threads; Mexican papyrus has 20-inch spheres of wiry foliage on stiff, erect, nonarching stems. Both are hardy in Zones 8 to 11 and grow in moist soil to 12-inch-deep water. They grow 5 to 12 feet tall and spread 4 to 5 feet.

Dwarf umbrella grass displays small, green flowers that turn tawny brown in summer.

Papyrus has much finer texture than many of the other cyperuses.

DICHROMENA COLORATA

White-top sedge

- Sun to part shade
- Zones 8 to 11
- Height: 1 foot to 2 feet
- Spread: running
- Water depth: moist soil to 1 inch

The seed bracts of white-top sedge resemble 3-inch stars floating above grassy foliage. The flowers are actually small fuzzy things clustered in the center of white bracts. After a time, both the flowers and the surrounding spikes turn light brown, retaining their starlike appearance. They make excellent cut flowers in both fresh and dried arrangements.

White-top sedge has a running habit and is best confined to a pot. Division after a few years is recommended; the plant grows in a circle around the outer edge and in a few years the center of the pot will have several sprouts of new foliage. It requires no other special care or maintenance but appreciates monthly doses of fertilizer.

D. colorata is closely related to *D. latifolia*, and the two are often sold interchangeably at nurseries and garden centers. The white seed heads of *D. latifolia* are about one-third larger than those of *D. colorata*. Plants overwinter well indoors or in a sunny greenhouse. Propagate by division.

The star-shaped flowers of white-top sedge float above the plants. The petals are actually bracts.

EQUISETUM FLUVIATILE

Water horsetail

Horsetails offer a stiff, upright form rare among water plants. A dwarf species is also available.

- Sun to shade
- Zones 4 to 11
- Height: 2 feet tall
- Spread: running
- Water depth: moist soil to floating

Water horsetail has green stalks with large, black bands accented by thin pink bands. It branches freely and grows long thin side shoots that radiate from each main stem. There are roughly 30 species of *Equisetum* but only a few are truly aquatic, although several adapt well to wet soils. They are easily identified by their straight, hollow stems, which are grooved. Each joint is a distinct part of the stem and has a black band at its edge. Plants reproduce by spores borne on cones that grow atop each stem and so are classified as cryptogams, plants that bear no flowers or seeds.

Equisetum earned the common name horsetail because the stem resembles the tail of a horse. The plant's uptake of silica, which is deposited as silica crystals in the tissue, causes its stems to be hard and gritty. Because of this, the plants were much favored to scrub pots and pans and earned the name scouring rush from early pioneers.

Cold-tolerant, horsetail survives winter at the pond edge. It is usually propagated by division of its underground rhizomes in spring.

GLYCERIA MAXIMA VAR. VARIEGATA

Variegated manna grass

Like many ornamental grasses, variegated manna grass spreads freely and needs restraint.

- Sun to part shade
- Zones 4 to 11
- Height: 1 foot
- Spread: creeping
- Water depth: moist soil to 3 inches

Variegated manna grass is a rambling aquatic with 2-inch-wide leaves that are usually a foot or so in height. Its foliage is striped in creamy white and bright green. In spring and fall, when the weather is cool, the leaves take on a delightful pink tinge. The plant spreads freely and should be restrained in a pot. In earthen plantings, it should be placed next to a mowed edge, which will keep it in check.

Manna grass generally overwinters easily in the pond. It requires submersion under only enough water to cover the crown of the plant, with no need to move it deeper into the pond. Plants grow by underground rhizomes that are easily divided in spring.

Although the species is an important food source for wildlife, the plant is not ornamental, and for this reason only the variegated cultivar is commonly available at nurseries or garden centers.

Water hibiscus is a true aquatic, tolerating water 2 feet deep during seasonal floods.

HIBISCUS SPP.

Hibiscus

- Sun to part shade
- Zones 5 to 11
- Height: 4 to 6 feet
- Spread: 2 to 4 feet
- Water depth: moist soil to 6 inches

Hibiscus are large coarse-textured perennials that resemble shrubs. Flowers are brightly colored and often as large as a dinner plate.

Water hibiscus (*H. moscheutos palustris*) is a true aquatic, thriving in wet soil to flowing water. It branches freely and has pink flowers with a rose throat. It tolerates seasonal flooding up to 2 feet deep.

Swamp mallow (*H. moscheutos*) has stunning, 10- to 12-inch flowers in colors ranging from white through deep red. It is usually larger-flowering and bushier than water hibiscus but not as water-tolerant.

It dies back to the crown in winter and may be slow to appear in spring. The plant attracts butterflies and hummingbirds. New cultivars with stunning summer-long blooms include 'Copper King' (red cutleaf foliage and red or pink 12-inch-wide blooms) and 'Blue Danube' (large, pristine white flowers). *H. militaris* also tolerates wet soil. It is hardy to Zone 6 and warmer regions.

HOUTTUYNIA CORDATA 'CHAMELEON'

Houttuynia

- Sun to shade
- Zones 5 to 11
- Height: 6 to 8 inches
- Spread: running
- Water depth: moist soil to 1 inch

This lizard's tail relative is a rampant runner in moist soil with the potential to become invasive. Confine its roots in a pot or with some other barrier.

Plants have heart-shaped leaves that form a dense mat and have a spicy fragrance when crushed. In fall, they turn dark maroon-purple. 'Variegata' is similar but has green and white leaves without maroon.

White, single-petaled flowers appear in late summer. The green form of houttuynia flowers freely, starting in summer and continuing through early fall. Double-flowering 'Flore Pleno' houttuynia has small white blooms that resemble rosebuds.

Houttuynias are excellent groundcovers. Try them under the upright stalks of iris or butterfly weed *(Asclepias incarnata)*. They grow well in a bog or other wet spot. Don't let plants freeze; submerge them in the pond.

Versatile 'Chameleon' houttuynia grows in sun or shade, soil or water. Blooms have less punch than foliage.

HYDROCOTYLE SPP.

Water pennywort

- Sun to part shade
- Zones 7 to 11
- Height: 1 inch to 4 inches
- Spread: running
- Water depth: moist soil to 4 inches

Pennyworts are low-growing aquatics with round, often toothed leaves that are fleshy and shiny and stand up straight from running stems. They may be a ½ inch to 3 inches in diameter. Plants quickly shade the pond as they grow running stems that float out over the water surface, scrambling between plants and making a soft edge between water and taller plants. In a container, they spill over and trail downward from the pot edge. They are usually grown for their foliage; flowers are inconspicuous white tufts that often remain underneath the round umbrella-like leaves.

For tender species grown in cold climates, bring the stem cuttings indoors. They will root in warm water on a sunny windowsill. Cold-tolerant species overwinter well at the bottom of the pond.

Hairy pennywort *(H. americana)* is one of few pennyworts with noticeable white flowers, which rise above ½-inch to 1¾-inch foliage in white tufts. It trails freely and is an excellent plant for waterfalls or pond edges or in a tub garden or tabletop pond.

'Little Umbrellas' pennywort is aptly named, although other pennyworts have similar, nasturtium-like leaves.

HYGROPHILA SPP.

Hygrophila

- Sun to shade
- Zones 9 to 11
- Height: 1 foot to 3 feet tall
- Spread: 1 foot to 2 feet wide
- Water depth: moist soil to submerged

Most hygrophila have tiny blue snapdragon-like flowers. Their leaves are usually long and narrow, becoming wider toward the middle. Some plants have ruffled leaves. Many species are sold as aquarium plants, some of which are also suitable as marginal plants.

Dragon lantern *(H. stricta)* is an upright fast-grower with purple-tinted foliage in cool spring and fall weather. It is free-flowering and tiny blue flowers often cover plants near the main stem year-round.

Water wisteria *(H. difformis)* has mintlike foliage and tiny blue flowers that hang from trailing stems. Plants will grow submerged in water, in which case their foliage becomes finely cut and fernlike. 'Variegata' has strong white leaf veins. Both green and variegated selections are excellent plants for containers or small ponds, trailing over the edge of the pot and filling in empty spots among taller plants. Propagate plants by stem cuttings.

Dragon lanterns bloom in summer. Cool weather brings out a purple tint in the foliage.

IRIS SPP.

Iris

DEPENDING ON SPECIES:

- Sun to part shade
- Zones 3 to 9
- Height: 2 to 4 feet
- Spread: 1 foot to 2½ feet
- Water depth: moist soil to 3 to 6 inches

Different types of iris grow in and near the pond. True water irises include yellow flag (*I. pseudacorus*), blue flag (*I. virginica*), southern blue flag (*I. versicolor*), rabbit-ear iris (*I. laevigata*), and some Louisiana iris (*I. brevicaulis, I. fulva, I.* × *nelsonii*, and others). These species grow best with water over their crowns throughout the year, even in fall and winter. Others, such as Japanese iris (*I. ensata*), Siberian iris (*I. sibirica*), and Rocky Mountain iris (*I. missouriensis*) tolerate wet soil for part of the growing season but prefer drier conditions.

Yellow flag irises are among the first marginal plants to bloom in the spring. They grow to 4 feet tall.

Rabbit-ear irises are the native plants often found growing along streams. Flower petals are small and upright.

The upright portion of an iris is called the standard, and the lower petal is called a beard or fall.

True water irises grow with water over their crowns. Plant irises of unknown heritage in shallow water.

COLORS: Iris was the Greek goddess of the rainbow. In keeping with their namesake, irises bloom in spring in colors spanning the spectrum from white to deep blue and dark purple. Some are deeply veined or marked with yellow toward the center of the petals. The flowers generally rise above the leaves of the plant, often appearing to float on water. The upright portion of the bloom is called the standard, and the lower part the beard or fall.

CARE: Water garden irises need minimal attention through the summer but are subject to a few maladies, such as thrips and root knot. Shelter them from wind and hot afternoon sun, and fertilize them monthly while they are growing. Plant and transplant them immediately after they have finished flowering. Mulch them heavily in late summer to withstand the winter cold. Propagate irises by division, or grow from seed after six weeks of cold, moist dormancy.

Tall marginals such as irises add vertical interest to the water garden, drawing the eye up and away from an expanse of nearly flat surface. Irises come in a variety of colors.

IRIS
continued

Louisiana irises grow well even as far north as Canada. They are smaller than other irises and offer the most distinctive red, yellow, and brown blooms of all iris species.

HYBRIDS: Despite their name, modern hybrids of Louisiana irises grow well in almost any climate. Look for those with *I. brevicaulis* in their ancestry, as they are most likely to be cold-hardy. Water depth needed is dependent on heritage, too; if you don't know what type you have, plant the rhizome just below the water's surface to be safe.

Louisiana irises are rampant growers and so should be potted when used in the pond. Their spectacular flowers, which come in a wide variety of colors, bloom best in full sun. 'Sinfonietta', a tall easy-to-grow hybrid, has medium-blue flowers with yellow signals. Another strong performer is 'Dorothea K. Williamson', with deep purple flowers. *I. fulva* cultivars bloom in shades of yellow, red, and copper.

Yellow flag iris owes its name to its bright yellow early-spring flowers. Growing as tall as 4 feet, it is suitable for larger ponds. 'Sulphur Queen' has pale yellow flowers, while 'Golden Queen' is a richer hue. 'Berlin Tiger' is yellow veined with brown. Both blue flag and southern blue flag have light blue flowers in mid-spring, and their blue-green sword-shaped leaves take on a dark red stain from the base to the tips. *I. versicolor* cultivars include 'Candystriper', with white flowers veined in red, and "Pink Peaks', a short variety with dark reddish-purple-veined dark pink flowers. If you live in a northern clime, try *I. virginica* cultivars 'Pond Lilac Dream', with lavender-pink blooms and creamy-yellow signals, or 'Dottie's Double', a double-petaled type with lavender veins.

Use Japanese irises outside the pond in the moist soil they prefer.

Keep Louisiana irises in pots if you use them in a pond. They are strong, rampant growers that can quickly outcompete their less vigorous neighbors.

Siberian irises grow best in moist soil with no water over their crowns. Use them in a bog garden or plant them in soggy areas of a perennial bed, but not directly in the pond.

Siberian irises (*I. sibirica*) work well in the bog garden or in moist areas of the perennial garden—close to but not submerged in water—and do best in full sun. The plants are hardy in many climates and their flowers bloom in late spring or early summer. Cultivars are available in white and yellow but most types bear two or three dark-veined purple flowers on each stem. 'Coronation Anthem' is indigo blue, shading to white toward the center. 'Shaker's Prayer' is soft periwinkle-blue freckled with white. Siberian irises grow 2 to 3 feet tall and about 1 foot across.

All irises grow best if planted in full sun. Although most Siberian cultivars bloom purple, those with light- or white-colored flowers benefit from afternoon shade that protects their blossoms from drying out.

Rabbit-ear irises have short rounded upright petals on white, elegant blue, or royal reddish-purple blooms. In areas with cool summers, they usually reach only 12 to 18 inches tall. Also called Japanese water iris, *I. laevigata* is the original native plant often seen in masses on stream banks. Its flowers may be smaller than those of its more terrestrial Japanese iris cousin. (*I. ensata* can also be distinguished by distinct midribs along its leaves.) Rabbit-ear irises have flowers 6 inches or more in diameter held above the foliage. They may be single, double, or multiple-petaled. Colors range from deep, velvety purple to the cleanest white. Generally, blooms are flat and petals hang downward. 'Colchesterensis' has white flowers mottled in blue; 'Regal' is magenta. 'Variegata' is prized for its white-striped foliage. The flowers are blue.

JUNCUS SPP.

Rush

- Sun to part shade
- Zones 4 to 9
- Height: 2 to 3 feet
- Spread: 2 feet
- Water depth: moist soil to 4 inches

Although rushes are grown for their stems, leave the brown flower heads on the plants for winter interest.

'Gold Strike' (left) and other upright rushes are favorites of dragonflies, who hide within the foliage while immature.

Many rushes have strong, upright foliage, which provides a useful background for other pondside plants with either a bolder or more delicate nature. Most rushes are noted for their long spiked stems, which are usually dark green but can be light blue. Foliage is stiff and hollow. Flowers appear as brown tassels that droop from near or at the tip of the leaves.

In many climates rushes are evergreen. They should occasionally be cut back to the ground to remove older, tattered growth. Plants may be grown in the perennial border as long as they are given adequate moisture.

Rush plants provide important shelter for fish, fowl, and insects. Stands of rush are useful in earth-bottom ponds, providing spawning ground for bluegills and sunnies. Dragonfly larvae often use the upright leaves to climb out of the water, clinging to the stiff foliage for camouflage while they metamorphose into adult dragonflies.

Most rushes are cold-tolerant and may be overwintered in the pond. Bring tender species such as Australian silver rush *(J. polyanthemos)* indoors and treat them as houseplants.

Rushes grow from underground rhizomes that are linked by stolons and are easily divided.

Soft rush *(J. effusus)* has stiff spines of green foliage. It often retains its color all year, even in cold climates. Corkscrew rush *(J. effusus* 'Spiralis') has tightly coiled foliage, which is excellent in fresh or dried floral arrangements. It is almost evergreen, even in cold climates. 'Gold Strike' has dark green leaves accented with gold stripes along their length. Both plants are hardy to Zone 3.

Blue rush *(J. inflexas)* has baby blue foliage that resembles that of blue fescue. It grows in full sun and takes moist soil to 2-inch-deep water. It is hardy to Zone 4.

The coiled foliage of corkscrew rush is evergreen in all climates. It is often used as an accent in floral arrangements.

JUSTICIA AMERICANA

Water willow

- Sun to part shade
- Zones 4 to 11
- Height: 1½ feet
- Spread: 1 foot
- Water depth: moist soil to 10 inches

A hardy relative to the shrimp plant, water willow produces masses of 1-inch clusters of white to pink flowers. The foliage is narrow, like willow leaves. Plants are shrubby.

Water willow grows about 18 inches tall in moist soil or in several inches of water. It also tolerates running water. It is useful in earth-bottom ponds and for erosion control.

Divide water willow rhizomes in early spring before new growth appears. Plants are also easy to propagate from stem cuttings.

For large ponds, water willow creates an edge that holds the soil, yet is so open that fishing lures will not snag or become hung up in it. Planted at the edge of the pond, it also helps to deter waterfowl, keeping them from wading into the water. Because water willow tolerates some disturbance and trimming, it can be grown around boat docks and landings and other wet recreation areas.

Water willows have white to pink blooms in summer on a versatile, easy-to-grow plant.

LOBELIA SPP.

Lobelia

- Sun to part shade
- Zones 5 to 11
- Height: 6 to 60 inches, depending on species
- Spread: 12 inches
- Water depth: moist soil

A favorite for the bog and perennial garden, lobelias are cherished for their brilliant flowers, which appear in late summer through fall. Their flowers, which have divided petals with two tips pointing upward and three downward, somewhat like a split-petaled snapdragon, attract butterflies and hummingbirds. Flower colors vary from bright red or bright blue through crimson and purple. Some have purple or dark red foliage. Plants do not usually branch; each stem grows from a separate crown.

Two of the most common lobelias are cardinal flower *(L. cardinalis)* and great blue lobelia *(L. siphilitica)*. Cardinal flower has bright crimson flowers July through September on 3-foot-tall stems. Great blue lobelia is similar to cardinal flower in form and habit, with bright blue blossoms July through October.

It is best to place plants deep in the pond for the winter or mulch them in a perennial bed. Lobelia is easily propagated by division in spring. Cardinal flower and great blue lobelia may also be propagated by floating mature stems in water; plantlets sprout at leaf nodes.

Late-blooming cardinal flower adds a bright splash of color to moist sites near ponds or in gardens.

LUDWIGIA SPP.

Ludwigia

- Sun to part shade
- Zones 6 to 11, depending on species
- 6 to 96 inches, depending on species
- Spread: trailing to 24 inches
- Water depth: moist soil to floating

Ludwigias range in size from huge (over 8 feet tall) to tiny (less than 6 inches tall). Leaves are usually rounded, toothed, and shiny. Flowers are mostly yellow, single, flat, and four-petaled. Often they form pneumatophores—spongy white spikes at the base of the stem that help plants absorb oxygen from water. Frost-tender species are best overwintered as houseplants in cold climates or as stem cuttings grown on a warm, sunny windowsill in a vase of water.

Primrose creeper *(L. arcuata)* is a good pond cover, creating an unusual visual effect in the water garden. As it floats out over the water, it holds the last 6 inches of its foliage straight up from the water surface. Flowers are bright yellow and about an inch wide.

Red ludwigia *(L. repens)*, a creeping form, has bright green leaves on red stems. This small plant is ideal near a waterfall or as groundcover at the edge of a pond or bog.

Primrose creeper is a short ludwigia that spreads to 2 feet wide. Its yellow flowers appear in summer.

MARSILEA SPP.

Water clover

- Sun to shade
- Zones 5 to 11, depending on species
- Height: ¼ inch to 6 inches, depending on species
- Spread: running
- Water depth: moist soil to 4 inches

Mimicking a four-leaf clover, floating water clover is actually a fern.

The distinct notch in the leaflets helps separate cutleaf water clover from other species.

Water clovers are the lucky charms of the pond. Their four-leaf, clover-shaped foliage belies the fact that they are really ferns, which reproduce by spores.

The plants are easy to grow and not particularly heavy feeders, so fertilize sparingly. They prefer shallow water that is rather still, and they are perfect for small ponds. Water clovers are not difficult to overwinter in cold climates, provided they do not freeze solid. Place them toward the bottom of the pond with other frost-intolerant aquatic plants such as hardy water lilies and lotuses.

Most species have foliage that emerges above the water surface; the leaves of one species float on the water. The emerged leaves open in the morning; when they close at night, they look like small butterflies at rest. All species have four lobes to each leaf. Some species have hairy leaves, others smooth.

In very cold climates, overwinter water clovers by bringing plants indoors and keeping them as houseplants. They are easily propagated from stem cuttings.

Floating water clover (*M. mutica)* has shiny waxy-looking leaves that grow from small clublike spore-bearing structures. Not a heavy feeder, it does best in still water and is grown easily from root cuttings. Plant it when the water temperature reaches 60° to 65°F. When crowded, it will send up leaves that stand 3 inches out of the water. Until then, the leaves float on the surface. In cold climates, bring it indoors and keep it in a bowl of water near a warm, sunny window. The cultivar 'Micro Mini' has dense leaves about the size of a dime that float on the water surface or rise slightly above the water. It is ideal for container water gardens.

The 1-inch-wide leaflets of butterfly water clover have wavy edges. Leaves open and close daily.

Hairy water clover (*M. drummondii)* has silvery cloverlike foliagethat is accented by brown stems. The leaves look like resting butterflies. It grows to 6 inches tall in moist soil to 1-inch-deep water.

Upright water clover (*M. quadrifolia)* has very upright, triangular leaves. It is good to grow near waterfalls and for giving small fish a place to hide. It is a rampant grower, hardy to Zone 5.

Butterfly water clover (*M. rotundifolia)* is covered in 1-inch leaves that open and close daily. Hardy to Zone 8, it grows to 6 inches tall in moist soil to 6-inch-deep water.

Cutleaf water clover (*M. schelpiana)*, has lacy, delicate, irregularly cut foliage. Hardy to Zone 6, it grows to 6 inches tall in moist soil to 6-inch-deep water.

MENTHA SPP.

Water Mint

- Sun to part shade
- Zones 5 to 11
- Height: 3 to 12 inches
- Spread: running
- Water depth: moist soil to 2 inches

Many mint species are highly fragrant and have long been used for their aromatic qualities. Several species are tolerant of wet soils, even those usually grown in the perennial border, such as spearmint. Mint has attractive, evenly green, lance-shaped leaves, which are often hairy, especially on the bottom. Flowers are clustered balls of tiny blue or pink flowers, appearing in midsummer and continuing through fall. Because of their running habit, mints should be kept in containers. They tolerate freezing temperatures and require no special care in cold climates. Water mint is easy to propagate, especially from stem cuttings or by division.

Aquatic mint (M. *aquatica*) is always a favorite with water gardeners. It is highly fragrant, flowers well, and attracts butterflies. The foliage is scented and can be used in teas and jellies.

Brook mint (M. *pulegium*), a ½-inch-tall version of aquatic mint, has airy, dainty flowers of sky blue. It is just as fragrant as other mints and attracts butterflies. It's perfect growing among rocks or in a bog.

Most mint species are tolerant of wet soils and freezing temperatures. They are easy to grow and divide.

MENYANTHES TRIFOLIATA

Bog bean (water trefoil)

- Part shade
- Zones 2 to 7
- Height: 6 to 12 inches
- Spread: creeping habit
- Water depth: moist soil to 3 inches

Perfect for container gardens and shady ponds, bog bean's fragant white flowers bloom in May through July on stalks held several inches above the dense foliage. Its soft three-lobed leaves grow from a creeping rhizome that floats along the water surface. The leaves have such a bitter taste that insects don't bother them.

Look for it by many common names, including moon flower, bog myrtle, water shamrock, buck bean, and marsh clover.

Although it tolerates full sun, bog bean is susceptible to burning, especially on hot summer days. Plants grow best in areas that receive some shade from the sun's late-afternoon rays. Bog bean can freeze solid during winter as long as it is in water. Propagate by dividing rootstock, or sow ripe seed after soaking it in refrigerated water for two months.

Perfect for shady ponds and container gardens, vanilla-scented bog bean is cold-hardy in water, insect-proof, and easy to propagate. Look for it by many common names.

MIMULUS SPP.

Monkey flower

- Part to full shade
- Zones 5 to 11
- Height: 12 to 36 inches
- Spread: 12 to 20 inches, depending on species
- Water depth: moist soil to 6 inches

Monkey flowers are best known for their tubular flowers, which resemble open snapdragons. They range in color from blue to lavender or purple or occasionally white and yellow. Although they grow adequately in full sun, they prefer part shade, where they grow taller and stay greener. Deadheading encourages more blooms and stretches their growing season.

Plants winter well in cold climates. Propagate by division or collect and sow the seed.

Sharp-winged monkey flower (M. *alatus)* has stalked leaves and winged stems. Flowers are usually lavender, but there is a rare white-flowering form, 'Snow Crystal'.

Lavender monkey flower (M. *ringens)* has profuse lavender flowers peeking out from between shiny jade-green leaves that are oblong, unstalked, and toothed.

Yellow monkey flower (M. *guttatus*), with yellow blooms, is not as cold-tolerant as other species.

Red monkey flower ('Lothian Fire') has bold, bright red trumpets with yellow throats.

Monkey flowers will grow taller and more verdant if planted in shade. Their blooms resemble snapdragons.

MYOSOTIS SCORPIOIDES

Forget-me-not

Forget-me-nots, with their small blue blossoms, like cool climates. Flowers have white, pink, or yellow eyes.

- **Sun to part shade**
- **Zones 5 to 9**
- **Height: 6 to 8 inches**
- **Spread: 12 inches**
- **Water depth: moving, such as streams**

This front-of-the-pond marginal rings in early summer with sprays of white, light blue, or bright blue flowers resembling small single roses. Plants have small, somewhat hairy, oblong green leaves. They form a dense mat that also grows well in a stream or waterfall.

Forget-me-nots often flower intermittently throughout the summer as long as it's cool. In warm humid climates, plants wither and leaves may turn dark. Trim wilted leaves; the plants will perk up when cooler days return. In southern climates, forget-me-nots are best grown as a winter annual.

It is difficult to distinguish the forget-me-nots that grow in water gardens from those that prefer dry land. If it grows in the pond, it is the aquatic form; if it withers and starts to die in the pond, it belongs in the perennial bed.

'Mermaid' has large blue flowers dotted with white eyes. 'Pinkie' forms a creeping cushion of cotton-candy-pink flowers. The crystal white flowers of 'Snowflakes' open in spring and continue blooming through summer.

MYRIOPHYLLUM AQUATICUM

Parrot's feather

Although similar to foxtail, parrot's feather grows only 6 inches tall and has denser foliage.

- **Sun to part shade**
- **Zones 6 to 11**
- **Height: 6 inches**
- **Spread: running**
- **Water depth: moist soil to floating**

Parrot's feather has whorls of feathery foliage that floats out over the water surface at the edge of the pond. Whorls may be 3 inches or more in diameter, growing on long trailing stems. Although some reference books list this species as a submerged oxygenating plant, foxtail (*M. heterophyllum* and *M. hippuroides*) and several other species are the ones that grow underwater.

Because parrot's feather grows rampantly, it has earned a place on the prohibited noxious weed list in some states. Before buying plants, check with authorities to ensure that it is allowed in your state, especially if you live in a warm climate. In climates where frost occurs, there is less chance of it escaping from your water garden and becoming a nuisance.

The plant may survive a winter freeze if submerged beneath the water, but it is not reliably hardy in cold areas. To ensure survival, overwinter parrot's feather by bringing stem cuttings indoors.

OENANTHE SPP.

Water parsley

'Flamingo' water parsley is nearly as colorful as houttuynia, but it grows much taller.

- **Sun to part or full shade, depending on species**
- **Zones 5 to 11**
- **Height: 6 to 12 inches, depending on species**
- **Spread: varies**
- **Water depth: varies**

Water parsley has finely cut foliage resembling leaves of celery or parsley. Leaves are aromatic and edible, having a peppery flavor suitable for salads and stuffings. Foliage grows from running stems that root quickly at the leaf nodes. Flowers are umbels of small white starlike blossoms appearing summer through fall. The plants are excellent for filtration, taking up nutrients that would otherwise contribute to algae. Water parsley winters easily in cold climates and withstands freezing.

Rainbow water parsley (*O. javanica* 'Flamingo') has pink, white, and green frilly foliage that resembles compact carrot tops. It grows well along the edge of the pond, stream, or waterfall or in a large container water garden. This cultivar exhibits a running spread and grows in moist soil or floats.

Common water parsley (*O. sarmentosa*), with its lush green foliage, provides an excellent foil to larger, more full-leaved plants. It grows rapidly and can cover a small pond in a single summer.

PENTHORUM SEDOIDES

Virginia stonecrop

- Sun to part shade
- Zones 4 to 11
- Height: 10 to 18 inches
- Spread: 10 inches
- Water depth: moist soil to 3 inches

In autumn, when many plants are going dormant, stonecrop's dramatic display is just beginning. A relative of sedums, this plant lacks the fleshy stems and leaves of its cousins. Instead, it is recognized by its unusual seed heads, clustered together like five-pointed stars. The petals are almost too small to see. As the seed heads mature toward autumn, their color changes from white or pale green to pale pink and then deep cherry red, and the star shapes become more visible. The stems develop a coppery color, and the leaves turn yellow, making the entire plant a vivid standout.

Stonecrop is not a target of pests. Its colors develop best in full sun, but it tolerates some shade. Unlike many other seed-producing marginals, stonecrop will not overrun the garden; in fact, it needs some protection from more vigorous plants. Best propagated by division.

Unusual star-shaped seed heads that change color as they mature make stonecrop eyecatching in the autumn water garden.

PHYLA LANCEOLATA

Frog fruit

- Sun to part shade
- Zones 5 to 11
- Height: 2 inches
- Spread: trailing
- Water depth: moist soil to 4 inches

An ideal groundcover for a wet spot in the yard or for a rocky margin at the edge of the pond, frog fruit tolerates some foot traffic and may even be mowed. It has small lance-shaped leaves that are toothed and an even green color. In fall, foliage turns a wonderful crimson.

Starting in early summer and lasting through fall, the plant is covered in tiny white flowers that resemble those of verbena. As the flowers mature, they change to yellow and then pink.

Plants overwinter well in northern climates without special care or attention. Leave them in the pond or along the water's edge. Propagate plants from stem cuttings.

Frog fruit adapts well to many conditions. In a container or tabletop pond, it will spill over the edge or tuck itself between more upright stems of other marginals. It's an excellent groundcover in a bog. In an earthen pond, frog fruit helps to control soil erosion around docks and boat landings. Regardless of its environment, it always attracts butterflies and skippers, which relish its sweet nectar.

An adaptable addition to any size feature, frog fruit bears white flowers and deep red fall foliage.

PONTEDERIA CORDATA

Pickerel weed

- Sun to part shade
- Zones 5 to 11
- Height: 24 to 30 inches
- Spread: 12 to 18 inches
- Water depth: moist soil to 10 inches

Pickerel weed, also called pickerel plant and pickerel rush, is favored for its shiny heart-shaped leaves and striking blue or white flowers in summer. It has a compact habit and a rhizome that grows like an iris near the soil surface. It has excellent filtration abilities.

The species has shiny jade-green heart-shaped foliage and large blue flower spikes. 'Alba' has flowers that are white rather than blue and tinged in pink. 'Pink Pons' has lavender-pink flowers. The flowers attract butterflies, skippers, and hummingbirds. Dragonfly and damselfly nymphs use the upright stems as safe perches above the moving water.

For optimum winter tolerance, buy plants that have been grown for the climate in which you will raise them. Plants overwinter best in cold climates if rootstocks are protected from freezing. Place rootstocks well below the frost line of the pond or remove plants and store them in cold, damp quarters until spring. Propagate pickerel weed by dividing rootstocks in spring. It may also be grown from seed but requires a period of cold, wet dormancy.

'Crown Point' pickerel weed grows to about half the size of standard pickerel weeds.

RUELLIA BRITTONIANA

Water bluebell

'Katie' is a dwarf bluebell. Look for named selections to ensure uniform flower color and plant size.

- **Sun to part shade**
- **Zones 9 to 11**
- **Height: 10 inches to 4 feet**
- **Spread: 1 foot**
- **Water depth: moist soil to 6 inches**

Ruellia that grow in wet soil are often sought by water gardeners. They are most noted for their large, petunia-like flowers that appear year-round in the tropical climates they prefer.

In cold climates, the foliage often turns dark purple when night temperatures cool. Because plants do not withstand cold temperatures, they must be wintered indoors as houseplants.

The species is a favorite; it is easy to grow and is covered with 1- to 2-inch lavender-blue flowers. 'Chi Chi' is a delightful pink variation with foliage that turns burgundy in fall. 'Katie' is a dwarf water bluebell with blue flowers that nestle tightly against the stems. It is compact, usually reaching no more than 10 inches or so in height, but its flowers are the same size as those of the standard water bluebell. 'Strawberries and Cream' is a new cultivar with variegated leaves speckled in cream, pink, white, and green. Flowers are soft purplish blue. Plants grow to 10 inches tall. Propagate them from stem cuttings and from seed.

SAGITTARIA SPP.

Arrowhead

Arrowhead earns its name from its distinct leaf shape. The summer-blooming plants are easy to grow.

- **Sun to part shade**
- **Zones 3 to 11**
- **Height: 3 to 24 inches**
- **Spread: running**
- **Water depth: moist soil to 2 inches**

Arrowheads contribute to the water garden landscape with their clean, geometric foliage and delicate white flowers. Named for their arrow-shaped leaves, arrowheads are highly ornamental at the pond edge and very easy to grow.

Foliage may be broad or narrow, depending upon the species; some have lobed leaves. Flowers are single, white, and held on a long stalk that rises from the center of the plant, appearing first in June and recurring through the summer.

Ruby-eye arrowhead, or giant arrowhead (*S. montevidensis*), has red dots at the base of each petal. It is 2 feet tall (Zone 8). Common arrowhead (*S. sagittifolia*) grows to 18 inches (Zone 3). Lance-leaved arrowhead (*S. lancifolia*) has yellow-centered blooms and grows to 2 feet (Zone 8). Red-stemmed arrowhead (*S. l. ruminoides*) has burgundy stems. 'Crushed Ice' (*S. graminea*) has white-variegated leaves. It does best with afternoon shade and grows to 1 foot tall (Zone 5). 'Bloom'n Baby' is a dwarf free-flowering arrowhead that starts to bloom when the plant is only 3 inches tall.

SARRACENIA SPP.

Pitcher plants

Pitchers are grown for their tubular leaves, but their dangling blooms are also exotic.

Depending on species:

- **Zones 3 to 11**
- **Sun to part shade**
- **Height: prostrate to 3 feet**
- **Water depth: continuously moist to 1 inch over the crown**

Although many pitcher plants are native to the southeastern United States, they will thrive in most zones—a few even as far north as Canada—and in poor soils with few available nutrients. To get the trace minerals they need to grow, these insectivores trap prey in their long, hairy tubular leaves to digest them.

Pitcher plants are slow to propagate. They are cultivated for their spectacular leaves, or pitchers, but their flowers are just as lovely, blooming just before the leaves begin to appear. They dangle face-down on their stems like paper lampshades, sometimes changing from creamy yellow to pink or red.

Pitchers do best in soft water and light continuously moist acidic soil. *S. purpurea*, the purple pitcher plant, grows in the widest range of climates. Its red-veined green leaves lie along the ground with the mouths turned upward. Flowers are white, pink, or red. *S. psittacina*, parrot pitcher plant, is the most water-tolerant. Its light green pitchers also repose on the ground, and its flowers are lightly fragrant.

SAURURUS SPP.

Lizard's tail

- Sun to part shade
- Zones 4 to 11
- Height: 1 foot to 3 feet
- Spread: running
- Water depth: moist soil to 6 inches

Lizard's tail species are known for their heart-shaped leaves that appear on tall stems growing from creeping rhizomes. The plant forms dense colonies of upright stems topped with drooping spikes of white flowers. Both the flowers and the stems are aromatic, with a fragrance similar to vanilla.

Although lizard's tails will withstand frost, they cannot tolerate being frozen in the pond. They must be placed so that their underground rhizomes won't freeze during winter. They grow well from stem cuttings or rootstock divisions.

Common lizard's tail (*S. cernuus*) is well-suited to the water garden, providing a tall backdrop for smaller plants. Its white flowers last from June through frost and return year after year. *S. cernuus ruminoides* has red stems.

Chinese lizard's tail (*S. chinensis*) has a white splotch on the topmost leaf, making the plant ornamental even when it is not in flower.

The goose-neck blooms of common lizard's tail last all summer. A vanilla-like fragrance comes from the stems as well as the flowers.

SCIRPUS SPP.

Rush

- Sun to part shade
- Zones 3 to 9
- Height: 2 to 6 feet
- Spread: running
- Water depth: moist soil to 6 inches

Rushes are excellent for shoreline stabilization in a natural pond or stream. They provide important cover for wildlife, such as birds, fish, and amphibians, as well as nesting grounds for wildlife.

Foliage is thin, narrow, and tall; flowers are brown clubs or plumes that appear in mid- to late summer. Many species are cold-tolerant and will survive a winter freeze. Most commonly propagated by division, rushes may be grown from seed.

Woolly rush (*S. cyperinus*) is distinguished by its fluffy silken tassels of tawny brown at the end of stiff dark green foliage. The plant forms a dense clump and does not run, unlike other species.

Giant nut grass (*S. fluviatilis*) boasts tall parasols of emerald green foliage. It grows 2 to 4 feet tall and does best in full sun. Zebra rush (*S. zebrinus* syn. *Schoenoplectus lacustris tabermaemontani* 'Zebrinus') is ornamental from spring through fall with white bands or markings every few inches along its tall green leaves. The white bands are more pronounced in cool weather or when the plant is actively growing.

Prized for its grassy growing habit, rush is grown more for its foliage than its flowers.

SIUM SUAVE

Water parsnip

- Sun to part shade
- Zones 4 to 11
- Height: 3 to 4 feet
- Spread: 2 feet
- Water depth: moist soil to 6 inches

Just when the pond begins to thaw in spring, the frilly first set of water parsnip's leaves start to grow. In a few weeks, the plant will form a low dense clump of feathery foliage similar to celery leaves, and from that the flower stalks will shoot up out of the water. The small white flowers—which look much like Queen Anne's lace—appear in broad umbels beginning in July and continue to bloom through September. Their strong fragrance attracts butterflies, especially swallowtails and hairstreaks.

Both leaves and flowers turn light brown in autumn but remain upright in the pond, even through winter. Water parsnip is in the same family as parsley and carrots, and has fibrous roots similar to its terrestrial parsnip cousin. However, it is also related to the highly toxic water hemlock, with which it can be confused. It is therefore best left in the pond and out of the kitchen. Propagate by seed or division.

The strong fragrance of water parsnip's white umbels attracts butterflies. Leaves and flowers turn brown but stay upright in autumn.

STACHYS PALUSTRIS

Marsh betony

Related to mint, marsh betony has dark green foliage and pink flowers.

- **Sun to shade**
- **Zones 4 to 8**
- **Height: 6 to 24 inches**
- **Spread: running**
- **Water depth: moist soil to 5 inches**

Prized by herbalists during the Middle Ages, marsh betony is now finding popularity among water gardeners. You may be familiar with this plant's close relative, lamb's ears. Marsh betony is much different. It has thick spikes of pink or purple flowers resembling those of snapdragons or penstemons.

Plants bloom throughout the summer into fall and are a welcome substitute for purple loosestrife *(Lythrum* spp.), a noxious prohibited weed that chokes out wetlands.

Marsh betony has hairy lance-shaped leaves with serrated edges. Bright green in summer, the foliage turns bright yellow in fall, adding interest to the pond even after flowers have faded.

Propagation is easy. Divide a clump in early spring when it first starts to sprout. You can also propagate plants by stem cuttings, which root easily. Perfectly winter-hardy, marsh betony requires no special care or treatment to survive freezing weather.

THALIA SPP.

Thalia

The flowers of thalia rise high above the leaves on long, arching stalks. It is grown primarily for its foliage.

- **Sun to part shade**
- **Zones 5 to 11**
- **Height: 2 to 9 feet**
- **Spread: 3 feet**
- **Water depth: moist soil to 12 inches**

Thalia (also called alligator flag) is grown primarily for its striking lush foliage. Leaves can reach 3 feet wide and over 3 feet long. Flowers are unusual silvery purple beads that droop from long arching stems.

Purple thalia *(T. dealbata)* overwinters in cold climates without protection. Alligator flag *(T. geniculata)* is more tender and will not survive frost. Bring it indoors for the winter. Thalias are propagated most readily by rootstock division.

'Blue Cup Leaf Form' purple thalia has blue leaves that are more cup-shaped than others. 'Broad Leafed Form' has flat leaves that are triangular. The foliage looks tropical and has a slight powdery blue color.

Alligator flag derives its name from the fact that the plant sways like a flag in the presence of alligators. As the gator swims through the glade, the current it creates rustles the plant, causing the leaves to swing back and forth. Foliage is more yellow-green than the hardy forms of thalia, and the plants grow 2 to 9 feet tall.

TYPHA SPP.

Cattail

Cattail's foliage offers a vertical focus in the water garden as well as a nesting place for many wild birds.

- **Sun to part shade**
- **Zones 3 to 11**
- **Height: varies**
- **Spread: running**
- **Water depth: moist soil to 4 inches**

Cattails grow in freshwater marshes and colonize wide areas with their stiff running rhizomes. They thrive in water over their crown and provide habitat for amphibians and fish. Their grasslike foliage serves as a nesting place for many species of wild birds, and their roots are often eaten by muskrats.

The leaves of cattails are 1⁄16 inch to 2 inches wide. They are generally flat on one side and more rounded on the other. Flowers are long catkins that turn brown as they mature, releasing downy seeds. There are also giant and dwarf forms; plant height can range from 6 inches to more than 12 feet.

Plants overwinter well in cool water and withstand freezing temperatures. Propagate by division or grow from seed.

Common cattail *(T. latifolia)* is the standard cattail seen in ditches and wetlands. It is excellent for water filtration. Graceful cattail *(T. angustifolia)* is narrow-leaved with foliage that arches and sways gracefully. Very elegant, it's suitable for most ponds and large container water gardens.

COMPANION PLANTS

AQUILEGIA SPP.

Columbine

- **Sun to part shade**
- **Zones 3 to 9**
- **Height: 1 to 3 feet**
- **Blooms: all colors; April to June**
- **Water depth: moist, well-drained soil**

Columbine's colorful, nodding flowers are held on upright stems above blue-green foliage. The blossoms are eye-catching, with hybrids offering single-, double-, and even tricolored flowers with long spurs. The plants are short-lived but self-sow easily. They will take root almost anywhere, even in pavement cracks, but are easily transplanted. They tolerate full sun but not hot temperatures.

A. candensis is a native North American wildflower that grows up to 3 feet tall and has large red and yellow flowers. *A. vulgaris*, European columbine, has smaller blue, purple, red, or pink flowers on plants about 2 feet tall. 'McKana' hybrids feature large vividly bicolored flowers with extra-long spurs. 'Music' series hybrids come in softer combinations. Leaf miners may cause damage; if so, cut the foliage to the ground and discard it. New leaves will develop. The foliage provides an attractive groundcover when blooming ends.

Columbine is easy to grow in almost any location. The flowers bloom in spring before the weather gets hot.

ASCLEPIAS SPP.

Butterfly weed

- **Full sun**
- **Zones 3 to 9**
- **Height: 2 feet**
- **Blooms: white, orange, red, purple; July to frost**
- **Water depth: moist, well-drained soil**

A relative of the common milkweed vine, butterfly weed is true to its name, producing nectar on its colorful blooms that attracts butterflies and also bees and hummingbirds. Unlike its invasive milkweed cousin, butterfly weed does not produce sticky sap. Instead it releases fragrance in the evening to attract moths and other pollinators. *A. incarnata* cultivars, such as 'Ice Ballet', can grow in water and are often called swamp milkweed. *A. tuberosa* types tolerate moist soil. *A. purpurascens* has purple flowers. *A. curassavica*, an orangey-red tropical hybrid, prefers standing water or continuously moist soil. The plants are cultivated as mounding shrubs.

Asclepias need no fertilizer or maintenance and are drought-tolerant. They die back in winter and re-sprout in spring from underground tubers. All parts of the plant are toxic.

Plant asclepias near your water garden for its scent and nectar that attract butterflies and hummingbirds.

ASTILBE ARENDSII

Astilbe

- **Sun to part shade**
- **Zones 4-8**
- **Height: 12 to 40 inches tall**
- **Blooms: white, pink, rose, purple; summer**
- **Continuously moist soil**

Astilbe's foliage is appealing even when the plant is not in bloom, forming a dense clump of finely cut leaves that are sometimes a copper color when immature. The plants are attractive interplanted with hostas and ferns at the shaded edges of the pond. The soft, feathery flowers are held on stalks above the foliage and bloom at various times in summer depending on the cultivar. The plants will tolerate a sunny location if the soil is kept continuously moist.

'Deutschland' grows to 24 inches and blooms white in early summer. 'Amethyst' has lavender-pink flowers in midsummer and grows 24 to 30 inches tall. Another midseason bloomer is 'Cattleya,' which grows to 36 inches and has rose-purple flowers. 'Venus' grows to 36 inches tall; its bright pink flowers bloom in late summer. Leave the dried flower heads on the plants for winter interest.

Astilbe's feathery flowers add color and texture in shady areas. Plant them with hostas and ferns.

The double-lipped pink flowers of turtlehead begin to bloom when other perennials are fading.

CHELONE SPP.

Turtlehead

- **Sun to part shade**
- **Zones 3 to 9**
- **Height: to 3 feet**
- **Blooms: pink, purple; summer to frost**
- **Water depth: moist soil**

A welcome bright spot in the late-summer garden, turtlehead gets its name from the way its upper petals arch over the lower ones, much like the shape of a turtle's head. When you remove a stand of purple loosestrife (a banned invasive), slow-growing, native turtlehead makes a perfect replacement with its similar upright habit and pink or purple flowers. It is tolerant of periodic drought but prefers continuously moist soil and shelter from afternoon sun.

Chelone glabra and *C. lyonnii* are hardy in Zones 3 to 8; *C. obliqua* is more reliably hardy in Zones 6 to 9. *C. lyonnii* is the least moisture-tolerant. The double-lipped pink, purple, or pink-and-white flowers bloom above the dark green, toothed leaves from July to first frost. Divide turtlehead rootstock in spring, making sure each piece has growing stems, or collect seed and keep in cold storage over winter before sowing.

Add the branching beauty of meadowsweet to the bog or pond edge for late-summer blooms.

FILIPENDULA SPP.

Meadowsweet

- **Sun to part shade**
- **Zones 3 to 9**
- **Height: 1 to 8 feet**
- **Blooms: white, pink, rose; late summer**
- **Water depth: moist, rich soil**

Meadowsweet is a tall, moisture-loving, bushy plant that works well around the edge of a pond or as a transition to landscaping. Sometimes called Queen-of-the-Meadow, it is a hardy pink- or white-blooming perennial that is most at home in boggy conditions.

F. ulmaria 'Variegata' gets its name from the plant's leaves, which are lemon-yellow near the stems. Creamy-white flowers bloom on branching stems in the summer. *F. purpurea,* Japanese meadowsweet, has maple-like leaves and rose-pink flowers on crimson stems. *F. palmata* 'Rubra' has tiny, hot-pink flowers that bloom in feathery plumes on long, branched stems. If planted in the wet humus it enjoys, 'Rubra' may grow to 6 or 8 feet tall. For smaller gardens, try *F. ulmaria* 'Aurea', a white-flowered cultivar that grows only a foot or so tall. Propagate *Filipendula* from seed or divide plants in autumn.

FUCHSIA SPP.

Fuchsia

Plant exotic fuchsias near the water garden to attract hummingbirds. Some cultivars are hardy.

- **Part shade**
- **Zones 4 to 9**
- **Height: to 4 feet**
- **Blooms: white, pink, red, purple, and bicolors; July to frost**
- **Water depth: consistently moist, well-drained soil**

Fuchsia plants grown in hanging baskets are heavy feeders that often dry up when temperatures rise. There are, however, herbaceous cultivars that thrive and may even overwinter when planted in the ground. Because they like moist soil, hardy fuchsias work well in the damp terrain near a pool or pond, where their bell-like blossoms can catch the water's mist. They are a favorite of hummingbirds.

A member of the evening primrose family, fuchsia has an upright, self-supporting growth habit that forms a fountain shape the first year and a rounded bush in successive seasons. *F. magellanica* 'Dark Eyes' has cascading red blossoms above violet-blue corollas. 'Hardy Tom Thumb' is a dwarf variety with rose-over-purple flowers. *F. triphylla* cultivars are tender perennials in Zones 9 to 11. 'Coralle' combines unusual salmon-orange blooms with bluish-green foliage. 'Firecracker' has salmon-pink flowers and gray-green leaves.

HEMEROCALLIS SPP.

Daylily

- Full sun to part shade
- Zones 4-9
- Height: 12 to 48 inches
- Blooms: all colors but blue
- Water depth: moist soil but is highly adaptable

So many thousands of daylily cultivars are available that it is possible to have a garden full of them alone. Not fussy about soil or light conditions, they will grow almost anywhere you plant them, but prefer moist soil. They do best planted away from broadleafed trees, whose shallow roots compete with them for moisture. Their long, medium-green, strappy foliage creates a natural transition between marginal pond plants and terrestrial flower gardens.

Daylily blooms come in white, cream, yellow, pink, peach, orange, red, lavender, and purple, as well as bi- and tricolor combinations. The flowers—highly fragrant in some cultivars—are borne on leafless stalks just above the foliage, and last for only a day. The plants have a long blooming season, however, and some varieties re-bloom after a period of rest.

Most daylilies spread rapidly on their own, but should be divided every four or five years to promote blooming. Aphids and mites are attracted to them but usually do no serious damage.

Daylilies will grow almost anywhere, and will bloom in the shade or in periods of drought.

HOSTA SPP.

Hosta

- Part sun to shade
- Zones 3-8
- Height: 12 to 36 inches
- Blooms: white, lavender; some are fragrant
- Water depth: moist soil

Grown primarily for their attractive foliage, shade- and moisture-loving hostas form large clumps that serve as groundcovers near the pond's edge. Trumpet-shaped flowers in white or lavender sway gently from stalks held well above the leaves. Many cultivars are available and all are easy to grow. The leaves come in a great variety of textures and colors, from lance-shaped and curving to broad and curly, in green, blue, chartreuse, and yellow, edged or streaked with cream or white. Propagate by division in spring. Watch for snails and slugs, which find hostas a tasty snack.

The mid- to late-summer lavender flowers of *H. plantaginea* are the most fragrant. *H. fortunei* 'Gold Standard' has yellow leaves with green borders, and tolerates more sun than other cultivars. *H. sieboldiana*'s leaves are softly puckered; 'Frances Williams' has blue-green leaves edged in a lighter shade of green.

Shade-tolerant hostas provide a natural transition between pond and landscape. They bloom in mid- to late summer, and some are fragrant.

IMPATIENS WALLERANA

Impatiens

- Part shade to full shade
- Zones 3 to 9
- Height: 6 to 12 inches
- Blooms: white, pink, red, orange, purple, bicolor; spring to frost
- Moist, well-drained soil

No shady garden is complete without the iridescent sparkle of impatiens. Tender perennials in their native Africa, impatiens have been hybridized for use as annuals in North America. Their succulent stems store moisture, but the shallow-rooted plants require continuously moist, well-drained soil in order to thrive. That makes impatiens a perfect choice for damp, shaded areas near the water garden.

Impatiens bloom from late spring until the first frost. Plants form compact mounds that rarely need attention, but if stems become leggy pinching back will result in new growth and flowers. 'Super Elfin' and 'Dazzler' hybrids are the most popular, bearing large blooms in electric colors that glitter against the plants' dark-green foliage. Newer hybrids offer yellow and apricot rose-type flowers, but the blooms are smaller. New Guinea impatiens, bred for use in sunnier spots, have attractive bronze-red or variegated foliage.

Moisture-loving impatiens are a must in the shady garden, blooming reliably from late spring to first frost.

Tropical shrimp plant will attract hummingbirds.

JUSTICIA BRANDEGEANA SYN. BELOPERONE GUTTATA

Shrimp plant

- **Sun to part shade**
- **Zones 5 to 11**
- **Height: 2 to 4 feet**
- **Blooms: shell pink, red, yellow; summer**
- **Water depth: moist soil**

Usually grown as a houseplant, shrimp plant can thrive in a moist garden and is hardy in Zones 9 to 11. Include it in your garden if you want to attract hummingbirds.

Shrimp plant gets its name from the pink bracts that overlap like segments of a shrimp's shell. White flower petals with purple spots protrude from between the bracts. 'Yellow Queen' has unusual chartreuse bracts. The flowering stems add a tropical look to cut-flower arrangements.

Shrimp plant is a member of the acanthus family and related to the water willow, so it prefers to keep its feet wet. It will tolerate periodic drought. Bring it indoors to a bright sunny location for the winter north of Zone 9. Propagate additional plants from stem cuttings when the plant is actively growing.

Plant lantana as an ornamental groundcover and enjoy its vivid flowers that attract butterflies.

LANTANA SPP.

Lantana

- **Sun to light shade**
- **Zones 4 to 10**
- **Height: to 3 feet**
- **Blooms: white, pink, red, yellow, purple, multicolor; spring to frost**
- **Water depth: moist, well-drained soil**

Sometimes called verbena, lantana is an ornamental shrub often found growing alongside streams in southern North America. Its dark green, hairy foliage is a good groundcover, but the leaves and stems smell bad when crushed. The brightly colored flowers produce nectar that attracts butterflies. Lantana is a tender perennial in Zones 8 to 10, and an annual in northern areas. Regular pruning encourages bushiness.

L. montevidensis 'Arlene Purple' is a trailing type suitable for planting on a berm or ledge where it can cascade. The vivid yellow blooms of *L. camara* 'Gold Rush' stand out in stalked clusters against the plant's leaves. The tropical look of 'Confetti' is popular for its pink, yellow, orange, and red flowers. New varieties, such as 'New Gold', do not produce the berry-like fruits that can make lantana invasive.

The bright yellow blooms of **Lysimachia ciliata** *'Purpurea' stand out against its maroon foliage.*

LYSIMACHIA CILIATA

Golden lanterns

- **Sun to part shade**
- **Zones 2 to 8**
- **Height: 1 to 4 feet**
- **Blooms: yellow; summer**
- **Water depth: moist soil**

A native U.S. wildflower related to primroses, *Lysimachia* is found in swamps and bogs and along shorelines in the continuously wet soil it requires. It is often called fringed loosetrife because of its toothed petals and fuzzy leafstalks. The plant has a slender, upright habit with nodding flowers along the length of the branches. It can become invasive in some regions if left unchecked. 'Purpurea', a form with purplish foliage, is more commonly available in nurseries than the green-leaved species.

L. punctata 'Alexander' ('Variegated Golden Candles') has creamy white variegated leaves and 1-inch yellow flowers on 2-foot stems. 'Firecracker' has dark green and purple foliage that makes the bright yellow blooms really stand out. *L. ephemerum* has long gray leaves and white, star-shaped flowers that bloom until the first frost. Propagate by root division.

MIRABILIS JALAPA

Four-o-clock

- **Sun to part shade**
- **Zones 3 to 9**
- **Height: 1 to 3 feet**
- **Blooms: white, pink, red, yellow, violet, bicolors**
- **Water depth: moist soil**

As the sun descends toward the horizon, four-o-clocks come alive in the garden with a fresh showing of new trumpet-shaped flowers each evening. The brightly colored, heavily fragrant blooms stay open all night, making them desirable companions to a waterscape that includes night-blooming lilies. 'Kaleidoscope' offers the most dramatic display of mixed bicolors.

Four-o-clock flowers are held on upright branches that may lean over as the plant matures. One large, black seed forms at the base of each spent blossom and will often overwinter if left to fall to the ground. The tubers themselves may survive in warm climates. Often called Marvel of Peru, four-o-clocks self-sow but can be successfully transplanted if their shallow roots are kept continuously moist.

Use four-o-clocks along a path to a pond full of night-blooming lilies. Their fragrance is delightful.

OSMUNDA SPP.

Fern

- **Part sun to shade**
- **Zones 3 to 8**
- **Height: 2 to 5 feet tall**
- **Water depth: moist soil**

Many ferns are appropriate companions to the water garden. Cinnamon fern's *(O. cinnamomea)* feathery foliage provides a perfect backdrop for hostas and irises. It tolerates some sun but will grow larger in cool shade, especially in a boggy site near the pond. Its rusty-brown fronds turn a tawny gold in autumn, adding bright color to the fading landscape.

Royal fern *(O. regalis)* tolerates sun and stays green until the first hard frost. The fronds of Himalayan maidenhair fern *(Adiantum venustum)* are 8 to 12 inches long and form arching mounds. It even tolerates semidry conditions if planted in the shade. Other good choices are holly fern *(Polystichum munitum)*, Japanese painted fern *(Athyrium niponnicum* 'Pictum'), and lady fern *(A. filix-femina)*.

Protect all ferns with mulch in winter. Propagate by division.

Plant shade-loving cinnamon fern with astilbes and hostas.

RUDBECKIA SPP.

Coneflower

- **Sun to part shade**
- **Zones 3 to 10**
- **Height: 1 to 3 feet**
- **Blooms: white, yellow, purple**
- **Water depth: highly adaptable, even drought-tolerant**

Easy to grow and long-blooming, coneflowers add color and attract songbirds to the perennial garden. They bloom in midsummer through autumn, often continuing their display when other plants are going dormant, and make excellent cut flowers. They tolerate some shade, and will survive a drought. Seeds borne on the cones are a favorite treat of songbirds.

Black-eyed susans *(Rudbeckia fulgida)* are often confused with their annual cousins *(R. hirta)* and are sometimes called by the annual cultivar name Gloriosa daisies. True yellow coneflowers are perennial; the hybrid most commonly found in nurseries is 'Goldsturm'. They grow 18 to 30 inches tall. Plants may be short-lived; they self-sow readily and thus seldom disappear entirely.

Purple coneflowers *(R.purpurea,* syn. *Echinacea purpurea)* thrive in full sun or light shade and are favorites of bees and butterflies. 'Bright Star' is an easy-to-find variety. Echinacea stems may reach 4 feet or more in the right conditions. They spread quickly and are easy to transplant by division in spring or late summer.

The seedheads of coneflowers are a favorite of songbirds. The plants are adaptable to moisture or drought.

SOIL, FERTILIZER, AND WATER

Many products are available to fertilize water garden plants. Use the liquid form in bogs and containers where you won't have to worry about causing an algae bloom. Tablet-form fertilizers can be used just about anywhere.

Water gardening begins with plants. Pot them up, then put the pots in the pond. Make sure that you fertilize correctly, the plant is at the right depth, and clean water is in the pond, and you're on your way to being an ace water gardener. There's no trying to figure out if you've overwatered or underwatered, if the soil is too dry or too moist, or if you've waited long enough to water again.

SOIL

The first step to growing water plants is planting medium. The best one for all water garden plants except filtrators is clay soil. That may come as a surprise to perennial gardeners because clay, with its dense, water-retentive nature, is the worst soil for perennials. These same qualities, however, make it ideal for water plants.

Clay stays soft in water, which allows roots to penetrate it. It is composed of small particles, which hold fertilizer like a sponge until the plant needs it, reducing the amount of fertilizer that leaches into the water. Sandy or loamy soil or even silt will work if it is at least half clay (or if you can add that much clay). You can tell if your soil is clay by making a small ball in the palm of your hand. Push your finger into it; if it doesn't break up, it's clay.

If you don't have clay soil or you're in doubt about the composition of your soil, add clay to the mix. Or add generic nondeodorized, nonscoopable kitty litter. It's nothing more than clay from decomposed limestone—perfect for most water plants. Also, it doesn't float once it's wet and won't dirty the pond the way soil does if spilled. Either mix kitty litter half and half with soil or use it alone in pots.

Some commercial water garden potting soils are available from manufacturers such as Fafard and Scotts. These are heavy unamended soils made specifically for water plants. Avoid potting mixes and other commercial soils for perennials or annuals, especially the lightweight mixes with peat moss, bark, perlite, vermiculite, and other lightweight ingredients. In water, these float out of the pot and create a mess on the water surface. Also, as the organic matter decomposes in warm water, it releases harmful amounts of organic salts and removes most of the oxygen in the root zone, killing roots.

Filtrating plants have different soil needs. Their roots take in unwanted nutrients in a pond with fish and so must be exposed to water. Alternative planting mediums for them include pea gravel, cocoa fiber, rock wool, synthetic fiber, baked-clay-based soil (Profile), and clay-sand-and-decayed-granite mixes. These allow roots of filtrators in open-weave pots to grow beyond the pot. Although you can use these materials with other water plants, they're not the best choice. Stick with clay, kitty litter, or commercial water gardening soils.

FERTILIZER

Water plants, like all plants, need nutrients. To ensure that they get what they need, fertilize them. The best kind of fertilizer is one designed specifically for water plants. It can be in liquid, granular, or tablet form.

Liquid fertilizers are good for container water gardens or plants you can take out

Clay

Kitty litter

Pea gravel

Commercial soil

Profile

of the pond and fertilize in a bucket of water. Don't pour liquid fertilizer into a pond. Algae will absorb most of the nutrients.

Use granular fertilizer to mix into potting soil when planting or dividing plants. Tablet (or tab) forms look like large pills. To use them, simply poke them into the potting soil.

Avoid "once-a-season" timed-release products. These work by osmosis or by having a coating that slowly dissolves. In a water garden, where the fertilizer is in constant contact with water, the pellets dissolve rapidly, adding too many nutrients to the pond at once. Also avoid using tree spikes and organic fertilizers. In water, tree spikes release their nutrients right away, burning the roots around them. They also leave behind hard spikes, which can accumulate. Cow, sheep, and pig manure, bat guano, and kelp extract are fine in cool water, but in warm water, they quickly foul a pond or rot roots.

Whatever you use, know how long it takes to dissolve so you will not add it too often. Drop a sample in a bucket before mixing it with the potting soil. Note how long it takes to dissolve completely. Most tablet forms should last two to three weeks underwater. Granular products last about six weeks.

WATER

Although you can't overwater plants in a water garden, you can underwater them. Each type of plant has its own tolerance for fluctuations. For this reason, keep your pond within 2 inches of its designed depth at all times.

Falling water levels expose the liner, which looks tacky. Worse, if you use a pot without a hole and the water level drops below the top of the pot, the plant can dry out in a day or two. Top off the pond, letting water trickle out of the hose at the pond bottom so that it doesn't dramatically change water temperature. Only add up to 10 percent new water at a time. On very hot days, oxygen levels drop. Splatter the water into the pond to mix air into it.

WATER QUALITY WITHOUT FISH: Except for floaters, pond plants tolerate water in a wide pH range—5.5 to 9.1—and aren't affected by the chemicals used to treat municipal water. However, they don't tolerate salt from excess fertilizer or water softeners. Planting directly into a clay-bottom pond buffers the water from wide pH swings. Even so, don't fill the pond with water recycled from a water softener.

WATER QUALITY WITH FISH: If the pond contains fish, water quality is a major concern. Before stocking the pond, treat the water with dechlorinator and chloramine remover to eliminate chlorine, chloramines, and heavy metals.

MYTH OF THE BALANCED POND

Sometimes water gardeners are led to believe that their pond will reach a "natural equilibrium" if they follow a mathematical formula of plants and fish—a state at which everything is in balance so the pond never needs cleaning or fertilizing. Not true. Backyard ponds are dynamic artificial environments. All parts of a pond contribute to overall health and well-being. Ponds change daily, and while ratios and rules of thumb are helpful guides learned from experience, they don't eliminate all the work. Your role is to direct the parts and take satisfaction in doing so.

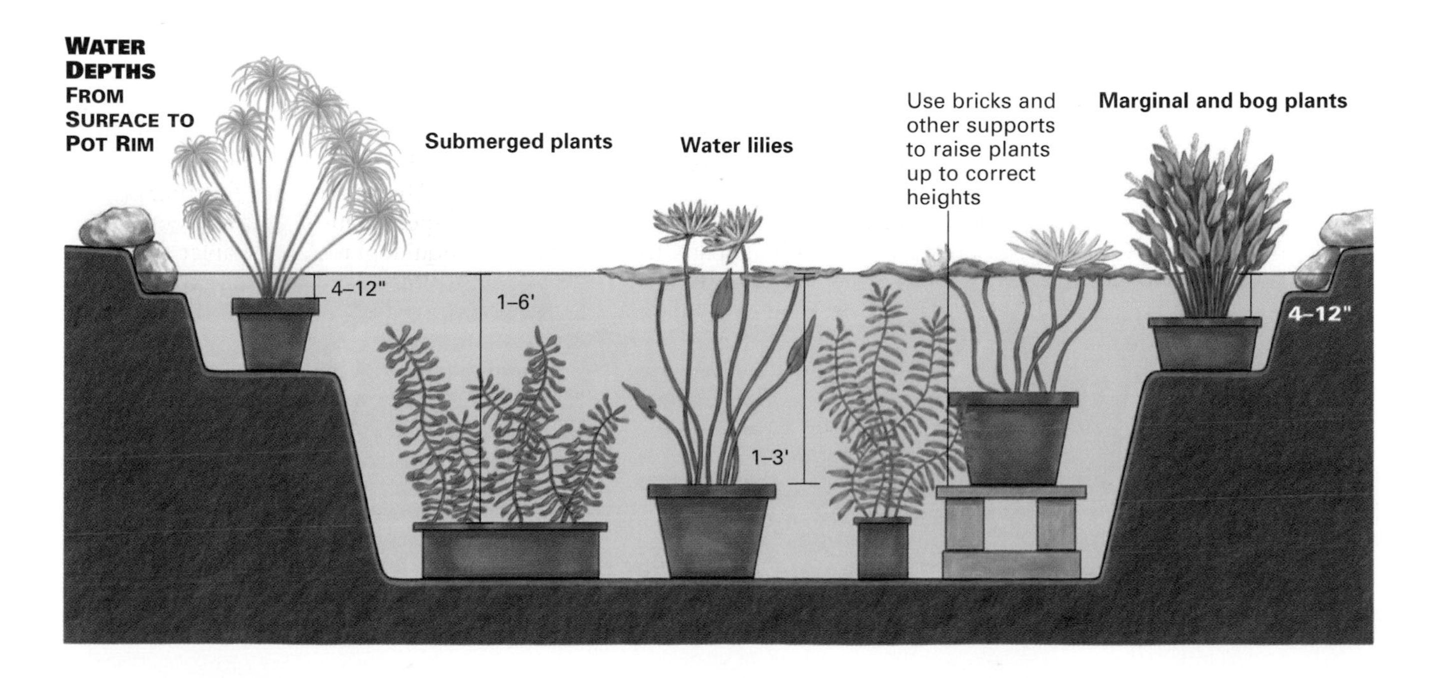

POTTING

Standard pots as well as newer designs can all be used to hold water plants.

The purpose of a water garden pot is to keep plant and soil together in the pond where you want them to be without dirtying the water or damaging the pond. Many types of pots are available, and most serve their function well. It's important to know the relative benefits and drawbacks of each type, so you can choose the one that's right for the way you want to grow the plants in your pond.

MESH CONTAINERS: Open-weave or plastic-mesh pots and fabric baskets are favored for filtrators because they allow roots to grow through them and have more contact with the water. These are the containers you often find for sale in the water garden section of a nursery.

Transplanting from an open-weave pot may be difficult because, as plants mature, their roots naturally grow thicker and may become entwined in the plastic. If you wait too long to divide and transplant nonfiltrating plants with running stems, such as lizard's tail, cattail, and rushes, their roots may grow together between pots, making them doubly difficult to remove from the pond. Such root growth is also a treat for large hungry fish, so if you don't want your aquatic plants to become a salad bar for koi, transplant as soon as you see the roots growing into the water.

GAUGING THE POT SIZE

Plant Type	Best Pot Size
Marginal	1 gallon
Water lilies	17 inch
Lotus	23 inch
Water-lily-like	1 gallon
Submerged, creeping	Cat litter tray
Submerged, noncreeping	1 gallon

TRADITIONAL POTS: Nursery containers and clay and plastic pots with single or multiple holes make good homes for most water garden plants, including water lilies and water-lily-like plants—even plants that run. Single-hole nursery pots are especially good for containing running marginals such as water mints and lizard's tail. The single hole prevents—or at least slows—plant roots from growing out of the pot. Containers without drainage holes, especially decorative pots, are excellent for miniature ponds on a tabletop or patio.

Because traditional pots let water in from the bottom, they also keep plants from drying out if the water level drops below the lip of the pot. If you use a container that has no holes in a large pond, take care that the lip of the container is always below the water surface so that the plant doesn't dry out.

SIZE: Pot size should be matched to the size and type of plant. Because most water plants grow only in the top 10 to 12 inches of soil, that's as deep as the container needs to be. Any deeper and the soil generally is wasted. Some plants don't need that much soil, growing only an inch or so deep. A few, such as lotuses and 'Victoria' water lilies, however, need a much deeper pot. In fact, lotuses will send roots as far down as 3 feet. For help in selecting the right size pot for your plants, see "Gauging the Pot Size" at left.

Basic Preparations

When you are ready to pot water plants, prepare a spot where you can set up everything you'll need. First, choose a shaded area in which to work. Direct sunlight beating down can be extremely damaging to water plants as you wash soil off their roots and transplant them. The location should be close to the pond, so you can easily get the plants back in the water. If there's no shade near your water garden, fill a wading pool with water and hold the plants in it until you're ready to restock the pond.

Next, gather your supplies. You'll need soil, pea gravel, pruners, and running water from a hose.

To pot water plants, the basic steps are to trim off any dead or damaged plant parts and then partly fill the pot with soil, set the plant in the pot, and finish filling the pot, avoiding covering the crown. Leave enough room to add a layer of pea gravel on top. How deep you set plants, where in the pot you set them, and how much fertilizer you mix in depends on the plant. You can mix fertilizer into the soil before filling pots, using amounts recommended on the label, or use tablets as shown in the illustrations on this and the next two pages.

Potting Water Lilies

Water lilies are easy to plant when they're small. The method you use depends upon whether they are hardy or tropical lilies. Hardy water lilies can be planted dormant, when they have few or no leaves, or when they are in active growth, with leaves and roots that have already sprouted. Tropicals are generally shipped—and planted—in full active growth, when they don't have a tuber. Although you can plant them while they still have tubers, it's more difficult.

Hardy Water Lily

Hardy water lilies: To plant a dormant or actively growing hardy water lily, fill a pot about two-thirds full of soil. Make a mound in the middle of the pot with a handful of soil. Place the rhizome on the mound; then spread any roots over the top of the soil so they are not under the rhizome. Sprinkle soil over the roots and around the rhizome, adding just enough to cover the rhizome. Do not bury the rhizome. It should have no soil on its crown; otherwise, it will have difficulty sprouting new leaves. Water the pot thoroughly; then top the soil with a layer of pea gravel, again avoiding covering the plant's crown.

Tropical Water Lily

Tropical water lilies: Tropical water lilies require a little detective work to plant at the right depth. Examine the lily's stems, starting at the base. Look for the point where the stem changes color from light to dark. This is the point from which the leaf emerged from the soil. When you plant the lily, the topping-off material must be even with this point. This will ensure that you have the plant's growing crown (the union where the roots meet the stems) at the right depth.

It's important that the main growing crown of a tropical be planted at just the right depth. If it is planted too deeply—especially on a night-blooming cultivar—it will usually stop growing in order to make new plants, taking energy from the main crown. You will eventually have more new plants, but they will be smaller, and by the time they reach the size at which they will bloom well, it may be too late in the season for them to set flowers.

The general planting procedure is the same as for hardy water lilies. Fill the pot about two-thirds full of soil, form a mound in the middle of the pot, place the base of the plant over the mound, and then spread the roots out and cover them with more soil. Leave enough room to top them off with pea gravel at the color change on the stem.

Both types: Water lilies are extremely buoyant when in leaf. Even rhizomes of dormant hardy water lilies have been known to suddenly pop out of the pot and float to the water surface after transplanting. If you are planting the lilies when they are actively growing, try to retain as many roots as possible and anchor them by firming the soil around the roots. For large plants, place a smooth rock on top of the soil over the rhizome (of a hardy water lily) or over the

Potting
continued

roots (of a tropical water lily). Keeping the plants just 4 to 6 inches below the water surface until their roots have a firm grip on the soil—three to four days in warm water—also helps to reduce buoyancy.

Potting Marginal Plants

Marginals grow in a wide variety of ways. Some develop from underground rhizomes, others from a central crown, and still others crawl across the soil surface. Here are the basic categories of marginal plant growth habits and the ways in which the types are planted. For all plants bought at a nursery, find out what material they've been transported in. If it's organic matter, such as peat moss or bark, shake the plant free of the bulk of the organic matter and pot in kitty litter or heavy clay soil. Pot them in at least a 1-gallon container. South of Zone 7, you'll need a 2-gallon container.

Marginal with Rhizome

Rhizomatous marginals: Water iris, sweet flag, and other marginals grow from rhizomes. To pot them, first fill the pot with soil about one-half to just under two-thirds full. Place the rhizome slightly off-center, with its cut end toward the edge of the pot. For water iris, especially, this allows the fan to grow toward the center of the pot. Next, spread the roots over the soil; then fill the pot with more soil to just cover the rhizome. Top off with pea gravel. If the water temperature is over 60°F, poke a regular dose of fertilizer tablets into the soil.

Single-stemmed marginals: Lizard's tail, houttuynia, water willow, and other marginals form a colony of individual stems that grow in a clump. Because all of these plants root from their stems, they should be planted with their roots well below the soil surface. Fill the pot about two-thirds full. These plants are sold in bunches of individual stems, or you can use cuttings. Select 5 to 15 rooted stems (fewer than 5 looks skimpy), poke a hole in the soil in the center of the pot, and place the stems in the hole. Firm the soil around them, adding more to fill the pot but leaving room to top off the pot with gravel.

The potting technique for Japanese sweet flag falls somewhere between that of water iris and lizard's tail. The plant looks like an iris, which is planted on the edge, but it actually needs to be planted in the center, like a lizard's tail. Plant several fans per pot; one fan alone looks sparse. Fill the pot two-thirds full of soil; then set the rhizomes in the center of the pot with their fans facing outward in a roughly triangular fashion. This helps them to branch out and fill the pot, and to form a cluster in the center of the pot. Finish filling the pot, using enough soil to anchor the fans firmly in place; then top it off with gravel mulch.

Grasses and Rushes

Marginals that grow from a central cluster of stems: Umbrella grass, sedges, and rushes send up clusters of stems from one central crown. Stems of umbrella grass and sedges generally sprout from the crown and grow in groups of three; rushes sprout any number of stems at the outside edge of the crown.

To pot these marginals, fill the container two-thirds full. Place the plant in the center, spreading the roots around the pot. Then cover the crown or rhizome with about an inch of soil to help anchor it. Top off the pot with pea gravel. Don't submerge the pot for the first week (at least); the stems are buoyant and may pop out. Instead, put the pot in water only as deep as the crown.

Marginals that grow from a single crown or tuber: Similar to the group above, these plants have multiple stems anchored in a central crown or tuber. Pickerel weed, water plantain, lobelia, and monkey flower are potted in much the same fashion as the other marginals discussed here. Fill the pot about two-thirds full of soil, place the plant in the center of the pot with its roots spread over the soil; then cover them. Make sure the crown of the plant is about an inch below the soil surface. Top off the pot with pea gravel.

Single Crown or Tuber

Arrowhead: When potting arrowhead that is actively growing, treat it as you would other plants that grow from a central crown. But when potting dormant tubers, you need to use a different technique, as follows.

In the fall, arrowhead forms a tuber. Technically a turion, it is the reason why arrowhead is often called duck potato. The turion resembles a small potato and is a favorite food of waterfowl. In spring the turion sprouts and sends a runner to the soil surface. Once it reaches the surface, the runner sprouts a single plant with a central crown. If you are potting turions, plant them well toward the bottom of the pot. Fill the pot one-fourth full with soil, set the tubers on the soil, and then finish filling the pot. The turion will elongate and grow a new plantlet at the top of the soil.

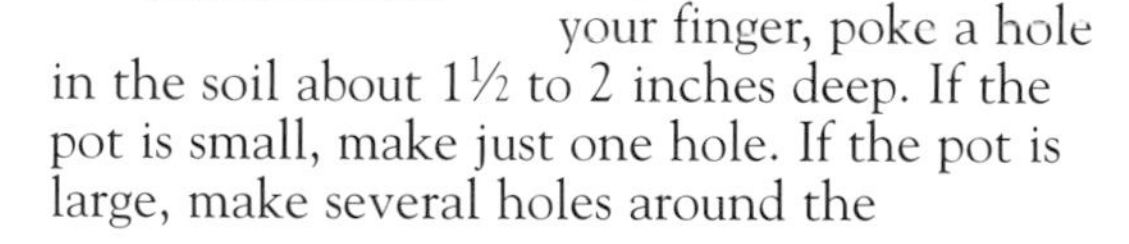

ARROWHEAD

RUNNING MARGINALS AND OXYGENATORS: All stem-cut oxygenators (plants that root from cut stems), such as foxtail, anacharis, and fanwort, and running marginals, such as cattails, are planted in a similar way. First, fill the pot with soil and top it off with sand or pea gravel. Water the soil thoroughly so it is easy to work. Using your finger, poke a hole in the soil about 1½ to 2 inches deep. If the pot is small, make just one hole. If the pot is large, make several holes around the perimeter as well. Insert anywhere from 5 to 10 stems into each hole. Firm the soil around the stems and submerge the pot in the pond. You can also plant oxygenators by gently tying them to a rock and placing the rock on the bottom of the pond. To ensure that the plants can overwinter, though, press their stems into the soil so that the plants root.

WATER-LILY-LIKE PLANTS: Treat water-lily-like plants much like oxygenators. The rule of thumb is one plant in a 6-inch pot, three in a 10-inch pot, and three to five in a 12-inch container. Fill the pot with soil, top with sand or pea gravel, and water thoroughly. Then make a hole in the soil, place the crown of the plant about an inch below the soil surface, and firm the soil over the roots. Submerge the pot in the pond roughly 6 inches below the water surface. Keep water-lily-like plants as moist as possible while you work with them because their stems are brittle and dehydrate easily. Return them to the pond as soon as they are planted.

TOPPING OFF

The final step of potting all water plants is to top off the soil with pea gravel or one of the commercial baked-clay-soil products. When dry, these products are lighter than gravel and may be easier to use. Topping off helps keep the soil from being disturbed by circulating water and discourages nosy fish from rooting around and spilling soil into the pond. Pour a 1-inch-deep layer of the topping-off material over the soil, or add enough to fill the pot even with or slightly below its rim. If you have large koi in your pond, use large stones, such as smooth river rock, to cover the soil.

WATER DEPTH FOR PLANTS IN POND BOTTOM

Most water plants benefit from being planted directly in soil on the bottom of the pond, giving the roots unrestrained growth. This is best in a pond for wildlife and one needing only minimal cleaning.

PROPAGATING PLANTS

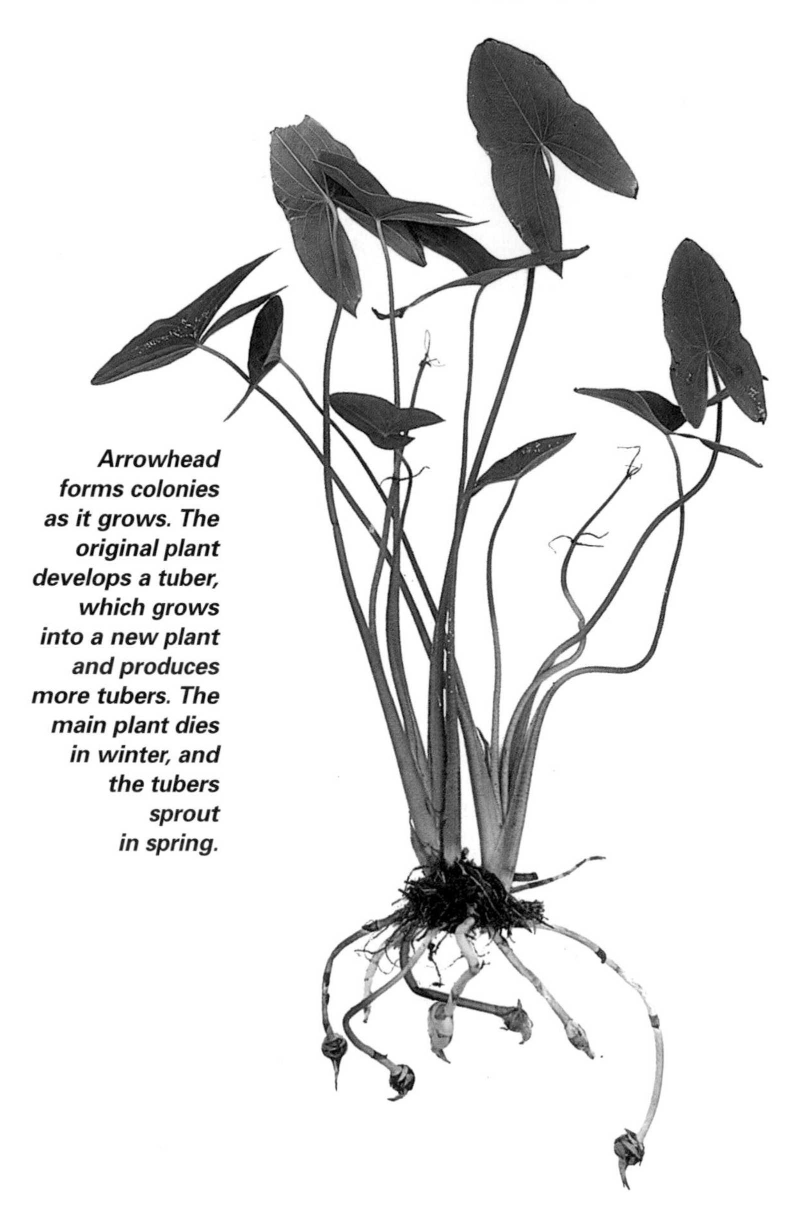

Arrowhead forms colonies as it grows. The original plant develops a tuber, which grows into a new plant and produces more tubers. The main plant dies in winter, and the tubers sprout in spring.

The easiest way to gain new water plants is to divide them. Just as when planting new water plants, choose a shady spot in which to work and have everything arranged for your propagating adventure. For container plants, your first step will generally be to remove the plant from the pot. To do this, gently roll the side of the pot on a hard surface and work the root ball out.

DIVIDING WATER LILIES

Water lilies are easy to divide. Do it in spring or early summer so the new plants have ample time to recover and harden off for winter. Wash soil from the rhizomes to find the small "eyes" that have sprouted here and there. Look for eyes that have a few leaves and roots; cut the entire eye, along with the roots and leaves, from the main root with a sharp knife. Let leafless eyes continue growing for later divisions. Plant the new starts in fresh soil so that the leaf sprouts are just at the soil level.

In early summer, some water lilies produce young plants in the center of their leaves called viviparous growth. Some day-blooming tropical water lilies are especially prone to doing this, as are a few hardy water lilies from time to time, and some water-lily-like plants such as water snowflakes and water poppies. Pin the leaves with plantlets to the soil with a rock. Once the plantlets sprout roots, cut off the old leaf and plant the new water lilies in their own pots.

DIVIDING MARGINAL WATER PLANTS

As you might expect, the techniques for dividing marginals fall into the same categories as for potting new plants.

RHIZOMATOUS MARGINALS: Divide these plants in summer after they flower. Break apart a large clump with a shovel or pitchfork; then replant each piece. For more precise division, wash the roots and look for the spot called the "fan," where the leaves emerge from the rhizome. If you want a good-sized plant in a 1-gallon pot, divide the rhizomes so that there are three fans to each pot.

SINGLE-STEMMED MARGINALS: Divide the clump of plants into four or five sections, slicing through the soil and roots as if you were cutting a thick pie into wedge-shaped pieces. Plant the sections as described on page 160.

Another propagation method is to take stem cuttings. Wash the roots and cut the rhizomes into 4-inch-long sections, each with a growing tip and a bit of runner. Plant them so the tips stand upright and the runners lie horizontally about an inch below the soil surface.

MARGINALS THAT GROW FROM A CENTRAL CLUSTER OF STEMS: Although all these plants are easily divided by splitting the crown with a sharp knife, members of the *Cyperus* family, such as papyrus, are also commonly propagated by soaking their "umbrella" cluster in a shallow bowl of water. New plantlets will sprout from the center and take root in just a few days to a week. Once they have grown a few inches tall, transplant them into a pot, where they will quickly take root and mature.

MARGINALS THAT GROW FROM A SINGLE CROWN: The crown of a plant is the point at which the roots and stems meet.

Propagate marginals that grow from a single crown by division in summer, which gives the new plants enough time to recover and harden off before winter.

First, wash the roots. Once the soil is gone, you will find new plants attached to the main, or mother, plant. Cut or split off any that have roots and leaves from the main plant and pot them, making sure the crowns are about an inch below the soil surface.

ARROWHEAD: In summer, divide arrowhead in the same way as you divide plants that grow from a single crown. In spring, propagate them from the turion, as described on page 161.

RUNNING MARGINALS AND OXYGENATORS: Because these plants grow readily from stem cuttings, they are most commonly propagated by simply snapping off 4- to 6-inch-long pieces of the newest growth at the point at which it joins the main plant. Bind several stem cuttings together with a rubber band, fill a pot with moist soil, and then make a hole and gently push the cuttings into the it. The stems will sprout new roots and overcome any transplant shock in just a few days.

WATER-LILY-LIKE PLANTS: These form individual plantlets right next to one another. To divide, simply remove each individual plant and pot it as for other plants.

VIVIPAROUS MARGINALS: Some water plants, such as melon sword, sprout new plantlets along their growing stem or along flowering branches, similar to the indoor spider plant. Separate this young growth from the main plant after it has sprouted a few roots. Or bend the branch so the plantlet is touching soil; pin it in place until roots have started to form.

Dividing irises: The plants form new fans with rhizomes that can be detached. First, identify the new fan and check it for roots. Then cut the new fan free from the original plant with at least 1 inch of rhizome and a few roots. Cut the foliage on the new transplant to about 3 to 4 inches tall. Pot the rhizome and place it in the shade for a few days to give it a chance to recover.

For plants that grow easily from stem cuttings, propagation is a snap. Simply cut 4 to 6 inches of new growth from the plant. Remove the leaves at the cut end of the stem, about halfway to two-thirds up the stem. Place the stem cuttings in water until they root, or plant the stems directly in soil, so that the bare stems are covered and the leaves are above the soil line.

For running plants such as clover, take a 6- to 12-inch runner and cut it free from the main plant. Wind it in a circle around two fingers with the leaves to one side (up) and the roots to the other (down). Now place the circle on the soil, leaves up, and hold it in place with a bent paper clip.

POTTING AND DIVIDING LOTUSES

LOTUS RHIZOME

Growing point or tip

Rooting at second node

First node or joint

Lotuses are running plants that produce new rhizomes every autumn. The rhizome is really a stem that grows horizontally in the mud. It consists of a growing point, followed by nodes or swollen lengths of stem, and joints. The rhizome usually consists of one to three of these joints. Small lotus varieties can be as short as 4 inches long, large varieties 2 feet or more.

Spring—before the rhizome has had a chance to sprout and grow—is the best time of year to plant or divide lotuses. Once the lotus has a few leaves, it's too brittle to survive being split apart and moved to new pots. Transplanting or potting a lotus in spring is easy. You just have to know what you're looking for: bright crisp white rhizomes similar to elongated potatoes.

POTTING LOTUSES

It's best to use a round pot when planting lotuses. The rhizome will run in the pot and may break and die if it encounters a hard corner that it is unable to turn. Larger lotuses can be planted in pots that are 2 to 3 feet in diameter and a foot or more tall.

Lotuses grow better when there is 12 inches of clay soil in the pot, so use deep pots for these plants. Because this means that the pot will be heavy, some water gardeners prefer to keep their lotuses in wheeled, decorative containers on their deck or patio. This is easier than trying to move heavy pots around in the pond.

It's not a good idea to grow lotuses directly in the soil of an earth-bottom pond because they run and can take over the garden in a couple of years. It's better to plant the tubers in a large container and sink it into the pond. Once a lotus has had one flower, it will produce one flower bud at every leaf axil—the point where the leaf joins the stem—that follows. In a pond, the leaf axils are often several feet apart. This means that the flowers will be several feet apart, too.

There is an old, reliable Chinese method of starting lotuses from bare-root rhizomes. The Chinese float them rather than plant them. Fill the pot in which you'll grow the lotus—one with no holes—almost full with soil, leaving room at the top of the pot for standing water. Pour enough distilled water into the pot so there's at least 2 inches of water over the soil. Drop the rhizome in the water; it will float.

It's best to use distilled water, as opposed to tap water or well water; distilled water is neutral—neither acidic nor alkaline—and sterile. Other kinds of water may contain contaminants or be too hard. Hard water contains many minerals that raise pH, and high pH inhibits lotus growth. Move the pot to a spot where the rhizome will be kept warm (around 70°F) and will have lots of sun.

Once it has sprouted a few leaves, gently push the rhizome down so that it just touches the soil. Anchor it with a flat stone. Don't bury the rhizome; it will grow roots and pull itself down into the soil. With this technique, you can count on a 99 percent success rate in starting your lotus. Even if the growing tip has broken—which generally means the rhizome won't sprout—this method works.

After the lotus sprouts, you can add it to the pond. Prop it up on bricks to bring it close to the water surface.

FERTILIZING

Lotuses are heavy feeders. Fertilize them regularly throughout summer, especially when they are in flower. But wait to fertilize until the tuber has sprouted at least three leaves. If you fertilize too soon, you can burn the plant.

When you do fertilize, follow the directions provided by the fertilizer manufacturer. You can use any material, as discussed on pages 156 and 157. If you use tablets, push them as far as possible into the soil, so the fertilizer reaches the lotus rhizomes at the bottom of the pot. Firm the soil over the fertilizer tablet so the fertilizer doesn't dissolve into the water and feed the algae in the pond.

DIVIDING LOTUSES

Lotuses are usually divided in early spring, before they have started to actively grow. First, gently turn the lotus pot upside down on a flat level surface. You want the soil from the bottom of the pot—where the lotus rhizomes grow—facing up.

Gently wash away the soil with a stream of water from the hose until all of the rhizomes are free. As you free them, you'll find joints where sections meet and growing points at the end, or tip, of each rhizome.

Starting at the tip, work your way back along the rhizome toward the center. Count back two joints; then cut into the next, or third, section with scissors or a sharp knife. Dividing the rhizome in this way protects the cutting if the sliced end rots. The joint prevents infection from spreading to either of the sections or the growing tip. Take special care not to break off the growing point; the plant may not sprout without it. Once you've made your divisions, follow the directions on page 164 for potting bare-root lotuses.

Your divisions should have at least one growing point, but often you'll have more. The more growing tips per division, the fuller the plant will be.

Turn the plant out of the pot, then gently hose the plant off to reveal the white rhizome, which grows on the bottom of the pot.

Lotuses grow well in their own bog garden. Scoop out a hole about 3 to 4 feet across and 2 feet deep. Line the hole with flexible liner and place a short piece of drain tile on end in the hole. Fill the hole around the tile with clay soil up to a few inches below the surrounding soil level. Plant the lotus rhizome so that it's just below the soil surface and fill the hole with water. The lotus will root and soon fill the bog. In cold climates, a lotus overwinters with little or no protection; its tuber migrates deeply into the soil to avoid freezing temperatures.

Find the end of the rhizome, using the photo on page 164 as your guide. Count back two sections and cut 1 inch to 4 inches behind the second node, or joint. You may find several sections to plant.

Fill a no-hole container to within 2 inches of the top with clay soil. Lay the tuber on top of the soil and fill the pot with water if putting it in a pond. Place a rock on the tuber between the nodes to hold it down. Don't bury the tuber.

PESTS AND DISEASE

Water garden plants are generally fuss-free, only occasionally falling prey to insects or disease. Animals may visit the pond, damaging plants when foraging for food or using the habitat. Here are the more common problems that can plague plants in and around a water garden.

Having a pond doesn't mean you have to have mosquitoes. Moving water and fish are two excellent ways to keep their numbers down.

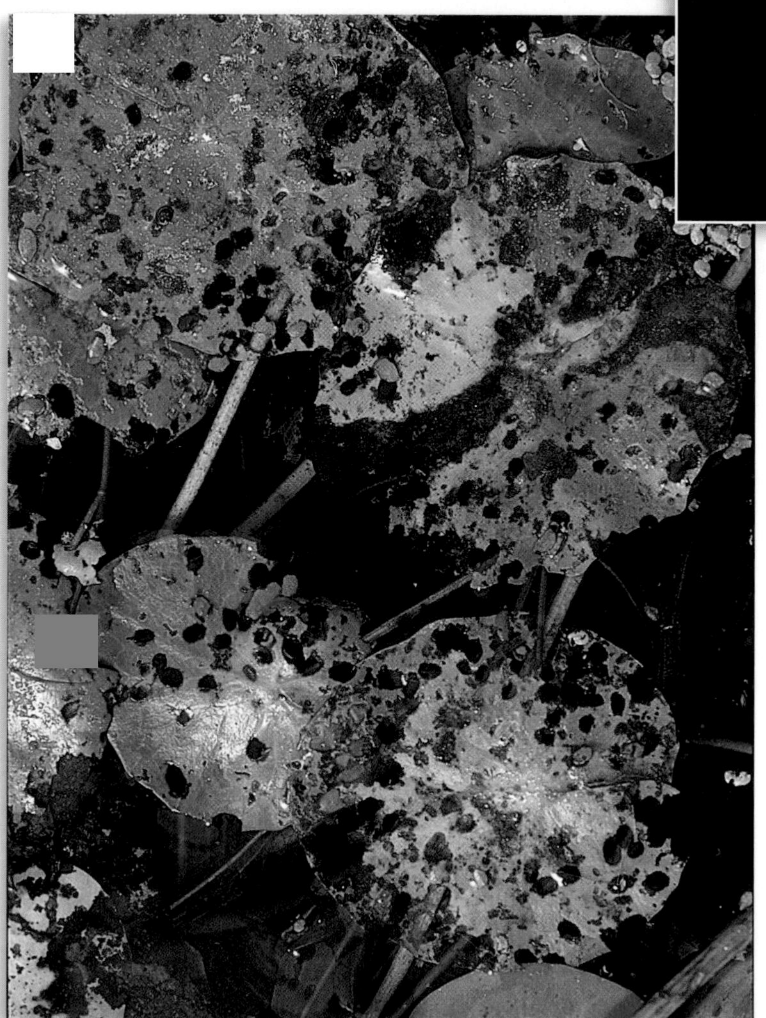

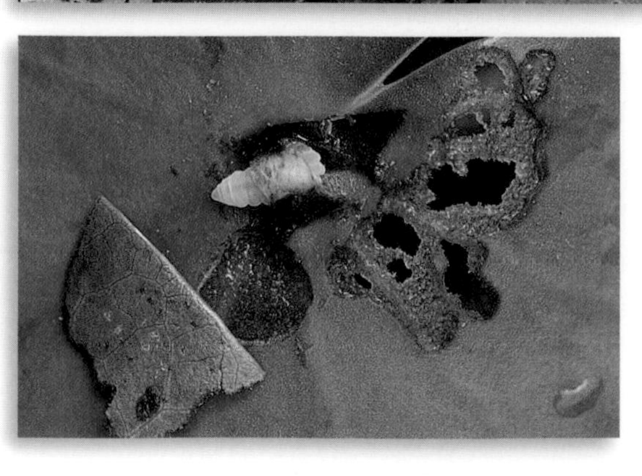

A severe infestation of China mark moths reduces plants to Swiss cheese (top). Unchecked, it can kill plants. The larvae (below) are destructive but easy to control.

CHINA MARK MOTHS

The most well-known pond insect pest is probably the China mark moth. Adult moths lay eggs on the leaves of water lilies, and the larvae drill into the central leaf stem, where they feed and grow for several weeks. The larvae may also chew small half-moon shapes from the outer edge of the lily leaf, using the cutout to make small enclosures on top of or on the underside of the leaf.

If only a few China mark moth larvae have attacked your lilies, remove and destroy the larvae by hand. If the infestation is large, chemical treatment may prove effective. A dusting of *Bacillus thuringiensis israelensis* (Bti) will eventually destroy a population of China mark moth larvae without harming fish.

LEAF MINERS

Several kinds of larvae generically called leaf miners also attack water lilies. These tiny creatures chew or burrow patterns in the leaf surface. If only a few leaves are affected, remove the leaves and throw them away.
A larger infestation may be more difficult to treat. Some homeowners report control by dusting the leaves with insecticide. However, some products are toxic to fish and are illegal to use on or near ponds. You can remove either the fish or the plants from the pond before beginning treatment, but first check the label to ensure you can return them to the pond after treatment.

APHIDS

Most plentiful in late summer when the weather is hot and humid and rainfall scarce, tiny insects called aphids attack new leaves and young flower buds as well as aging, yellowed foliage. They especially go after water lilies and marginals. Aphids draw fluids and sugars from the plant, and in small numbers they are more unsightly than harmful. Left alone, their numbers can grow rapidly and soon harm the plant's growth and overall health.

The easiest treatment is to submerge the plant entirely below the water surface for a day or so. The aphids cannot survive underwater and will float to the top, where you can skim them off. A dusting of diatomaceous earth will also kill the aphids, although it may have to be repeated over several days in order to be effective.

JAPANESE BEETLES

Japanese beetles seem to prefer the leaves of thalia, curling the edges and creating an open-weave pattern in the foliage. They also damage cannas, especially those with red or orange flowers. If only a few beetles are affecting your plants, remove them by hand. Use a Japanese beetle trap for large numbers. Follow the manufacturer's directions and hang it away from the pond so it won't attract more beetles to the pond. Neem-based repellents (from neem trees) are also effective.

Japanese beetles chew holes in leaves. Here one is feeding on the foliage of water hyacinth.

CROWN ROT

Crown rot is a fungal disease that attacks rhizomes. Water lilies suffering from this disease often lose their central crown and leaves, creating a tell-tale open circle of lily pad leaves floating on the water. By the time the disease is diagnosed, the entire plant is already infected, so you must remove the rhizome and destroy it. Some gardeners have had success using fungicides, but these are recommended only as a last resort for difficult-to-replace lilies. Some fungicides are toxic to fish; check the label for warnings.

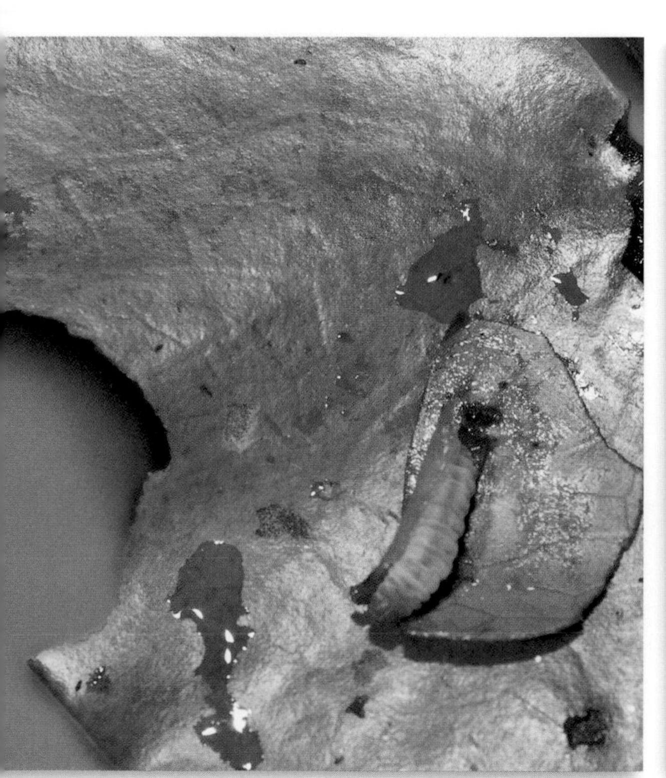

Remove and destroy the work of leaf cutters (left). Water lilies suffering from fungal crown rot (right) must also be discarded.

WATER WILDLIFE

IN THIS SECTION

It's the creatures living in and near the pond that transform a picture-perfect water garden into a vibrant, dynamic ecosystem. Children and adults can spend hours watching the acrobatic antics of fish and frogs. It's relaxing, too, to see koi and goldfish gliding effortlessly through the water like little jeweled submarines. With practice, you can even teach the fish to feed from your hand.

Other animals are drawn to the pond by the sight and sound of running water and are fun to observe. Many birds use small ponds as birdbaths. Herons, egrets, and kingfishers visit larger water gardens in search of food. Hummingbirds dart through the spray from a waterfall. Butterflies draw minerals from the wet sand near the edge of the pond; many are attracted to the color and fragrance of flowering water plants as well as to the cooling environment the pond creates.

Animals you probably would rather avoid come too. Raccoons and opossums visit to

Frogs hunt among lily pads for insects. You can train them to come to you by using live crickets. Some frogs will even come hopping out of the pond when they hear the door open.

forage for a meal, looking for snails and insects in the soil and fish in the water. If your pond has an earthen bottom, muskrats will think it's a great place to build a home. Snakes warm themselves on the rocks and eat small prey—they are especially attracted to the calls of frogs in the water.

Fish top the list of desirable critters in a pond. Goldfish, koi, bass, bluegill, and rosy red minnows are all popular. How do you choose? Goldfish are usually the easiest to find and prettiest to keep in a backyard pond. Koi are also colorful and popular, as are schools of rosy red minnows. Even tropical fish can be kept in the pond in summer. Not all fish are showy on top. Because you see the fish in the pond only from the top, not from the side as you do in an aquarium, check the fish from all angles before buying.

There are other critters too. Dragonflies start their lives deep underwater, hiding among decaying leaves at the bottom of the pond. Several varieties of snails call ponds their home. Tadpoles hatch all through the summer as different kinds of frogs and toads use the pond for an amorous getaway. Clams help keep water clear and clean. Even crayfish can live in a backyard pond, although they might consider the plants a delectable salad bar.

This section offers information and ideas on stocking and caring for animals in your pond, plus some tips on dealing with problems.

Dragonflies are a sign of a healthy pond. They are attracted to ponds with plants. They lay eggs on lily pads and use upright rushes to get out of the water when they become adults.

Fish can be trained to eat out of your hand and may become quite tame. They can live for many years.

GOLDFISH AND KOI

Fish bring both color and movement to your water garden. They also keep the mosquito population in check. Start with just a few fish; then gradually add more.

Goldfish and koi are popular because they are large, colorful fish that are highly visible from above. They are easily trained to take food from your hand. They grow quickly, are generally pest-free, and come in many bright, cheerful colors.

Stocking a pond requires careful planning. Fish can't tolerate the chemicals commonly found in municipal water supplies, so you'll need to neutralize these chemicals before introducing fish to the pond. Also, choose fish with your climate and pool size in mind. Certain species fare better in certain climates and pool depths than in others.

Shubunkin goldfish

The type of fish you stock determines whether you can grow plants in the water garden. Be aware that the diet for both goldfish and koi includes plants, and they can decimate a pond unless you plan for their needs from the start. If the fish are native species, you're safe, at least as far as plant cuisine goes, because native fish eat other fish. But also for this reason, you can't put native fish in the same pond as goldfish, koi, and tropical fish.

Feed your fish at the same time every day, and you'll soon see them eagerly awaiting you in the pond. Give them as much as they'll eat in 10 minutes or so. Use floating pellets or flakes so that when they're done feeding, you can skim leftover food from the pond. Uneaten fish food will decompose and foul the water, leading to poor water quality as well as algae blooms.

Sarassa comet goldfish

Even if you feed koi and goldfish regularly, they may look for supplemental meals in your plants. Goldfish tend to stay small, up to 10 inches or so in length. Stocking the pond with these smaller fish will keep you from having to worry about your plants.

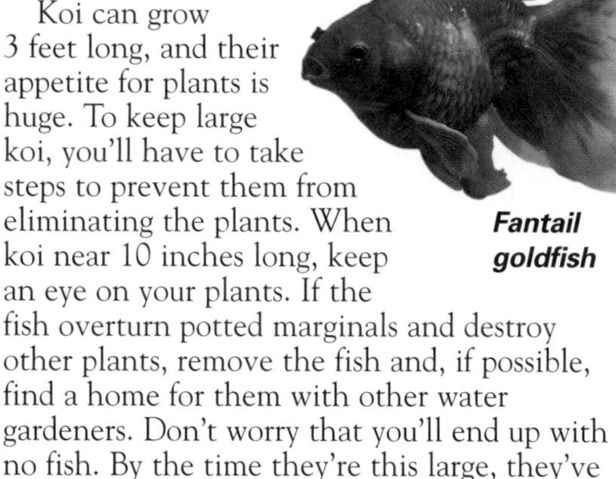

Fantail goldfish

Koi can grow 3 feet long, and their appetite for plants is huge. To keep large koi, you'll have to take steps to prevent them from eliminating the plants. When koi near 10 inches long, keep an eye on your plants. If the fish overturn potted marginals and destroy other plants, remove the fish and, if possible, find a home for them with other water gardeners. Don't worry that you'll end up with no fish. By the time they're this large, they've already made more.

If the goldfish are causing problems, the pond has too many fish and too few submerged plants. Rather than removing fish, you can add more plants. Other solutions include constructing a separate fish-only pond.

With proper management, goldfish and koi make wonderful outdoor pets in the backyard water garden. Because koi have voracious appetites for plants, goldfish may be better choices for small to medium water gardens.

TIP

To keep the filtration needs of the pond within the abilities of your filtrator plants and pump filters, follow these guidelines:
GOLDFISH: Supply at least 5 gallons of water per inch of fish.
KOI: Supply at least 10 gallons of water per inch of fish.
Fish longer than 6 inches need substantially more water.

GOLDFISH

Goldfish originated in the Orient and have been prized in China and Japan for centuries. Asian cultures have practiced refined breeding programs to develop many beautiful goldfish forms and varieties. Goldfish are classified by their color, body shape, and finnage. Those known as fancy have long trailing fins and rounded bodies. Some varieties have unusual eye shapes or forehead flares. Although goldfish can overwinter outdoors, some people bring them indoors for the winter to enjoy their delicate features year-round.

Pearlscale goldfish

The best-known goldfish is probably the comet, which is similar to the orange or red goldfish that many of us had as children. Comets are usually bright orange-red, with long flowing fins. They have torpedo-shaped bodies and swim quickly, adding a special grace and elegance to the water garden.

Yellow and white yamabuki hariwake

There are two other types of comets. Those with red and white markings are known as sarassa comets. Shubunkins are calico-colored. They have a white body with red, blue, orange, yellow, or black markings on their scales.

Other goldfish are fatter and more rounded than comets. Perhaps the best known of these fancy goldfish is the red-cap oranda, with a pearl white body and a red cap, or hat, on the front of its head. All orandas have long, flowing fins; the caudal fin is double and very long and draping.

Orandas come in many colors, including red, black, and white. They may be calico-colored, too, with tricolored scales (Dutch calico oranda) or brown (known as chocolate oranda). Pearlscale has scales that resemble pearly white half-moons.

When you're shopping for fish, you may find some irresistible goldfish with unusual eyes. Bubble-eye goldfish have large sacs that protrude around their eyes. When the eyes extend from the side of the fish's head, the fish is called "telescope" or "dragon-eye." A fish with eyes turned upward is called "celestial." Because the eyes and the areas around them are easily damaged, it is not recommended that these types of fish be kept in an outdoor water garden.

Gin rin koi

Asagi koi

KOI

Sophisticated relatives of the common carp, koi also have their origins in the Orient. Highly prized and sometimes extremely expensive, koi come in a wide range of colors. Their overall shape and color and their markings and scales are called their conformation and are the attributes judged in koi shows all over the world.

With coloring similar to that of shubunkin goldfish, sanke (the large fish in the center) are among the most popular koi.

Koi are classified into categories according to conformation. Distinguishing one type of koi from another requires a keen eye and many years of practice.

The preferred colors are white, red, and black. Blue and silver tones and metallic colors are also possible. Butterfly koi, first introduced and raised in the United States, have long flowing fins. They are more popular with Americans than with koi fanciers in other countries.

One of the most popular categories is the kohaku; these koi are white with red markings. Another favorite is the sanke, which have a white body with red and black markings. Showa have a predominantly black body with red and white markings. Asagi are pale blue with red along their belly and fins. Yamabuki are yellow. Gin rin means the diamond-shaped scales have a sparkly, glittering appearance, regardless of color. Koi with scales that are black in the center are said to be matsuba; those with metallic scales are classified as hikari, and metallic koi of a single color, such as white, are called ogon, or hikarimono.

This specimen is typical of the hybrid koi that result when fish breed in home ponds.

FISHPOND FILTRATION

Because of their large fish load, koi ponds often must have sophisticated filtering systems. Extremely large fishponds, such as you may see in parks, need so much external filtration that the system is housed in a small building.

Fishpond filtration can include skimmers and bottom drains, settling tanks, sand filters, UV clarifiers, diatomaceous earth filters, polishers, biological filters, bead filters, wet–dry filters, aeration towers, up-flow filters, and charcoal filters. Ponds with all of this in place keep the koi or other fish clean and healthy. They are akin to fish swimming pools; the water is so clear that it is transparent, and the fish appear as though they are floating in air.

For most pond owners, such complicated filtration systems are unnecessary. Fish require water that is clean, with perhaps a slight green tint. This more natural design has a charm and beauty all its own, too.

TROPICAL FISH

Guppies and fancy aquarium fish can be brought outside for a summer vacation. Some even help control mosquitoes and other insects.

Tropical fish are good candidates for the pond, whether they're on vacation from the home aquarium or new purchases from the pet shop. When the water temperature warms up to 70°F and above, tropical fish from indoors benefit from an extended excursion to the pond. With more room and more varied foods to choose from, many even breed and exhibit improved vigor.

Most tropical fish peacefully coexist with goldfish and koi. They may try to eat the same food you feed your goldfish and koi, but it will probably be too large for them to manage, and you will still need to feed them flaked food. Tropical fish also control mosquitoes. They love mosquito larvae, as well as adult mosquitoes that land on the water to lay their eggs.

Small fish such as neon tetras or small guppies can fall prey to dragonfly naiads (immature dragonflies). Brightly colored small (minnow-size) fish also attract the attention of kingfishers. Most small fish can keep their numbers relatively stable, though, by constantly producing offspring. Not all tropical fish coexist peacefully. When purchasing fish, ask the supplier which ones can be combined.

Smaller ponds and container water gardens often have highly fluctuating water temperatures that would be detrimental to koi. But many tropical fish thrive in these conditions. They also are more tolerant of the reduced oxygen levels in small water gardens, unlike koi, which require higher oxygen saturation in the pond water.

Any tropical fish is fine for the pond in terms of adapting, but many look like minnows when seen from above. If you are purchasing fish to add to the pond, find a way to get above them to see how they will look in the pond.

Mollies, swordtails, and platys are probably the best choices for a backyard pond. Resembling miniature goldfish, they come in many sizes, shapes, and colors. They reproduce well, are easy to care for, and accept a wide range of habitats. With colors in bright red, orange, yellow, green, black, and white, they are highly visible. Relatively wide-bodied, they are easy to see in the pond. Guppies are difficult to see in the pond because they are generally gray-tan on top. Remember to bring tropical fish indoors when pond water dips below 70°F.

These black mollies, along with orange and green mollies as well as platys, are ideal for small and large water gardens. They form schools without overloading the pond.

NATIVE FISH

Bluegill

Raising native fish in the backyard pond may be a novel idea to some, but it has been done successfully for many years, especially among those who are conservation-minded. It's sensible, too, when you think about it. Native fish are accustomed to the local climate and weather conditions. They prefer the area's flora and fauna for their daily dinner. With the proper protection, they will withstand both the winter freeze and the summer heat and humidity.

Game fish such as bass, perch, crappie, bluegill, and catfish are all predatory fish. They eat the other fish in the water and are not suitable for a pond with ornamental fish such as koi or goldfish. When they're all mixed together, the less aggressive fish (including the koi and goldfish) will tend to "disappear" or become injured, no matter how small the predatory fish may be.

Native fish come in all sizes, shapes, and colors. In a deep pond, the family anglers can practice their casting talents for bass, bluegill, and even pike. In a shallow pond, children can enjoy watching the schooling habits of tiny sunfish, also known as bream.

Some of the more common or popular native fish include top minnows, shiners, and killifish. Top minnows, so named because they live in the top few inches of water along the pond surface, are long, thin, colorful fish that consume several times their weight in mosquito larvae.

Sunfish are more rounded than top minnows. Living deeper in the pond, the various species of sunfish are brightly colored on their sides and often have differing temperaments. Some are outgoing and gregarious; others are shy.

Keeping native fish in your backyard pond is an ideal way to appreciate and learn about your local environment and habitat. Be sure to find out from the appropriate wildlife authorities which species are allowed and which are protected. Learn about the fish species' particular requirements for food and water conditions so they will be safe and thrive in your pond. You might even be able to collect native fish from local waters. Contact your state's natural resources department for the most up-to-date information and follow all regulations regarding licenses and netting.

Native fish, such as this largemouth bass, grow quickly in a water garden. If included in your pond, they will likely eat other fish.

PRAISE FOR THE MOSQUITO FISH

Although water attracts many desirable creatures, it draws one insect that no one enjoys—the mosquito. These pesky biters come to the water to lay their eggs, which hatch into younglings that live in the water for a while before they transform into adult winged mosquitoes. Most species of mosquitoes prefer still, even stagnant, water, but some will lay their eggs in moving water, including a stream in your backyard. Mosquito fish (*Gambusia* spp.) are considered effective in ridding the water of mosquito larvae. You need only a few in a normal-sized backyard pond. In some states, mosquito fish are used as a nonchemical method of mosquito control. In fact, the fish are released by plane into the marshes and everglades of southern Florida. The fish make a free-fall to the water below, where they live and breed, consuming large quantities of mosquito larvae.

STOCKING THE POND

Local and mail-order sources of fish and other living pond creatures abound, so search out a reputable dealer—ideally, someone you know and trust. When working with a local supplier, you have the opportunity to check out the animals before buying. Look for fish that are alert and swim freely in the tank. Avoid fish that swim sideways or those that seem to have trouble navigating. All animals should be free of spots, sores, or ulcers, and fish fins should be clean and full, not tattered or worn.

SAFELY TRANSPORTING FISH

Bringing home new fish can be a stressful time for them and you. To keep problems to a minimum, plan well. Fish are usually transported in plastic bags; for the journey home, place the bag in a polystyrene box which will act as an insulator and reduce changes in water temperature. A sturdy cardboard box will also suffice. Keep the fish cool and in the shade. If traveling by car, don't put the bag in the trunk or in direct sunlight where it could overheat.

It's best to take the fish straight home. The longer they are in the bag, the more stress they have to endure. If the fish will be in the bag for more than a half hour or so, have the store add extra oxygen to the bag; otherwise the fish will use up the available oxygen during transport. For extra-long trips, it's advisable to add a nontoxic disinfectant to the transport water. Some suppliers even add a medication that acts as a mild sedative.

Each of the water creatures you buy for your pond should have its own bag with plenty of air inside. Keep the animals cool and take them right home.

MAIL-ORDER CRITTERS

If ordering by mail, request the fastest shipping possible—overnight is best. If you're buying snails or other aquatic animals as well as fish, ask that each type of creature be shipped in a different bag with oxygen and water. That way, they can't bump into or attack one another during the trip.

Snails are sometimes shipped with plant material in their container, but this isn't the best shipment method. Plants use oxygen when they're in the dark, so when they're in the transport box, they will use up the oxygen the snails need.

Tadpoles are usually shipped like fish, in bags. Offer them plenty of food—crushed dry fish food, or small flaked fish food—as soon as they arrive. Any interruption in their food supply may hasten their development into frogs, and you don't want them to transform into frogs right away, especially if you bought them to eat algae or to scavenge in the pond.

ADDING CRITTERS TO YOUR POND

As a general rule, it's best not to introduce fish or other creatures to the pond during excessively hot or freezing weather or during early spring when temperatures fluctuate greatly. All of these conditions stress the animals, causing them to succumb to disease or illness and ultimately leading to their premature demise.

When you add a new fish to the pond, you must acclimate it gradually because its swim bladder, an internal organ that controls buoyancy, could expand and burst if subjected to extreme changes in water temperature. To acclimate the fish, float the unopened bag in the pond for a few minutes. Do not release the fish into the pond until the temperature of the water in the bag is within 2°F of the pond temperature.

Floating the bag helps to even out the water temperature. If the bag is in the sun, put a damp light-colored towel over it so that the rays from the sun don't heat up the bag. After a few minutes, use a net to gently remove the fish from the bag and place it in the pond.

If your new fish isn't in a bag but is in a bucket or other container, add some of your pond water gradually to the container so the fish becomes acclimated to the pond water temperature. Then gently net the fish and move it to the pond. Very large fish can be lifted with a special sling net that will lessen the possibility that the fish will flip out or thrash around, hurting itself in the process.

Snails don't need to be acclimated to the water because they don't have a swim bladder. Tadpoles also don't have a swim bladder, so they will acclimate to the new pond temperature without needing to be floated.

Unless you know that the bag water the fish, snails, and tadpoles arrive in is safe, it's best not to add it to your pond water. Water from another pond may contain chemicals or diseases that aren't present in your own pond, and you don't want to introduce them. Fish transported over long distances are often sent in water that has been specially treated to keep the fish sedated and medicated. Don't taint your pond by adding this water.

Some authorities recommend that new fish be treated and/or quarantined before they are added to the general fish population. One precaution is to treat the fish by dipping them in a low-salt solution or a special chemical mixture such as formalin for the most common forms of fish diseases. Other treatments may be appropriate if you already have many fish in your pond. Follow the manufacturer's directions very closely with respect to any chemical treatment, and set up a separate quarantine tank for such treatment, leaving your main pond unaffected.

Rather than adding water from another pond or stream to your pond, use a net to place the new wildlife into your pond or pool.

When stocking fish, place their unopened bag in the pond for several minutes so they can adjust to the water temperature.

FISH DISEASES AND PARASITES

Never buy a sick fish, no matter how beautiful, with the thought that you'll be able to treat it. Ulcer disease, such as this, is a serious condition that needs treatment and vigilance until cured.

Goldfish and koi may fall victim to several parasitic or bacterial infections. These may occur because a new fish, infected with a disease, has been introduced to the pond. Many times, however, it's simply something outside the water gardener's control. For example, several kinds of parasites and bacteria occur naturally in pond water. Although present, they generally don't harm fish because the fishes' immune system wards off any attack. When the immune system becomes compromised, fish may become sick.

The most effective way to ensure the fish stay healthy is to practice good pond maintenance. Keep the water clean. Don't allow uneaten fish food, dead leaves, or other organic debris to remain in the pond. Test the water periodically for nitrite, ammonia, and nitrate levels with an accurate test kit. If you refill the pond with municipal tap water, use chloramine remover and dechlorinator to remove chlorine, chloramines, and heavy metals from the water.

Keep your pond clean to avoid fish disease problems. A water test that measures various forms of nitrogen is a good indicator of potential problems that may develop.

One common fish ailment is anchor worm, caused by a parasite that attaches to the fish's skin, leaving a small red mark. The parasite may be visible. Remove it with tweezers and treat the wound with a small swab of a topical medication, such as Betadine. Small ulcers or lesions may appear, especially in spring when fish are spawning. These, too, may be treated with Betadine or a similar medication.

Some illnesses become noticeable because they change fish behavior. Fish gasping near the water surface, especially near a waterfall or fountain, may signal oxygen depletion, nitrite toxicity, or gill flukes (flatworm parasites). Nitrite toxicity is more common in summer when the pond water temperature soars, causing a sudden rise in nitrite levels. Lower the nitrite level and add oxygen with a partial water change and increased aeration.

Fish that suddenly swim very quickly, scraping themselves against the pond sides, may have "ich," a common parasitic infection that manifests itself as small white dots on the fishes' skin. Ask your dealer for medication.

Fish gasping at the surface of your pond indicate one of several possible problems. First try aerating the water to add oxygen. If the gasping persists, test for elevated nitrite levels. Yet another possibility is an infestation of the gill fluke flatworm.

TREATING ILLNESSES

Whatever the ailment and the treatment, closely follow the manufacturer's directions whenever you use a medication. Don't use more than the recommended dosage or use it more often than what is called for. If the disease is contagious, move the ill fish to a quarantine tank to protect the rest of the fish in your pond, or follow label directions for treating the entire fish population.

Consult your fish supplier to help you diagnose the disease and select the proper treatment for your area and conditions. Many diseases are seasonal; temperature and climate changes can cause an outbreak. If your fish are ill with a disease, it is likely that other local pond owners are having similar difficulties. Talking to a reputable supplier as well as neighboring water gardeners will bring common problems and cures to light.

QUARANTINE

When fish fall ill or develop signs that they may be ailing, it's wise to place them in quarantine to treat them. This hospital pond should be completely independent of the main pond. Place it several feet away from your main pond so water spray won't drift from the hospital pond and infect the main pond. Don't use the same pump or filter, or even the same nets, in both the quarantine pond and your water garden.

The quarantine pond should have all the attributes of a regular pond. Depending on its size and the type, number, and size of fish in it, the hospital pond should have a pump to circulate the water and a filtration system to clean the water. It may be necessary to place a net over the pond to prevent fish from jumping out; koi especially are prone to jumping in an effort to escape their new confines. Use bleach or chlorine to disinfect any equipment used in the quarantine pond.

FROGS, TURTLES, AND OTHER CREATURES

Frogs are the most musical addition to the pond. During spring, the breeding calls of mating frogs can be quite loud. If you get too many, bless a park pond with the extras.

Many types of amphibians are attracted to water gardens. They are a sign of a healthy, balanced pond ecosystem and provide hours of enjoyment for you and your family.

FROGS

Some frogs come to live in the water; others just visit to sample the local insect fare. Most toads spend only enough time in the water to lay their eggs, leaving afterward for their preferred terrestrial surroundings. They, too, enjoy munching on the many insects drawn to the water and will do their part in eliminating any mosquitoes around the pond.

If you notice frogs or toads in or near your pond, you are in for a treat. Some homeowners have been able to tame the visitors by feeding them live bait such as crickets or earthworms. It's delightful to sit near the pond and listen to their calls, trying to distinguish each species by its unique sound.

Frog and toad tadpoles appear in the water garden in late spring and intermittently throughout the summer. The adults' early-spring mating calls signal the tadpoles' later arrival. Some tadpoles, such as those for spring peepers or tree frogs, are less than a quarter inch long. They live in the water for a few days or weeks and then transform into frogs. Other frog species spawn tadpoles that remain in this stage longer. Bullfrog tadpoles, for example, spend up to two summers as tadpoles before maturing.

Once grown, adult green frogs and bullfrogs live in the pond year-round. Leopard frogs spend some time in or near the water but spend most of their time on dry land.

Frogs require little attention from the pond owner. Plant the edge of the pond with sedges or arrowhead to provide the frogs with shade and cover. Before mowing the lawn, walk the area around the pond to shoo frogs back into the water. In cold climates, you can build a mound of twigs and leaves near the edge of the pond so the toads will have a place to burrow during the winter. Frogs will bury themselves in the pond mud for the winter.

Not all frogs are neighborly inhabitants in the water garden. Although green frogs and leopard frogs eat only insects, bullfrogs are voracious and omnivorous. Adult bullfrogs have been known to eat goldfish and koi. They will snatch small birds that come to drink or bathe. It's best to relocate a full-grown bullfrog to a natural body of water, unless you have a very large pond and don't mind losing a few of your smaller fish to its rapacious appetite.

TURTLES

Some species of turtles are water-loving amphibians that are delightful, but hungry, pond inhabitants. Red-eared sliders, painted turtles, and snapping turtles all enjoy the water in a backyard pond. They also consider your favorite koi or goldfish as prime fillet for

Someday your pond will have tadpoles. You'll see then in late spring not long after you hear the adult frogs' mating calls. If the tadpole population becomes too large, net some and deposit them in a nearby stream or pond.

dinner, with snails as the hors d'oeuvres. Turtles love to snip water lily pads and oxygenator plants from the bottom of the pond. And snapping turtles live up to their name if disturbed.

If you want turtles in your water garden, create a separate pond just for them. You will have to build a fence or other enclosure to prevent them from wandering away. To learn how to properly care for turtles throughout the year, check with a herpetology club in your area or look on the Internet. Also ask your state's natural resources department whether keeping a turtle is allowed in your area. Many new laws are being passed that restrict or prohibit catching and keeping native fauna, including turtles.

Turtles like to wander off. If you move a pet turtle outdoors for the summer, build a fence to keep it in a protected area by the pond. Remember, raccoons eat turtles, and turtles eat fish.

SNAILS

Snails help control algae. However, they are not the turbocharged algae cleaners that some people make them out to be. If you added enough snails to keep your pond algae-free, there would be little else in the water. An optimum ratio of at least one snail for every square foot or two of water surface is required to keep algae growth down. At that rate, a 2-foot-deep, 10×10-foot pond would need 100 to 200 large snails.

Carefully choose which snails you add to the pond. Avoid Columbian ramshorn and apple snails. They eat water plants, especially water lilies. Japanese snails, northern ramshorn, which are about the size of a dime, and trapdoor snails leave plants alone, preferring instead surplus fish food, fish excrement, and algae that grow on the sides of your pond.

SHELLFISH

Mussels and clams are ideal in water gardens. They are eager cleaners of pond water, filtering up to 200 gallons a day and combing out the pea-soup algae. They provide a fine service to the pond because of their natural filtering abilities, and they live for many years. They are easy to care for, too. Just place them in a pot or tray of soft sand at least 6 inches deep. They will bury themselves until just their tips stick out.

It is illegal in some areas to remove a freshwater clam or mussel from the wild to place in your pond, so contact your state's natural resources department to become aware of local restrictions.

Crayfish tend to be plant eaters as well as scavengers, and so are not recommended for ornamental ponds. If you add one, give it a place to hide, such as a clay tile or a rock pile.

DRAGONFLIES

Dragonflies and damselflies are so adept at snatching mosquitoes on the wing that they are known as mosquito hawks. They consume up to 200 mosquitoes a day. More than 450 species of dragonflies exist in North America alone. They usually find ponds on their own and do not need to be introduced to yours. Even so, many water garden suppliers and mail-order sources carry the juvenile forms of dragonflies and damselflies.

These juveniles may take a year or more to mature. They are carnivorous at this stage, living underwater and feeding on insects as well as very small fish. The adults live for three to four months and will guard a territory around the pond against others of the same species. Adults lay eggs on the undersides of water lily leaves or directly on the surface of the water. These eggs hatch in late summer, and the juveniles overwinter in the pond, even in cold climates.

ATTRACTING BIRDS TO THE WATER GARDEN

This male cardinal is attracted to the fresh water of a water garden. Remember to also provide nesting sites and sheltered feeding locations to draw birds to your garden.

Wild birds flock to any source of water to drink and bathe. The garden pond is a welcome invitation and a gracious change from the roadside puddles they may otherwise be forced to use. Not only do birds drink and splash in the refreshing water, they also eat the insects and use the plants in the area as food, nesting material, and cover from predators.

PLANTS

Vary the heights and textures of plants in your garden to attract the widest variety of birds. Tree branches that overhang the pond by 15 feet or so allow birds to perch and check for predators before flying down for a drink. Leafy tree canopies and brushy shrubs provide safe places to retreat and preen. Tall grasses and other marginal plants around the pond create places for insect-eating birds to forage. Plants with berries and prominent seed heads will guarantee visits from songbirds.

POND DESIGN

Many constructed ponds don't adequately meet birds' vital need for water. Often the sides drop away at a sharp angle, making it impossible for small birds to reach the water. Sometimes young birds fall in and drown. Bird-conscious construction features will make your pond attractive and safe for a wide variety of avian species.

Trickling or splashing water will make your water garden irresistible to all kinds of wild birds. They appreciate the sound of a waterfall or fountain as much as you do. A bamboo spout pouring clear water into a shallow pool is sure to become a popular gathering spot for birds. Consider adding a small waterspout on a sculpture and angling it to spray across the surface of a flat rock at the pond's edge. Small birds especially will appreciate your effort.

Place a birdbath where you can see it from your outdoor seating areas, but where your movements won't disturb the birds. Consider, too, the views from inside the house so that you can fully enjoy the beauty of the bird sanctuary you provide.

An easy way to add a bathing area for birds to an existing water garden is to place a large

A POOL TO ATTRACT WILDLIFE

Build a water feature and birds will come. Water is instantly attractive to all wildlife.

rock with a flat surface 1 inch to 3 inches below the water surface. Place a scrap of extra pond liner underneath the rock to prevent damage from sharp edges. A thin flat stone can be supported by bricks or a plastic crate, which also will provide refuge for your fish.

ADD A BEACH

Add a sand or pebble beach to create a natural-looking and safe spot for birds to walk on. A gentle slope into the water provides a variety of water depths for different size birds. Dig the pond with this in mind and purchase enough liner to cover the extended area. (If your pond is already in place, you can use two-sided liner tape to seam an extra piece onto the existing edge.)

Dig out an area at the side of your pond at least 2 feet square. Leave the outer edge at the same height as the ground and make a gradual slope toward the pond that increases in depth no more than 1 inch for every 8 inches of distance. Dig the inner edge of the beach about 5 to 8 inches below the pond's water level.

Cover the excavated area with the flexible liner. Along the deep edge, place a row of stones large enough to keep pebbles from rolling into the water. Fill in the beach area with enough pebbles to create a maximum water depth of 3 inches, suitable for avian bathing and drinking. Add flat edging stones at the perimeter to provide a landing and preening area.

ADD A BIRDBATH

To create a birdbath that blends with your landscape but does not share water with your water garden, you can make an adjacent miniature pond. Dig out a tapered indention in the ground, to a center depth of roughly 12 inches. Line the hole with pond liner. Fill this with a layer of river rocks or pebbles and add water. If necessary, add more stones until there are bathing areas ranging from 1 inch to 3 inches deep.

For an aboveground birdbath, find a thick, flat stone with a natural depression in one side that will hold water. Add other stones or bricks underneath to raise the bathing stone to the desired height. Locate this in an area near plants or shrubbery so birds will feel safe using it. If you can't find a suitable stone, use an old sink or cement trough sunk into the ground and filled with stones to create the right water depth. Even a large, shallow flowerpot saucer will work. Add marginal plants to soften the edges.

Any birdbath should be cleaned regularly to prevent buildup of bacteria and algae. Vigorous spraying with a sharp stream from your garden hose will probably be sufficient. Loose interior rocks can be scrubbed individually if necessary.

Birds need fresh water year-round. If water freezes in winter where you live, consider installing an electric deicer to keep your birdbath thawed. To discourage mosquito breeding during summer, add a dose of Bti to the water. Available at garden centers, this biopesticide is harmless to fish and animals but will kill mosquito larvae.

Waterfowl such as these mallard ducks appreciate open water for swimming, shallow pools for bathing and preening, and rock ledges for sunning themselves.

ATTRACTING HUMMINGBIRDS TO THE WATER GARDEN

Hummingbirds are naturally attracted to ponds because, like all birds, they need ready access to water. Their arrival in the garden is the highlight of the year for many pond-keepers. These butterfly-sized birds with iridescent feathers beat their wings so rapidly that they can hover around water and desirable flowers. You may see them refresh themselves by flying through the fine spray created by a waterfall splashing against stones. If conditions are suitable, they may even set up housekeeping in your garden and lay their pea-sized eggs in nests the size of walnut shells.

Pond-keepers who want to create an inviting hummingbird habitat must think in terms of scale. Hummingbirds can't withstand torrents of water and need only the shallowest of drinking places. Except for the fine mist that may spray from waterfalls or fountains, most pond features are simply too large for a hummingbird's use.

MINIATURE WATER FEATURES

To create a hummingbird-sized water feature, install a small misting station over a flat rock at the edge of your pond. Hummingbirds will delight in flying through the spray, and small indentations on the rock will collect puddles of water just the right size for them to drink and bathe. Mist attachments for garden hoses are available in most garden centers, and smaller versions specifically intended for use in birdbaths can be found. These misters are easily adapted to work with a small pump at the pond's edge. It takes very little water pressure to create a fine mist, but be sure to turn the mister off at night and when you will be away. Even a fine mist can result in unnecessary water loss from your pond.

Another water feature to tempt hummers is a dripping spout. Use a small pump, or feed from the same pump you've used for your misting station. Run the pump's hose through a small pipe or a length of bamboo and adjust the flow to low. Position a flat rock beneath the trickling or dripping outlet. Angle the rock so any excess water runs back into the pond.

FOOD

To accommodate the rapid metabolism essential to fuel their rapid wing-flapping, hummingbirds feed every 10 minutes throughout the day. Provide them with a steady supply of hummingbird-sized nutrition along with plentiful water and they will probably visit your garden every day.

Hummingbirds will visit and even land where the water is shallow enough for them to get a drink. Even a small indentation in a rock holds just enough. Keep the birds' tiny size in mind when creating a habitat for them.

Include plants near your water garden that have trumpet-shaped red and orange blooms. Hummingbirds will come to dine on the nectar and insects in the flowers. Provide fresh drinking water at a small misting station near the edge of your pond. Hummers enjoy flying through the spray.

Hummingbirds' first choice of food is the nectar of flowering plants. They are particularly drawn to trumpet-shaped blooms. Although red is a preferred color, they will feed from blossoms of other colors as well. Among their favorite plants are honeysuckle, trumpet vine, cardinal flower, lantana, columbine, fuchsia, and impatiens. Flowering shrubs, such as azaleas, weigela, and quince, and flowering trees, such as crab and tulip poplar, will entice them too. The blossoms provide nectar and also attract insects that make up the balance of a hummingbird's diet.

Hummingbirds will reward your efforts to attract them. They appreciate supplemental nutrition from your hummingbird feeder when no flowers are in bloom. Put your feeder up a week or two before the birds are expected to arrive in your area on their northward migration. This may be as early as January in Florida and other southern states, and as late as May in Michigan and other northern states. Maps are available on the Internet to help determine when to expect hummingbirds in your area.

Hummingbird feeders are designed with red on them because hummers find that color so appetizing. To draw even more attention to the feeder, tie a red ribbon to it. To help the birds make the transition to your feeder, hang it near their favorite flowering plants or hang a flowering potted plant near the feeder.

Some hummingbirds are territorial, so if you hang more than one feeder, space them well apart. Many species, such as the ruby-throated hummingbird, will fight to protect their favorite feeders from other hummers.

Hummingbird nectar can be purchased premixed, or you can make it yourself by combining 1 part sugar with 3 parts water and boiling it. Allow it to cool before filling the feeder. Store the leftover portion in the refrigerator. Don't add food coloring to the nectar: The effects of dyes on hummingbirds are unknown and it isn't necessary if you use a feeder with red on it. Do not add honey or artificial sweeteners. Honey ferments easily and artificial sweeteners may harm the birds. Fill the feeder only half full or less because the tiny birds cannot drink more than that before the rest ferments. Clean the feeder with hot water and vinegar every few days. Use a bottlebrush to scrub the inside.

Avoid yellow feeders because they are more likely to attract wasps and bees. To prevent wasps and bees from overtaking your feeding station, use a doughnut-shaped saucer-type feeder. It has a guard around the top that allows hummingbirds to reach the fluid but keeps wasps and bees out. Bees and wasps can reach in only about a quarter inch, but a hummingbird can reach in an inch or more.

Take the feeders down about two weeks after you see your last hummingbird. An old myth says that if a feeder is still available too late in the season, hummingbirds will not migrate but instead will linger and freeze to death in cold weather. This is not true. They are driven by instinct to start flying south at the proper time, and a full feeder will ensure that they are well fed before they start their long journey south.

ATTRACTING BUTTERFLIES TO THE WATER GARDEN

Nectar on the flowers of **Asclepias incarnata** *attracts monarch butterflies. Birds, especially hummingbirds, enjoy it too.*

Butterflies come in a breathtaking array of colors and sizes. Gardeners take pleasure in watching them flit from flower to flower. A water gardener can create an especially appealing butterfly habitat near the backyard pond. A butterfly garden is easily incorporated into the areas in and around existing pond features.

PUDDLES

Like all living things, butterflies need water, food, shelter, protection from predators, and a place to raise their young. Some butterflies linger only while as they migrate through the area with the seasons. Others remain in one vicinity throughout their lifetimes, as long as all their needs are met there.

Butterflies drink from only the shallowest of puddles, hoping to keep their wings dry. They cannot risk the deep water in the water garden, but wet surfaces and tiny puddles created by the spray from fountains or waterfalls serve them well. Even water droplets on marginal plants will be inviting.

Create a drinking station quickly and easily by filling a shallow flowerpot saucer with smooth river rocks. Place it at ground level or raised slightly on a layer of stacked bricks among some blooming plants. Fill it with fresh, cool water just to the point where water is visible between the rocks but does not cover them all. This leaves places on the rocks for sure footing while the butterflies sip.

For an irresistible butterfly attraction, create a pint-sized puddle by digging out a shallow indentation in the ground near your pond. Line it with a scrap of pond liner and an inch or two of sand. Cover any exposed liner with stones. Add just enough water to keep the sand wet. If possible, position this miniature water feature so that it collects water droplets from your pond's waterfall or fountain spray. Make sure that the butterfly puddle area is safe from gushing or rapidly moving water. Puddle visitors may include swallowtails, whites, sulphurs, blues, brushfoots, admirals, and skippers.

Some male butterflies need to drink from mud puddles in order to replenish the salts their bodies need for reproduction. Create a butterfly puddle using mud instead of sand to help them perform this essential function. Expect to be rewarded with visits from a variety of mud-puddlers, including whites, sulphurs, and swallowtails.

PLANTS AND FLOWERS

Butterflies spend their days looking for food and mates. They often collect nectar from a variety of flowering plants, but some species prefer or require a specific type. Likewise, most butterfly caterpillars need a specific kind of host plant. For a garden that butterflies will find most appealing, it helps to use both host and nectar plants. Check on the Internet or at the library for a list of plants best suited to butterflies in your locale.

Plant several different kinds of flowers in your butterfly habitat. Use plants of varying heights with blooms of different colors that flower at different times during the growing season for a continuous supply of butterfly food. Mist plants during dry weather so that butterflies can drink from the water droplets on the leaves.

Wildflowers are a favorite feast for butterflies, and a wildflower garden near your pond will encourage them to visit often. Most wildflowers grow well in the kinds of sunny areas favored by butterflies. Choose native plants and those that are well-adapted to your area's conditions. They not only will require less care from you but also will be more likely to attract local butterflies. Among the best nectar plants to attract butterflies are azalea, black-eyed susan, butterfly weed, butterfly bush, lantana, echinacea, zinnia, verbena, aster, and phlox. Additional food sources are fruits and tree sap.

Provide a secluded area of the garden specifically for host plants. Some hosts are not the most attractive plants, so this careful planting can hide the hosts as well as the damage caterpillars do as they eat them. Host plants include milkweed, snapdragon, thistle, fennel, alfalfa, willow, and sassafras.

Avoid using pesticides in your butterfly garden. Such products are not specific about which bugs they kill, and will eliminate desirable insects such as butterflies in addition to pests. Also, pesticide runoff into your pond can kill your fish. Release beneficial nematodes and ladybugs in the garden to manage pests organically.

Butterflies drink from and bathe in tiny puddles of water in order to keep their delicate wings dry. Droplets on rocks are more than enough.

SHELTER

Creating wind blocks in the area will improve the butterfly habitat. Delicate butterflies, especially those that have just emerged from their cocoons, have trouble flying in harsh or gusty wind, so trellises or rows of plants to divert it are helpful. A wooden privacy fence is a good start.

Butterflies need a safe place to sleep at night, and species that don't migrate must find a place to hibernate during winter. You can encourage them to stay near your water garden by keeping a log pile close by. Although a stack of logs may not be as appealing to you as a little wooden butterfly house, the butterflies know and appreciate the difference. A log pile more closely replicates fallen branches and trees in the woods, where butterflies naturally seek shelter. Stack layers of logs as you would firewood. Elevate the pile according to pest-control codes in your area and cover the top of it to keep out rain.

A shallow birdbath or fountain ledge away from moving water but near blooming plants or wildflowers will bring butterflies to your yard to dine and drink.

CONTROLLING CARNIVORES

RACCOONS AND MUSKRATS

The most frequent animal pests at the pond are raccoons and muskrats. Raccoons don't usually eat water plants; instead, they knock them over and tear them apart searching for snails and insect tidbits in the soil. They also enjoy hunting frogs, and love to catch a koi or goldfish that is unlucky enough to swim by. Raccoons aren't choosy; all fish are fair game.

Raccoons will come around dusk or in the early hours of the morning to feed on insects and small snails. Raccoons eat live fish, so they will try to catch those in your pond. Slow-moving fish, such as fancy goldfish, are easy prey and need particular protection.

One way to deter raccoons is to design the pond so they don't have easy access to the fish in the first place. Raccoons like to wade in shallow water and are reluctant to venture into water that's more than 6 to 8 inches deep. Shallow ledges invite the raccoon to wade into the water, knocking over potted plants and generally wreaking havoc. If raccoons are common where you live, build the pond more than a foot deep, without shallow shelves along the edges. Locate marginal plants away from the edges and support them at the correct depth on bricks. These measures are also effective against opossums, which will search the pond for food, whether insects, frogs, or fish. A net covering the pond or a motion-sensitive impact sprinkler attached to the garden hose may also be deterrents.

Muskrats view water lilies and marginal plants as a food source. Emerged water plants, especially cattails and rushes, that aren't eaten will be stripped to the ground and torn to shreds to build a nest. A small muskrat can easily destroy several plants in a single night's work. Muskrat burrows can lead to multiple holes in the liner, collapsed sides, and lots of mud—in other words, a devastated pond. Either place a motion-sensitive impact sprinkler near the pond or hire someone to legally remove the muskrat. Live traps are an option but their use is regulated in some states; check with your state's department of natural resources for details.

Raccoons can destroy a pond in one night. Attracted to the sound of water or frogs, raccoons topple plants and stones, eat fish and frogs, and tear apart water hyacinth.

BIRD PESTS

Herons and egrets are also fish predators. Unlike raccoons, they are not dissuaded by straight pond sides or deep water. Various products are offered as heron guards, with varying degrees of success. These include an artificial but real-looking heron that can be placed on a post along the edge of the pond. Because birds are territorial, they will not approach when they see another of their kind already near the pond—until they realize that the bird is just a decoy. However, in times of scarce food, hungry herons will give in and feed side by side.

Other fake pond critters can sometimes be helpful in deterring herons. A plastic goldfish glued securely to a rock in shallow water may capture a heron's attention. Real fish can take cover in deeper water while the heron tries to get the impostor to cooperate.

Some homeowners have kept herons away with artificial alligators, made of hard plastic or stone. Such success may be dependent on geography; herons that live year-round in the north may not know what alligators look like.

Kingfishers dine almost exclusively on small fish, so they will see your fishpond as an invitation to a meal. You may hear their loud, rattling calls before they arrive. Like herons and egrets, kingfishers are not deterred by deep water, and will even dive completely underwater to catch a choice morsel. They watch for prey from nearby perches or hover in flight 10 to 20 feet above the water. They also eat frogs and turtles. Use 1-inch or 2-inch mesh netting stretched and supported across your pond to keep kingfishers out. Birds may become entangled in finer mesh.

A backyard pond or water garden where fish live is a magnet for hungry herons like this Great Blue. Give your fish aquatic plant cover or another place to hide from birds.

The Belted Kingfisher watches from a perch above the water until it sees a fish, then dives down into the water to catch it in its bill.

CONTROLLING CARNIVORES

continued

SOLUTIONS

Occasionally, your water garden may be visited by the neighbor's dog or cat. Some homeowners have had to reline entire ponds after a dog's nails punctured the flexible liner. Depending on where you live, deer may also stop by. Although not necessarily harmful to the pond, they can be a nuisance. Nearly every suburban gardener has a story of walking out to the pond one morning ready to work or just relax, only to find that the local deer had munched on most of the water lily pads and flower buds that would have bloomed that day.

Large blankets of netting, such as that used to protect fruit trees from birds, may keep deer, dogs, raccoons, opossums, herons, and egrets at bay. It's usually effective but always unattractive. If you use it, float a large beach ball in the pond so the netting does not sink. If the only concern is night-marauding raccoons and opossums, the netting can be placed over the pond in late evening and removed in the morning. If birds are the culprits, the netting will have to remain over the pond day and night. Secure it all the way around with bricks or heavy stones so that would-be diners can't wiggle under the protective netting.

A 6-inch-tall, low-voltage electric fence also can prevent access to unwanted visitors. Be sure to turn it off when you're working near the pond.

Crisscrossing the pond with string or clear fishing line is effective against certain birds, including Canada geese. The birds land on the lawn near the pond, but the string prevents them from reaching the water. Unable to traverse the fishing line "fence," they become disenchanted and leave the pond alone.

Perhaps the most effective deterrent is an impact sprinkler with a motion-sensitive device attached to the garden hose. When activated, it sprays a strong jet of water in a wide circle. Startled by the spray, the intruder runs or flies away. The sprinkler can be left on all the time to ward off many sorts of pests. Remember to turn it off, so you and your friends don't get soaked when you go out to admire the waterfall.

Motion-detector sprinklers can deter herons, deer, raccoons, and opossums; however, they're not 100 percent effective. Use more than one to help protect a large pond.

Streamers across a pond help scare off birds. They are a quick solution, but not a permanent one; the birds may adjust to their presence after a few weeks.

SNAPPING TURTLES

While turtles are an important indicator of a healthy ecosystem, they can be devastating to a small water garden. All turtles enjoy a tasty water lily bud or a bite of submerged plant. But snapping turtles in particular, which eat fish, frogs, snails, and beneficial insects, can cause serious problems in a backyard pond.

It is nearly impossible to keep turtles from finding a way in. They are drawn to the sound of moving water and can sneak under a fence gate or bird netting. If your water is clear, you may be able to see a snapper at the bottom of the pond. More likely, however, you will know you have one when you see half a fish float by.

A snapping turtle will be as eager to get away from you as you are to get away from it. Snappers are not usually aggressive toward people who aren't bothering them. However, one that feels vulnerable—especially on land—presents a challenge. Snapping turtles have strong beaks and sharp claws that can cause serious wounds. They can quickly turn their long necks all the way around to face backward. When confronted, they may also emit a foul-smelling orange ooze from the back edge of their shells. The best advice is not to touch one unless you absolutely must, and then only by grabbing the turtle's tail and hindmost edges of its shell.

Because common snapping turtles can live to be 50 years old and weigh about as many pounds, it is important to remove them from small ponds as soon as they are detected. Check with your state department of natural resources for the most recent regulations and recommendations on trapping and relocating snapping turtles.

MOSQUITOES

There may be nothing more disruptive to an evening's quiet contemplation by the pond than the persistent whining of hungry mosquitoes. Born in and attracted to water, they will surely be a part of your waterscape. Mosquitoes prefer still or stagnant water for breeding, such as rainwater caught in old tires, flowerpots, and gutters. Even birdbaths can be attractive spots, so keep them clean and change the water often.

One of the best mosquito controls may already be in your pond: your fish. Fish eat mosquito larvae, thereby reducing the potential population. Also, moving water makes the pond's surface a less desirable breeding ground. A waterfall or other feature that breaks the surface tension will be an effective deterrent.

Bats eat mosquitoes, so consider putting up a bat house for them near your water garden. If bats make you uncomfortable, perhaps a house for purple martins would be a better choice. They eat mosquitoes too.

If your water is obviously infested, you may want to add the biopesticide Bti. It is deadly to mosquito larvae but will not harm plants, fish, or other wildlife.

PROJECTS

The most successful water garden follows a plan and has a design that weaves together the entire project. The plan and design need to be integrated with the contours and style of the overall landscape and with the gardener's individual lifestyle.

The best plan, therefore, will always reflect a balance of both practical and aesthetic elements. For example, the size and shape of your water garden should conform not only to the scale of your yard but also to the amount of time and funds you can devote to the maintenance of its plants and wildlife.

If you have less than an hour each week to devote to caring for your pond, consider a small installation, even if you have a large backyard. Similarly, if your schedule allows you to enjoy your pond only in the evening and on weekends, your best bet might be to have a "moon garden," with tropical water lilies and other plants that bloom at night.

If your primary interest is attracting birds and butterflies, you'll need to include design features such as a sandy butterfly beach or a shallow area at the pond edge that will serve as a birdbath.

Families with young children might take comfort in the safety of a shallow bog garden. Container water gardens are also perfect for family-oriented yards or in small urban spaces.

Gardeners who enjoy entertaining outdoors might choose to build a small, formal pool within a well-planted seating area. Others might create multiple ponds connected by streams and waterfalls in a natural setting. Hobbyists may want to focus on features most compatible with fish.

Look through the projects that follow for inspiration and guidelines.

If you already enjoy gardening, the tools you keep on hand will be just what you need to begin many of the water garden projects on the following pages. Most are do-it-yourself designs that can be completed in a few hours to a few weekends. The rewards will last for years.

IN THIS SECTION

ENLISTING PROFESSIONALS

If you don't have the time or inclination to construct a water feature, consider hiring a contractor. The growing demand for water features has attracted the attention of many landscapers and building contractors. Local home and garden shows present an excellent opportunity to meet water feature installers. Seek out those with whom you can easily discuss your project. Examine their portfolios of finished projects and ask for references. Visit several projects that have been in place at least two years. Remember, even though a water feature's portfolio photos may exceed your expectations, arrange to inspect the feature in person to make sure that it functions properly. It is important to inspect contractors' work and talk with their clients.

DEALING WITH CONTRACTORS

Get a written estimate of the project; be aware that the final cost may vary. Many landscapers offer to bill you based on hours of work plus materials and markup for overhead and profit. Request price quotes from several contractors. In some areas, specialized firms send a skilled team to install a complete water feature in a day. Verify that the contractor has a license (where applicable) and insurance, and that all permits will be secured.

Agree on a final price with payment subject to completion of the project, and get a contract that details the terms. A contract should state the exact price agreed upon, subject to a timetable as well as to completion of the project. If you make any changes from the agreed-upon specifications, be prepared to pay the contractor's asking price. If timely completion is crucial, include a financial penalty if work is not finished within the agreed number of workdays. If a project takes weeks, provide partial payment as the work meets important defined points, holding back full payment until satisfactory completion of the project.

DESIGNS

Some contractors employ designers. For a modest fee, they create a plan in tune with your ideas. If you accept the plan, the design fee is applied to the overall price of the project. You can engage your own designer to make the detailed plan. Most designers work closely with landscapers and builders and can recommend contractors. Some designers will oversee the project for you if you want. Large or complicated designs often work best when built by skilled professionals. However, if you have experience as a do-it-yourselfer, you will find most of the projects on the following pages to be well within your abilities.

Building a water feature can often be an excellent do-it-yourself project. But for more complex pool and pond construction, hiring professional help can make the job even easier. Be sure to check contractors' references and visit some of their completed projects before signing a contract.

CONTAINER GARDENS

Container water gardens are perhaps the easiest to start with. You can create one in an hour or two with no digging and little expense. And you can put them anywhere.

Virtually any kind of container works for a water garden. If it holds water—or can be made to hold water—it can become a water garden. Here are some suggestions: whiskey half barrels, galvanized buckets, livestock troughs (older ones that are no longer shiny; otherwise they can be toxic); oversize dishes and bowls, boulders or rocks with hollows, black plastic tubs designed for water gardens, wooden buckets, iron kettles, and old claw-foot bathtubs.

With a pond in a pot, you can have a water garden anywhere, even on a balcony.

TABLETOP GARDENS

After choosing a container, check it for watertightness. Fill it with water and place it on a dry surface, such as a sidewalk or driveway. Let it sit for a full day, checking occasionally for leaks. If it does leak, seal minor cracks from inside the pot with aquarium-grade silicone sealant or caulk.

Make wooden and porous containers watertight with a flexible liner or a brush-on sealant designed especially for water gardens. (You must seal or line whiskey barrel halves if they smell of whiskey to keep impurities in the wood from killing fish.) If using flexible liner, fold and tuck it carefully into all recesses; staple or glue edges to the container with silicone sealer or rubber adhesive.

You may want to seal your container with spray urethane, even a pot that is glazed or galvanized. The urethane keeps terra-cotta pots from weeping, and it protects galvanized and iron containers from rust. Apply three coats to the inside of the pot.

PLANT THE CONTAINER

PLANTS: Choose plants for your container in keeping with its scale, such as fairy moss, miniature cattail, water iris, or 'Spiralis' rush. Plants that trail over edges, such as parrot's feather, with its feathery leaves and curling stems, also work well. Miniature water lilies such as 'Helvola', 'Rose Laydekeri', or 'Perry's Baby Red' are also good. Water-lily-like plants, such as water poppy or water snowflake, are good substitutes in container gardens. Frogbit makes a wonderful addition as a floating plant. Miniature umbrella grass is in keeping with the container's small scale.

1. Plug drainage holes with a scrap of liner spread with caulk. Fix cracks with caulk or sealant (aquarium-grade for pots with fish). Waterproof the inside of the pot with water-garden paint. It comes in black, white, or gray. Seal wooden containers with flexible liner.

2. Use a small fountain or aquarium bubbler to aerate the water. You'll need to match the pump's size to the pot's volume. To measure volume, fill the pot from 5-gallon buckets. Conceal the pump's cord with plants and plug it into a GFCI outlet.

CONTAINER GARDENS
continued

FISH: If you plan to stock your mini pond, you'll need to balance plant needs for sun with fish needs for oxygen. Most water garden plants do best with six hours or more of full sun per day. That much sun on a hot day heats up water significantly. In turn, the water becomes oxygen depleted, which stresses fish. You can help fish get enough oxygen even in a warm site by positioning the container garden where it receives afternoon shade. Keep a thermometer in the water, and never let the water get warmer than 85°F. If fish surface to gasp for air, aerate the water immediately.

***3.** Fill the container with water and let it sit for five to seven days to dissipate chlorine and stabilize water temperature. (Or use chlorine remover.) Treat for chloramines if needed. Add a small battery-powered air stone or pump to provide adequate aeration for fish.*

***4.** Choose plants with a variety of shapes, textures, and colors. Include some that dangle over the edge and others, such as sedges, that are tall and spiky. You may need to set smaller pots on bricks or flat stones to achieve the correct depth.*

***5.** Add fish. Fish make an ordinary garden extraordinary. Let them adjust to the water by floating them in their water-filled plastic bag for 10 minutes before you release them.*

Use a small, battery-powered aeration pump or an air stone, a device with a small external pump that's placed in the water.

Stock the pot with tropical fish or small goldfish. Mollies, platys, and swordtails are good choices for container water gardens. They handle high water temperatures and dine on mosquito larvae. Cover the container with netting to keep the fish from jumping out. Don't try koi in a container; they don't survive in such small areas.

Because the container garden will hold only a few fish, control the population by relocating offspring.

FOUNTAINS: Fountains help oxygenate water. The fountainhead and volume have to be just right, however. Avoid large, high sprays; choose a spray pattern in keeping with the container style. Small spitting fountains, such as a small fish or frogs that gently spray water into the pond, are well-suited for containers. Remember, too, that most floating plants don't like their leaves splashed, so you may have to choose between having fish and plants or a fountain.

You'll need only the smallest of pumps—a bubbler is a good choice. The pump should have an adjustable spray to fit the container. Drape its electric cord over the back, and hide it among plants or bury it under gravel.

PLANT LIST FOR THE CONTAINER GARDEN

Code	Plant Name	Number
A	Water lettuce	5
B	Umbrella grass	1
C	Horsetail	1
D	Moneywort	1

CONTAINER PLAN

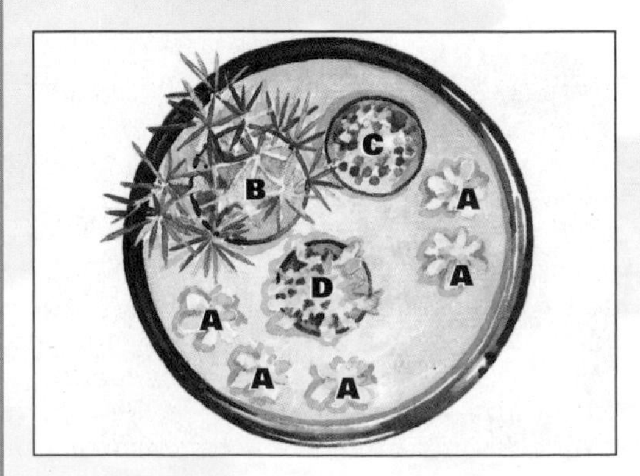

You Will Need

- Container as desired
- Floating plants
- Miniature water lily or other plants
- Garden soil or aquatic-mix potting soil
- Pea gravel

For a trailing effect, plant parrot's feather to one side (above). Turn a terra-cotta pot into a tiny garden by planting a miniature water lily in 3 to 4 inches of soil. Add water almost to the rim (left).

TABLETOP GARDEN

Dip into water gardening in a small way by creating a tabletop design. You can use many of the same plants you would in a larger garden; in fact, some that become invasive in a pond behave better in the restricted space of a container.

Choose any container that does not have drainage holes in the bottom. Use floating plants in water. Or treat the plants as if they were marginal or bog plants, and plant them in a layer of soil topped with a layer of pea gravel. Then fill the container with water.

Plants for Tabletop Gardens

- Floating fern
- Miniature water lily
- Parrot's feather
- Water fern
- Water lettuce
- Water snowflake

Water lettuce and white-flowered water snowflake thrive in a container set on a patio table (right). Combine plants with a variety of foliage markings, textures, and heights to create a pleasing miniature garden.

CONTAINER GARDENS
continued

YOU WILL NEED

- 10- to 14-inch-diameter ceramic or stone pot at least 12 inches deep
- 1 to 2 tablespoons crushed charcoal (aquarium type)
- Pebbles or river stones (optional)
- Floating plants

Water hyacinth's bright leaves are the just the right size for a small, decorative pot (above). Other good choices for container gardens include water poppy, water fern, and duckweed.

CERAMIC POT

Potted water gardens accent a perennial border or bed, become a focal point in a planting of herbs, or brighten a lightly shaded patio or balcony.

Creating a potted water garden is easy. Any container (except metal, which can heat the water in summer) will do, as long as it does not have any drainage holes at the bottom. The delight of having the plants at eye level more than makes up for the increased care, which includes keeping a watchful eye on the water level.

If you'd like to include oxygenating plants or fish, you'll need a container that's at least 12 inches deep. To keep the water fresh and clear, add some crushed charcoal, top with a layer of pebbles or river stones, and fill the pot with water.

Floaters are the easiest water garden plants to use since they don't require potting. Spread out or untangle the roots and set the plants on water.

SEASONAL CARE

Check the water level and top the water off periodically, especially during the hot days of summer.

When cool autumn weather arrives with temperatures 55°F or lower, move the plants—or the entire container—indoors for the winter.

WHISKEY BARREL

Whiskey barrels lend themselves to all kinds of plantings, and water gardens are no exception. Their size accommodates several plants as well as a few goldfish and snails.

YOU WILL NEED

- Half whiskey barrel
- Flexible or rigid plastic liner
- Bricks or cinder blocks
- Potted plants
- 3 to 4 goldfish (optional)

SETTING UP

Whiskey barrels are watertight as long as they are wet, but to be safe—and to prevent toxins from leaching into the water—line the barrel with a sheet of PVC or EPDM plastic, or a rigid plastic liner (available at nurseries and garden centers). Staple the liner about 2 to 3 inches below the rim, where it won't show.

Plant all the plants in garden soil in plastic pots. You can either float the floating plants or pot them. Placing the floaters on top of the water is the simplest way to maintain them; if they grow too vigorously, remove some from the barrel.

Set the plants in the barrel, placing them on bricks or prewashed cinder blocks to bring them to the correct depth under the water's surface. (See individual plant entries on pages 112–150 for the preferred depths.)

FISHY BUSINESS

A whiskey barrel can support three or four small fish—ordinary goldfish. Exotic fish, such as koi, need a larger pond to survive. A location with some shade, particularly at midday, will help the fish survive in water that is often subject to sudden and extreme changes in temperature. In colder zones (below Zone 6), bring the fish indoors to an aquarium for winter.

Water cannas, dwarf papyrus, caladium, and water lilies bring color, height, and texture to a barrel garden.

CONTAINER GARDENS
continued

Tuck a small container garden into an existing flower bed. Dwarf papyrus, elephant's ear, and water fringe grow well in areas of dappled shade, where impatiens and ferns also thrive.

YOU WILL NEED

- 12- to 16-inch-diameter container
- Garden soil
- Crushed charcoal
- Sand or pea gravel
- Bricks or cinder blocks
- Water plants

CONCRETE CONTAINER

Plant containers such as the one shown above following the directions for the whiskey barrel on page 197. Do not use small pots like these for fish. When winter approaches, bring the plants indoors to a cool, frost-free location. If you leave the container outdoors, empty it of water and clean it.

Fill a plastic pot with heavy garden soil. Avoid commercial potting mixes because they contain additives that might separate and float out into the water. (See page 156 for soil suggestions.) Hollow out a planting hole in the center with your hands.

Set the plant in the hole; untangle and spread out the roots. If the plant has a lot of stems and foliage, cut them back a little to make handling easier. Add soil and gently work it around the roots with your fingers. Tamp the soil firmly but don't compact it. Water thoroughly.

Cover the soil with ½ inch of sand or pea gravel, and water again. Sink the potted plant into the container so the rim of the pot sits 4 to 6 inches below the water's surface. If the container is too deep, put a brick beneath the pot to raise it to the correct level.

PLASTIC CONTAINER

When the plants in your water garden begin to look crowded, it is time to divide them. Share some with other aquatic gardeners, and use some to plant a container water garden to use on a deck or patio.

By the time a marginal plant is ready to divide, it may be root bound. With a sharp knife, cut the plastic pot down the side to remove the plant and its root ball intact. Gently loosen any roots that have grown through the pot's drainage holes.

Slice through the root ball, cutting it in half. Depending on the size of the plant, you may want to divide it further. You'll want fairly small divisions to start in your container garden, but make sure they have ample roots attached. (See pages 158–165 for information on dividing and potting plants.)

Plant the divisions in new plastic pots filled one-quarter to one-half full of garden soil. Center a division in the pot and fill in around the roots with more soil. Water thoroughly and cover the soil surface with pea gravel.

Fill a wide plastic container with water deep enough that your newly potted divisions will sit several inches below the water surface. Sink the pots in the container, using bricks or upturned clay pots to support any that need to be raised. Choose a variety of plants for texture and color, and add a floating or trailing plant.

Chameleon plant, dwarf cattail, four-leaf water clover, and a water lily create a lush container garden suitable for use on a deck or patio or in a perennial bed.

YOU WILL NEED

- 24-inch-diameter plastic container
- Bricks or upturned pots
- Garden soil
- 5–6 tablespoons crushed charcoal (to help maintain water freshness)
- Pea gravel
- Potted plants
- Floating plants

PLANT LIST FOR THE CONTAINER GARDEN

- Chameleon plant
- Dwarf cattail
- Four-leaf water clover
- Hardy water lily

CONTAINER GARDENS

continued

A TASTY GARDEN

A water garden can provide plants that are interesting to grow and eat as well as ones with beautiful flowers or handsome foliage.

You can eat the leaves of water fern, water spinach, and chameleon plant (although some people find it too bitter). The leaves, tuberous roots, and seeds of lotuses are mainstays in Asian cuisine. Add the leaves of water celery to soups for a mild celery flavor. Use the leaves of water mint as you would other mints. Harvest the tubers of duck potato and roast them. Use peppery watercress in salads and sandwiches. It does best in moving water but can be grown in a container.

Plant water chestnuts in the spring in any shallow container that will hold water but does not have drainage holes in the bottom or sides. Put 2 to 3 inches of soil in an 18-inch container that is at least 6 inches deep. Place the corms an inch or two apart and cover with a couple of inches of soil. Gently firm the soil on top of them.

Fill the pot with water so that the surface of the water is at least an inch above the soil. Place the pot in full sun, and feed once a month with liquid fertilizer.

Water chestnuts mature in about 6 months. When the foliage turns brown, lift the plants out of the soil. Wash off the soil and rub the foliage off the chestnuts.

With a sharp knife, peel the chestnuts and use them in stir-fries or hors d'oeuvres.

The grasslike foliage of water chestnuts will turn brown when the corms are ready to harvest.

YOU WILL NEED

- Plastic pots or tubs
- Garden soil
- Pea gravel or pebbles
- Tubers, corms, plants
- Fish emulsion

Peel the chestnuts and cook them in stir-fries or wrap them with bacon and grill for a crunchy treat. Re-plant some of the smaller, unpeeled corms in fresh soil for next year's harvest.

SUNKEN GARDEN

Insulate your container garden against temperature changes by sinking a pot in the ground rather than placing it on a deck or patio. The result is a miniature pond that looks particularly attractive at the edge of a path or surrounded by other plants.

Visit architectural salvage yards and flea markets for discarded items that can hold water. A plastic washtub, a galvanized feed trough from an animal supply store, or even an old ceramic sink can be transformed into a sunken garden. Be sure to plug any holes so that water is not lost.

When you've chosen your container, use it as a guide to dig the hole. Excavate an area slightly larger and deeper than the container so that when you fit the pot in the hole its rim will sit flush with ground surface. Add a layer of sand or gravel to help level the bottom of the hole.

Set the container in the hole and fill in around it with sand, gravel, or excavated soil to secure it. Disguise the edges with flat rocks or marginal plants.

Fill the container with water and let it stand several days before planting to stabilize the temperature and allow excess chlorine to evaporate. Then add a water lily or lotus and a half dozen or so potted and floating aquatic plants.

YOU WILL NEED

- Shovel
- Plastic planter
- Sand or gravel
- Flat stones or flagstones
- Marginal plants
- Floating plants

Make sure the rim of the container is slightly above ground level. Otherwise, water will seep into the adjacent soil.

Almost any container can be turned into a sunken water garden—even an old sink or a metal horse trough. Camouflage the rim with rocks and plants.

BOGS AND STREAMS

BOG AT POND'S EDGE

This is a gardener's bog built to enhance the safety of a water garden. Because the owners were fearful that visitors or children might slip and fall into the water, they rebuilt the pond to make it more stable and added a bog as a buffer between visitors and open water.

The pond is approximately 10 feet wide by 12 feet long and 2 feet deep. A 3-foot by 4-foot header pool, also 2 feet deep, is connected to the main pool by a three-step waterfall. Along one edge the bog provides ample room for marginal water plants. Large flat stones on the other edge provide a stable area for visitors to walk up to the water.

The bog planting pocket is roughly 2 to 3 feet wide, 6 to 10 inches deep, and about 6 to 10 inches above the water line at the edge farthest from the pond. Pond underlayment and liner were placed in this pocket and then held in position at the far edge of the pocket with fieldstone. The pocket was filled in with clay soil. The pocket's pondside edge is below the water line, so water filters into the pocket and keeps the soil moist.

NATURAL BOG

Instead of filling your bog with soil, use silica sand—the kind used in sandblasting or in pool filters. Limestone-based sand is harmful to the plants because the lime forms compounds with other minerals in the sand, making nutrients unavailable to plants.

For a natural bog you'll need to plant sphagnum moss, which is the best indicator of the health of a bog. If it is turning brown and having trouble growing, other bog plants won't grow either. If the moss is growing well, other bog plants will also flourish.

First, place a few inches of premoistened long-fiber dried sphagnum moss on the surface of the soil. On top of that, place live sphagnum moss. You can use just the dry sphagnum moss, provided it has some green tips, which provide spores that will grow into live sphagnum moss. You may also find that additional sphagnum moss is likely to be attached to small carnivorous plants from the store.

Irrigate natural bogs with acid (pH 6) water low in minerals. Distilled water or rainwater are good sources to start the bog with.

A bog garden can keep visitors from getting too close to the water's edge.

The acid soil in a true bog leads to a much different planting. Venus flytraps, sundews, and pitcher plants are typical of a true bog. Even the peat moss thrives.

Create a bog garden to solve the problem of a low spot in the yard, ease the transition from pond edge to landscape, or simply provide a place to grow wet-soil lovers.

FREESTANDING BOG

The bog garden forms a natural transition between a wet area and dry land. This freestanding bog includes water-loving marginal plants that thrive in moist soil. Exotic-looking plants add an element of the unexpected to the residential landscape. A bog provides an ideal opportunity to turn a poorly draining site into a beautiful asset.

BUILDER'S NOTES: Excavate to 16 inches deep; line the site with a 2-inch layer of sand topped with a flexible liner. Install a perforated PVC pipe in the bottom of the bog, extending one end of it just above where the soil will be level so that you can connect it to a hose to keep the soil saturated. Cover the bottom of the bog with a 3-inch layer of gravel. Refill the bog with the soil saved from excavating; mix in generous amounts of peat moss.

APPROXIMATE SIZE: 10×15 feet

VARIATIONS: Make the bog a narrow strip, a small pocket adjacent to a pond or stream, or a sprawling wetland. Plant a bog garden in a large plastic tub sunk into the ground; fill it with a collection of carnivorous plants. Substitute leaky hose for PVC pipe.

Primroses and irises thrive in and near the water of a bog garden, while forget-me-nots, loosestrife and rhododendrons make excellent companions in moist soil nearby.

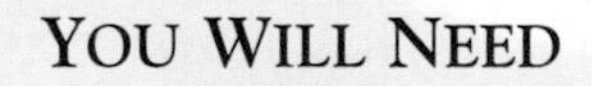

YOU WILL NEED

- 1 EPDM rubber liner, 15×20 feet
- Geotextile underlay (optional)
- 12 feet of 1½-inch PVC pipe
- Elbow fitting
- Hose fitting
- PVC sealant
- 1 ton sand
- 1 ton gravel
- Rock for edging
- 1 bale peat moss
- Immersible containers (optional)
- Plants: ligularia, taro, thalia, arrowhead, parrot's feather, rush, ludwigia, yellow iris

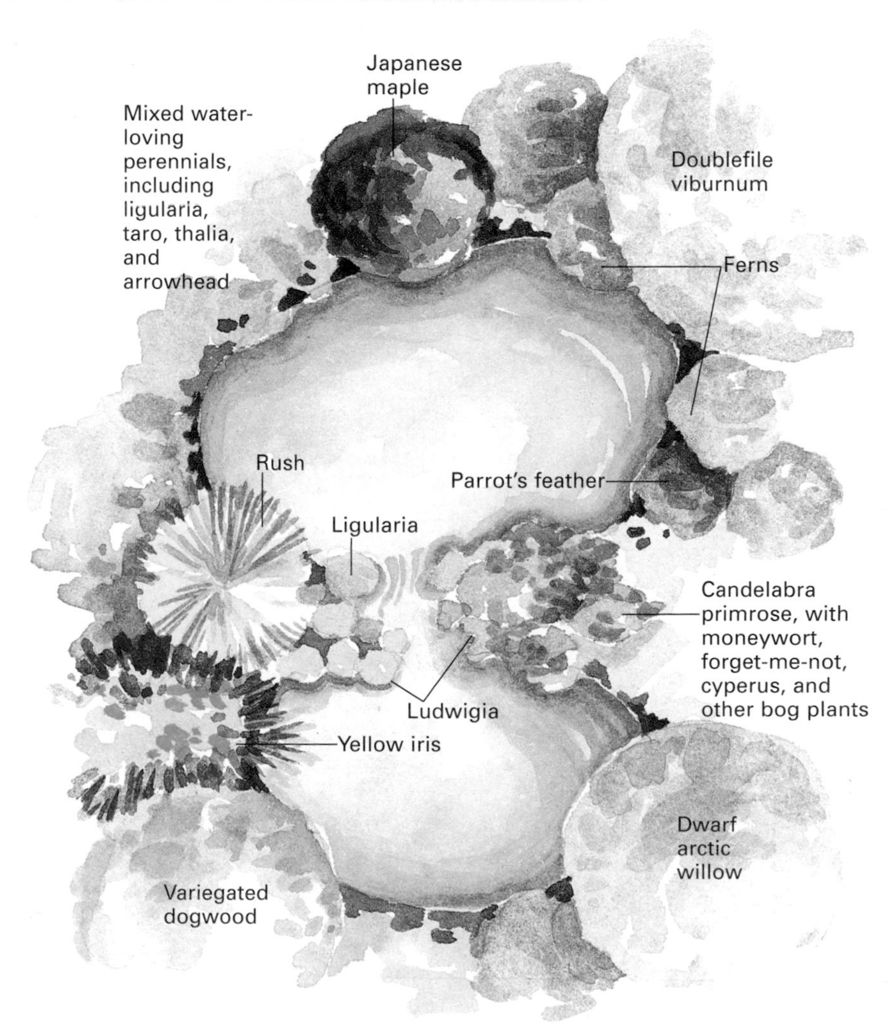

BOGS AND STREAMS
continued

Transform a low spot in your yard into a lotus bog. All it takes is a little digging and a scrap piece of flexible liner to create the warm, shallow garden that lotuses love. Choose a sunny location; lotuses thrive in hot weather. Skip the pots and plant them directly in the bog.

LOTUS BOG

Lotuses love warmth. They bloom best in summer sun and hot temperatures. However, those grown in pots in the pond can be a time-stealing maintenance chore. Since they grow well in just a few inches of water, it's not really necessary to pot them and lug them into the pond. Find a scrap of EPDM liner and locate a good place to dig a hole, and then make your own lotus bog.

DIG THE HOLE: Is there a low spot in your yard or garden where water always collects after a hard rain? Do you have an empty corner by your front porch where nothing but weeds seem to thrive? Just about any place where you can dig a 2-foot hole will probably work for your lotus bog.

Choose your site and dig your hole, reserving the soil for backfilling later. In Zones 5 and colder, dig about 6 to 8 inches deeper than your average frost line. Even in warmer zones, make your hole 18 to 24 inches deep to give the lotus ample growing room. In colder climates the depth will keep the lotus warm in winter; in warmer areas it will keep the water cool during the growing season. If your soil is heavy clay, angle the sides of the hole slightly outward from bottom to top.

INSTALL THE LINER AND DRAIN TILE: Sculpt a collar around the top of the hole about 6 inches wide and deep. Then place the liner into the hole, making small pleats in the excess so that it all fits securely. Use river rocks or other stones to hold the top of the liner in place inside the sculpted collar.

Cut a few notches in one end of the drain tile and place the tile notched-end down onto the bottom center of the lined hole. Secure the tile in that position with the pea gravel. This allows water to flow out of the drain tile into the bog but keeps dirt out of the tile.

FILL AND PLANT: Backfill the hole with the excavated soil to within 6 inches of the collar. Add extra stones to disguise any liner that still shows. If you're transplanting a lotus that is already growing, put it in the soil a few inches deep. Then fill the hole gently from a garden hose, letting some of the water enter through the drain tile. If you're planting a dormant, bare-root rhizome, fill the bog with water first. After the dirt is thoroughly saturated, plant the lotus rhizome.

FERTILIZE: Fertilize the lotus during the growing season by dropping fertilizer tablets into the drain tile. Mulch the bog with straw in winter if it is sited in an exposed area.

YOU WILL NEED

- EPDM liner, about 10×10
- Corrugated, nonperforated drain tile, 4 inches in diameter and 2½ feet long
- 3 gallons of pea gravel
- Large river rocks or other heavy stones
- 1 lotus rhizome

A stream attracts wildlife and offers visual interest all year long.

STREAMS

Two streams become one as they rush to two ponds below. A small waterfall connects the ponds; another small waterfall splits the stream in two. The rushing water draws attention to its beauty and sound. A strategically placed, comfortable chair invites the visitor to linger. The feature attracts wildlife and offers year-round interest. Landscaping includes trees, shrubs, and perennials suitable for shade.

BUILDER'S NOTES: Every stone is carefully selected and placed with consideration of how it will affect the water's flow. Excavating the 6-inch-deep stream takes one day; digging the double pond takes another day. Use an algaecide for a feature that doesn't include fish.

VARIATIONS: Use a simpler design, including one pool and a single stream. Aquatic plants, such as iris and pickerel rush, could be added to quiet nooks in the stream. Water lilies, submerged plants, and marginal plants could inhabit the two ponds. Divert one-third of the water to run through a UV clarifier, enabling you to use a smaller pump and save money.

YOU WILL NEED

- 1 EPDM rubber liner, 5×45 feet
- 2 EPDM rubber liners, 10×15 feet
- Geotextile underlayment
- 2 tons sand
- 1 ton washed gravel
- 2 tons river rock
- 4,000 gph pump
- 70 feet of 2-inch PVC pipe; 30 feet of 1½-inch PVC pipe
- Fittings: one 2-inch PVC T-fitting; two 2×1½-inch PVC reducers; 2 gate valves; PVC elbows, as needed; connector to pump (varies with pump)
- PVC glue
- UV clarifier (optional)

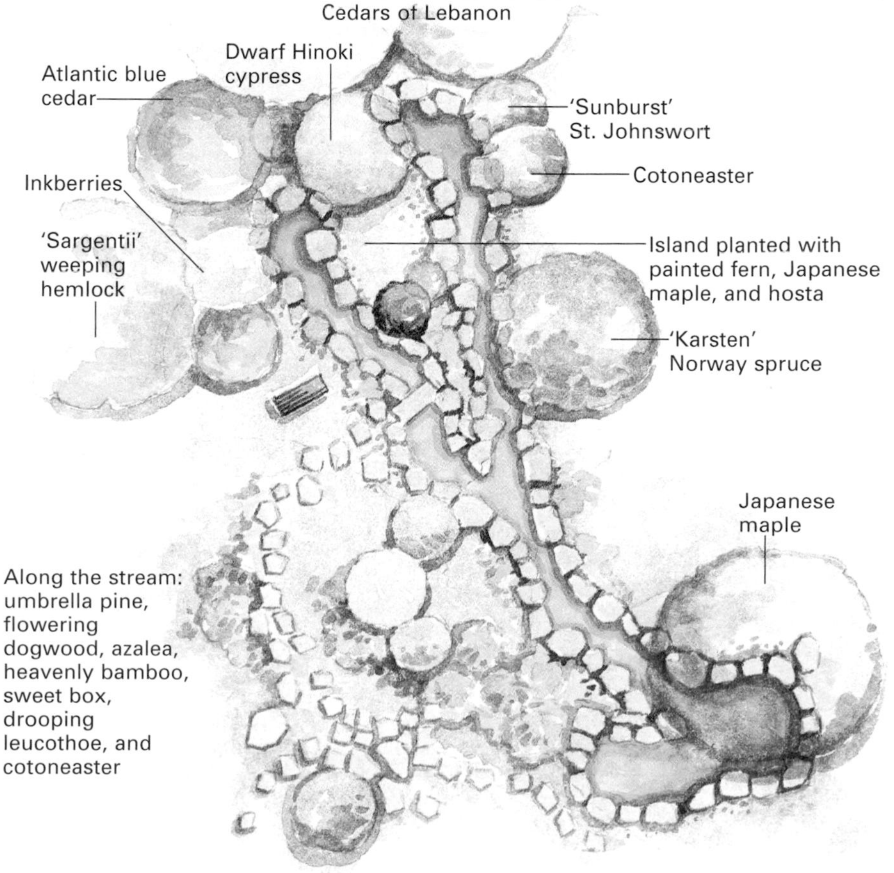

PONDS

CLAY POND

A natural clay-sided pond has several distinct and desirable advantages if you have good clay soil in which to build one. First, the soil can stabilize an eroding bank while it keeps the area as natural as possible—no plastic rims or concrete sides to contend with. You can turn a much-used drainage ditch into an attractive asset rather than an eyesore by emptying it into a clay pond.

A FEW POINTERS: Use any lumber for the sides because it won't rot under water. If a nearby stream is the source of water, direct the water from it through a pipe to the pond to avoid any sediment buildup. Close off the pipe to drain the pond for cleanup.

SET PLANKS: Dig out the shape. Lay the planks on edge and hammer the pipes 18 inches into the ground to hold the frame in place; in a section by a slope, stack two planks. For curved sections, soak thin planks in water overnight to soften them; then bend them into a curve. Set them on top of thicker straight planks.

WATER: Fill the pond with water; the planks will not show because they will be at least an inch below the surface. Even if water seeps out—and it will, despite a packed clay bottom—bog plants should survive. To accommodate water lilies, floating plants, and fish, keep a garden hose handy for topping off the pond.

YOU WILL NEED

- Shovel
- Bald cypress or other planks: 1 inch thick by 12 inches wide; thinner for curved sections
- 30- to 42-inch-long pipes (iron water pipes)
- Sledgehammer
- Shovel
- Marginal and aquatic plants

If you have an existing pond you can improve it by reinforcing the sides in the same way that you construct the sides in a new natural clay pond.

SIMPLE LINED POND

A basic pond, adjustable to a large or small scheme that fits the site, provides an opportunity for diving into water gardening. This pond operates as a well-balanced system with neither a pump nor a filter. The design combines an informal pool that features plants and still-water reflection. Add goldfish for more enjoyment.

BUILDER'S NOTES: Easy to construct and maintain, this classic water garden with a winding path to the house provides outstanding views from indoors. The pond's mortared stone edging encourages access for maintenance and closer viewing. No special equipment is needed for this project.

APPROXIMATE SIZE: 10×15 feet

VARIATIONS: A wildlife pond, including a shallow beach and a variety of plants attractive to wildlife; a hidden garden with mysterious appeal that offers a quiet retreat in an enclosed, out-of-the-way spot. The path could be traded for a bermed area with a waterfall. Add a stream, an adjacent paved entertainment area, or a fountain. Alternative building materials include preformed liner; cut stone, concrete pavers, or wood decking for edging; and endless variations of plants.

No pump and filter are needed for this informal pool. Aquatic plants, goldfish, and snails keep it in balance.

YOU WILL NEED

- 1 rubber pond liner, 15×20 feet
- 1 geotextile underlayment
- 2 to 3 tons sand
- 5 bags ready-mix mortar
- 1 ton washed gravel
- 1½ tons river rock
- 3 potted water lilies
- 10 potted marginal plants, such as cattail, rush, cardinal flower, and papyrus
- 36 bunches submerged plants, such as anacharis and cabomba
- 20 black Japanese snails
- 6 goldfish

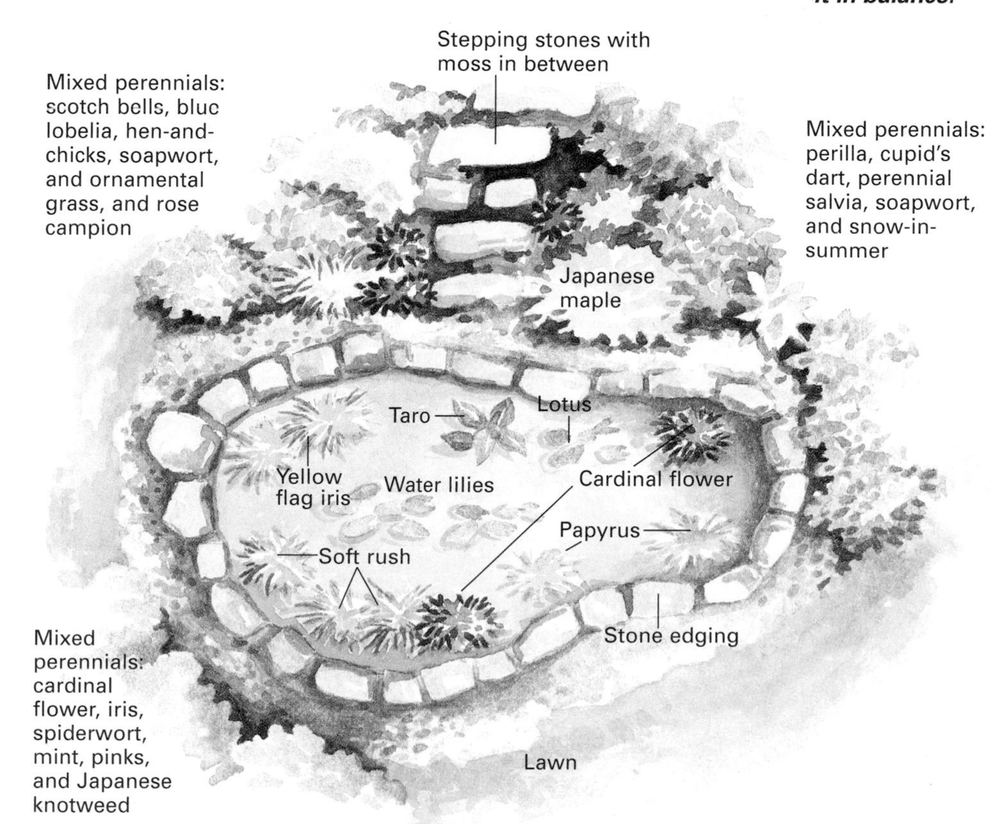

PONDS
continued

POND WITH FLEXIBLE LINER

You have many more options for shapes and sizes when you build a pond with a flexible liner, but it does take planning and some additional building time. Although you can make any shape you want, simple shapes are the easiest to excavate and set up. A pond with a flexible liner is much easier to install than a rigid, preformed pond liner, which requires more precise excavation.

Flexible liners make building a water garden easy, allowing you to create a simple pond in almost any shape. Add a small circulating fountain or some garden sculpture to complete the scene.

PLANT LIST FOR THE FLEXIBLE LINER POND

- Lily-of-the-Nile
- Yellow flag iris
- Water lettuce
- Tropical water lily

1. SELECT A SITE: Select a site that is away from deciduous trees so you won't be constantly cleaning out fallen flowers in spring and leaves in autumn—a wise precaution no matter what material you are using for your water garden. Even though you will pad the ground underneath the pond before laying down the liner, avoid rocky areas. Rocks can puncture the liner.

Choose a location in direct sun or with midday light shade if you live in warmer zones. Most water plants grow best with at least 6 hours of sun daily. Don't place the pond at the lowest point in the yard. Water runoff from heavy rains can cause problems.

2. OUTLINE: Decide on the shape of the pond. (Make a preliminary drawing on paper, indicating the pond's relationship to other areas in the yard.) Use a garden hose, lime, or flour to outline curved sections. If your design includes straight edges, stretch a length of string between stakes for those sections.

Look at the pond's shape and location from afar—from the patio, the deck, even inside the house—to get a feeling for how the finished project will look. Rearrange the outline until you have a shape you like.

3. DIG: Excavate the hole at least 18 inches deep, preferably with the assistance of a couple of helpers. Slope the sides and keep the bottom flat.

At one end, along one side, or all around the pond, dig a 1-foot-wide terrace 8 to 12 inches deep to hold containers of marginal plants. If you plan to edge the pond with flat stones or bricks, dig a ledge 3 to 4 inches wide for that purpose.

4. LEVEL: Lay a 2×4 across the pond and set a carpenter's level on it to check that the edge is the same height all around. Keeping the edge level will prevent the liner from showing when you have filled the pond.

If the pond is too wide for the 2×4, attach a line level to a length of string; pull the string taut at different points across the length and width of the excavation.

YOU WILL NEED

- Flexible liner, 20 to 45 mil thick
- Garden hose or lime
- String and stakes
- Shovel, carpenter's level
- 2×4 (for leveling)
- Builder's sand
- Geotextile fabric or other underlayment
- Stones, pavers
- Pump-and-fountain kit

Add or remove soil until the edge is level. Then lower a small section of the edge by an inch to allow overflow to drain off during heavy rains.

5. UNDERLAYMENT: If the soil is very rocky, spread 2 inches of sand over the bottom before laying down the underlayment.

Cover the bottom and sides of the pond with an underlayment of several layers of newspapers spread in full sections, old carpet, or geotextile fabric to protect the liner from protruding rocks and roots.

6. LINER: To figure out the liner size you need, measure the pond length and width; then add twice the depth plus 2 feet all around to allow for overlap. Move the liner gently into place in the excavation. Leave wrinkles for slack along the curves. Anchor the edge of the liner with stones temporarily.

Slowly fill the pond with water; ease, fold, and smooth the liner as needed. The wrinkles will not show when the pond is full.

A site away from tree roots will make it easier to dig the hole. Locating the pond away from trees will also reduce the time you spend on maintaining the pond in autumn.

Protect the liner from sharp rocks and roots by covering the excavated area with layers of newspaper or geotextile fabric before you put the liner in position.

Make sure the edges are level all around so that no water seeps out after you fill the pond.

PONDS
continued

Secure the edge of the pond liner with flat stones fit together as securely as possible.

When all the stones are in place and the liner is secure, trim all but 1 foot off the excess.

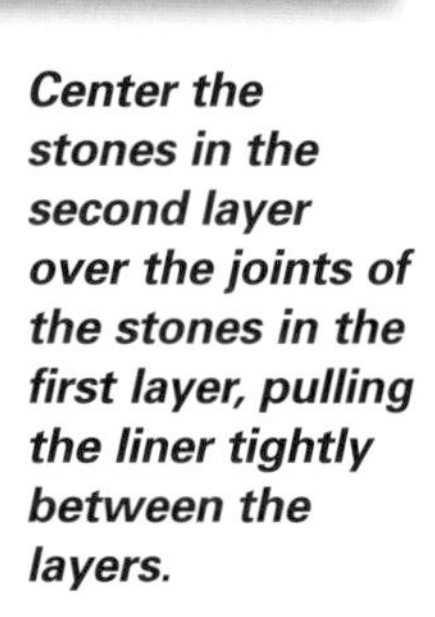

Center the stones in the second layer over the joints of the stones in the first layer, pulling the liner tightly between the layers.

Add more layers of stones for a drystack edging effect, or create a raised wall at one end to hold a fountain or other ornament.

POND WITH FLEXIBLE LINER

continued

7. EDGING: Remove the stones you used to temporarily hold the liner in place. Set flat stones around the rim of the pond on the 3-inch ledge and secure the edge of the liner under them.

Abut any irregularly shaped stones as if they were pieces of a puzzle. They should form a fairly level first course (layer). Use pavers, bricks, flagstones, or cut stones to build the edge. If you want, position some of the pavers or stones so they overhang the rim of the pond a little.

8. TRIM: Using sharp scissors, trim the liner all around to within 1 foot of the edge of the first course of stones.

9. SECOND COURSE: Set a second course of stones on top of the first, pulling the liner securely under the stones as you lay them. Center each stone over the joint of a stone in the first course. Double edging ensures that the liner will not slip.

The liner is invisible from the pond side. To hide it on the exterior side, use edging plants. Take your time in deciding on the plants to place around the pond. Good choices to consider are daylilies, hostas, and yellow or purple coneflowers.

10. ADDITIONS: If you want, add one or more courses of stones to create a decorative edging, which will have the appearance of a drystack stone wall. This raised wall is perfect for holding a larger fountain or a small spitter (a decorative object that sprays water into the pond). Plan for that before you place the second course of stones. Leave a small opening through which to guide the tube from the recirculating pump to the fountain.

11. PUMP: If you include a pump and fountain in the pond, rest it on the bottom of the pond—in the center, off to one side, or near one end. Bring a small pump closer to the surface by putting it on bricks or cinder blocks. (Scrub cinder or concrete blocks with a stiff brush dipped in a solution of 1 part vinegar and 3 parts water; then rinse.) Keep the fountain away from water lilies, which prefer still or nearly still water.

12. PLANT: Use a dechlorinating product to treat the water. Then set in plants.

Raise plants, such as water lilies, to correct heights by placing the pots on bricks or concrete blocks.

Place marginal plants, such as irises, papyrus, and cattails, in pots on the terrace created as you dug the pond (see pages 208–209). Wait for a week or two for the water to stabilize before adding fish.

You'll spend more time excavating for and building a pond with a preformed liner, but you'll earn more space for plants.

Pond with Rigid Liner

A pond with a rigid liner is like a large sunken container, with subtle differences. A preformed pond offers more space for plants and it takes more time to dig. Although you can work to approximate the exterior shape, you need to be more exact with the length, width, and placement of the interior shelf.

Turn the preformed liner upside down on the pond site and trace around its perimeter with lime, spray paint, or flour. Then turn the liner right-side up and set it nearby so you can refer to its interior contours as you dig. Excavating the hole will be easier if you avoid rocky areas and large tree roots. Once you've placed the liner, backfill around it with sand.

Camouflage the rim of the liner by laying rocks and flat stones on it; place some so they overhang the water for a natural look. Turn some of the flat stones into shelves for potted flowering and foliage plants.

Rock edging and marginal plants help to hide the rim of a preformed liner and blend the aquascape into its surroundings.

You Will Need

- Preformed pond liner
- Lime, paint, or flour
- Stakes
- Shovel
- Sand
- Pump
- Assorted rocks and flat stones
- Potted plants
- Floating plants

Plant List for Rigid-Liner Pond

- Water lilies
- Duckweed
- Water hyacinth

PONDS
continued

The flexible liner in this water garden is disguised by the exterior wood edging. You can pull your chair right up to the side of a raised pond to feed the fish or watch the lilies bloom. The pond's height also makes it easier to clean and maintain.

PLANT LIST FOR THE RAISED POND WITH FLEXIBLE LINER

- Tropical water lily
- Water hyacinth
- Parrot's feather
- Floating fern

RAISED POND WITH FLEXIBLE LINER

Easy to build and just right for a small patio, this project is smaller and takes less time than a similar pond built with a preformed liner. This raised pond's flexible liner leaves room for less-than-perfect measuring. If you want to put it on your deck, remember that it will be heavy when filled with water—at least 600 pounds. Be sure the deck can support it.

SETTING IT UP: The best plants for a pond this size are miniature water lilies and a single full-size hardy or tropical lily. Wait to buy plants until the pond is finished and filled with water. Use water from a garden hose; then dechlorinate it with one of the many available treatments. Plug in the pump after planting. Wait one to two weeks before adding fish or snails. The pond will accommodate two or three, goldfish; koi need a larger, deeper pond.

1. BASE FRAME: Refer to the illustration on the next page as needed. Cut the 2×2s into 36-inch lengths for the base frame. Assemble the frame with 3-inch deck screws, first drilling countersunk pilot holes for all screws to avoid splitting the lumber.

2. BASE: Crosscut three of the 2×8s to make five 36-inch-long pieces. Place the pieces edge to edge. Mark the last board so the overall width of the base is 36 inches; cut all boards to size. Place the base frame on a flat work surface. Center the boards on top, and drive 2½-inch deck screws through the base into the base frame. Take the base and position it where you want the water garden to be.

3. SIDES: Crosscut the remaining four 2×8s into 36-inch lengths for the eight side pieces. Assemble them into two boxes, using 3½-inch deck screws. Place one box on the base assembly. Miter the 1×2 banding to run around the perimeter of the box. Center the banding on the joint line between the box sides and the base; fasten it with 2-inch deck screws, driving some screws into the box sides, others into the base.

4. ASSEMBLE: Stack the second box on the first. Screw on two more sets of banding: one straddling the joint line, the other flush with the top of the sides. Cut a ½×½-inch notch at one corner for the pump's electrical cord.

5. LINER: Cut the flexible pond liner to a manageable size. A 66-inch square will provide you with a 1½-inch allowance on all sides. Put the liner in the box and roughly center it. Divide the surplus of the liner into equal pleats on each side (left side in illustration) or pleat all of it to one side (right side in illustration). Drive staples through the liner all along the sides near the top. Trim the liner flush with the top of the sides, using heavy scissors or a utility knife.

6. PUMP: Position the pump where you want it inside the box, centered or off to one side. If you will plant water lilies, place the pump in the corner opposite the plants because they prefer still water. Raise the pump on stacked bricks so the fountain will be above the surface of the water. Guide the electrical cord through the notch you made.

7. CAP: Crosscut the 2×4 lumber into four cap strips, to the lengths indicated in the diagram below, and screw them in place with 3-inch deck screws. Double-check the location of the completed box before you fill it with water, making sure it's near a GFCI electrical outlet. Because of its weight, it will be difficult to move after filling. Level the pond with wood shims if necessary. Paint or stain the outside of the pond, if you want, or let it weather naturally.

YOU WILL NEED

- Pressure-treated lumber: two 2×2s, 8 feet long; seven 2×8s, 8 feet long; six 1×2s, 8 feet long; two 2×4s, 8 feet long
- Deck screws (corrosion-resistant flathead screws) in 2-, 2½-, 3-, and 3½-inch lengths
- Wood shims
- Flexible liner at least 66 inches square and 35 mil thick
- Staple gun, table saw, drill, screwdriver
- Scissors or utility knife
- White stain or exterior latex paint (optional)
- Pond pump-and-fountain kit (optional)

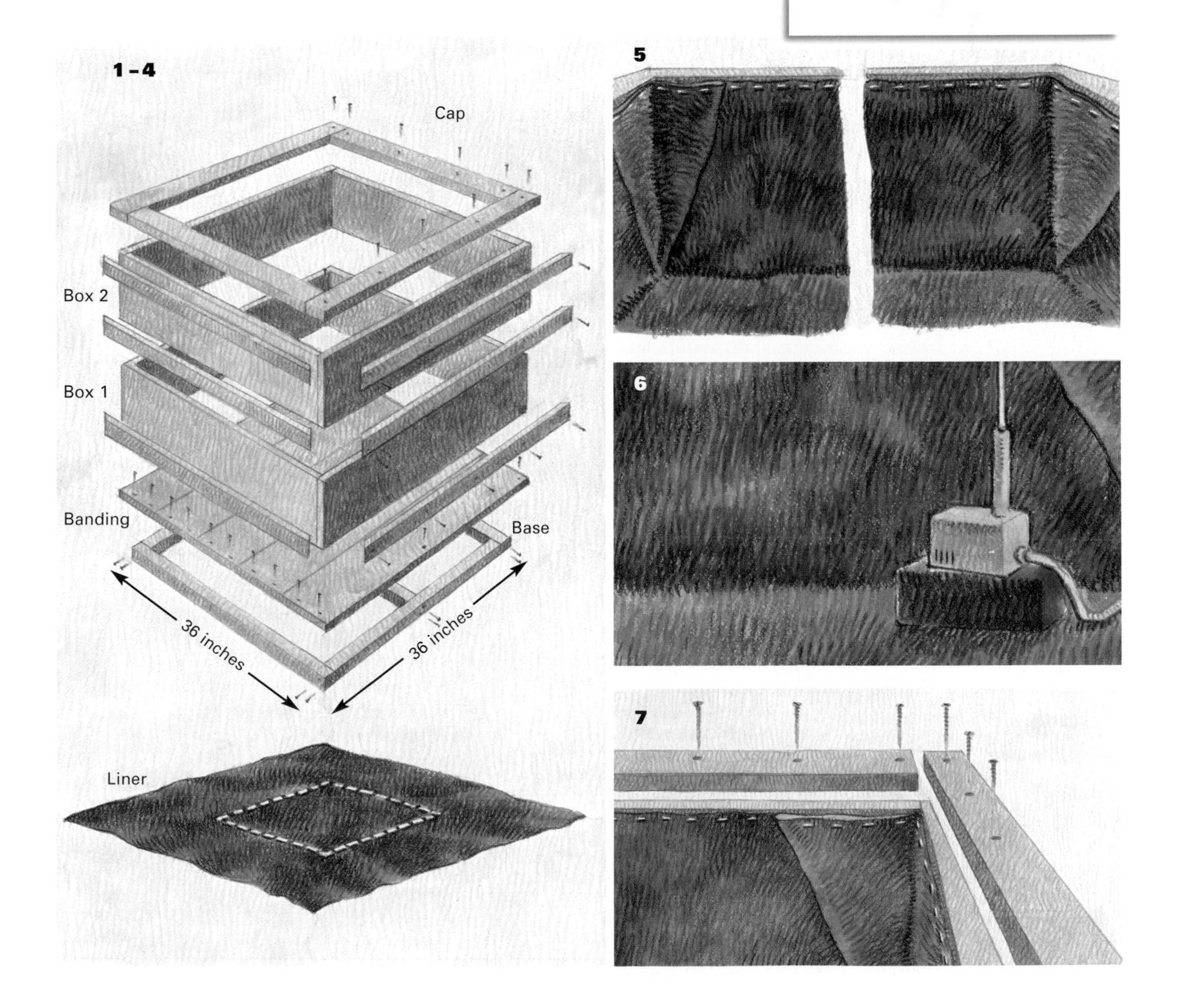

PONDS
continued

A wide ledge around the rim of a raised pond provides a shelf for potted annuals or even a place to perch and admire your handiwork. You'll appreciate the ease of cleaning a water garden without having to wade in or bend down too far.

RAISED POND WITH RIGID LINER

There are a number of reasons to build a raised pond rather than set one in the ground. First and foremost are the aesthetics—the view. A raised pond is closer to eye level, so you can enjoy it when you sit on its edge or nearby on a deck or patio.

Also, it's easy to maintain. You don't need to bend over far to care for the plants or to clean the surface. Finally, there is the ground itself: Your soil may be too moist (strange as that may sound when talking about a pond) or too rocky to dig out a level area.

DAY ONE: Build the raised wood pond on a level surface so that the framing will be square. For the 82×49-inch base, nail together a frame with two long and two shorter 2×4s, using simple butt joints. Mark the short sides one-third in from each end and nail the remaining two 2×4s in as supports. Nail the pressure-treated plywood on top. Then build the side panels with the redwood 2×2s; space the 2×2 uprights about every 12 inches and nail them in. Reinforce the corners by adding a 2×2 upright 2 inches from each corner. Make the end panels with 2×4s for the corner uprights and 2×2s for the top and bottom rails; add 2 spaced 2×2 uprights to each end panel. Finally, nail side and end panels onto the base, butting and nailing the corners together.

1. Cut a 2-inch-thick piece of plastic-foam insulation to fit inside the framework and set it down on the base. Lay the CDX unfinished plywood on top of the insulation. Put the pond liner inside the frame, resting the liner lip on the 2×2 top rail.

2. Butt and nail 1×4 cedar trim at the corners, using one straight piece and one ripped piece for each corner. Cut the cedar lap siding to fit between the trim pieces and nail it in place to the frame uprights; toenail the siding to the corner trim. Leave slightly open at the top on each side.

PLANT LIST FOR THE RAISED POND WITH RIGID LINER

- Hardy water lily
- Tropical water lily

ANNUALS FOR COLOR

- Yellow culinary sage
- Globe amaranth
- Purple culinary sage
- Begonia

DAY TWO: Move the pond to its final location while it's light enough to transport easily. Select a site that is level and has access to a GFCI outlet (for pump and filter). When the pond is in place, fill the cavity between the siding and liner with masonry insulation.

3. Nail on the top pieces of lap siding. Finish filling the interior cavity with insulation by pouring it in with a dustpan.

4. Build a cap with mitered corners, using cedar 2×8s; remember to measure the length at the longest point of the miter. Attach the cap to the frame with galvanized deck screws placed about every 12 inches. Add cedar 1×8 trim boards around the entire structure just below the cap to cover gaps; nail them to the frame.

5. Fill the pond with water and treat to dechlorinate it. Add a pump and filter to keep the water oxygenated and clean, a small fountain for aeration and pleasant sound, and a pond heater if you plan to overwinter fish.

6. Set water lilies and other water plants in the pond. Wait a couple of weeks before adding fish. Dress up the perimeter of the pond with containers of annuals, perennials, and herbs for all-season color.

YOU WILL NEED

- Preformed polyethylene pond liner (holds 150 gallons), 82×49 inches exterior measure (includes 2½-inch lip); 77×44×18 inches interior measure
- Pressure-treated 2×4s (base): 2 pieces, 82 inches long; 4 pieces, 46 inches long
- ¾-inch pressure-treated plywood (base), 82×49 inches
- ¾-inch CDX unfinished plywood (base), 79×46 inches
- Sheet of 2-inch-thick plastic-foam insulation, 79×46 inches
- Redwood 2×2s (sides and ends): 4 pieces, 82 inches long; 4 pieces, 46 inches long; 20 uprights, 17¾ inches long
- Redwood 2×4s (end corner uprights): 4 pieces, 17¾ inches long
- Cedar 1×4s (corner trim): 8 pieces, 23 inches long; 4 of them ripped down ¾ inch on one side to make the corners equal
- 5½-inch cedar lap siding (measure first, cut to fit): 10 pieces, 76½ inches long; 10 pieces, 43½ inches long
- Cedar 2×8s (mitered cap; measure to the long point of the miter): 2 pieces, 88½ inches long; 2 pieces, 55½ inches long
- Cedar 1×8s (trim boards): 2 pieces, 85 inches long; 2 pieces, 50½ inches long
- Masonry insulation for cavity walls
- 1 pound of No. 7 galvanized nails
- 1 pound of 2½-inch galvanized deck screws

PONDS
continued

CONCRETE POND

Long before preformed and flexible liners came into existence, concrete was the material of choice for ponds. It is inexpensive and long-lasting if you take precautions and some extra care in building and maintaining the concrete.

DIG AND PREPARE: Decide on the shape of the pond, using a garden hose or rope. Remember to consider the thickness of the concrete and add about 6 inches all around. Outline the shape with lime, flour, or spray paint. Excavate the soil, digging to the depth you want plus 6 inches for the concrete; slope the sides to about a 20-degree angle. Dig a shelf for edge plants, if desired. Compact the earth on the bottom and especially on the sides. Make sure the top edges of the pond are level. If you include a pump and fountain, decide where to place the electrical cord and water-return line.

REINFORCE: Contour concrete reinforcing mesh in the hole. About 12 inches above the bottom, drive in 6-inch metal stakes to hold the mesh. The stakes also help to guide you in keeping the concrete a uniform 6 inches thick on all surfaces.

POUR: Pour the ready-mix concrete into one part of the pool at a time (concrete sets up quickly) and pack it into the mesh with a trowel. When you reach 6-inch thickness, pull out the stakes or drive them into the ground; fill the stake holes with concrete. Pour the next portion. Dampen the concrete periodically to retard the curing process.

A waterfall-type fountain adds sound and movement to this reflecting pool. Pavers hide the waterfall mechanics.

YOU WILL NEED

- Garden hose or rope; lime, flour, or paint
- Shovel and carpenter's level
- Masonry trowel and mortar
- Ready-mix concrete
- Concrete reinforcing mesh
- 6-inch metal stakes
- Polyethylene sheets
- Bricks, pavers, or cut stones
- Pipe or conduit
- Stiff-bristle brush
- Pool paint (optional)

A pond with sloping sides is easier to build than one with straight sides, which requires the use of wooden forms. Build the pond in mild, dry weather so that the concrete will cure properly.

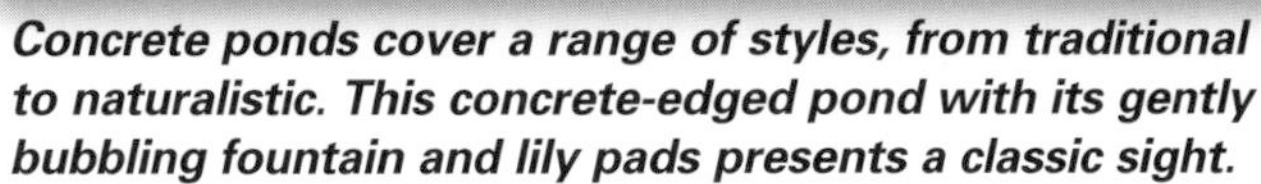

Concrete ponds cover a range of styles, from traditional to naturalistic. This concrete-edged pond with its gently bubbling fountain and lily pads presents a classic sight.

The mortarless drystack stone wall surrounding this concrete pond matches other walls on the property. Plantings accent the pond's edge. The water is open to the sky, reflecting trees and shrubs through the changing seasons.

PROTECT: After you have poured all of the concrete and smoothed its surface with the trowel, cover the pond with a sheet of polyethylene, holding it in place with a few strategically placed bricks. The polyethylene slows the curing process and keeps rain out of the pool until the concrete has completely hardened. Concrete that has cured slowly is stronger than concrete that cured quickly in hot weather.

CURING: The concrete will take a week to cure completely. Remove a 4- to 12-inch area of sod surrounding the pool to make room for a rim; then mortar a coping of brick, pavers, or cut stone around the edge to provide the lip. Place a length of pipe under the section closest to the GFCI electrical outlet when you mortar so you have housing for the wiring of a recirculating pump. Use a level to make sure the coping is even all around.

FINISHING: Fill the pool with water; let the water stand at least 24 hours and then drain. Scour the concrete with a stiff-bristle brush to remove cement residue; rinse well. You can seal the surface with pool paint or plaster made from white marble powder and cement. Cleaning and sealing prevent concrete from leaching into the water and making it cloudy and an undesirable environment for plants or fish.

Even a small pond will accent a garden or patio. With room for just a few plants and goldfish, this pond brings serenity to a lightly shaded patio. The bluestone ledge provides a welcome place to relax and watch the fish in action.

PONDS
continued

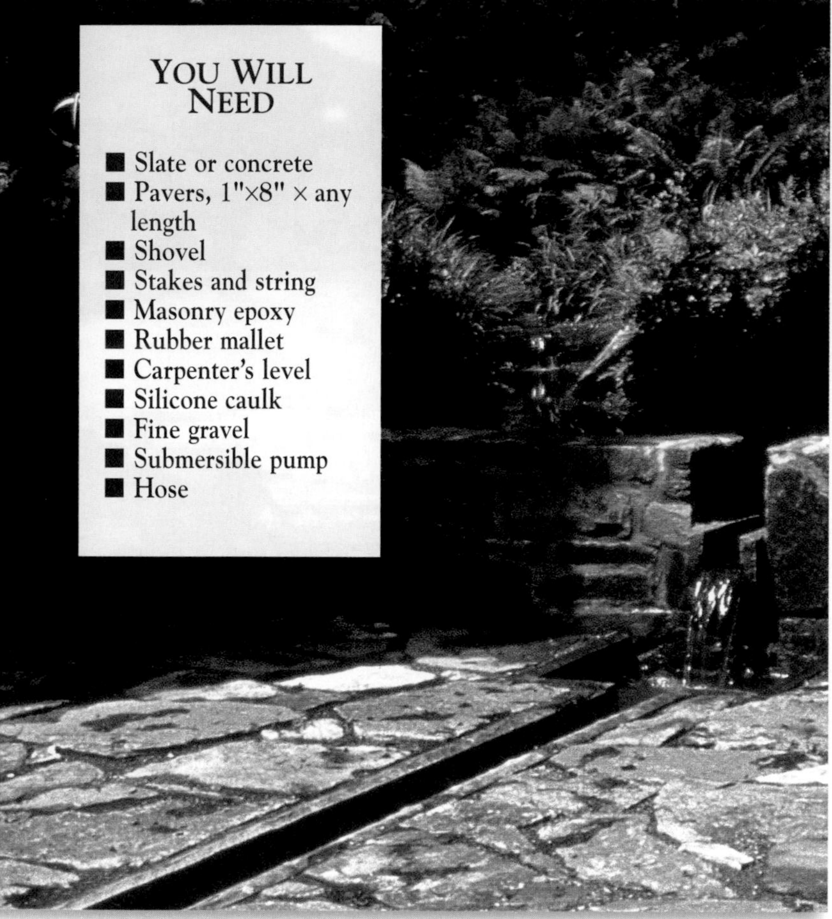

YOU WILL NEED

- Slate or concrete
- Pavers, 1"×8" × any length
- Shovel
- Stakes and string
- Masonry epoxy
- Rubber mallet
- Carpenter's level
- Silicone caulk
- Fine gravel
- Submersible pump
- Hose

Add the sound of trickling water to formal terraces or courtyards with a runnel. A recirculating pump keeps the water flowing.

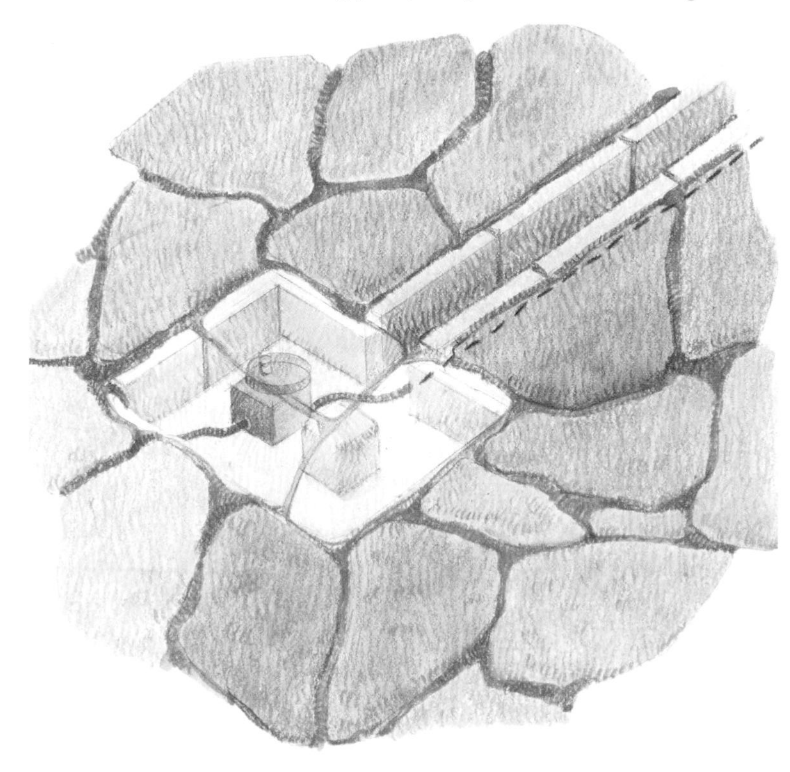

RUNNEL

A runnel is a small channel through which water flows. It connects two ponds or stands alone as a unique water feature. You can make it as long or short and as high or low as you want. The only limiting factor is the hose length for the recirculating pump. Runnels provide a rather formal look to landscape design. They look good in courtyards, on terraces, and along entry walks. Building a runnel is easiest if you plan for it from the beginning, although you can add one to an existing walkway.

MEASURE STONES: Use pieces of slate or concrete pavers 1 inch thick by 8 inches wide for the sides and bottom of the runnel. The pieces can be any length. Have the stone cut to fit the exact dimensions you want for the runnel, or build it based on the size of the stones. Have at least eight pieces of stone cut in half lengthwise.

DIG TRENCH: Dig a trench at least 10 inches deep and 12 inches wide. Use a string tied between two stakes to keep the line straight. Add 2 inches of fine gravel to the bottom of the trench.

LAY STONES: Lay stones flat on the gravel to form the bottom of the runnel. Apply masonry epoxy between all joints. Use a rubber mallet to tap the stones into place; check that each stone is level. To make the sides, start with a half-piece of stone so the joints of the bottom pieces don't overlap with those of the side pieces. Set the stones on edge, flush with the outside edge of the bottom piece. Cap one end with a half-piece. Build a 16-inch-square return box for the pump at the other end.

INSTALL PUMP: Leave a ½-inch gap between two of the edging stones for the pump cord. Once all stone is in place, use silicone caulk to seal joints that will be under water. Place the pump in the return box and plug it in. Depending on the size of the pump, you may want to attach a return line (a hose for the water to run in) to the pump. Placed at the far end of the runnel, it will move the water the entire length of the feature.

SEASONAL CARE

Although the pump will recirculate water, you may need to replenish the water supply occasionally. Unplug the pump in autumn in zones where winter temperatures fall below freezing for days at a time.

Use a naturally sloping property to best advantage by building a series of cascading pools highlighted by a waterfall. Splashing sounds make a water garden irresistible to all kinds of visitors, including birds and other wildlife. Add colorful marginal and perennial plants along the watercourse to make it even more compelling.

POND WITH WATERFALL

A natural, gentle slope in the landscape makes an ideal setting for a watercourse. Take advantage of the change in elevation to join two or more ponds with a waterfall in between. In this project, waterfalls link three stone-lined ponds. Careful planting around and among the rocks blends the watercourse with the landscape.

BUILDER'S NOTES: Perennials and upright evergreens surround the feature, linking it to the site and making it look natural. Large, flat stones provide spillways for the waterfalls and spots along the edge of the pools for sitting.

APPROXIMATE SIZE: About 20×50 feet overall (two pools 15×15 feet; one 20×20 feet)

VARIATIONS: The feature could include two or three ponds with linking waterfalls, or a stream with cascading ponds. Make small or narrow bogs along the ponds to transition to surrounding plantings. Extend the planting materials into the ponds, including water lilies and other aquatic plants. Add fish to the lower pond.

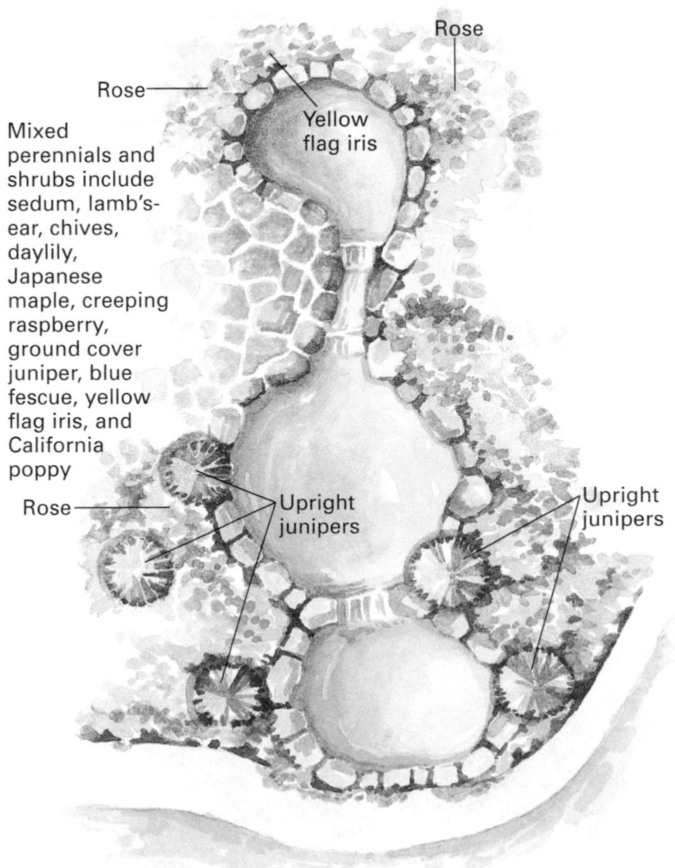

MATERIALS

- 2 EPDM rubber liners, 20×20 feet
- 1 EPDM rubber liner, 25×25 feet
- Geotextile fabric
- 2 to 3 tons sand
- 40-pound bag of gravel (for filling pots)
- 4 tons rock
- 55 feet PVC pipe or kink-free tubing
- Fittings: L's, T's, and clamps
- Black urethane foam
- 50 bunches submerged plants
- 50 black Japanese snails
- 8 comet goldfish
- Yellow irises
- 2,000- to 4,000-gph submersible pump
- Biological filter

PONDS
continued

A waterfall enhances the design of an aboveground, formal pond by adding music and movement to the patio or yard where it is installed.

RAISED POND WITH WATERFALL

This striking two-level pond, situated on a patio next to a Victorian-style home, takes a contemporary approach to the classical lines of a formal design. Besides providing the customary attraction of sparkling water, the waterfall with its music camouflages traffic noise and soothes the owners to sleep at night. Located in a frequently used area near the house, the raised pond provides hours of enjoyment while owners are dining or entertaining on the patio. The stone-capped walls provide seating and protect against an accidental plunge.

BUILDER'S NOTES: The centerpieces of the pond include a fountain and a waterfall. A 3-foot-wide sheet of water spills 18 inches into the lower pond and recirculates to the upper pool. The feature's stacked-fieldstone veneer and flagstone edging repeat building materials used to construct the nearby walls, steps, walkways, and patio. Plantings include submerged oxygenators, water lilies, irises, and rushes. Statuary adds charm.

APPROXIMATE SIZE: 15×15 feet

VARIATIONS: The project could be located at the edge of a deck. Or make the pond a different shape lined and edged with concrete, tile veneer, or brick edging.

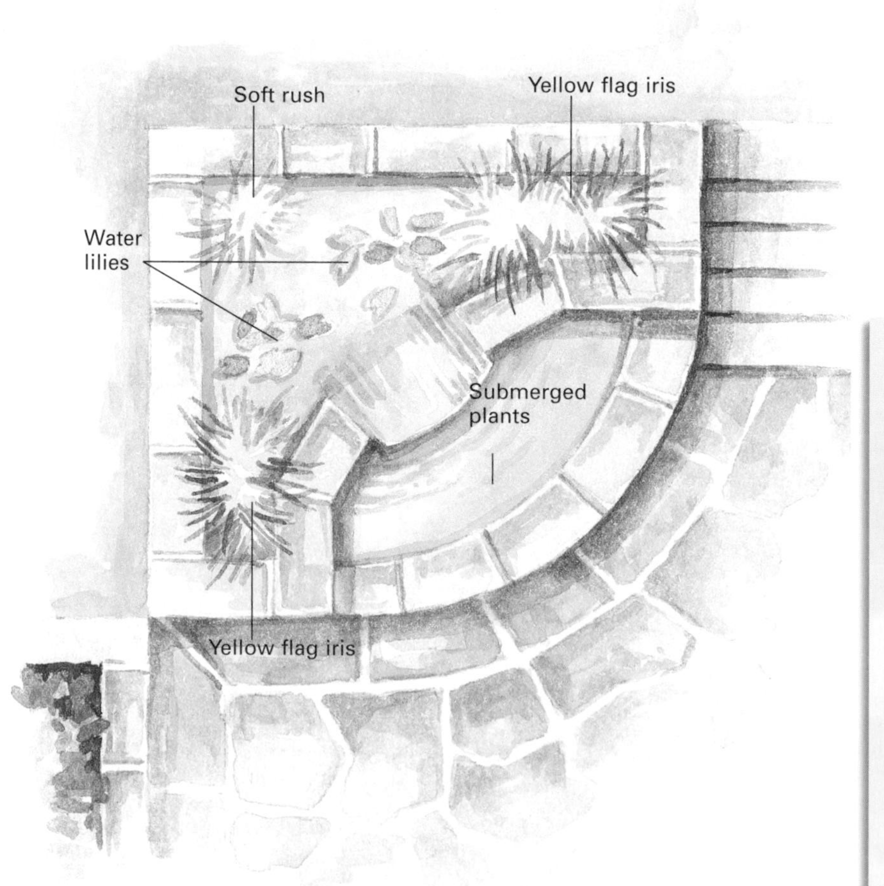

MATERIALS

- 1 EPDM rubber liner, 20×20 feet
- 1 EPDM rubber liner, 10×15 feet
- 70 feet flagstone
- 3 tons fieldstone
- 5 hardy water lilies
- 15 irises
- 6 rushes
- 4 decorative stone or metal frogs
- 12 comet goldfish
- 50 bunches submerged plants
- 50 black Japanese snails
- Submersible pump for the waterfall
- Submersible pump for the piped statuary
- 2 piped ornamental statuary pieces

FOUNTAINS

Even if you enjoy the simple, peaceful calm of still water, in time you may be unable to resist adding a fountain to your water garden. If you live in a busy suburban or urban neighborhood, you may find a fountain invaluable because it masks the surrounding street noises with the sound of running water. Putting a fountain in your pond is an easy project. So many kinds of fountains are available; you may have a difficult time deciding which one to choose. There are gentle bubblers and mushroom or bell-shape sprays, gushers, upright sprays and jets, fountains that sit on pumps just below the surface of the water, and others that pour water from classical statuary. Let the style of your pond and landscape guide you.

Whatever type you choose, it will need the same basic equipment: a pump, sized according to the size of the pond and the fountain; tubing to connect the pump to the fountain; and a nearby electrical outlet that has a GFCI.

ELECTRICITY: Any time you combine electricity and water, you have a potentially dangerous situation. Always connect electrical plugs to outlets that are equipped with a GFCI.

RAISE IT UP: Most ponds are deeper than 18 inches (the shallowest recommended), and the mechanics of most fountains are relatively small. This is especially true of the small sprays or bubblers that attach directly to a pump. To raise them to the surface, set them on concrete blocks or on bricks.

FILTERS: Consider adding a filter to your pond pump to help extend its life and to keep the fountain nozzles clear of debris. (Pump or modular filters are different from pond filters.

HOSES: The hose that circulates the water between the pump and the fountain may be black or transparent. Use clamps to make a water-tight seal between the hose ends and the pump and fountain. If you purchase a pump-and-fountain kit, the hose and fixtures will be included. You may need a flow control valve, depending on your water pressure.

FOUNTAIN PATTERNS: Fountains are available in many spray patterns and sizes. Consider the size of your pond to decide which to install.

Installing a fountain in your pond can be a simple but rewarding project. Even a small bubbler or light spray adds visual interest to an aquascape and oxygen to the water. It can also help to mask street noises.

PLANT LIST FOR THE POND WITH FOUNTAIN

- Dwarf cattail
- Hardy water canna
- Pickerel rush
- Siberian iris
- Hardy water lily
- Creeping jenny

YOU WILL NEED

- Pump and fountain or pump-and-fountain kit
- Concrete or cinder blocks or bricks
- GFCI outlet

FOUNTAINS
continued

A large ceramic bowl offers a dramatic alternative to a millstone. If you live in an area with freezing winters, drain the fountain and bring the bowl inside for the winter.

Adjust the height of the fountain to fit the mood you want to create. Place small stones near the hole to diffuse the spray and add to the compelling sound.

MILLSTONE FOUNTAIN

A spray of water adds immeasurably to any yard or garden. You can create such an ornament with a millstone or grindstone. Or drill a hole in the center of a flat stone or slab of concrete. For a more contemporary look, drill a hole in the bottom of a large ceramic or concrete bowl.

1. BASE AND LINER: Use a shallow whiskey-barrel liner that is slightly larger in diameter than the largest millstone or the grindstone and deep enough for you to submerge the pump. The water from the pump will spill over the stone into the liner, and the pump will recirculate it. Choose a location near a GFCI electrical source, whether in a garden bed, alongside a patio, or near a walkway. Dig a hole slightly wider

YOU WILL NEED

- 5-foot-diameter, 18-inch-deep plastic tub
- Pump and fountain jet
- Shovel
- 3- to 4-foot length of pressure-treated 1×4 board
- Sand or gravel
- 4-foot-diameter millstone or other large, flat stone
- Decorative stones

than the liner and deep enough to set the liner in flush with the ground.

2. LEVEL: Set the liner in the hole, making sure it is level. If it isn't, lift out the liner and spread sand, gravel, or soil in the bottom of the hole to create a level surface. Replace the liner in the hole and fill in with soil around its sides to hold it in place. Remove any soil you accidentally spill in the liner.

3. PUMP: Place the water pump in the center of the liner. This project requires only gentle water pressure; choose the smallest pump available. Arrange river rocks or bricks under the pump to lift it nearly level with the top of the liner. Make sure it is secure by surrounding it with more rocks or bricks.

4. SUPPORT: Lay a board (either pressure-treated, cedar, or redwood to prevent rotting) across the top of the liner and mark the spot where the board matches up with the pump. Cut a hole at that spot large enough for the pump spray to bubble through. Notch the ends of the board so it will sit securely atop the liner. Put the board back on the liner. The board will distribute the weight of the stones and leave the liner unharmed.

5. MILLSTONE: With help from an assistant, position the millstone over the board, matching the holes with the hole in the board over the pump. Gently lower the stone; then fill the liner with water.

6. FINISHING: Connect the pump to the electrical source. Adjust the water flow as desired; use a flow restricter if necessary. Conceal the ends of the board and the rim of the liner with mulch, rocks, or spreading plants. Keeping soil out of the liner will keep the water clean. Even though the pump will recirculate the water, add more periodically to offset evaporation, especially on hot summer days. If you live in an area where winter temperatures consistently drop below freezing, remove the pump before the first fall frost.

Choose the smallest pump available to keep the water pressure in the fountain low. Adjust the flow to minimize water loss. Use moisture-loving plants around the millstone to help conceal the base and liner.

FOUNTAINS
continued

As the water from the spout fills the bamboo hammer, the balance shifts and the hammer tips down. It strikes the rock as it rights itself.

SHISHI-ODOSHI: JAPANESE FOUNTAIN

Shishi-odoshi, or deer-scarer, is a Japanese ornament designed to keep animals away from rice paddies and other cultivated areas. Also called a water hammer, shishi-odoshi's simple form and operation make it a popular water garden feature as well. It may not ward off deer in your yard, but the sound of trickling water is soothing.

A traditional deer-scarer is made from bamboo poles cut to balance in a special way. One length of bamboo is positioned opposite another—much like a seesaw—below a water source. Bamboo is hollow except at its nodes, the dark rings that circle the stems. The bamboo hammer is attached to its cradle just in front of one node. Water drips into the lever from a spout above, filling to that node. As the hammer fills with water, the balance of its weight shifts forward and it tips down. The water spills out in a reservoir below; as the bamboo tube empties and grows lighter, it returns to the original position. As it rights itself, the bottom of the bamboo lever strikes a strategically placed rock, producing the rhythmic clacking sound that the shishi-odoshi is famous for.

A deer-scarer is easily scalable to almost any size water garden, and is especially suitable for use as the focus of its own container. A shishi-odoshi that is too large for its container or pond may cause water loss, so plan carefully. One that is too small for its surroundings may become lost among plants or be difficult to hear.

The most difficult step is working with bamboo, which has tough canes. You can accomplish this project with a hand-held drill and a hacksaw, but a drill press and a bandsaw will make it easier. If bamboo is hard to find in your area, check the phone directory for rattan and bamboo furniture repair suppliers.

PREPARE THE CONTAINER: Choose a site near a GFCI outlet and put a half whiskey barrel in place. Fill it with potting soil or

Although the canes are hollow, bamboo can be tough to cut. Use a hacksaw or bandsaw on a level surface to trim the pieces to the size you need for your fountain. Sand the rough edges.

leftover excavated garden soil from another project. Scoop out a depression in the middle and push in a plastic bucket or tub.

PIPE AND SPOUT: Cut one of the large bamboo pieces 1 foot long, measuring it carefully so that one of the nodes will be at the top. This will be the water-source pipe.

Cut a piece from the narrower bamboo about 4 inches long and without nodes so that it is entirely hollow. Cut one edge square and angle the other sharply to form a spout. Sand the rough edges.

Drill a hole 2 inches from the top of the source pipe big enough to accommodate the smaller spout pipe. Run the vinyl hose through the source pipe, drilling through nodes as needed. Leave 4 inches hanging out of the hole near the top of the source pipe and thread that excess through the back of the spout. Then push the spout into the hole in the source pipe. Add bamboo shims if necessary to make it a snug fit.

Glue the source pipe to a wooden anchor with waterproof adhesive in order to keep it upright, or simply stick an 18-inch length of metal rod 7 or 8 inches into the dirt in the container. Slip the source pipe over the rod and press it into the dirt an inch or so. Run the vinyl hose into the plastic tub and trim any excess. Install the pump in the tub and fill the tub with water. Turn on the pump and check the stream of water from the spout to make sure it flows back into the tub. It may be necessary to adjust the position of the source pipe or the flow control of the pump.

HAMMER AND CRADLE: Cut a foot-long piece of the narrower bamboo and find a spot to cut another spout that will be 4 inches or so from the nearest node. Angle your cut sharply as you did with the first spout. This is the hammer. Next, cut an 8-inch piece from the wider bamboo. Cut a slot into one end that is wide enough to cradle the hammer. Sand the rough edges.

Cut a 4-inch-long piece of ⅜-inch dowel, or use a brass pin of the same dimensions, to create a pivot rod for the hammer. Drill holes in the centers of the cradle arms large enough for the pin; then put the pin in place.

Rest the hammer in the cradle on top of the pivot pin; then slide the hammer back and forth until you find the spot where it sits in balance. Drill a hole through both sides of the hammer between the balance point and the node below the spout lip. Remove the pivot pin, put the hammer in the cradle, and run the pivot pin through both pieces.

Sink another piece of metal rod, about 12 inches long, into the dirt where the cradle will sit, then secure the cradle and hammer over it. Turn on the pump and let the spout fill the hammer with water. If the hammer won't drop, saw off a little of the closed end; then let the water fill the spout again. The hammer should drop on its own, empty the water, and return to the upright position without any assistance. If the hammer is too heavy to right itself when empty, trim a little off the angled spout end. When the hammer is trimmed to the correct length and you have sanded any rough spots, position a rock under the closed end of the hammer so that it can make the clacking sound. Trim the excess off the pivot pin and add caps to keep it from sliding out.

FINISHING TOUCHES: Plant the area around the plastic tub with a few small marginal plants and top the dirt with a layer of pea gravel or small rocks.

If your shishi-odoshi sits in an open area, check it after stormy weather to be sure it is still operating correctly. During hot weather, add water to the plastic tub if the level gets too low.

Vinyl tubing for the water supply must fit through the bamboo pipe and spout pieces. Use a hand-held drill or drill press to rout through the cane nodes where necessary.

YOU WILL NEED

- Half whiskey barrel or other similar-sized container
- Potting soil or garden soil
- 5-gallon plastic bucket or tub
- Bamboo, 2½ feet of 2 inch diameter and 2 feet of 1 inch diameter
- Vinyl hose, 3 feet, sized to fit your pump
- Slim metal rod, 2½ feet
- Pump sized for container garden
- Dowel rod or brass pin, 4 inches long
- End caps for rod or pin
- Small marginal plants
- Pea gravel or other small rocks

FOUNTAINS
continued

A simple wall fountain brings the music of moving water to small spaces such as patios and balconies. If you can't drill through a wall to install a fountain, use mounting hardware to attach it to the surface.

WALL FOUNTAIN

An elegant wall fountain can be installed in just a couple of hours or over a few days, depending upon the complexity of your plan. Preassembled easy-to-install kits in a variety of styles and sizes are commercially available. More complex fountain plans may require professional help or advice and may call for a second set of hands. You can design and install your own wall fountain to bring grace and beauty to your outdoor living area by using the following basics.

CHOOSING A DESIGN: Determine the style and design of the fountain you wish to install. Some wall fountains consist of a one-piece unit that contains the spout as well as the water basin and may have the pump included. Others have two visible parts—the basin and the spout ornament (the decorative object, such as a lion's face, spitting fish, or bamboo tube, through which the waterspout emerges)—in addition to the pump and hosing. Water is pumped up through a hidden or disguised hose or pipe from the basin to the spout, where it spills back into the basin below. In some wall fountain designs the basin rests on the ground below the spout, while in others it is mounted on the wall.

If the fountain you choose does not include a pump, select one calibrated to move enough water for your project. A pump that moves too few gallons per hour will result in too little or no flow. A pump that moves too many gph may spray the water out too vigorously, and ruin the affect you are trying to achieve, while losing water in the process.

THE SITE: Choose a wall for your fountain sturdy enough to safely bear all the necessary components: the spout ornament, the basin full of water (unless it will be on the ground), the hosing or pipe, and the pump. Traditional stone and concrete fountains are available at nurseries and home improvement centers. The weight of these fountains will require great stability in the supporting wall; a wooden wall will be insufficient. Many decorative fountain elements are now produced in lightweight resin or fiberglass. They provide an authentic look and durability without the weight of stone or concrete. Depending on the size, some wooden walls may support these lighter-weight designs. If your wall will support a spout mask but not the water receptacle, choose a basin, large vase, or trough that can sit on the ground below the spout.

Decide whether you will drill holes through the supporting wall so that you can run the plumbing line and the pump's electrical cord

YOU WILL NEED

- Spout ornament
- Basin, pot, or trough
- Flexible tubing
- Pencil
- Pump and hosing
- GFCI outlet
- Drill
- Masonry or wood bits and screws
- Plumber's putty
- T-brackets*
- U-brackets*

*if required

behind it or run them on the exterior side of the wall. If you run them on the exterior, you may want to disguise them later with plants, a trellis, or other decorative items.

PLUMBING AND ELECTRICAL: An electrical outlet for the pump's plug must be accessible on the appropriate side of the wall. Install a GFCI at the outlet to protect against electric shock.

If your plan requires that you drill through a wall, decide first where you want the spout ornament to be mounted. With a pencil, mark the location where the hole should be drilled. Position the basin so that when installation is finished the basin will catch the water that falls from the spout.

Put the pump in the basin and run its cord and flexible outlet hose over the top edge. You can minimize the appearance of the cord and hose by drilling a third hole through the side of the basin. If you do this, drill the hole so that it will end up on the side of the basin that is against the wall. Place it an inch or more higher than the top of the pump so that if water escapes, the basin will still contain enough water that your pump will not run dry. Seal the hole around the cable and hosing using plumber's putty.

With a pencil, mark the location for the lower hole in the wall. Move the basin and check the spout ornament and basin marks to ensure that they are properly aligned.

Using a masonry bit for a stone or brick wall, or a wood bit for a wooden one, drill the two holes through the wall at the pencil marks you made. The lower hole must be large enough for the head of the pump's electrical cord and hose to pass through. The upper hole should be big enough for the hose alone.

The fountain components are attached to the wall using mortar and wall plugs or T-brackets. Double-check the stability of the basin because its supports must hold its own weight plus the water. If you use a freestanding basin or ceramic pot, place it on a level surface, such as a concrete pad or patio stone. Align it below the waterspout so that little or no water splashes out. Too much splashing will cause your reservoir to lose water, risking damage to your pump.

With your pump in the basin, run the flexible black hosing up to the spout, going behind the wall if your design calls for it. Securely attach it to the spout ornament. If your hose will be on the wall's exterior, bracket it into place using U-brackets and screws or provided kit hardware.

Fill the basin with water. Plug in the pump. Make any necessary adjustments to the basin, pump, hose, and spout to get the stream of water to fall at the right speed and location.

After you have drilled the holes for the spout and basin, run the tubing from the pump in the basin through the back of the wall ornament. You can disguise the cord later with vining plants. Align the basin beneath the spout and check to be sure it is level and secure, in order to avoid damage and water loss.

Run the pump's electrical cord to a nearby GFCI outlet. Fill the basin with water, install the pump, and turn it on. Check to be sure that water from the spout is pouring at the desired volume and falling into the basin in the correct position. Adjust the flow as needed.

FOUNTAINS
continued

FREESTANDING FOUNTAIN

One of the simplest water features you can make is a fountain in a container. Use any large pot. Terra-cotta is particularly handsome. If the container does not have a drainage hole in the bottom, drill one (using a masonry bit) or drape the pump's electrical cord over the rim. Disguise the cord by guiding a few stems of one of the surrounding plants along the rim.

Set the freestanding fountain in a garden bed or border that has an electrical outlet nearby; using an extension cord is unsafe and not recommended.

If you think you will have a problem with mosquitoes, add a few small goldfish, which will eat the mosquito larvae. The number of fish you can use—probably not more than three—will depend on the size of the container.

1. Set a submersible pump in the bottom of the container. Using a pot that is at least 30 inches in diameter makes a splash and requires less water refilling than a smaller pot. Pull the pump's electrical cord through the drainage hole of the pot.

2. Pull out enough cord to be able to connect it to the outlet—don't plug it in—and leave sufficient slack to raise the pump in the pot. Close the drainage hole with premixed quick-drying cement. Let the cement dry thoroughly; follow directions on the package.

3. Seal the inside of the pot—whether it is terra-cotta, wood, or some other porous material—with a liquid water sealant that is labeled for use on wood. Let the sealant dry completely.

4. Elevate the pump in the center of the container: Place it on bricks to bring it within a few inches below where the water's surface will be. Fill the pot with water and connect the pump to the GFCI outlet. Be sure the water level does not dip below the pump.

Put the pump in the bottom of a pot at least 30 inches in diameter. Pull the electrical cord through the drainage hole.

Pull out enough cord to reach the GFCI outlet, but leave enough slack to raise the pump for maintenance. Plug the hole with cement.

Seal the inside of the container with a liquid water sealant made for wood, even if your container is not wood. Allow to dry thoroughly.

Place the pump on bricks to bring it within a few inches of the water's surface. Fill the pot and plug in the pump.

YOU WILL NEED
- Container 30 inches or larger in diameter
- Pump-and-fountain kit
- Premixed quick-dry cement
- Liquid water sealant
- Bricks
- Outlet with GFCI

SPECIAL PROJECTS

BIRDBATH

This handmade birdbath belongs nestled in a flower bed, where thirsty visitors will be attracted. You don't need a fancy mold to fashion the 18- to 20-inch basin. You can even use a cardboard box instead of the ground, as long as the box is at least 4 inches wider than the basin width. Fill it 10 inches deep with soil; then scoop a basin shape in the soil.

CREATE THE MOLD: Dig and shape a hole in the ground (or in a soil-filled cardboard box) to use as a mold. Sprinkle the shape with water and pack the soil firmly. Tamp a flat area in the center so the finished basin will sit securely on a flat base.

MIX CONCRETE AND PEAT: Wear gloves and a dust mask. Mix 3 gallons of premixed concrete with 2 to 3 cups of peat moss in a wheelbarrow. Add about 2 gallons of water and mix with a hoe to make a stiff batter. If it is too thin, add more concrete; if too thick to hold together, add water.

FORM THE BASIN: Work quickly—concrete starts to set in minutes. Shovel the wet mix into the mold; pat it into place. Conform it to the basin shape; scoop concrete from the center of the basin to the outside rim. Pat smooth. Spritz with water to keep concrete moist.

DECORATE: Sprinkle crushed glass on the wet mix; gently press into place. Press in other decorative pieces such as stones. Cover basin with a plastic sheet to cure for 3 to 7 days. Uncover; remove it from the ground. Age a month before filling with water.

Wear rubber gloves and a dust mask to prepare the concrete and peat moss mixture for this simple birdbath. The concrete sets rapidly, so be sure to work quickly.

Spread out the wet mixture in a hole in the ground that is the size and shape you want the birdbath to be. Smooth it from the center to the sides.

Press crushed bottle glass or colorful stones into the wet mix, then cover with plastic while the concrete cures. In a week, dig the birdbath out of the dirt; in a month, fill it with water.

YOU WILL NEED

- Hoe or shovel
- Rubber gloves
- Safety glasses
- Dust mask
- Spray bottle and water
- 3 gallons premixed concrete
- Peat moss
- Crushed, colored, recycled glass; stone specimens
- Plastic sheet

SPECIAL PROJECTS
continued

DRY CREEK

Sometimes all it takes is the impression of a stream. Many people have unused areas in the yard because these spaces do not seem to lend themselves to a pretty garden design. The most common unused spaces include a wet expanse of ground at the rear of the property and a side yard. Both places present an opportunity to take advantage of design challenges in the landscape.

A dry streambed can function as a drainage ditch for the wet area, while its beauty masks the utilitarian aspect. A well-planted dry creek can filter obtrusive street noises in the side yard. A winding trail of polished or rough stones bordered by hedges and beds of colorful annuals and perennials invites visitors to take a relaxing stroll.

Side yards and rear property lines often include fences, which make excellent backdrops for plantings. The addition of a dry creek is a perfect opportunity for designing a special, private garden retreat.

A dry streambed provides a peaceful path through the garden in sunny weather and a convenient drainage ditch when it rains.

A FEW POINTERS: To save money, put in an underlayment of ordinary rough stones and use polished river stones for the top layer only. The subdued gray color of the river stones, *below left*, beautifully offsets the greens and floral hues of the plants.

Utilize plants that live naturally beside a real stream such as irises, cardinal flowers, hostas, and astilbes. Summer some of your houseplants, such as clivia and orchids, outdoors in the shelter of a fenced dry-creek garden. They will appreciate the heat reflected from the stones and the shelter from the wind and hot sun.

1. DESIGN AND DIG: Using rope or a garden hose, lay out the contours of the stream in a meandering, casual style. Vary the width. To make digging easier, you may rototill the creek bed first. If the stream is very large, you may want to rent an earth-moving tractor to cut the initial swath. Use the excavated soil to mound a creek bank or to fill low spots elsewhere on your property. Dig the bed to a depth of 6 to 8 inches. Even on flat property, the bed should run slightly downhill, so it can carry a stream of water during heavy rains.

2. SHAPE: It's visually interesting to have some straight, deep sides and some that curve. Shape and smooth the sides and the bottom; they do not need to be perfectly smooth. Remove twigs, roots, stones, and other objects that might puncture the landscape fabric. Remove weeds and plants. Chop through large roots with an ax.

3. LAY FABRIC: Working on a still day, spread at least two layers of landscape fabric, such as permeable polypropylene fabric. With two layers, your dry creek will last a long time, eliminating the need to remove the covering rock and replace the fabric if it wears out. If you want the creek to carry water, use some solid plastic sheeting. Place stones to secure the fabric. Smooth out each layer and overlap the bed edges.

4. STONESCAPE: Select stones in scale with the size of the stream. Smooth river rocks give the illusion of a more active creek;

YOU WILL NEED

- Rope or garden hose
- Shovel
- Rototiller (optional)
- Permeable landscape fabric
- River stones, rough rocks, pebbles
- Boulders
- Flat stones (stepping-stones)

Rototill the creek bed to make it easier to excavate. Remove any rocks or other sharp objects that might puncture the landscape fabric. Make sure to dig the bed so that it runs slightly downhill, to carry water away when it rains. A curving shape is natural-looking and pleasing to the eye.

rough stones give the impression that the creek has been dry for quite a while. Use a depth of 4 inches along the base of the stream; mound the stones 6 to 8 inches deep along the edges to meet the banks. Place stepping-stones, if you wish, or add another point of interest, such as a waterfall made of stacked stones.

5. ANCHOR: Use boulders to anchor the landscape fabric that drapes up the sides and over the bank. Fill in with smaller boulders and river rocks to hide the fabric. Add more stones to the creek and up the sides.

6. LANDSCAPE: Create a natural look along the edges of the stream, keeping the edges a little rough and irregular. Bury larger stones at least half their height in the soil rather than laying them directly on top of the soil. Soften the edges of the creek with groundcovers and perennials that will spread—most won't root in the stream itself. If some do, prune them occasionally to keep them overhanging instead of invading. Plant a few evergreen shrubs and dwarf trees along the creek and in beds nearby. Fashion a stepping-stone bridge or a raised wooden bridge, if you want.

PLANT LIST FOR DRY CREEK BED

- Japanese pittosporum
- Impatiens
- Sweet flag
- Kaffir lily

SPECIAL PROJECTS
continued

An artful path across water is practical as well as attractive. Stepping-stones let you view aquatic life up close, and make maintenance easier.

STEPPING-STONES

Easier maintenance and increased viewing pleasure are the practical and aesthetic reasons for installing stepping-stones. No matter the reason, remember two things for safety: Use stones with a rough surface so they will not be slippery when wet, and securely fasten the stones to a solid base.

It is easier to install stepping-stones in a pond without water than a filled one. Plan for and construct them as you build the pond; otherwise, drain the pond first.

STEP PLACEMENT: Be aware of changes in levels on the bottom of the pond and any challenges they may pose. For safety and aesthetics, it is important that you have a level surface on which to walk.

WATER SURFACE: When you have an idea of approximately where you want the stones, drive a stake on either side of an imaginary line passing through the center of where the steps will be. Run twine between the stakes and use a line level to adjust the twine so it is even with where the surface of the water will be.

SPACING: Lay the pavers on a driveway following the configuration laid out above, and position them so you can walk across them comfortably. Sketch the layout on paper, marking all dimensions.

FOUNDATION: Place a scrap of carpet or cardboard where each stepping-stone will be. With the sketch as a guide, put the large concrete blocks on their sides on top of the carpet; stack them until they are ½ inch below the string. (The half inch allows for the mortar that will be between each of the concrete blocks and the pavers.) You may need to use narrower capstones to get the exact height. Put the pavers in place.

BUILDING: Mix several batches of mortar. Take apart the piers; then reassemble them using ½ inch of mortar between any blocks all the way up to and including the stepping-stones. Allow the mortar to set for 3 days. Cover everything with a tarp if it rains.

YOU WILL NEED

- Line level, stakes, and twine
- Nonskid pavers, at least 2 inches thick and 18 inches wide
- Carpet or cardboard scrap pieces
- 24×24-inch concrete blocks
- 24×24-inch capstones (if needed)
- Premixed mortar

The simple architecture of a well-constructed bridge can transform a common stream into the focal point of a landscape. The bridge's function may be less compelling than its subtle symbolism.

ARCHED BRIDGE

Bridges are among the most spectacular examples of humanity's desire to build. This span will turn your landscape into an object of admiration. The design features arched construction for appearance and strength. Copper spindles and copper post tops complement the cedar components perfectly.

LAMINATE THE BEAMS: Each beam is made from five 5/4×6 cedar boards 10 feet long. Put one board on a laminating jig, and spread glue on its upper face with a 3-inch paint roller. Stack a second board face to face atop the first, and align their ends, edges, and centerlines. Use a pipe clamp to pull the pair of boards down into the jig so the boards' centerlines align with the jig's centerline. Make certain that the edges are still aligned, then add a second pipe clamp at the centerline on the opposite side of the boards.

Clamp the arched boards together along their length. Always place clamps in pairs on opposing sides of the stack to keep it stable.

Secure the boards together by driving a double row of 1⅝-inch deck screws along their length spaced 1¼ inches from each edge and 6 inches apart. Countersink each screw head so it doesn't interfere with the next lamination. Allow this assembly to dry for at least eight hours, then remove the clamps.

Repeat this process to add the third, fourth and fifth boards to the beam. Repeat the sequence to make the second beam.

TOOLS YOU WILL NEED

- Measuring tape
- Hand saw, circular saw, and band saw
- Level
- Framing square and pencil
- Power drill and drill bits
- Pipe clamps
- Screwdriver
- Paint tray and 3-inch paint roller
- Plumb bob and string
- Tube cutter
- Router
- Laminating jig

MATERIALS YOU WILL NEED

Use cedar or other rot-resistant lumber.

- Two 4×4 posts 10 feet long
- Ten 5/4×6 decking 10 feet long
- Twelve 5/4×6 decking 8 feet long
- Sixteen 1×4 boards 10 feet long
- One 2×4 board 8 feet long
- Four 2×6 scrap pieces 10 inches long
- One piece of scrap ¾-inch plywood
- Twelve ½×10-inch carriage bolts with nuts and washers
- Five pounds #8×1⅝-inch deck screws
- Three pounds #6×1¼-inch deck screws
- Two pounds #8×2½-inch deck screws
- Eight ¾-inch-dia. copper pipe 10 feet long
- Four copper post tops
- Four concrete patio paving blocks
- Weatherproof glue

SPECIAL PROJECTS
continued

Glue together two thicknesses of 2×6 and secure them in place on two 10′-foot-long posts to form the laminating jig. To laminate the rails, clamp from the center toward each end of the jig. Scrap blocks align the boards while you drive the screws in place.

LAMINATE THE RAILS: Rip twelve 10-foot-long cedar 1×4s to 3 inches wide to make the bottom rails, the center rail, and the handrails.

Leave the second completed beam in the laminating jig while you screw a temporary ¾×1½×8-inch scrapwood spacer near each end of the beam.

Lay one piece of rail stock on the beam with the ends resting on the scrapwood blocks. Spread glue on the rail stock; then place another piece of rail stock atop it. Align the centerlines of the rail stock with the beam's centerline and clamp in place.

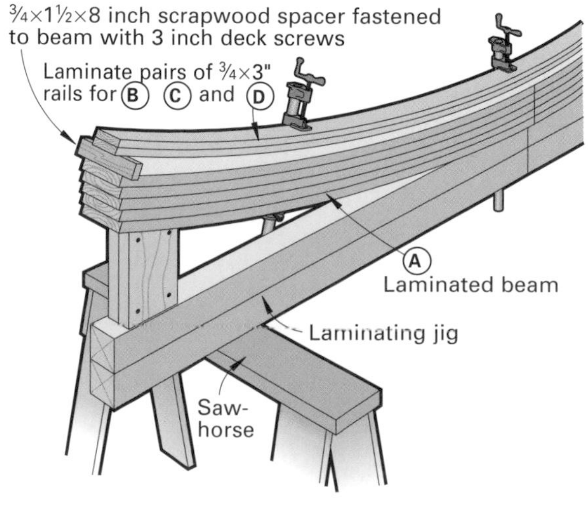

¾×1½×8 inch scrapwood spacer fastened to beam with 3 inch deck screws

Laminate pairs of ¾×3" rails for (B) (C) and (D)

(A) Laminated beam

Laminating jig

Saw-horse

Use additional clamps to laminate the two pieces of rail stock tightly together.

Secure the two boards together by driving a double row of 1⅝-inch deck screws along their length spaced ½ inch from each edge and 6 inches apart. Allow the assembly to dry for eight hours, then repeat the process for the remaining five pairs of rail stock.

DRILL THE RAILS: Level the setup before you drill. The copper-pipe spindles fit into holes drilled through the bottom rail and partially into the center rail. Stack and clamp these rails inside the curve of the beam with all of the centerlines aligned.

Stretch a string between the ends of the setup. Make adjustments so that the setup is level, both end-to-end and side-to-side. Clamp the pair of rails to the beam at its midpoint, then drive a pair of 2½-inch deck screws 2 inches from each end of the rails to keep each pair in position until sawed apart.

MARK THE RAIL HOLE CENTER POINTS: Suspend a plumb bob from a ladder placed 5 feet from the setup. Sight the shaft of your 1-inch drill bit to match the plumb line. Drill holes 2¼ inches deep into both sets of bottom and center rails. Be careful not to drill too deeply, or the point of the spade bit could go through the center rail. Repeat for the other set of rails.

MARK AND CUT BEAMS: Remove the beam from the laminating jig, and place it on the floor with the arch facing upward. Clamp a scrap board along the beam's centerline.

Clamp the rail assemblies to the bridge's floor, and you can mark the cutlines easily and accurately.

Place a 20×20 square of ¾-inch-thick plywood under each end and add shims under the plywood to make it level.

Measuring from the centerline of the beam, make a mark at each end cutline. Use a pencil and framing square to complete these vertical lines. Use the same method to mark the location of the end posts.

Use two thicknesses of the ¾ cedar stock that you'll use for the floorboards as a gauge to mark the horizontal cutlines. Using a circular saw, cut just to the waste side of each of these cutlines. Use each kerf as a guide for a handsaw to complete the cuts. Repeat for the other beam.

MAKE POSTS: Cut the end and center posts to length. Mark and drill holes. Mark centerlines along each post edge that will attach to the beam.

Put one of the beams on the plywood squares you used when you marked cutlines on the beam, and adjust it with shims so that the centerline is plumb. Clamp the end posts and the center post to the beam, aligning the centerlines. Check that each post is plumb. Use the holes in the posts as guides to drill into the beam. Bolt the posts to the beam. Repeat for the remaining posts and beam.

ADD FLOORBOARDS: Place the two beam assemblies parallel with their outer edges 35½ inches apart. Using shims, adjust both assemblies so that the posts are plumb. Screw scrapwood spacers between the beams to keep them aligned while you prepare floorboards.

Cut floorboards from 5⁄4×6 cedar to 42½ inches long. Notch the center floorboard to fit around the center posts, and fasten it to the beams with 2½-inch deck screws. Screw in the remaining floorboards, spaced ¼ inch apart. Notch floorboards around the end posts, and screw them in place. Rip and crosscut the end caps to size, then attach them to the posts.

MAKE THE MOUNTS: Rip stock for the end and center mounts. Cut a 15-degree bevel at the lower end of each blank for the end mounts. Mark and drill the holes, and cut the parts to length. Mark the shape at the top of the end mounts, and cut it with a bandsaw.

Clamp the end mounts to the end posts and the center mounts to the center posts. Clamp the bottom-and center-rail assembly to the bridge's floorboards, and mark cutlines where the rails meet the end and center mounts. Unclamp the rails, and use a pencil and square to extend the cutlines around the rails. Use a handsaw to cut the rails. Keep the bottom rail and center rail together in pairs. Mark them so that they'll be assembled between the same posts used to mark them for cutting. Rout a ¼-inch round-over along all of the edges of the bottom and center rails.

BUILD SIDE ASSEMBLIES: Unclamp end and center mounts. Position a pair of bottom and center rails between them. Position the rail ends and drive 2½-inch screws to secure the assembly. Repeat the steps for the remaining three assemblies.

SPECIAL PROJECTS
continued

Use a tubing cutter to cut the spindles to length from ¾-inch copper pipe. Drill a hole through one wall of each spindle near the end of the pipe. Insert the spindles through the bottom rail and into the center rail. Fasten each spindle by driving a screw through the spindle into the bottom rail.

Position each side assembly into its opening. Clamp each assembly into place, but do not drive in any screws yet.

FIT AND ASSEMBLE THE HANDRAIL: Clamp a pair of 8-inch-long scrap boards flush with the top of each center post. Place a handrail on the scrapwood, aligning the handrail's centerline with the centerline of the center post. Align the handrail with the end marks you previously made on the end mounts. Mark cutlines on the handrail.

Rout the round-over along the edges of the handrails, then cut these parts to length with

EXPLODED VIEW

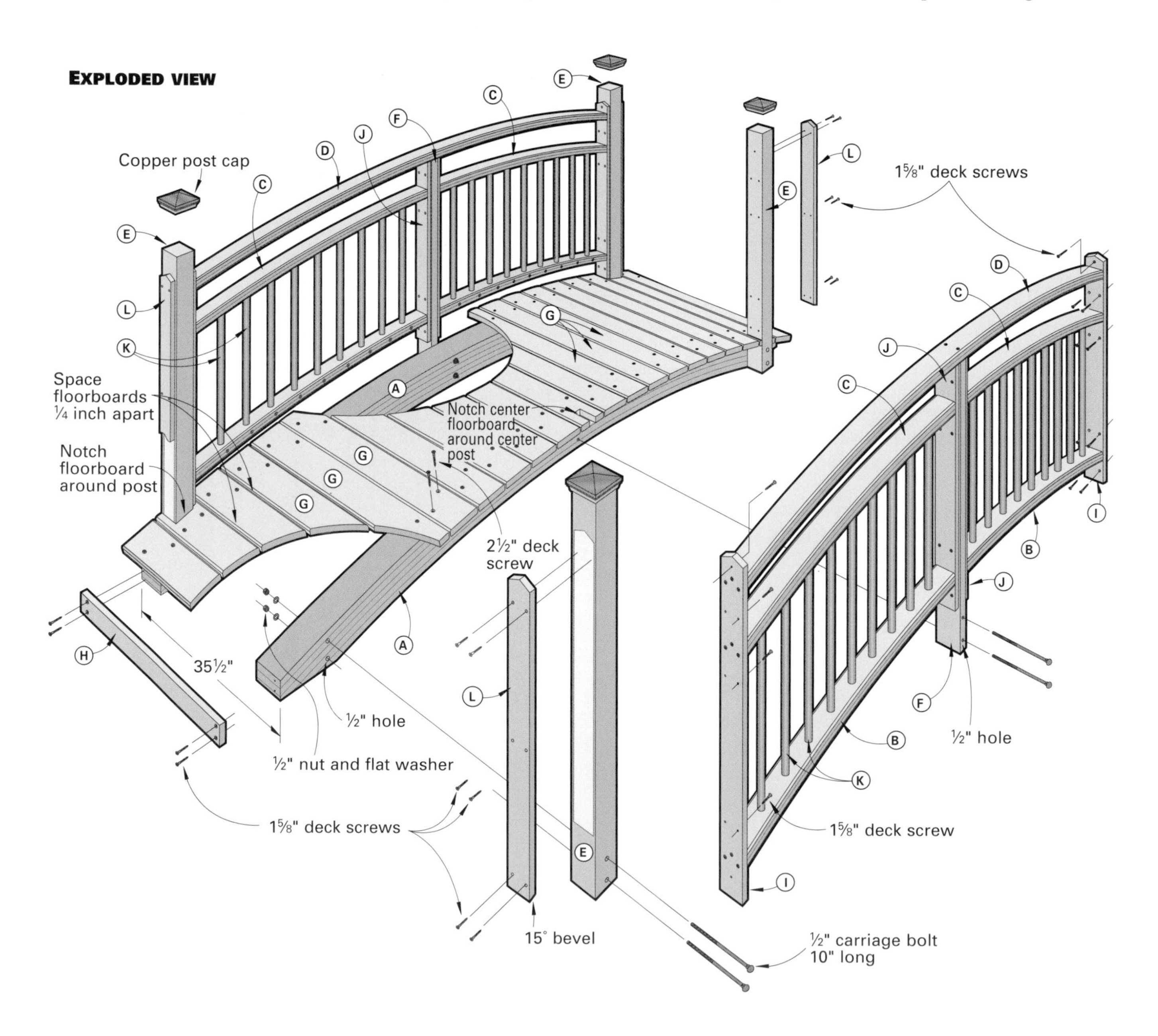

a handsaw. Tilt the top of the side assemblies outward to provide clearance to drive the screws. Clamp the assemblies in this position while you drive the screws through the end mounts into the handrail. Unclamp and plumb the end and center mounts, then drive screws through these parts into the posts. Drill pilot holes for the 4-inch deck screws that attach the handrail to the center post, then drive these fasteners. Repeat the fitting and assembly steps for the other handrail.

FINISHING TOUCHES: Cut the post strips to size; then drill the holes. Screw the post strips to the end posts. Apply your choice of finish to the bridge. Install the bridge by setting each beam end on a 2×12×12-inch precast concrete patio paving block.

Mark the handrail's length against the end mounts to ensure they fit snugly together.

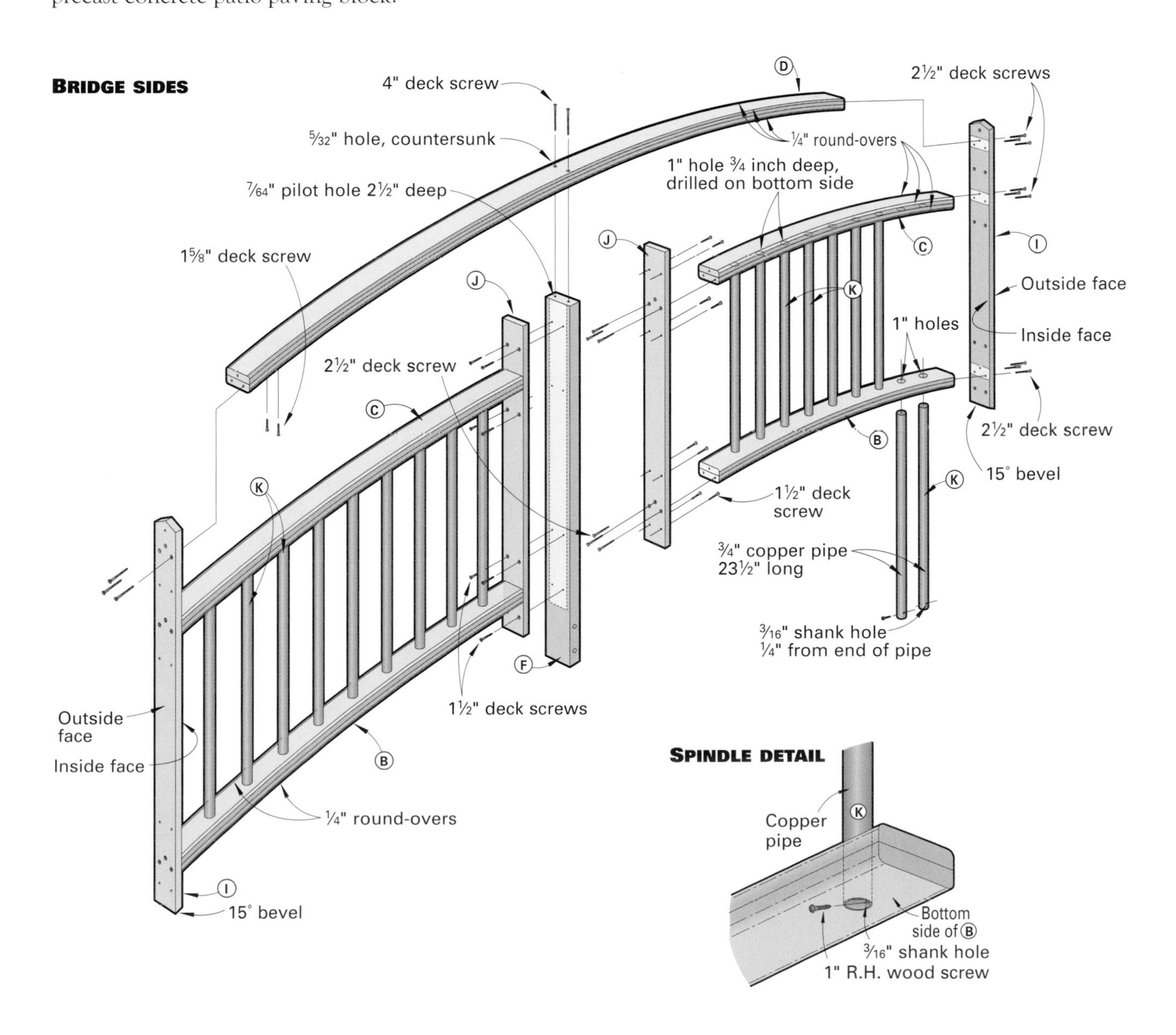

SPECIAL PROJECTS
continued

CONVERTING A POOL TO A POND

Do you have an old swimming pool on your property that's just gathering leaves? Don't backfill it. You can easily transform it into a large water garden.

It may be made of gunite and reinforced steel, but even if it's a liner pool or in need of replastering and retiling, you can still convert it to a koi pond or other waterscape. Most of the hard work is already done. The hole is dug, the dirt has been hauled away, and the plumbing and electrical are in place. All you need are a design idea and the energy for a bit of cleanup and mechanical modification.

CLEANING: A chief concern in converting a swimming pool to a working water feature is the removal of chemicals and residues from the surfaces. Pool chemicals such as cyanuric acid and conditioner, chlorine, and bromine are general biocides that kill all forms of life. Remove them completely.

Accomplish this with a procedure called acid/bleach washing, used in both swimming pool and ornamental aquatics maintenance. Drain the system, apply a water-diluted solution (about 1⁄10 muriatic acid) to the basin, plumbing, and mechanical surfaces (making sure to remove filter cartridges first); then rinse and drain two more times.

Wear rubber gloves, old long-sleeved shirts and slacks, and eye protection. Once you've tackled this cleaning, it will seem simple and straightforward. Basin re-coating, plastering, and retiling will probably not be necessary as the coating from algae in the pond will eventually hide any flaws. The algae makes surfaces slippery, so be careful when walking in the pond for maintenance and other tasks.

CIRCULATION AND AERATION: Pump size and installation depend on what you want in your pond. For full-blown koi systems, the pump needs to run continuously. The pumping mechanisms installed for the swimming pool are likely not the best available or most appropriate technology to use with your conversion. Most fully rated swimming pool pumps are designed to produce relatively high volume at high pressure. You will want some volume at not much pressure for your pond—to protect aquatic life as well as save on electric costs. Do your homework here, as there are some good choices in fractional and multiple horsepower pumps for ponds that can be retrofitted to the existing pool plumbing. Compare power curves, water moved per kilowatt consumed, and service factors because the pump operation will probably be your greatest ongoing expense.

On the other hand, if you will operate your waterfall only when guests visit, or if the pond will be a reflecting one only or a heavily planted water garden, your current pump may work just fine operated manually as needed or for a few minutes to a few hours daily on an automatic timer.

For koi and other vigorous oxygen users you may need to turn the water over frequently, whereas systems with mostly plants need far less circulation. Generally, you can continue to use the main drain on the bottom of the pool as the pump's principal intake, rather than supplying another mid-depth intake. If you circulate your water daily and regularly remove sludge and leaves, you will probably avoid difficulties with stagnant water or stratification in your system. If you live in an area where freezing is a concern, consider deicing mechanisms, surface agitation, air stones, or the use of a small submersible pump to keep your water moving in cold weather.

FILTRATION: Swimming pool filters are made to remove small amounts of small debris from the water. Biological ponds call for

Swimming pool chemicals such as chlorine and bromine are powerful biocides that can harm fish and other aquatic life. The most important step in this project is to thoroughly clean any such residue from all pool surfaces with an acid/bleach washing and several rinses.

Replace the old swimming pool pump with a pond pump designed to move less water at lower pressure.

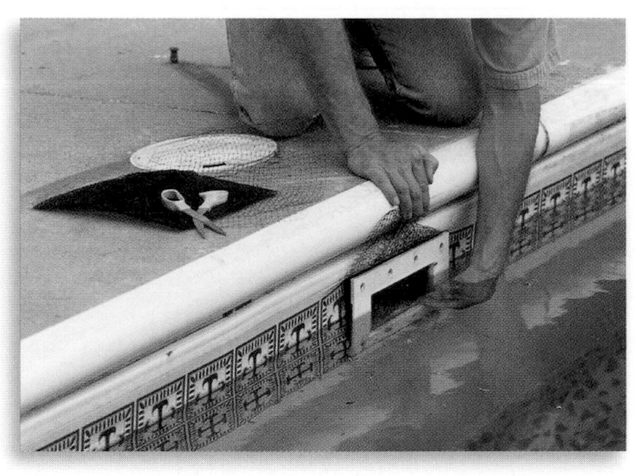
The contents of a biological pond may overwhelm a swimming pool filter. Cover the skimmer intakes with sturdy plastic mesh to keep fish and floating plants from being pulled in. Add a fish filter.

extraction of larger quantities of larger matter. If your pond does not collect many leaves and has adequate biofiltration from aquatic plants, you may be able to remove the existing swimming pool filter media (diatomaceous earth sleeves, cartridges, or sand) and instead use plastic biomedia, ceramics, fused glass beads, or batting material.

A filter designed specifically for ponds is definitely required for koi ponds and other more serious applications. Construct a large container inside a new waterfall, or use an in-line series of plastic troughs. Even in-pond filters will work; plan them carefully to expedite maintenance tasks.

RETROFITTING: Your conversion may need new plumbing for intakes or discharges, such as waterfalls, to improve circulation or to allow for the passage of more water without resistance. If so, use schedule 40 PVC pipe and fittings. Copper pipe already in place is safe for your aquatic animals; because of its patina, any copper ion released will be an insoluble solid.

If your pool has a heater, leave it and its plumbing as is or remove or retrofit them to lessen pumped-water drag. If you decide to retrofit your existing pump's plumbing, don't miss the chance to cut in barbed intake and discharge fittings on Ts and valves on the new pump's intake and discharge lines. These can be a real boon in regular vacuuming maintenance and occasional large water changes, allowing you to pull out the water and place the waste where you want it.

Skimmer intakes can be problematic in pool-to-pond conversions. An excess of floating matter and even fish can become trapped in such areas. Screen the skimmers with plastic mesh of sturdy construction to prevent a tragedy.

Maintain your new pond the same as you would any other irregular-sized and -shaped biological pond. Fish feeding, plant potting, re-potting, and fertilization will all follow the same schedules.

An unused swimming pool is easily updated from an eyesore or safety hazard into a lush aquascape you can enjoy all year long.

WATER GARDENING RESOURCES

You'll find a tremendous variety of equipment, building supplies, plants, and aquatic animals at water garden centers and nurseries. The following suppliers sell by mail order, and most sell on the Internet too. Many also offer colorful, free catalogs with detailed information.

These resources are listed for your information only; no endorsement is implied or intended. Look in your local phone directory or on the Internet for water gardening clubs in your area. Other pond-keepers can provide you with advice on water gardening in your region.

RETAIL & MAIL ORDER

Al Zimmer's Ponds & Supplies
6271 Perkiomen Ave.
Birdsboro, PA 19508
800/722-8877
www.azponds.com
Supplies

Avian Aquatics, Inc.
P.O. Box 188
Harveson, DE 19951-0188
800/788-6478
www.avianaquatics.com
Water features for songbirds

Aqua Art Pond Specialists
11-G Poco Way, #154
American Canyon, CA 94503-1071
800/995-9164 (order line)
707/642-7663 (Helpline)
www.aquaart.com
Equipment, statuary, and ornaments

Busse Gardens
17160 245th Ave.
Big Lake, MN 55309
800/544-3192
www.bussegardens.com
Perennial plants

California Carnivores
2833 Old Gravenstein Hwy. S.
Sebastopol, CA 95472
707/824-0433
www.californiacarnivores.com
Carnivorous plants and supplies

Crystal Palace Perennials, Ltd.
P.O. Box 154
St. John, IN 46373
219/374-9419
www.crystalpalaceperennial.com
Plants

Escort Lighting
51 N. Elm St.
Wernersville, PA 19565
800/856-7948
www.escortlighting.com
Garden lighting

Fairweather Gardens
P.O. Box 330
Greenwich, NJ 08323
856/451-6261
www.fairweathergardens.com
Plants, including carnivorous

Gilberg Farms
2172 Highway O
Robertsville, MO 63072
800/423-4717
www.splashplants.com
Aquatic plants

Girard Nurseries
P.O. Box 428
6839 N. Ridge East
Geneva OH 44041-0428
440/466-2881
www.girardnurseries.com
Plants

Green & Hagstrom, Inc.
P.O. Box 658
Fairview, TN 37062
615/799-0708
www.greenandhagstrom.com
Plants and fish

Hemphill's Water Gardens
2222 Fallston Rd.
Fallston, MD 21047
410/803-1688
www.pond-people.com
Equipment, fish, plants, and supplies

Heronswood Nursery Ltd.
7530 NE 288th St.
Kingston, WA 98346
360/297-4172
www.heronswood.com
Plants

Klehm's Song Sparrow
Perennial Farm
13101 East Rye Rd.
Avalon, WI 53505
800/553-3715
Plants

Lilyblooms Aquatic Gardens
932 S. Main St.
North Canton, OH 44720
330/499-6910
800/921-0005
www.lilyblooms.com
Plants and supplies

Lilypons Water Gardens
6800 Lilypons Rd.
P.O. Box 10
Buckeystown, MD 21717-0010
800/999-5459
www.lilypons.com
Plants, equipment, and supplies

Lilypons Water Gardens
139 FM 1489 Koomey Rd.
Brookeshire, TX 77423-0188
800/999-5459
www.lilypons.com
Plants, equipment, and supplies

Maryland Aquatic Nurseries, Inc.
3427 North Furnace Rd.
Jarrettsville, MD 21084
410/557-7615
www.marylandaquatic.com
Plants, equipment, and fountains for indoors and out

Millstone Koi
153 Stillhouse Rd.
Freehold, NJ 07728
732/431-9300
www.millstonekoi.com
Goldfish, koi, and pond supplies

Mystic Koi and Water Gardens
1250 W. Arrow Highway
Upland, CA 91786
909/920-3767
www.mystickoi.com
Koi, plants, and supplies

Niche Gardens
1111 Dawson Rd.
Chapel Hill, NC 27516
919/967-0078
Plants, including carnivorous

Pacific Water Gardens
354 Pacific St.
San Luis Obispo, CA 93401
805/594-1693
www.pacificwatergardens.com
Koi and pond supplies

Paradise Water Gardens
Route 18
Whitman, MA 02382
781/447-4711
800/955-0161
www.paradisewatergardens.com
Fish, plants, equipment,
and supplies

Patio Garden Ponds
P.O. Box 892396
Oklahoma City, OK 73189
800/487-5459
www.patio-garden-ponds.com
Plants and supplies

Perry's Water Gardens
136 Gibson Aquatic Farm Rd.
Franklin, NC 28734
828/524-3264
www.tcfb.com/perwatg/
Lilies, lotuses, plants, supplies

Pet Warehouse
P.O. Box 752138
Dayton, OH 45475
800/443-1160
www.petwhse.com
Equipment and plants

Plant Delights Nursery
9241 Sauls Rd.
Raleigh, NC 27603
919/772-4794
www.plantdel.com
Plants, including carnivorous

Scherer Water Gardens
104 Waterside Rd.
Northport, NY 11768
631/261-7432
www.netstuff.com/scherer/
Equipment and plants

Signature Ponds, Inc.
418 Liberty Ln.
Jasper, GA 30143
706/692-5880
www.signatureponds.com
Lightweight alternative stones
and boulders

Simple Gardens
615 Old Cemetery Rd.
Richmond, VT 05477
800/351-2438
www.simplegardens.com
Plants, containers, supplies

Slocum Water Gardens
1101 Cypress Garden Blvd.
Winter Haven, FL 33884
863/293-7151
www.slocumwatergardens.com
Plants, equipment, goldfish, koi

Tilley's Nursery/The Water Works
111 E. Fairmount St.
Coopersburg, PA 18036
610/282-4784
www.tnwaterworks.com
Equipment, plants, supplies

Tranquil Lake Nursery
45 River St.
Rehoboth, MA 02769-1395
508/252-4002
www.tranquil-lake.com
Daylilies and irises

Tropical Pond & Garden
17888 61st Place North
Loxahatchee, FL 33470
561/791-8994
www.tropicalpond.com
Equipment, plants, supplies

Van Ness Water Gardens
2460 N. Euclid Ave.
Upland, CA 91784-1199
800/205-2425
www.vnwg.com
Equipment and plants

Varsity Pond Supplies
2112 Omega Dr.
Santa Ana, CA 92705
800/700-1720
Pond and koi supplies

The Water Garden
5594 Dayton Blvd.
Chattanooga, TN 37415
423/870-2838
www.watergarden.com
Equipment and plants

Water Garden Gems, Inc.
3136 Bolton Rd.
Marion, TX 78124-6002
800/682-6098
www.watergardengems.com
Equipment and plants

Waterford Gardens
74 East Allendale Rd.
Saddle River, NJ 07458
201/327-0721
www.waterford-gardens.com
Plants, equipment, books, supplies,
and fish

Western Outdoor Aquatics
16150 Highway 7
Brighton, CO 80602
303/255-7081
888/277-3227
www.westernpond.com
Equipment, koi, plants, supplies

Wildlife Nurseries, Inc.
P.O. Box 2724
Oshkosh, WI 54903-2724
920/231-3780
Native wetland plants

William Tricker, Inc.
7125 Tanglewood Dr.
Independence, OH 44131
800/524-3492
www.tricker.com
Plants, fish, supplies

WATER GARDENING RESOURCES

continued

SUPPLIERS AND DISTRIBUTORS (WHOLESALE)

Beckett Corp.
5931 Campus Circle Dr.
Irving, TX 75063-2606
888/232-5388
www.888beckett.com
Water garden products

Cal-Pump
13278 Ralston Ave.
Sylmar, CA 91342
800/225-1339
www.calpump.com
Pumps and accessories

Charleston Aquatic Nurseries
3095 Canal Bridge Rd.
John's Island, SC 29455
800/566-3264
www.charlestonaquatic.com
Plants

DMF Gardens, Inc.
2511 E. 21st St.
Des Moines, IA 50317
515/266-2488
Plants

Little Giant Pump Co.
P.O. Box 12010
Oklahoma City, OK 73157-2010
405/947-2511
www.littlegiant.com
Submersible pumps and related equipment

Pond Supplies of America
1204A Deer St.
Yorkville, IL 60560
888/742-5772
www.pondsupplies.com
Skimmers, pumps, and other pond equipment

Tetra Pond
3001 Commerce St.
Blacksburg, VA 24060-6671
800/526-0650 Ext. 5433
www.tetra-fish.com
Aquatic planters, liners, pumps, and fish supplies

United Pump
1772 Buerkle Circle
White Bear Lake, MN 55110
651/770-7810
www.unitedpumpinc.com
Equipment

Water Creations, Inc.
2507 E. 21st St.
Des Moines, IA 50317
800/475-2044
www.watercreations.com
Equipment, fish, plants, and supplies

Wicklein's Water Gardens
1820 Cromwell Bridge Rd.
Baltimore, MD 21234
410/823-1335
800/382-6716
www.wickleinaquatics.com
Plants and supplies

INTERNET ONLY

Aqua-Mart, Inc.
P.O. Box 547399
Orlando, FL 32854-7399
800/245-5814
www.aqua-mart.com
Plants and water features

Fish2U.com
P.O. Box 851
Gibsonton, FL 33534
813/677-3003
www.fish2u.com
Fish, koi, scavengers, and supplies

Pond and Landscape Solutions, Inc
2899 E. Big Beaver, #238
Troy, MI 48083
888/750-4805
www.pondsolutions.com
Equipment, plants, and supplies

PondMart
P.O. Box 1802
Beltsville, MD 20704-1802
301/931-9395
www.pondmart.com
Equipment, plants, and supplies

WetWebMedia.com
www.wetwebmedia.com
How-to information and articles about ponds, aquariums, and fish

MAGAZINES

Pondkeeper
1000 Whitetail Court
Duncansville, PA 16635
888/356-9895
www.pondkeeper.com
Trade magazine for aquatic plant nurseries, ornamental fish hatcheries, landscape installers, and retailers

Koi USA
P.O. Box 1
Midway City, CA 92655
888/660-2073
www.koiusa.com
Bimonthly magazine for koi enthusiasts

Water Gardening magazine
P.O. Box 607
St. John, IN 46373
800/308-6157
www.watergardening.com
Bimonthly magazine for pondkeepers

CLUBS, ASSOCIATIONS, AND SOCIETIES

Aquatic Gardeners Association
71 Ring Rd.
Plympton, MA 02367
206/789-5840
www.aquatic-gardeners.org
Publishes a bimonthly journal, *The Aquatic Gardener*, devoted primarily to aquarium plants

International Waterlily & Water Gardening Society
1401 Johnson Ferry Rd.
#328-G12
941/756-0880
Marietta, GA 30062
www.iwgs.org
Publishes a quarterly journal; holds annual meetings; offers chat rooms

National Pond Society
3933 Loch Highland Pass NE
Roswell, GA 30075-2029
800/742-4701
www.bandd.net/nps/
Publishes a bimonthly magazine

USDA Plant Hardiness Zone Map

This map of climate zones helps you select plants for your garden that will survive a typical winter in your region. The United States Department of Agriculture (USDA) developed the map, basing the zones on the lowest recorded temperatures across North America. Zone 1 is the coldest area and Zone 11 is the warmest.

Plants are classified by the coldest temperature and zone they can endure. For example, plants hardy to Zone 6 survive where winter temperatures drop to –10° F. Those hardy to Zone 8 die long before it's that cold. These plants may grow in colder regions but must be replaced each year. Plants rated for a range of hardiness zones can usually survive winter in the coldest region as well as tolerate the summer heat of the warmest one.

To find your hardiness zone, note the approximate location of your community on the map, then match the color band marking that area to the key.

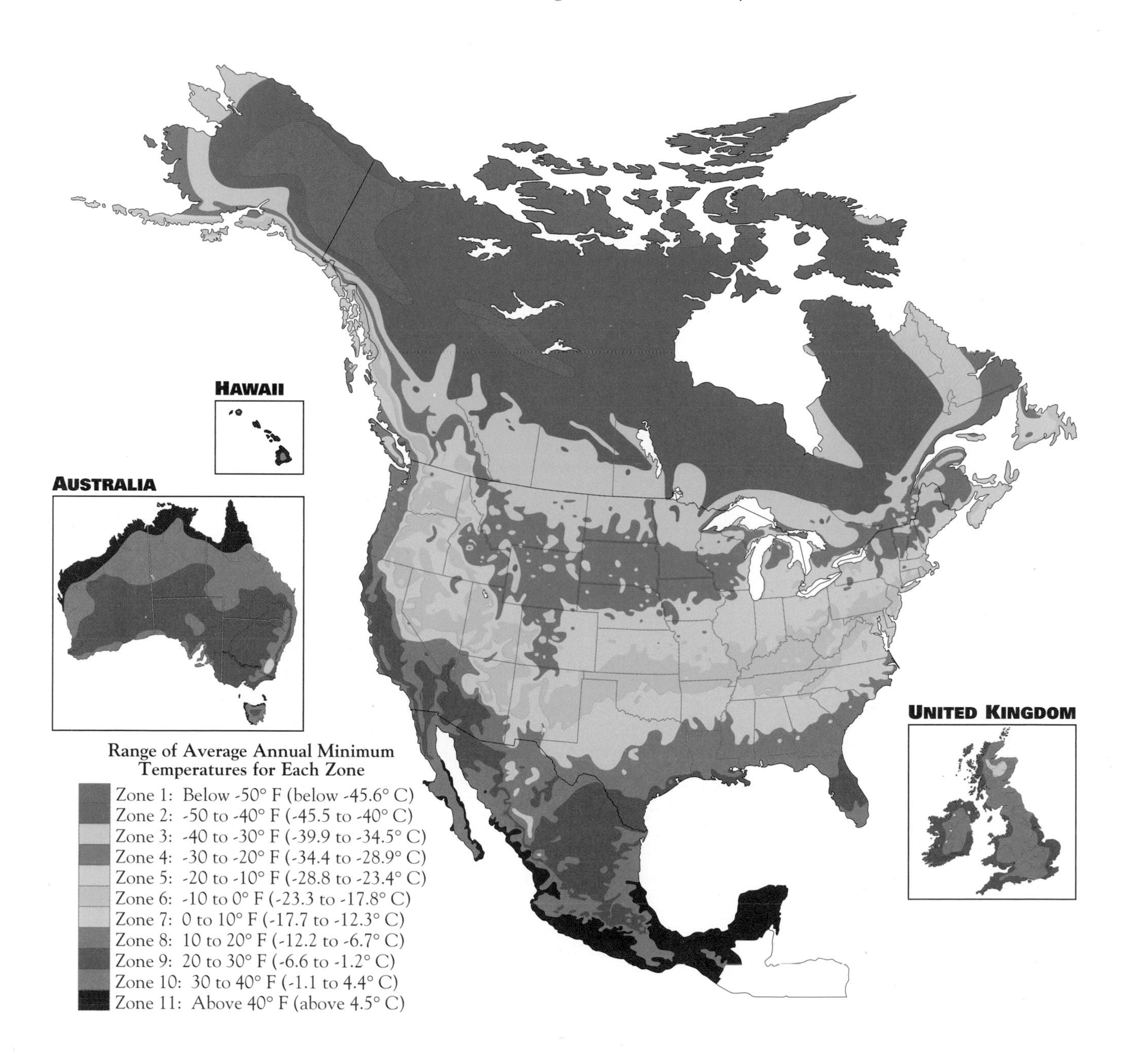

SPRING AND AUTUMN FROST DATES

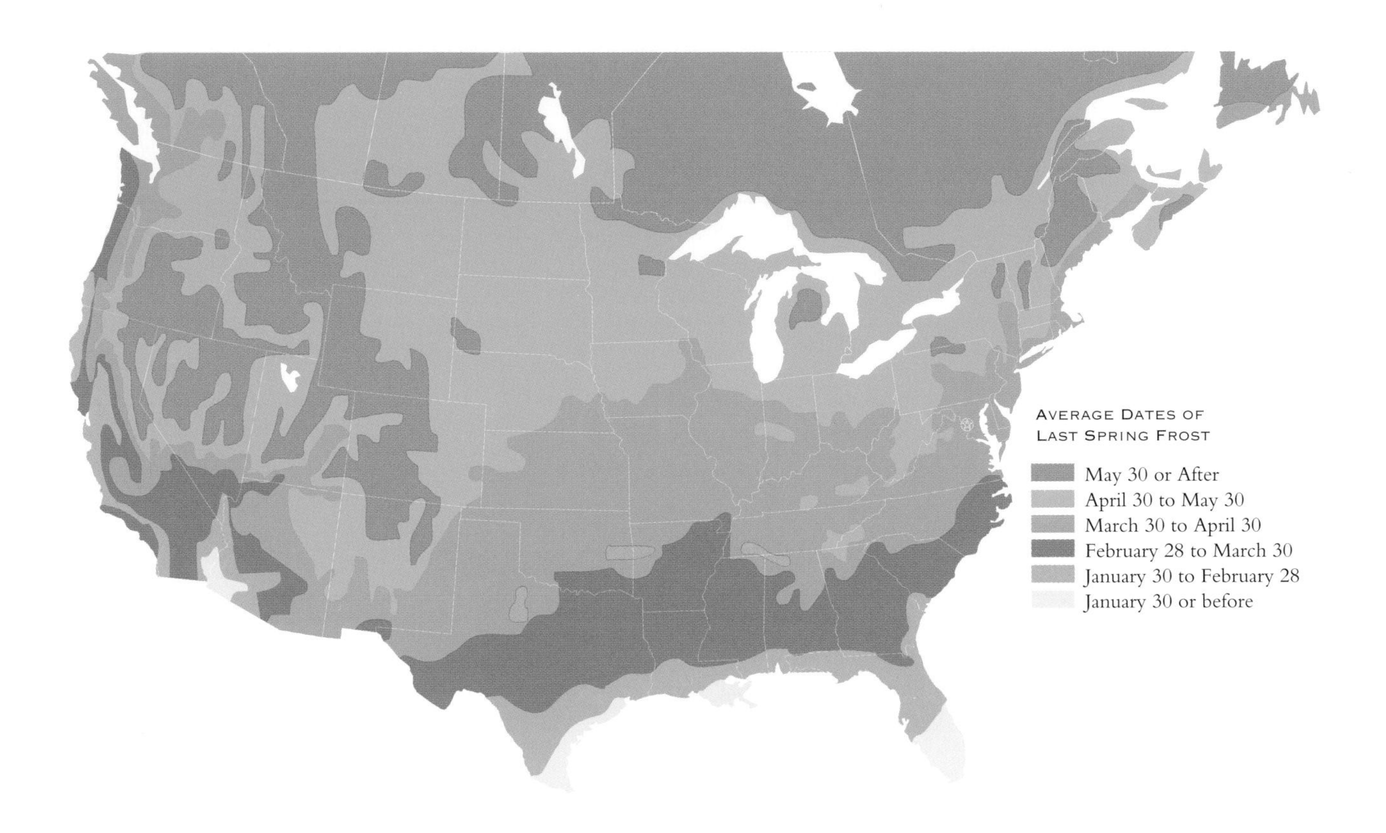

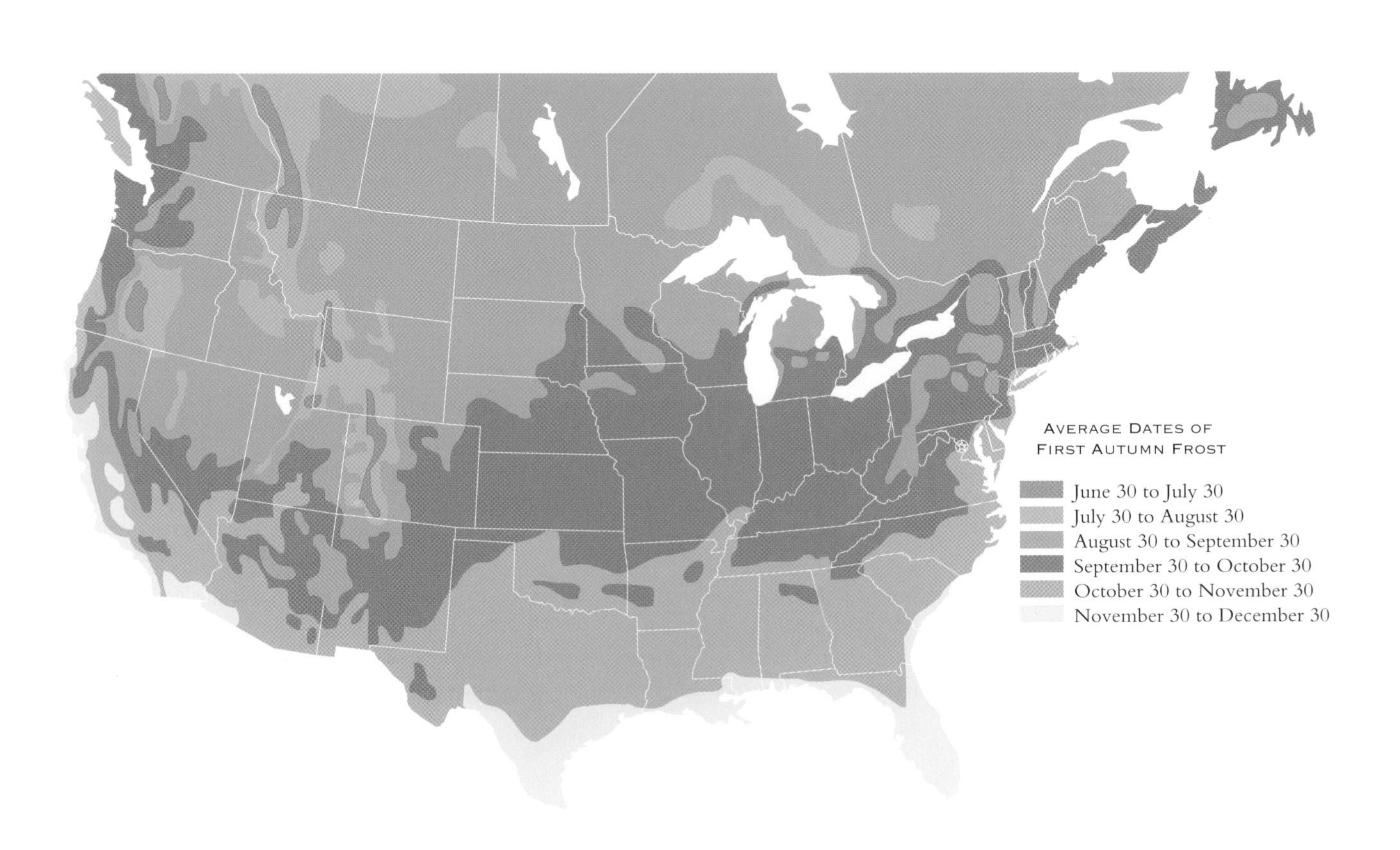

INDEX

Page numbers in **bold type** indicate main descriptions of plants and generally include a photograph. Page numbers in *italic type* indicate additional photographs and illustrations.

T

Metric Conversions

U.S. Units to Metric Equivalents			**Metric Units to U.S. Equivalents**		
To Convert From	Multiply By	To Get	To Convert From	Multiply By	To Get
Inches	25.4	Millimeters	Millimeters	0.0394	Inches
Inches	2.54	Centimeters	Centimeters	0.3937	Inches
Feet	30.48	Centimeters	Centimeters	0.0328	Feet
Feet	0.3048	Meters	Meters	3.2808	Feet
Yards	0.9144	Meters	Meters	1.0936	Yards
Square inches	6.4516	Square centimeters	Square centimeters	0.1550	Square inches
Square feet	0.0929	Square meters	Square meters	10.764	Square feet
Square yards	0.8361	Square meters	Square meters	1.1960	Square yards
Acres	0.4047	Hectares	Hectares	2.4711	Acres
Cubic inches	16.387	Cubic centimeters	Cubic centimeters	0.0610	Cubic inches
Cubic feet	0.0283	Cubic meters	Cubic meters	35.315	Cubic feet
Cubic feet	28.316	Liters	Liters	0.0353	Cubic feet
Cubic yards	0.7646	Cubic meters	Cubic meters	1.308	Cubic yards
Cubic yards	764.55	Liters	Liters	0.0013	Cubic yards

To convert from degrees Fahrenheit (F) to degrees Celsius (C), first subtract 32, then multiply by $\frac{5}{9}$.

To convert from degrees Celsius to degrees Fahrenheit, multiply by $\frac{9}{5}$, then add 32.

Ortho® Books
An imprint of Meredith® Books

Creating Water Gardens
Project Editor: Elsa Kramer
Editor: Denny Schrock
Contributing Editor: Marilyn Rogers
Contributing Writers: Richard M. Koogle, Eleanore Lewis, Kellie Sisson Snyder, Greg and Sue Speichert, Charles B. Thomas
Senior Associate Design Director: Tom Wegner
Assistant Editor: Harijs Priekulis
Copy Chief: Terri Fredrickson
Copy and Production Editor: Victoria Forlini
Editorial Operations Manager: Karen Schirm
Managers, Book Production: Pam Kvitne, Marjorie J. Schenkelberg
Contributing Copy Editor: Jay Lamar
Contributing Proofreaders: Becky Etchen, Fran Gardner, Sharon McHaney, Barb Stokes
Contributing Photographer: Marty Baldwin
Contributing Illustrators: Mike Eagleton, Thomas Rosborough
Contributing Map Illustrator: Jana Fothergill
Contributing Prop/Photo Stylist: Susan Strelecki
Indexers: Ellen Davenport, Kathleen Poole
Electronic Production Coordinator: Paula Forest
Editorial and Design Assistants: Kathleen Stevens, Karen McFadden

Additional Editorial Contributions from Art Rep Services
Director: Chip Nadeau
Designers: lk Design
Illustrators: Rick Hanson

Meredith® Books
Editor in Chief: Linda Raglan Cunningham
Design Director: Matt Strelecki
Executive Editor, Gardening and Home Improvement: Benjamin W. Allen
Executive Editor, Gardening: Michael McKinley

Publisher: James D. Blume
Executive Director, Marketing: Jeffrey Myers
Executive Director, New Business Development: Todd M. Davis
Executive Director, Sales: Ken Zagor
Director, Operations: George A. Susral
Director, Production: Douglas M. Johnston
Business Director: Jim Leonard

Vice President and General Manager: Douglas J. Guendel

Meredith Publishing Group
President, Publishing Group: Stephen M. Lacy
Vice President-Publishing Director: Bob Mate

Meredith Corporation
Chairman and Chief Executive Officer: William T. Kerr

Chairman of the Executive Committee: E.T. Meredith III

Library of Congress Control Number: 2002109100
ISBN: 0-89721-492-7

Thanks to
Catherine Hamrick, Mary Irene Swartz

Photographers
(Photographers credited may retain copyright © to the listed photographs.)
L = Left, R = Right, C = Center, B = Bottom, T = Top

Debbie Adams: 179BR; **Aquascape Designs, Inc.:** 40T, 101, 102; **John Baker/Garden Picture Library:** 145B; **Liz Ball/Positive Images:** 90; **Cathy Barash:** 26B, 206T, 211B, 224T; **Bill Beatty:** 178B; **R. A. Behrstock:** 169T; **Mark Bolton/Garden Picture Library:** 141T; **Kate Boykin:** 172T; **Gay Bumgarner:** 155B, 180, 181TL, 181B, 185T; **Gay Bumgarner/Positive Images:** 14, 16L, 187T; **Les Campbell/Positive Images:** 183; **David Cavagnaro:** 25B, 31B, 123TL, 132T, 138TL, 144TL, 149T, 149C, 199; **Patrice Ceisel/John G. Shedd Aquarium:** 172B; **Rosalind Creasy:** 200; **Charles Cresson:** 206BL, 206BR; **Eric Crichton/Garden Picture Library:** 145T; **R. Todd Davis:** 181TR; **Catriona Tudor Erler:** 2, 13B, 17T, 33T, 122B, 125T, 139, 171TR; **Derek Fell:** 22R, 96, 120, 122TR, 136C, 136B, 143C, 148B; **Robert Fenner:** 43, 44, 239B; **Jan Fetler:** 74; **Vaughan Fleming/Garden Picture Library:** 137T; **T. L. Gettings/Wildlands Conservancy:** 176B, 179TL; **Mark Gibson:** 84B; **Susan Glascock:** 132B, 147C, 173B; **John Glover:** 6, 12T, 15R, 18T, 30R, 32B, 111BL, 121, 124C, 125BL, 135T, 153T, 153C, 155C, 203; **Marcus Harpur:** 135C; **Jerry Harpur:** 13T (Design: Jeff Mendoza, N.Y., The Schneider Garden), 23B, 25T (Dennis Lochen), 29; **Jessie M. Harris:** 143T, 186; **Lynn Harrison:** 135B, 171BL; **Inger Hogstrom/Danita Delimont, Agent:** 179BL; **Neil Holmes/Garden Picture Library:** 133T; **Saxon Holt:** 9B, 128T, 130TL, 136T; **Jerry Howard/Positive Images:** 28B, 30L, 131T; **Bill Johnson:** 122TL, 129B, 166T; **Dency Kane:** 196, 198, 201B, 216T; **Mark Kane:** 195T, 195B; **Rosemary Kautzky:** 32T, 38, 98, 106, 127TL, 140BR, 150T, 151, 152T, 152B, 153B, 154T, 154C, 168, 175T; **Donna & Tom Krischan:** 33B, 110B; **Andrew Lawson:** 28T (Designer: Wendy Lauderdale), 84T (Designer: G. Robb, Hampton Court Show 1999), 133B, 152C; **Scott Leonhart/Positive Images:** 187B; **David Liebman:** 95T, 124B, 148C, 150C, 167BR, 177; **Lilypons Water Gardens:** 46B, 62R; **Edward G. Lines/John G. Shedd Aquarium:** 170BR; **Janet Loughrey:** 18B; **Charles Mann:** 222TR; **Hanson Mann:** 170TL, 170TR, 170BL; **Steve & Dave Maslowski:** 173C, 184; **Ivan Massar/Positive Images:** 130B; **Marilyn McAra:** 20, 23T; **Brad McLane, Florida Aquatic Nursery:** 113TR; **Charles W. Melton:** 182; **William H. Mullins:** 178T; **Clive Nichols:** 65B (Designer: Richard Coward), 169B; **Philip L. Nixon:** 167T, 167BL; **Jerry Pavia:** 8, 42, 91, 97T, 124T, 131BR, 140T, 141B; **Courtesy of Trevor Pearson/East Riding Koi Co.:** 55B; **Emma Peios/Garden Picture Library:** 142B; **Ben Phillips/Positive Images:** 134T, 134B, 150B; **Howard Rice/Garden Picture Library:** 133C, 145C; **Jeff Rugg/Pond Supplies of America, Inc.:** 171C; **Julie Maris Semel:** 22L; **John G. Shedd Aquarium:** 171TL, 171BR; **Richard Shiell:** 155T; **Rob & Ann Simpson:** 176T; **Garold Sneegas/Aquatic Kansas Images:** 173T, 179TR; **Pam Spaulding/Positive Images:** 123BL; **Greg & Sue Speichert:** 112B, 113B, 147T; **Albert Squillace/Positive Images:** 126T, 143B; **Joseph G. Strauch, Jr.:** 149B; **Ron Sutherland/Garden Picture Library:** 24; **Peter Symcox/gardenIMAGE:** 31T (Designer: Robin Hopper); **Brigitte Thomas/Garden Picture Library:** 204; **Charles Thomas:** 127R, 127BL; **Michael Thompson:** 26T, 85, 111T, 119T, 123TR, 123BR, 125C, 130TR, 132C, 137C, 138B, 138R, 140BL, 142TR, 144B, 146, 154B; **Connie Toops:** 111BR; **Rick Wetherbee:** 185B; **Justyn Willsmore:** 81, 148T; **Gary G. Wittstock/Pond Supplies of America, Inc.:** 7, 109

On the cover: Tropical water lily 'Marmorata' by Jessie M. Harris

All of us at Ortho® Books are dedicated to providing you with the information and ideas you need to enhance your home and garden. We welcome your comments and suggestions about this book. Write to us at:
Meredith Corporation
Ortho Gardening Books
1716 Locust St.
Des Moines, IA 50309–3023

If you would like to purchase any of our gardening, home improvement, cooking, crafts, or home decorating and design books, check wherever quality books are sold. Or visit us at: meredithbooks.com

If you would like more information on other Ortho products, call 800-225-2883 or visit us at: www.ortho.com